HOME
OF THE
BRAVE

A Patriot's Guide
to American History

John Alexander Carroll
Odie B. Faulk

UNIVERSITY
PRESS OF
AMERICA

University Press of America,™ Inc.

4720 Boston Way
Lanham, MD 20706

Library of Congress Cataloging in Publication Data

Carroll, John Alexander.
  Home of the brave.

  Reprint. Originally published: New Rochelle, N.Y.   :
Arlington House Publishers, c1976.
  Includes index.
  1. United States – History. I. Faulk, Odie B.
II. Title.
E178.C287   1984   973   83-23305
ISBN 0-8191-3628-X   (pbk. : alk. paper)

All University Press of America books are produced on acid-free
paper which exceeds the minimum standards set by the National
Historical Publications and Records Commission.

Contents

tion . . . The First Continental Congress . . . The War Begins . . .
British and American Advantages . . . The Declaration of Inde-
pendence . . . The Revolutionary War . . . The Peace Treaty . . .
The Impact of the Revolution

The Responsibility of Freedom . . . The State Constitutions . . .
The Articles of Confederation . . . The Financial Crisis . . .
The Western Lands . . . Toward a New Government . . . Ratifying the Constitution . . . The First President . . . Foreign Entanglements

The Second President . . . Problems with France . . . Jefferson
Elected . . . Jefferson and the Federalists . . . Jefferson and the
Courts . . . Jefferson and Foreign Affairs . . . Exploring the West
. . . The Burr Conspiracy . . . European Entanglements . . . Madi-
son Elected . . . The Road to War . . . The War of 1812 . . . The
Peace Treaty . . . The War in Retrospect . . . Changing Political
Alliances

Decades of Change . . . Monroe's First Administration . . .
Monroe and Foreign Affairs . . . The West Explored and Exploited
. . . The Election of 1824 . . . The Adams Administration . . .
The Election of 1828 . . . Jackson Inaugurated . . . Public Lands
and Tariff . . . The American System . . . Industrialization of the
North . . . Western Farming . . . The Bank War . . . The Van
Buren Administration . . . The Election of 1840 . . . The Fur
Trade . . . The Santa Fe Trade . . . The Settlement of Texas . . .
The Election of 1844 . . . The Oregon Question . . . Causes of the
Mexican War . . . The Mexican War . . . The Treaty of Guada-
lupe Hildago . . . The Boundary Survey . . . The Gadsden
Purchase . . . The Election of 1848 . . . The Compromise of
1850 . . . Beginnings of Disunion

The United States at Mid-Century . . . The Kansas-Nebraska
Act . . . Bleeding Kansas . . . The Republican Party . . . Buchanan
and Kansas . . . Douglas and Lincoln . . . John Brown's Raid . . .
The Election of 1860 . . . Attempts at Compromise . . . Secession
. . . North and South in 1861 . . . Battles and Leaders . . . Diplo-
macy During the War

Maps and Graph

Prepared especially for this book by Don Bufkin

Preface

FROM total wilderness to world leadership in less than five centuries—such is the history of the United States. Some viewers of this phenomenon have tried to explain it in terms of abundant raw materials: the nation rose to prominence because its resources, unlike those of Europe, had not been depleted in developing a high civilization. Others have characterized the American success story as one of divine guidance: the "God-looks-after-fools-and-the-United States" syndrome. Still other viewers have asserted that America became rich because of isolation: it did not suffer the periodic destruction visited on Europe through war. Finally, some have sought to explain the nation's rise in terms of a frontier that challenged its citizens.

All of these views hold some truth. America is a land of great natural resources; it has not been wracked by periodic destruction through war; it did have a frontier for more than four hundred years. As for the amount of divine protection and guidance, only God knows.

Yet the history of the United States has been more—much, much more. Born from the refugees and cast-offs of Europe, the population has proved remarkably inventive, optimistic, hard-working, thrifty, and pious—while simultaneously being pessimistic, hedonistic, spendthrift, and impious. This has been a land of contradiction and contention, of questioning and questing, of virtue and villainy. Yet withal it is a nation without parallel, one whose inventions have benefited the entire world and whose culture is imitated by more people than any before it.

To write the history of one's own country is a high pleasure for any historian, and we hope the reader enjoys the reading as much as we enjoyed the writing.

Introduction

MAN looks at raw, undeveloped land as through a pair of spectacles—eyeglasses that allow him to see only in the light of his society, his culture, and his technology. Every man who has ever lived has had to contend with this handicap; it is simultaneously his birthright and his curse. Much of the history of the world consists of man's struggle to enlarge his vision by finding new ways to exploit his environment in order to enrich the quality of his life.

What the first Europeans who viewed America saw seemed good to them within the framework of their society, their culture, and their technology. The New World of the Atlantic Seaboard, the Gulf Coast region, and Latin America was timbered, well watered, and fertile. In climate and resources it differed little from Western Europe, except that it was still unexploited, still virgin, still waiting for labor and capital to possess and use it. Those European explorers and colonizers little realized at first what a vast prize they had found, for to them the continent at first seemed only an impediment to their goal of discovering the spice-laden, jewel-rich Orient.

The geography of the land that these European explorers found was varied beyond their imagination, for what they saw was a coastal plain extending inland, sloping very gradually up from the sea. Beyond the prime forests that covered this tidewater section was a chain of mountains stretching from New England to Georgia on a northeast-southwest line; on the far side of this chain of mountains, which would bear the name Appalachians, was a river valley, the Mississippi, which drained the heart of the continent. Beyond the Mississippi and its tributaries were vast plains stretching from Canada southward to Texas, and to the west of that yet another range of mountains, the Rockies, whose peaks rivaled and even exceeded the Alps of Europe. West of the Rockies was a high desert country, the inter-mountain basin, bounded on the west by yet another chain of mountains, the Sierra Nevadas. At places the Sierras came down to the Pacific in jagged cliffs, but generally there was a coastal plain of high fertility along this western sea. More than 3 million square miles of land were encompassed in the region that would come to be the United States, and in this were mountains and valleys, lakes and rivers, deserts and forests, canyons and plains—in short, a land of infinite variety and beauty.

Living on this land were the first discoverers of America, the Indians, a people of limited technology. These were hunting-and-gathering nomads from the Steppes of Siberia. Although the evidence is not yet fully marshaled, these nomads probably crossed a land bridge where the Bering Strait now exists. They came in waves of migration beginning as early as 30,000 years ago. Once in the New World, they moved southward in search of warmer climate and game until they had thinly populated both North and South America from Alaska and the Hudson's Bay region southward to Tierra del Fuego and the Straits of Magellan. These people were from several linguistic stocks and many cultures, and in their new homeland they evolved variant cultures from what they had brought with them—tribal bands of differing levels of civilization. But nowhere did they have the wheel, the plow, iron instruments, or a written language. Nowhere in North America did they even have livestock beyond the domesticated dog. But they did learn to use and respect the land. They had made advances in pottery, weaving, and government, although they had not developed a high sense of private property. They learned to use the game animals wisely, to do intricate woodwork, and, among some tribes, to cultivate certain native plants.

What they failed to do within the present limits of the United States, however, was to develop beyond the tribal stage into national states such as those in the Europe of the 1500s, or to evolve a technology that would enable their warriors to withstand European armies. The spear and the bow and arrow were their major weapons, for gunpowder and its myriad uses were unknown. Yet English, Spanish, French, Russian, Dutch, and Swedish settlers would borrow heavily from the Indians. From them the newcomers learned woodcraft, agricultural techniques, and pioneering concepts—and might have learned far more except that they despised the Indians as people of some culture and education always despise savages. Because the Indians had not developed national states or an advanced technology capable of meaningful resistance in battle, the Europeans derided the natives—even denied their humanity. These newcomers would use the old, would borrow from the Indians and trade with them, would seek friendship and treaties with them—until they gained military supremacy, when they would turn against them with intent to destroy them.

Ambrose Bierce, a wit of the post–Civil War period, in his delightful *Devil's Dictionary* defined aborigines as "persons of little worth found cumbering the soil of a newly discovered country. They soon cease to cumber; they fertilize." The heart of Bierce's humor was its bite of truth. Estimates of the total number of Indians within the present United States who were cumbering the soil vary tremendously, ranging from one to five million. Even more conjectural than the number of Indians prior to Columbus' voyage was exactly who among white men first discovered America. That was a process of several centuries.

12

Chapter One

To the Ends of the Earth

THE quest is an enduring theme of literature and poetry. Man always is striving to achieve some new frontier of physical or spiritual experience. Never content with the old, the ordinary, the known, he must seek the new, the original, the unknown. Perhaps it was this quality that impelled our ancestors to stand upright, develop tools, plant crops, and tend domesticated animals. Perhaps it was this—or something so ordinary as a need for more food—that sent them from their old homes in search of new. Whatever the reason, they did expand from wherever it was that man originated, outward across mountains and valleys and deserts and swamps until they came to the ocean. Crude rafts then were constructed, and in these flimsy vessels that proved man to be more courageous than cautious, they set out to find what was on the other side of the water. Few records of such voyages were kept; rather, the results of these quests became part of the folklore and legend of each people. Periodically today in the United States, particularly in the Midwest, some farmer or another in plowing his field turns up an artifact of unknown origin. Examined by some local "authority," each is proclaimed to be of Chinese or Viking origin; perhaps the writing is in Runic or Phoenician or Chinese, but somehow the authenticity of each such relic is debatable—and these in turn become part of the legend about the discovery of America.

Early Explorations

One of the first expeditions to reach America about which there is more than legend was that led by Fusan, a sixth-century Buddhist missionary who reportedly reached the West Coast. Prince Murdoc of Wales possibly reached the East Coast that same century, as possibly did St. Brendan, an Irish monk. Shreds of intriguing evidence also open doors of speculation about the Phoenicians and others. However, about the Vikings the evidence is more than speculative. Norsemen settled in Iceland beginning about 870 and were exploring the coast of Greenland a century later. Before the year 1000 a Norse trader, Bjarni Herjulfson, sighted the mainland when his ship was blown off course. In 1003 Leif Ericson explored the North American coast somewhere between Newfoundland and Virginia, and others followed in the next decade. The Norse explorations came to naught, however, for

Western Europe was unready to exploit a new world. It had to pull itself out of the doldrums of the Middle Ages before it could turn outward.

By the late 1400s, however, Europe was developing to the extent that it was ready to undertake exploration and colonization. The Crusades had revealed the wealth of the Orient and had created a desire for spices, perfumes, silks, and jewels. The Crusades also had reanimated a missionary zeal for spreading the gospel message to non-Christian parts of the world. The Renaissance, which began in Italy in the 1200s, likewise was spreading, thereby stimulating a renewed interest in classical learning. For example, Ptolemy's *Geography* appeared in translation in 1410 and showed the world as round, although it estimated the globe to be five-sevenths its actual size and omitted North and South America.

Portugal and Spain took the lead in this exploration because they were the first to unify and become modern national states. They also were peninsular and thus isolated from European wars. And they had been fighting the Moors for centuries, producing a class of adventuresome fighting men in the process. Prince Henry, designated The Navigator by historians, stimulated Portuguese exploration by establishing a school at Cape St. Vincent in 1415; from it he sent mariners to seek a water route around Africa to the Orient. This process took eighty-four years to culminate in Vasco da Gama's 1498 voyage to India. Prince Henry and his heirs made use of new inventions—the compass, the astrolabe, time-keeping devices, and innovative sailing methods—to widen the frontiers of geographical knowledge and to spread the use of such inventions. They also employed the caravel instead of the carrack, thereby popularizing new methods of shipbuilding that provided greater stability, safety, and capacity.

Spanish Colonization

Where the Portuguese pioneered, the Spaniards soon followed. In the spring of 1492, led by Ferdinand and Isabella, Spanish forces drove the Moors from Granada, their last stronghold on the Iberian Peninsula, and thus were ready to channel their energies in new directions. On April 17 Ferdinand and Isabella commissioned Christopher Columbus, a Genoese shipmaster, Admiral of the Ocean Sea and, together with private sources, financed an expedition that was to go west with the hope of reaching the Orient. In the *Niña*, the *Pinta*, and the *Santa Maria*, Columbus and his men departed Palos, Spain, on August 3. Despite threats of mutiny, Columbus drove westward, and on October 12 they sighted land (presently called Watling Island). On that voyage Columbus also discovered and briefly explored the Bahamas, Cuba, and Santo Domingo before returning to Spain in March, 1493.

Columbus' discoveries raised grave questions of ownership of newly discovered lands, and in May, 1493, the Pope issued a decree granting Spain all discoveries west of a north-south line one hundred leagues west of the Azores and Cape Verde islands, Portugal all land east of that line. Subsequently, the Treaty of Tordesillas (June 7, 1494) redrew this line 370 leagues west of the Cape Verde Islands. With their rights to new lands thus secured, the Spanish monarchs pushed voyages of exploration, hoping to open commerce with the Orient. Columbus made three subsequent voyages, the first in 1493, during which he planted the colony of Isabella on Santo Domingo (January 2, 1494), the second in 1498, during which he explored the mouth of the Orinoco River in South America and was arrested to be sent home in chains because of unrest and uprisings in Santo Domingo, and the third in 1502, during which he explored the coast of Central America southward from Honduras to Panama. Returning to Spain in 1504, he died there two years later.

Subsequent Spanish exploration produced sufficient information to prove that Columbus' discovery was a New World, not the Orient. And, thanks to German geographer Martin Waldseemüller, that new world was named America after Amerigo Vespucci, an Italian explorer. From the original Spanish colony on Santo Domingo, settlement spread to Cuba and other islands in the Caribbean, and exploration spread to the mainland. While Vasco de Balboa was earning great fame in Panama, Juan Ponce de Leon, governor of Puerto Rico, was exploring the coasts of the Florida peninsula, creating the legend of the Fountain of Youth. Then in 1519–21 Hernán Cortés penetrated the Halls of Montezuma, defeated the Aztec Indians, and established Spanish domination of Mexico. From Mexico City, Spaniards moved northward in search of precious metals and mines, as well as a harvest of souls; thus they felt themselves to be serving their Spanish and heavenly monarchs simultaneously. A desire to conquer, a love of adventure, and a zeal for battle inspired these proud dons. Individual daring and initiative were rewarded during these formative years in the New World as never before in the history of Spain. Ambitious but poor young Spaniards fought for the wealth of Mexico and Peru and took fortunes from the ancient inhabitants. Men rose to positions of undreamed wealth and power within the span of a few years as a result of their own strength of arms and feats of valor. Thus there were years of gigantic gains for Spain during what came to be called The Golden Age of Discovery. Yet the men who entered what presently is the United States profited little.

In February, 1528, in search of another Mexico City, Pánfilo de Narvaéz led 400 men to Tampa Bay in Florida. After a fruitless trek up the peninsula, the explorers were disheartened by the failure of their ships to meet them. Constructing five ungainly barges, they drifted westward, hoping to reach Mexico. Three barges were lost, but two reached Galveston Island. Only fifteen Spaniards survived that first winter, and after six years as prisoners of the local Indians, four of the fifteen fled on foot. Led by Álvar Núñez Cabeza de Vaca, the four walked for eighteen months before finding a Spanish outpost. Taken to Mexico City for questioning by the viceroy, Cabeza de Vaca said truthfully that he had seen no gold or silver, but that he had heard of seven rich cities to the north, the Seven Cities of Cíbola. The viceroy tried to persuade Cabeza de Vaca to lead an expedition in search of these cities, but he refused, as did two of the other survivors. The fourth member of that party was a Moorish slave named Esteban, who could not refuse. The viceroy purchased him and used him as guide for the expedition in 1539 headed by Fray Marcos de Niza, a Franciscan missionary. Fray Marcos journeyed north through present Arizona to view from a distance a pueblo he took to be one of the Seven Cities of Cíbola; he did not enter because he had heard that Esteban and several Indian allies had been killed by the natives. Fray Marcos returned "with much more fear than food," as he said, so that he might make a report.

Fray Marcos' report stirred young Spaniards to enlist in a major expedition to conquer the Seven Cities. Leading this expedition was Francisco Vásquez de Coronado, a rich and promising young governor of one of the provinces. With 336 Spaniards and about 1000 Indian allies, and guided by Fray Marcos, Coronado in the spring of 1540 journeyed northward to the city viewed by Fray Marcos. There a battle was fought on July 7, eventuating in Spanish victory. The pueblo proved to be a Zuñi Indian village named Hawikúh, not a golden city. Parts of Coronado's expedition visited westward to the Hopi pueblos and even reached the brink of the

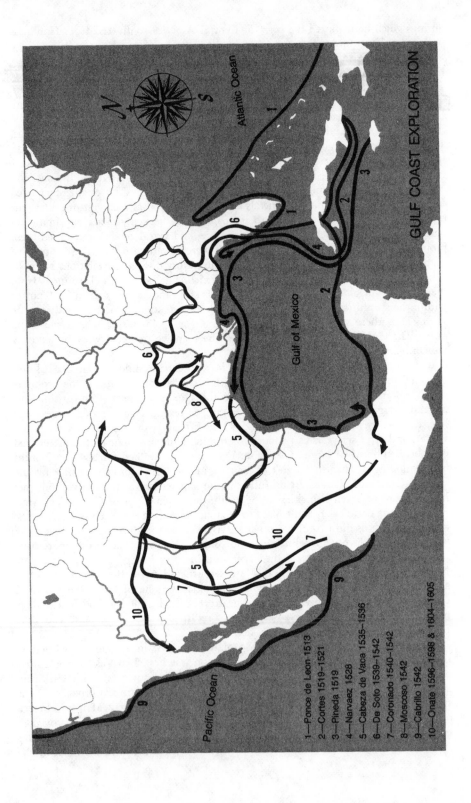

GULF COAST EXPLORATION

Atlantic Ocean

Gulf of Mexico

Pacific Ocean

1—Ponce de Leon 1513
2—Cortes 1519–1521
3—Pineda 1519
4—Narvaez 1528
5—Cabeza de Vaca 1535–1536
6—De Soto 1539–1542
7—Coronado 1540–1542
8—Moscoso 1542
9—Cabrillo 1542
10—Onate 1596–1598 & 1604–1605

Grand Canyon before the expedition moved eastward to winter with pueblo natives in New Mexico along the Rio Grande in the vicinity of the present Albuquerque.

During that winter Coronado heard tales of a rich land to the east, known as the Gran Quivira, that caused him in the spring and summer of 1541 to journey eastward across the Panhandle of Texas and northward across Oklahoma and into Kansas. Still no gold or silver was found, no second Mexico City to exploit. Tired and discouraged, the expedition returned to Mexico in 1542. Coronado's report stressed that he had found no precious metals and no Indians easily exploited.

Almost simultaneous with Coronado's epic trek and momentous report were the explorations and report of the Hernán de Soto–Luís de Moscoso expedition. De Soto in 1536 received a commission from the Spanish king, Charles V, to govern Cuba and to explore Florida. With 600 men he landed at Tampa Bay in 1539. His search for precious metals led him northward into the Carolinas and then westward across Georgia, Alabama, Mississippi, Louisiana, Arkansas, and the plains of Oklahoma. In the process, he discovered the Mississippi River. On the banks of that river on May 21, 1542, he died and was buried in "The Father of Waters." His successor, Luís de Moscoso, took command and led the expedition to the southwest into Texas before returning to the Mississippi to build seven crude rafts. On these the Spanish explorers drifted downriver to the Gulf and then westward around the Gulf to Tampico, which they reached in 1543. Only 320 survived. The report of this expedition, like that of Coronado, stressed that no source of quick riches had been found, only Indians willing to fight for their scant supplies of food.

Because of these two reports, Spanish interest in further exploration in what is now the United States declined. It was fear of foreign intruders that brought the first permanent colonization; because this fear was of Europeans, that first colony would be in Florida. The first attempt to colonize in this region had come in 1526 when Vásquez de Ayllón established a settlement on the coast of North Carolina; after a very hard winter, the colony failed. Then in 1562 French Huguenots under Jean Ribaut, fleeing religious persecution at home, attempted a settlement at Port Royal (near present-day Charleston). It was unsuccessful, but two years later René de Laudonnière established a colony of French Huguenots at St. Johns River in Florida. In 1565 Pedro Menéndez de Avilés of Spain sailed from Spain with 2600 soldiers and orders to drive out the French. He founded St. Augustine in September and subsequently drove out Laudonnière and the Huguenots. In 1566 and 1567 Spanish settlements were planted at Charlotte Bay, Tampa Bay, Miami, and other points in Florida to prevent future French colonization. Settlements on Florida's west coast subsequently were abandoned, but the remaining outposts were reinforced by the construction of Jesuit missions. These Jesuits gradually pushed their work as far north as present-day Georgia and even the Carolinas, although those advances proved abortive and were withdrawn.

Far to the west, in present New Mexico, settlement occurred likewise for defensive reasons. From 1577 to 1580 the English seadog Francis Drake piloted a ship through the Straits of Magellan and up the west coast of South and Central America, pillaging Spanish treasure ships and ports; then, pausing to rest and refit in California, he circled the globe to return to a royal welcome and a knighthood in England. Spanish officials, who had waited fruitlessly for him to return the way he had gone, decided that he had found the long-sought and fabled Northwest Passage, for the Pacific was too vast for anyone to cross. Confident that Drake had found the Northwest Passage, they named it the Strait of Anián, and they determined, for defensive reasons, to control it. Therefore, preliminary reconnaissances occurred in the 1580s that led to the granting of a contract of settlement in 1595 to Juan de Oñate. These preliminary searches had convinced Spanish officials that the strait did not exist, but they had found thousands of Indians willing to be converted and some economic potential in the form of cotton blankets. Oñate, the son of a silver magnate, began colonizing New Mexico at his own expense. In 1598 he moved north from Mexico with some 400 followers and laid out the little capital village of San Juan de los Caballeros (near the present Santa Fe). Like Coronado he sought the Seven Cities of Cíbola and the Gran Quivira; like Coronado he failed. Also, he was plagued with an Indian revolt and unhappy colonists who wished more freedom to exploit the natives. In 1608, as a result of charges of mismanagement and cruelty, Oñate was removed. The following year, under a new governor, the capital was ordered moved and renamed Villa Real de la Santa Fe de San Francisco de Asis, soon shortened to Santa Fe.

Thus by 1610 Spain had a firm foothold, not only in South and Central America, but also inside the present United States. By that time there were more than 150,000 settlers in New Spain (as Mexico was then called). The Gulf of Mexico had become a Spanish lake, although plagued somewhat by buccaneers from Holland, England, and France. But other nations were jealous of the golden stream of wealth pouring into the Spanish royal treasury from the New World, and they determined to gain a share of that wealth.

French Colonization

✦ France was the second nation to establish colonies in North America and claim land now within the United States. As the French monarch Francis I put it in the early 1500s: "The sun shines on me as well as on the others. I should be very happy to see the clause in Adam's will which excluded me from my share when the world should come to be divided." Acting on that premise, he sent Giovanni de Verrazano in 1524 to seek a water route to the Indies; Verrazano visited the coast of New England and entered the present New York harbor, thereby staking France's claim to the region. Ten years later Jacques Cartier, likewise flying the French emblem, sailed to Newfoundland and Prince Edward Island, claiming them for his sovereign. The following year Cartier entered the St. Lawrence River, sailed beyond the rock of Quebec and past a site he named Montreal, and reached rapids he thought prevented his continuing to the Orient; those rapids he named La Chine ("China Rapids"). He wintered at the site of Quebec before returning home in 1536. Cartier made a final voyage up the St. Lawrence in 1536, during which he opened a fur trade with the local natives. After Cartier's voyages, Frenchmen came to dominate fishing off Newfoundland and would trade regularly with the Indians near Quebec for furs.

No permanent French settlements followed immediately, however, for France was engaged in interminable wars, both foreign and civil, during most of the remainder of the century. Much of this warfare was religious in nature, as Catholic fought Protestant Huguenot; on St. Bartholomew's Day, 1572, 10,000 French Huguenots were slain by their Catholic countrymen. Such strife led to the Huguenot colonies in the Carolinas and in Florida. Unity and peace came at the end of the sixteenth century under Henry IV; in 1598 he issued the Edict of Nantes, which restored religious harmony in France, and permanent settlement in the New World quickly followed, principally for economic reasons.

18

Mercantile companies were chartered by the crown to exploit the fur trade. One of these companies, composed of private French capitalists, hired Samuel de Champlain and in 1603 he made his first voyage to the St. Lawrence. Champlain was patriotic, desiring greatness for his nation; he was religious, desiring to convert the natives to Catholicism; and, greatest of all his attributes, he was curious, desiring to increase his knowledge of geography, the Indians, and the animals, whatever the cost in hardship and suffering.

Champlain's first voyage, during which he questioned the Indians extensively, would bear fruit five years later. The following year, 1604, the company that employed him decreed a settlement on an island at the Bay of Fundy. That first winter saw thirty-five of seventy-nine colonists die, and in 1605 the settlement was moved to Port Royal. This colony would take root as the first permanent French settlement in North America. Yet the fur trade there was poor, and Champlain left the infant colony at Port Royal in 1608 to establish a base nearer the beaver. Without hesitation, he chose the natural fortress of Quebec, and there in 1608 he moved "to lay the foundations of a permanent edifice, as well for the glory of God as for the renown of the French." That same year he received a call for military assistance from the Montagnais (Algonquin) Indians against their traditional enemies, the Iroquois. Champlain made a fateful decision: he would aid these Indians. He depended on them for the furs brought to his trading post; he needed their aid if his secret desire to explore was to be realized; he wanted security for his post; and he desired to convert the local Indians to Christianity. Little did Champlain realize that he was involving Frenchmen in a large-scale Indian war for control of the St. Lawrence Valley—and that he had chosen the weaker of the two contending factions as an ally.

In July, 1609, on a hunting and exploring trek with the Montagnais, he moved southward by way of the Richelieu River into upstate New York. There he discovered the lake that would bear his name, and he learned the route to Lake George and the headwaters of the Hudson. But there also, at the southern end of Lake Champlain, he aided his Indian allies in a battle with the Iroquois; in fact, he won the battle for them by using his firearms. Perhaps more than anything else, Iroquois hatred of the French prevented their movement southward and thereby determined the lines of expansion of New France. Also, the Iroquois would contribute significantly to the ultimate defeat of the French in their quest for North America.

English Settlements

England was the last of the major powers to enter the race for colonies in the New World. England was unified as a nation in 1485 under the Tudor dynasty that began with Henry VII. He strengthened the monarchy in England, and he increased the wealth in the national treasury. His sole gesture, upon hearing of the discovery of the New World, was to send John Cabot, a naturalized Venetian, in 1497 to seek the Northwest Passage. Cabot sighted either Cape Breton Island or Newfoundland, which he claimed for England in June, then sailed south. Seeking the passage to Japan, Cabot explored as far south as Chesapeake Bay before returning to England in May, 1498. More than three-quarters of a century would pass before Englishmen would again visit the New World; thus Cabot established England's sole claim for many years.

Great changes in England during the 1600s eventually would bring total British domination of the colonial race and make England the foremost world power. Religious nationalism engulfed the isle after 1534, when Henry VIII broke away from the church of Rome to establish Anglicanism. This break not only released men and capital for other endeavors, but it strengthened the monarchy. But religious wars undermined the monarchy during the mid-1600s, which saw Bloody Mary return England to the Catholic fold, only to die for her efforts, and Elizabeth I ascend the throne and reestablish Protestantism. Parliament assumed a greater role in governing the nation, and civil liberties were established in law. Another development during this period was the rise of the middle class, which believed in the merits of hard work and thrift. The result was the belief, reinforced by Protestantism, that commercial success in this world indicated God's favor in the world to come. In short, England became a nation of shopkeepers and manufacturers, and Spanish wealth from the New World found its way into English cash registers. England also concentrated on building its merchant fleet and navy, and thus gained an increasing share of the carrying trade of Western Europe.

In England during this period the concept of the joint-stock company was developing. Economic endeavors of the day were risky. Ships sent on far voyages, with the potential of great profit, had a corresponding likelihood of not returning. If several merchants invested in several such ventures, some of the ships would return, making sufficient profits to pay a dividend to all, whereas each financing his own would result in a few rich merchants and some bankrupt ones. Joint investment in speculative ventures gave rise to the joint-stock company, each investor buying shares and sharing correspondingly in the profits. The Muscovy Company and the East India Company were such endeavors. This development led to a search for resources and for markets—both of which colonies could supply.

Mercantilism and Colonization

While religion was a cause of growing nationalism in Europe, so also was economics. The prevailing economic theory of the day was mercantilism, which held that a nation grew rich through a favorable balance of trade—with more gold coming into the nation than going out. Also, mercantilism stressed a high degree of preparedness for war. The tenets of mercantilism included: (1) national encouragement of manufacturing through such devices as the tariff, (2) national encouragement of agriculture to insure a food supply without the necessity of imports, (3) national encouragement of the growth of population to supply manpower in case of war, (4) national encouragement of the growth of the merchant marine to transport goods between nations (thus keeping for the country gold that would otherwise have to be paid out for this purpose) and provide trained sailors in time of war, (5) national encouragement of a favorable balance of trade as a means of increasing the amount of gold and silver in the country, and (6) national encouragement of the development of a colonial empire as a source of raw materials, thereby bringing national self-sufficiency and supplying a market for products manufactured in the home country.

Thus, by the late 1500s, England had many motives for colonization. These would check the growing power of Spain, which until 1588 and the War of the Spanish Armada, was the most powerful nation in Europe. Colonies would increase English prestige—and nationalism demanded this. Colonies might allow the conversion of heathens to Christianity, and the fervor of the Reformation favored this.

Colonies might provide a cure for pauperism and overpopulation, which had developed in England as a result of the growing demand for woolen cloth; this had led to the conversion of tenant farms to sheep runs, thereby forcing peasants into the cities where they became public charges or criminals in order to survive. Colonies likewise might provide a refuge for divergent religious sects, especially for Puritans who refused to accept the ways of the Church of England. Finally—and perhaps most important—colonies would improve English commerce and thereby make the nation more wealthy. Thus there were social, religious, political, and economic reasons for colonization by the end of the sixteenth century, and, as a result, colonies were developed.

British buccaneers had kept alive English interest in the New World by their exploits during those years when events at home precluded colonization. These sea-dogs had raided Spanish treasure ships regularly, bringing home a vast booty. In the process, they spread the impression that America was synonymous with easy wealth and quick riches, a place where gold and silver lay about on the ground just waiting to be picked up. Men such as Francis Drake gained wealth and knighthoods for their efforts. The first serious effort at exploration since John Cabot's try in 1497 came in 1576, when Martin Frobisher was dispatched by the Cathay Company, a joint-stock venture formed to develop trade with China, to seek the Northwest Passage. On his epic voyage, Frobisher reached Baffin Land, discovered Frobisher Bay, and sailed through Hudson Strait. He failed, however, to open a quick route to China, and the Cathay Company lost interest. Similarly, John Davis made three unsuccessful attempts to find the Northwest Passage in 1585–87. These were the last will-o'-the-wisp attempts at finding the long-sought water route around North America. Thereafter the stress would be on colonies for mercantile reasons, financed by joint stock companies.

Humphrey Gilbert in 1578 secured a charter from Elizabeth I for settlement in North America. His goal was Newfoundland (possibly lurking in his mind was the thought of the Northwest Passage and the chance of emulating Francis Drake's raids on Spanish treasure ships). Gilbert's efforts are shrouded in mystery, and he died on his second voyage in 1583. His half-brother, Sir Walter Raleigh, thereupon took up the task, but the goal was Roanoke Island, discovered accidentally in 1584 by Raleigh's captains. Their flattering report of that location caused Raleigh to name it Virginia after Elizabeth, the Virgin Queen. He sent a hundred colonists there in 1585, but mismanagement and Indian hostility caused the settlers to abandon it the following year. Raleigh's final attempt there came in 1587, when he sent 120 settlers under John White to build a colony. White deposited them at the site, then sailed home for supplies. His return was delayed by the War of the Spanish Armada; when he returned in 1590, he found the colony deserted, its fate a mystery.

A friend of Gilbert and Raleigh, Richard Hakluyt the younger, would do more to encourage colonization of North America than either of the other two men, however. Hakluyt sent no settlers to foreign lands, nor did he receive a charter from the king. Instead, he published everything he could find about the New World in a series of volumes that described this new land as "more like the Garden of Eden than any part else of all the earth." Hakluyt's *Principall Navigations, Voiages, and Discoveries of the English Nation,* which began appearing in 1589, also contained his editorial recommendation that colonies in the New World would relieve unemployment, provide raw materials and a market, and empty the overcrowded prisons.

21

James I, who succeeded to the throne in 1603 following Elizabeth's death, took advantage of this interest, for he was a strong advocate of mercantilism.

James I was free to encourage colonization because his accession to the throne brought external peace to England for the first time in years. In 1604 he negotiated a peace treaty with Spain, followed by commercial agreements that insured prosperity. Furthermore, as he also was king of Scotland, his accession brought peace with the neighbor to the north. Thus Englishmen felt secure enough to hazard such risky ventures as colonies in North America. Attention was drawn to this region in 1605 by the return of Captain George Waymouth, who had sailed to the coast of Maine in search of a refuge for Catholics; on the trip he kidnapped five Indians, whom he exhibited in London upon his return. In September of that year, two different joint-stock companies petitioned James I for a charter to colonize Virginia. In April, 1606, the king signed the final draft of this charter, which provided that colonists were to take with them the "Liberties, Franchises, and Immunities" of Englishmen at home. This charter actually franchised two companies: the Virginia Company of London, which could establish settlements between thirty-four and forty-one degrees north latitude, and the Virginia Company of Plymouth, which could colonize between thirty-eight and forty-five degrees north latitude. To avoid arguments over jurisdiction, the charter stipulated that in the overlapping region between thirty-eight and forty-one degrees north latitude, no colony could be within a hundred miles of another settlement.

The merchants, knights, and gentlemen of the Plymouth Company made the first attempt. In August, 1606, an expedition was sent, only to be captured by Spaniards in the West Indies. Then in May and June, 1607, Sir Ferdinando Gorges sent two ships to the coast of Maine. There, on the Sagadahoc River, a colony was started, but the harshness of the winter so discouraged the settlers that they abandoned the attempt in 1608.

The Settlement of Virginia

Meanwhile, the London Company had been readying its venture, and in December, 1606, *Discovery, Godspeed,* and *Susan Constant* departed. The 160 men sailed fifty miles up a river they named the James and on May 14 established a settlement they called Jamestown. That first summer was a disaster. The site the colonists had chosen, despite warnings to avoid low, swampy places, proved malarial and the water bad. By 1610 only sixty settlers survived.

Only in part can climate and water be blamed for the high mortality rate. The major causes were the purposes of the colony and the intentions of the settlers. The original instructions to these men had been to search for a water route to China, to trade with the Indians, and to search for gold, iron, and copper mines. The colonists had been filled with stories of easy wealth in the New World, to the extent that they sought gold rather than planting crops. Their supply of food from England was soon exhausted. In the winter of 1608–09 came the "starving time." Their failure to build stout homes and plant crops—in short, to work—brought such famine that one colonist was executed for cannibalism. In this desperate situation, Captain John Smith exerted a positive influence by instituting a "no work, no eat" policy. His tyranny saved the colony from total extinction, but in 1609 Smith was injured and returned to England, bringing on yet another and worse starving time. Moreover, the colonists had angered the local Indians by this time, causing still more deaths.

In June, 1610, the survivors decided to abandon the colony and started floating downriver, hoping to be picked up by fishing vessels and taken home. Instead they met a large fleet under the command of Sir Thomas Gates. He had new and wide-ranging powers, given him by the London Company, which had secured them in a new charter of 1609. Gates faced the difficult problems of company policy that dictated total company ownership of the land; settlers had to work the land in common and then draw from the common store—a plan that killed incentive. What saved the settlement was two-fold: peace with the Indians and the discovery of a cash crop.

The key to peace with the Indians was to find some type of appeasement for their chief, Powhatan. He was the son of a chief (reportedly driven from Florida by the Spaniards) who had settled in Virginia and there conquered five local tribes, banding them under his leadership. Powhatan had inherited this union at the death of his father, and he continued the policy of conquest; by the time of the British arrival, he ruled about thirty tribes composed of some 8000 people. He made his headquarters at Werococomoco, a village on the north side of the York River fifteen miles from Jamestown. However, his home was at the falls of the James River (near the present Richmond). This site was known as Powhata, and thus the English called him Powhatan. In 1607 Powhatan was described by John Smith as a "tall, well proportioned man" with gray hair, thin beard, and an aura of sadness about him.

The early colonists had come to Powhatan to beg for corn, for, as the Indians later said, they were yet too weak to steal it. Powhatan was suspicious of the newcomers and refused to sell them corn. He also ordered ambushes of small parties of Englishmen, and several workers were murdered in the fields. In 1608, according to a story of debatable authenticity, Captain John Smith was captured and was about to be clubbed to death when he was saved by Powhatan's daughter Pocahontas. Yet this incident, if true, did not change Powhatan's attitude toward the English.

Then came the abduction of Pocahontas. As a child she often had played at the fort at Jamestown—giving some basis to the legend that she saved John Smith's life. Then in 1613, when she was visiting the village of the Potomac Indians, Pocahontas was captured by Captain Samuel Argall of the vessel *Treasurer;* he held her as security for several Englishmen known to be in Indian hands and for tools and supplies that the Indians had stolen. Taken to Jamestown as a hostage, Pocahontas was treated with courtesy by Governor Sir Thomas Dale, who was touched by her gentility and intelligence. After instruction in the Christian religion, she was baptized and took the name Rebecca.

John Rolfe, a gentleman at Jamestown, fell in love with the Indian princess and asked Dale for permission to marry her. Dale readily agreed in order to win the friendship of the Indians (despite his knowledge that Pocahontas may already have been married to a chief named Kocoum). Powhatan also gave his consent, and the marriage took place at Jamestown in 1614 in the Anglican church. Powhatan did not trust the English sufficiently to attend in person, but he did send his brother. After the marriage Powhatan made a formal treaty of peace with the colonists, which he kept until his death in April, 1618. He was succeeded by his second brother, Itopatin (or Opichepan), who was freed to go to war again by the death of Pocahontas.

In 1616 the Virginia Company expressed to Rolfe and his bride its desire that the Indian princess visit England; officials of the company thought this would aid the company in securing funds from British financiers. Rolfe, Pocahontas, her brother-in-law Tomocomo, and several Indian girls sailed for England, where Pocahontas was received as a princess, entertained by the bishop of London, and presented to James I. Early in 1617 the party prepared to return to Virginia, but at Gravesend Pocahontas developed a case of smallpox and died. Her only child, Thomas Rolfe, was educated in England and later returned to Virginia to leave many descendants bearing the name Rolfe.

John Rolfe, besides marrying Pocahontas, also is credited with cultivating the first crop of tobacco. A variety imported from Trinidad grew well, and the spread of the habit of smoking and dipping snuff in England brought high prices. By 1618 so much tobacco was being grown in Virginia that 30,000 pounds were exported to England that year.

The following year, 1619, came two momentous events for the colony. A Dutch privateer stopped in Virginia with twenty-one Negroes aboard. They remained, some as indentured servants, others completely free. Nonetheless, this was the first step toward the introduction of slavery in the colony. The second major event was an end to the communal system of landholding. Each colonist was granted fifty acres as a headright, and future settlers arriving at their own expense would be so endowed. John Rolfe wrote that this policy excited "great content," for freemen would be far more inclined to work—to clear land and plant crops. Likewise, that same year the company governors in London determined to allow local self-government on the English model. A general assembly was to be held each year, consisting of a two-house legislative body empowered to pass laws "thought good and proffittable." The lower house of this legislative body was representative in nature. Called the House of Burgesses, it met for the first time in 1619, as a result of what, loosely construed, was constitutional government; but the constitution was written and promulgated by the London Company, not by the governed.

Despite these changes, the colony failed to prosper greatly. Then in 1622 came an Indian uprising that saw 347 settlers massacred by the natives. Virginians retaliated by making vigorous war on all natives, and thereafter the colony followed a policy of relentless war against Indians. This Indian war of 1622 was followed the next year by a disease that killed 500 more settlers. As a result, a royal investigation of the London Company followed. This investigation revealed that 6000 colonists had departed England for Virginia, but that 4000 of them had died; that the population of the colony stood at only 1275; and that the investors in the company had paid in 200,000 pounds but had received not a single dividend. Such failures caused the crown to revoke the London Company's charter and make Virginia a royal colony.

Thus by the very early years of the seventeenth century, colonies had been planted on North American soil by Spain, France, and England, and already certain patterns were emerging. The Spaniards came to settle for God and king, and in the process they mixed their blood with the natives to produce a new race subordinate to the old. The French came also for religion and to mix their blood with that of the Indians, but not to subjugate the natives; rather they sought furs to export. The Englishman came to carve out another England, a replica of home. The Indians, who at first were needed for technical advice, were soon regarded as an impediment to plowing, planting, and constant expansion. Three nations and three philosophies were planted on the North American continent in the first century and a quarter following Columbus' discovery, but it was a large continent capable of sustaining all three without major conflict for almost another hundred years.

24

Chapter Two

Reflections of the Old World

Expanding Colonization

EUROPE at the turn of the seventeenth century seethed with excitement. French and English settlements might yet be tenuous, but combined with the colonies of Spain they were providing an outlet for aggressive young men who otherwise might have turned their energies to less constructive enterprises. The New World also was sending the Old a continuous stream of gold and silver, thereby generating a new class of wealthy people. The supply of precious metals had been relatively stable since the fall of Rome; the infusion of the new gold and silver unsettled the financial and economic structure of Europe and triggered an inflationary spiral that would last for centuries. But perhaps most important, the discovery of the New World had unleashed imagination, which had lain dormant for centuries. Novels almost of a science fiction nature were written of lands yet to be found and inhabited by near-humans of fantastic proportions. The myth of El Dorado, men made of gold, was only one such story; the land of the Amazons was another. The combination of a rebirth of imagination along with an economic boom triggered rapid development in the New World, especially when coupled with continued religious bigotry and strife.

In the first years of the seventeenth century, even minor European powers such as the Netherlands and Sweden entered the colonial race, entranced with the thought of quick wealth from the New World. The Dutch had revolted against their Spanish masters and had won their independence during the last years of the sixteenth century. Quickly they took advantage when Portugal became part of Spain in 1580, and they came to dominate the trade with the Orient and with Brazil. To consolidate this traffic, they created the Dutch East India Company in 1602. Handsome dividends followed for the investors. Still, the company wanted a quicker route to the Orient—and thus larger profits. Therefore in 1609 Henry Hudson was commissioned to seek the Northwest Passage. Sailing in the *Half Moon,* he entered New York harbor and proceeded up the river that would bear his name. In the vicinity he gave gifts to Mohawk Indians, members of the Iroquois confederacy, and thereby won their friendship.

Five years later that friendship proved very valuable. In 1614 a party of Dutch-

25

men established Fort Nassau (later renamed Fort Orange) near present Albany and began trading for furs with the Iroquois. In return, these Indians received firearms that enabled them better to fight the French in Canada. When this colony proved profitable, the Dutch West India Company was chartered with rights to establish colonies and trade in the New World. Approximately thirty families arrived in 1624 to settle at Governor's Island, along the Delaware River, and at Fort Nassau. Then in 1626 Peter Minuit became governor; his reign lasted five years, but he is chiefly remembered for an event that occurred shortly after his arrival. He purchased Manhattan Island from the Indians for some twenty-four dollars worth of trinkets and renamed it New Amsterdam. Negro slaves were introduced in 1628.

In formulating a philosophy of colonization, the Dutch decided to transfer to the New World the land-holding system of the Old World. Wealthy men, called Patroons, were granted large estates, which they were expected to people with tenants. Huge grants were made along the Hudson River and outward to Hartford on the Connecticut River, as well as on Long Island. But as the Dutch expanded, they came into contact with another colony, this one belonging to Sweden.

Swedish merchants established a settlement, New Sweden, along the Delaware River in 1638. These Swedes made one important contribution in their brief tenure. They developed the log cabin as an architectural form. By 1655 there were some 8000 residents in New Sweden. That year Peter Stuyvesant, who governed the Dutch colony from 1646 to 1664, took control of New Sweden after a conflict between the two colonies that had raged intermittently since 1643. Thus by 1655 Sweden had been eliminated as a colonial power. Significantly, the Dutch West India Company had found it necessary to extend some measure of self-government to the growing colony centered at New Amsterdam. Dutch householders were allowed to elect nine men to advise the governor and council, and certain of the larger towns enjoyed limited local self-government as well.

The Plymouth Bay Colony

Unfortunately for Dutch expectations for the New World colony, it came into conflict with European rivals mightier than the Swedes. What had started at Jamestown as a small endeavor, and which almost died of starvation in its first two years of existence, proved but an advance guard for a mighty tide of Englishmen—Britishers who came only in part for economic reasons. Religion likewise proved a mighty force in driving them westward from their home island. During the reign of Elizabeth I (1558–1603), Protestantism had taken firm root in England. There was an official Church of England, or Anglican Church, but a growing number of the people subscribed not to it but to Calvinism, known locally as Puritanism. These Puritans thought that a more thorough reformation was needed than that provided by the state church. They especially wanted the hierarchy abolished, for they believed every man to be his own priest. Additionally, they wanted a sterner moral code enforced.

Two branches developed within the Puritan faction, one called Nonconformists and the other Separatists. The Nonconformists wished to remain within the Church of England and change it from within; the Separatists saw no hope of changing the state church from within and so broke away to form their own congregations. So long as Elizabeth reigned, the Puritans were not persecuted—and by 1603 their appeal was such that they probably outnumbered Anglicans in England. When Elizabeth died, however, James I came to the throne. An absolutist who believed in the divine right of kings, James intended all his subjects to be Anglican, for as king, he was head of that church, a position that strengthened his authority. James announced that he would "harry" the Puritans out of the land if they would not conform to the established church. One group of Separatists at Scrooby (in East Anglia) felt so persecuted that in 1609 they determined to move to Leyden in Holland. This they did, led by William Brewster, a Cambridge-educated theologian; John Robinson, their pastor; and William Bradford, a scholar.

Ten years passed in Leyden, ten years during which these English refugees saw their children growing up speaking Dutch and marrying local girls. They saw their English customs and habits disappearing, to be replaced by foreign customs and habits. Horrified, they approached a leading member of the London Company, Sir Edwin Sandys, a Puritan, and petitioned for the right to colonize in the New World. This was granted, and after interminable delays their small ship, the *Mayflower*, departed England on September 16. Brewster led the Puritans, while Captain Myles Standish sailed as military leader. The trip across the Atlantic was difficult for the 102 "ancestors," and their ship was driven far north of its intended destination. On November 21 they entered Cape Cod Bay, where they decided to stay and colonize. However, their patent from the London Company was invalid, for Cape Cod was north of the forty-first parallel. Fearful of the result of no authority whatsoever, the forty-one adult males joined together to formulate and sign the Mayflower Compact before they landed. This compact called for all to obey laws formulated "for the generall goode of the colonie"—in short, they would be governed by the will of the majority until permanent provision could be made for their settlement. This agreement in essence was a constitution drafted by the governed.

In December the colonists went ashore at Plymouth and began constructing houses. That first winter over half the settlers died of disease. Fortunately, the Wampanoag Indians in the vicinity proved friendly. The almost-legendary Squanto and his tribesmen showed the Pilgrims how to plant corn and shared food with them. The Wampanoags actually were in no condition to oppose the new settlers, for three years previously a third of their number had died of a plague (probably left by visiting Europeans) ; the Pilgrims commented that this plague was the gift of "divine providence" for thereby God had "made way for the quiet and peaceable settlement of the English in those nations." In the fall of 1621, just as famine again was gripping the colony, the ship *Fortune* arrived with supplies, an event that triggered the first Thanksgiving.

The question of government was resolved on June 1, 1621, when the Council for New England (which was the Plymouth Company reorganized) granted the Pilgrims a patent to settle at Plymouth. Five years later the Pilgrims felt sufficiently prosperous to purchase all rights to the colony from the Council for New England. The price was raised by fifty-three residents of the colony and five like-minded men in England. These fifty-eight individuals became the shareholders of the company —or freemen—and constituted a corporate colony. Corporation and colony had merged. Under the inspired leadership of William Bradford, who was elected governor in 1621 and thereafter (with the exception of but five years) until 1657, the colony continued to prosper, chiefly from fur and fish. Greater participation in government gradually was extended to nonshareholders, so that governor and assembly were elected popularly. But religious freedom did not come to America with the Pilgrims. They wanted only the freedom to impose their own tenets. Troublesome questioners of doctrine were ejected.

Difficulties in England

Plymouth Plantation existed as a separate colony, despite the fact that it never received a royal charter, until 1691, when it was absorbed by a larger and stronger neighbor, Massachusetts, another Puritan colony. In fact, Plymouth by its existence and by its success had inspired the founding of Massachusetts. But Massachusetts grew from more complex antecedents than did Plymouth.

The land between the colony of Virginia and the French settlements to the north was named by Captain John Smith, the same man who had brought Virginia through its starving time. Employed in 1614 by London merchants to seek gold mines, he returned with furs and fish only, but his map labeled the region "New England." The name stuck to the region authorized for settlement and exploitation by the Plymouth Company. Sir Ferdinando Gorges was the leader in this concern. His plan was to divide the region into vast estates and sell them to aristocrats. This never materialized, although the company was reorganized in November, 1620, as the Council of New England. In 1623 this company allowed a group known as the Dorchester Adventurers to establish a permanent fishing village in New England. The village became a reality, but when no profits were forthcoming, the settlement was withdrawn in 1626. Some of the settlers refused to leave, however, and under the leadership of Roger Conant they moved and established the village of Salem.

John White, a pastor high in the Dorchester group, believed Salem a good beginning for missionary work, and in 1628 he and a group of Puritan gentlemen and London merchants formed the Company of New England to take over the Dorchester project. They received confirmation from the Council of New England for land from three miles south of the Charles River to three miles north of the Merrimack River. However, Sir Ferdinando Gorges protested that the title was illegal. Therefore the New England Company petitioned the king for its own charter, and on March 14, 1629, it received a royal charter merging the New England Company into the Massachusetts Bay Company with the same land rights as before. That same year, a split developed in the Massachusetts Bay Company. One faction consisted of Nonconformists who wanted to remain in England; the other faction, principally Separatists headed by John Winthrop, wanted to leave England because of political pressure.

James I had died in 1625, mourned by very few Englishmen. He had squandered his initial popularity by pursuing his strong desire to govern absolutely. In the process he had encroached on parliamentary powers. He also had been unwise with his funds and was constantly searching for more and yet more taxes. James was succeeded by his son, Charles I, who likewise was welcomed to the throne enthusiastically. Soon that support turned to hatred. When Parliament refused to vote new taxes, Charles resorted to "forced loans," and his compliant clergy declared nonpayment a sin. Archbishop William Laud, installed by Charles, intensified the persecution of Puritans (the name derived from their desire to "purify" the Church of England of its papist ways). When Parliament in 1629 attempted to curb these tendencies, Charles dissolved it. Eleven years passed before another Parliament was called. The Puritans became so disheartened by these events that they determined to migrate to the New World, as had their brethren to Plymouth in 1620.

The Massachusetts Bay Colony

In August 1629, John Winthrop and eleven like-minded men signed a document known as the Cambridge Agreement. This stated that they would migrate to the New World provided the charter and officers of the Massachusetts Bay Company migrate with them. Between March and October of the following year, more than a thousand Puritans emigrated in seventeen ships, founding Boston, Charlestown, and Watertown. Winthrop became governor, and the other eleven stockholders became his assistants (or council). The transfer of this charter and the company officials to America made the colony practically independent of England. Subsequent liberalizations enlarged the number of freemen, and representative government was instituted. All voters had to be members of the church, however, for, as in Plymouth, the founders did not want religious freedom, only the dominance of their own brand of orthodoxy. The religious requirement for voting gave the clergy an unhealthy dominance in the colony, even as tyranny in the Mother Country during the decade of the 1630s brought increased settlement. So many came, in fact, that the phenomenon was labeled the Great Migration.

Connecticut Colonized

Dissatisfied residents of Massachusetts did take action. In 1636, under the leadership of the Reverend Thomas Hooker, one congregation moved to the Connecticut River valley and founded Hartford. Other settlements, such as Wethersfield and Windsor, sprang into existence. Similarly the Reverend John Davenport and Theophilus Eaton moved from Massachusetts in 1638 and established settlements in another region, which in 1643 were drawn together to form the colony of New Haven.

All those who split away from Massachusetts did not do so on a friendly basis. Between 1631 and 1636, Roger Williams, a Cambridge-educated theologian, developed heretical ideas. He preached opposition to the theocracy and advocated religious liberty; he asserted that the land belonged to the Indians, not the crown; and he opposed the right of the colony to tax those not belonging to the church. For such sins, he was tried by the general court and sentenced to banishment. In 1636 he moved southward, purchased land from the Narragansett Indians, and founded a tiny settlement he named Providence. Anne Hutchinson, another religious rebel who believed that every person was his own priest guided by an inner light, was expelled in 1638 and founded Portsmouth. Another town in the vicinity, Newport, was established in 1639. Eight years later Williams, Hutchinson, and the Newport settlers would band together to form the colony of Rhode Island.

There were also illegal settlements in the areas that would come to be Maine and New Hampshire. The Company of New England in 1635 granted New Hampshire to Captain John Mason, while Sir Ferdinando Gorges controlled Maine after 1620. Thus the two men had title to the land between the Merrimack and Kennebec rivers. Settlers moved into the area without permission and founded towns, while the colony of Massachusetts refused to recognize these grants and tried to acquire

29

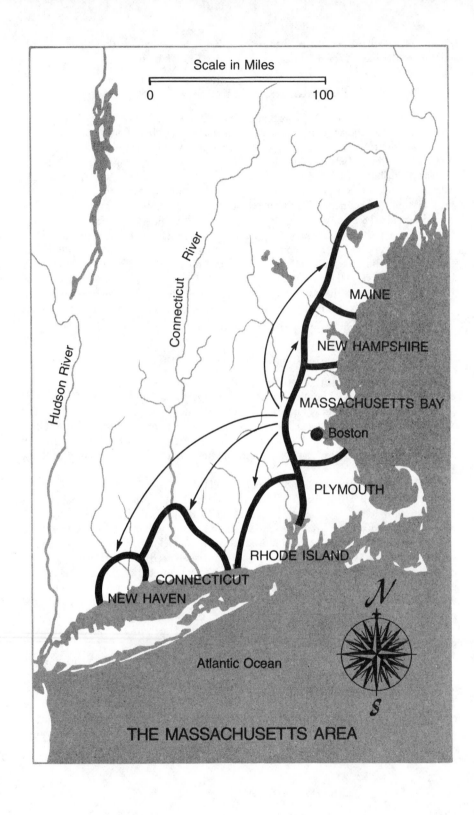

Scale in Miles

0   100

Hudson River

Connecticut River

MAINE

NEW HAMPSHIRE

MASSACHUSETTS BAY

Boston

PLYMOUTH

RHODE ISLAND

CONNECTICUT

NEW HAVEN

N

S

Atlantic Ocean

THE MASSACHUSETTS AREA

title to them. In 1640, upon the death of John Mason, New Hampshire came under the ownership of Massachusetts, as did Maine in 1688.

The Establishment of Maryland

Another colony quite distinct from the Puritan settlements of New England likewise sprang from the religious and political struggles in the Mother Country during the reign of Charles I. While Puritan and Anglican quarreled with one another, both turned viciously on the few Catholics yet in England. The most distinguished English member of that church was George Calvert, Lord Baltimore, who was converted in 1625. Calvert had a long interest in North America; indeed he had been a subscriber to shares in the London Company, and in 1622, for services to the crown, he had been given the entirety of Newfoundland by James I. After his conversion to Catholicism, he attempted to plant a colony in Newfoundland as a refuge for his fellow religionists. The hard winters there spelled disaster for the attempt, however, and in 1628 it was abandoned.

George Calvert died in 1632. To his son, Cecilius Calvert, second Lord Baltimore, Charles I on June 30, 1632, made a proprietary grant of the land between the Potomac and forty degrees north latitude. The only restriction placed on Calvert was that he had to govern with the "advice and consent of the freemen." On December 2, 1633, 200 colonists sailed under the direction of Leonard Calvert, brother of Cecilius, for the colony called Maryland, in honor of the king's wife, Henrietta Maria. The group landed and established the village of St. Mary's after purchasing the land from the Indians. Because they arrived in the spring and because they immediately planted corn, they did not suffer a "starving time" as had their neighbors across Chesapeake Bay in Virginia. And because they bought their land from the Indians, they did not have the wars that plagued the Virginians. In 1635 an assembly of freeholders was called, bringing representative government to the Catholic colony. Maryland prospered despite some boundary disputes with Virginia, and tobacco farming brought economic security. The major threat to the colony came not from events in the New World, but from the Puritan Revolution in England, an event that would have great significance for all the English colonies in America.

The Puritan Revolution

Charles I, like his father, James I, wished to rule without Parliament as an absolute monarch. The "Short Parliament" of 1629, which attempted to restrict the king's collection of taxes without the consent of Parliament, was dissolved, and another meeting of the body did not take place until 1640. That year Charles had to call another session of Parliament because of his pressing need for money. That meeting, generally referred to as the "Long Parliament," refused to raise taxes. Instead it raised an army under Puritan leadership and began a revolution that culminated in Charles' capture and execution. England then became a Puritan republic under the leadership of Oliver Cromwell, an event that virtually halted the migration of Puritans to the New World and which caused considerable worry to Marylanders, who feared their right to worship as Catholics would be endangered. As a result, Maryland's assembly in 1649 passed the Toleration Act providing for complete freedom of worship for all Christians, but a death penalty for non-Christians.

31

John Underhill

THE confused state of affairs in New England, religiously and politically, produced such men as John Underhill, whose life certainly reflected his times. Underhill's family was English, but his father was a mercenary soldier for the Dutch. John possibly was born in Holland, and there he became a Puritan, although not one of great conviction.

In 1630 Underhill went to Massachusetts to settle in the Bay Colony and to help organize the militia, in which he served as one of the captains. Four years later he became a selectman of the town. However, he was not happy. Puritans had little love for the military, and Underhill constantly had to fight for supplies. Then came the Indian wars of 1637. Underhill fought in Massachusetts and in the Pequot wars in Connecticut. Returning to Boston in 1638, he was arrested and tried before the General Court for making contemptuous speeches about the leaders of the colony. Found guilty, he was banished and fled to Dover, New Hampshire, just in time to avoid trial for adultery. At Dover he became governor of the colony and stoutly resisted Massachusetts' claims to the region. He begged forgiveness of the Boston church for his adultery, however, and even returned to confess it publicly. But he was adjudged insincere and excommunicated. Finally he was reinstated in the church, and in 1641 his sentence of banishment was removed.

At the invitation of the New Haven Court, Underhill in 1643 moved to Stamford in Connecticut and became a captain of militia. He soon resigned that post to take employment with the Dutch in New Amsterdam, where an Indian war was raging. He settled on Long Island and became a member of the Council of New Amsterdam, but when he denounced Governor Peter Stuyvesant as a tyrant he was almost tried for sedition and had to flee. Moving to Rhode Island, he was commissioned a privateer in 1653 and seized the property of the Dutch West Indies Company at Hartford, Connecticut. Then, during the Anglo-Dutch War of 1665–67, Underhill fought for the British to conquer New Amsterdam, and there in 1665 he was named surveyor of customs for Long Island. He died at his Long Island estate in 1672.

Virginia benefited from the Puritan Revolution at first. Sir William Berkeley, a staunch royalist, had offered refuge to royalists from republican England. He also waged a successful war against the Indians, forcing them to cede much land between the James and York rivers in 1644. However, in 1652, the House of Burgesses overthrew Berkeley's iron rule.

Puritan New England, as might be expected, suffered little during the Cromwell era. In fact, the region became almost self-governing and made the first steps toward confederation. The threat of the nearby Dutch, coupled with menacing Indians, at a time when England could offer no aid, revived a scheme first proposed by Connecticut in 1637. This proposed union of the Puritan colonies had been rejected at first, but in 1642 Massachusetts expressed an interest in the project. The following year commissioners from Massachusetts, Connecticut, Plymouth, and New Haven met in Boston and formed the United Colonies of New England. Matters such as fighting the Dutch and the Indians were to be dealt with by concerted effort under the guidance of an eight-man council composed of two representatives from each colony. Local matters were to be left to each colony. No mention was made of the English government in the drafting of this document, nor was Rhode Island, considered a haven for heretics, included. The United Colonies of New England did settle some boundary disputes between the four members, and it negotiated with the Dutch to some extent. But from the outset Massachusetts, the largest and most powerful of the four signatory colonies, dominated the council. Therefore by 1652 the other three allowed it to languish, although it did not die until 1686. Its finest hour came in 1675–76 during an incident known as King Philip's War, a bitter fight with the Wampanoag and Narragansett Indians.

King Philip's War grew out of the Indians' gradual realization that the growing number of British colonists would contest ownership of the land with them—and out of the hatreds of the Indian leader of this war. Philip was born at the tribal village of the Wampanoag Indians at Mount Hope, Rhode Island. His father, Massasoit, the tribal chief, took two of his sons to Plymouth and asked that they be given English names: the elder son was named Alexander, and the other was called Philip. Alexander became chief of the Wampanoag upon his father's death. In 1661 he was arrested by the Plymouth Bay colonists, who feared an uprising was planned; on the way to Plymouth, Alexander became ill and died, causing the Indians to believe that he had been poisoned. The next year Philip became sachem of the tribe.

As such, he renewed his father's treaty with the colonists and lived peacefully with them for nine years, but gradually he became hostile to the whites because their increasing numbers made game scarce, the fisheries to fail, and Indians to have difficulty retaining sufficient land. The Indians were being pushed into marginal swampland, for every time they wanted to purchase English goods they were asked to pay by signing away yet more of their land.

Philip's arrogance exacerbated the growing tensions. On one occasion he declared himself to be the equal of his "brother," Charles II. And he began plotting against the whites. In 1671 he was summoned to Taunton and confronted with evidence of his plots. He was released, however, after signing a statement of submission, paying a fine, and surrendering part of his tribe's firearms.

The open break between the two races came in 1675. Philip's former secretary, Sassamon, was murdered by the Wampanoag, who believed that Sassamon had betrayed Indian secrets to the whites. Three Wampanoag braves were executed for

34

this crime, whereupon Philip reacted by sending his tribe's women and children to live with the Narragansett Indians and by making an alliance with the Nipmuck. On June 24, 1675, their attack on a colonial village triggered King Philip's War.

The fighting quickly spread to Plymouth and Massachusetts Bay colonies, west to the Connecticut River, and north to Vermont. The Indians in this war killed men, women, and children. At this juncture, the United Colonies of New England rose to the emergency. It sent a combined army to try for a decisive battle, but Philip preferred stealth, ambush, and surprise raids. In these he displayed wily and effective leadership. However, he was unsuccessful in persuading the Mohegan and Mohawk Indians to join him.

Failing to get a decisive battle, the colonials tried a new strategy. In December, 1675, Governor Josiah Winslow and 1000 troops attacked the Narragansett village, killed 1600 Indians, and sold the captured Wampanoag women and children into slavery in the West Indies and South America. The colonials also destroyed Indian crops, offered amnesty to deserters, and advertised a reward for any Indian killed in battle. These measures caused Philip's army to dwindle. With a few faithful followers, he was pursued from place to place—while his wife and son were captured and sold into slavery. In the swamps near Mount Hope he was shot in August, 1676, by an Indian serving the colonials. His body was beheaded and drawn and quartered, his head to be exhibited at Plymouth for twenty years.

King Philip's War proved the effectiveness of the Council of New England by showing that unity was necessary in the face of major adversity. And it foreshadowed future developments and showed that common interests demanded compromise and confederation under a written agreement.

Oliver Cromwell died in 1658, leaving a power vacuum that was filled two years later when Charles II, son of Charles I, was invited to reestablish the monarchy. This change presaged great turmoil in the New World colonies. In Virginia, Sir William Berkeley was restored to the governorship and proceeded to hang several of the ringleaders of the rebellion against his authority. In Maryland, where the Calverts had been deprived of their proprietorship and the Toleration Act had been repealed during the Puritan era, Charles Calvert, son of Cecilius, was named governor. However, pro-Catholic policies caused great discontent in the colony during the next fifteen years, especially when coupled with low tobacco prices. Connecticut was the first New England colony to make overtures to the restored monarch of England, and in 1662 it was granted the Fundamental Orders of Connecticut, a royal charter making it a corporate colony and allowing it to absorb New Haven. Rhode Island likewise received a charter; granted in 1663, this charter included a statement of religious toleration and provided for self-rule. Massachusetts grudgingly received four commissioners in 1664, who recommended that landowners be given the vote, that laws against the crown be repealed, and that religious freedom be allowed. Massachusetts refused, however, and nothing was done.

Charles II and Colonization

New English colonies were swiftly added during the period of the restoration, again bringing change to the direction of these settlements. In 1664 Charles granted the area of Maine (north of the Kennebec River) to his destitute brother James, Duke of York. Also, he gave James the land from the western boundary of Connecticut to the east shore of the Delaware. In April that year James sent Colonel

Richard Nicholls to conquer the area between Connecticut and Delaware, the region known as New Netherlands. Governor Peter Stuyvesant surrendered to Nicholls, a surrender confirmed by the Second Anglo-Dutch War of 1664–67, and the New Netherlands became New York. In 1665 James issued the "Duke's Laws," a code allowing self-government with elective officials. The Dutch Patroons accepted this transfer, for they found the autocratic James agreed basically with their methods and their philosophy. New York briefly was reconquered by the Dutch in 1673 during the Third Anglo-Dutch War of 1672–74, but it was returned to England at the termination of that conflict.

To the south, new colonies began with the restoration of Charles II. In April, 1663, as partial payment for debts he had incurred, Charles granted the land between thirty-one and thirty-six degrees north latitude to eight proprietors, whose only restrictions were that they had to govern with the consent of the freemen and religious liberty had to be granted. The northern part of this grant, which eventually became North Carolina, had already been colonized by refugees from Virginia; in 1664 the proprietors named a governor for this region, called Albemarle, and malcontents from Virginia continued to settle there, growing tobacco. Albemarle also became a haven for pirates, runaway slaves, defaulting debtors, and other undesirables. When in 1691 it became North Carolina, it was regarded by Virginians and South Carolinians as a haven for heretics and scum, but it did have its own governor and assembly.

The proprietors began settlement of South Carolina in 1665 by bringing in colonists from Barbados. When that failed, John Locke, the famed English philosopher, was persuaded to draft the Fundamental Constitutions of Carolina, a document that provided for a hereditary nobility, each to have 12,000 acres, a governor, and a one-house legislature. Charleston was established in 1670, and the following year the assembly met in that city. The people intended as vassals for the huge estates resisted payment of their rents to such an extent that the constitution had to be liberalized. A bicameral legislature was granted, with the lower house assuming more and more power, but in South Carolina the aristocratic heritage would linger long; the colony, for example, maintained the highest property qualification for voting of any colony in the New World. French Huguenots, who fled continuing religious wars in their homeland, arrived in South Carolina in 1680, and they added a distinctive flavor to the colony. Also, the continued importation of Negro slaves brought a planter economy principally devoted to tobacco and indigo.

Quaker Colonies

Religious persecution in England likewise brought colonists to the New World during the period of the restoration. Two colonies resulted, one new and the other the outgrowth of an older colony. In 1664, James, Duke of York, paid off some of his debts by giving John Lord Berkeley and Sir George Carteret the land between the Delaware and Hudson rivers. This land, which became known as New Jersey in honor of Carteret's home on the Isle of Jersey, was governed under a document known as "Concessions and Agreements," which provided for a governor and assembly and for religious freedom. Elizabethtown was established in 1665 by Governor Philip Carteret. However, there soon was a protest against the rents exacted by the proprietors, and in 1674 Berkeley sold his interest to members of the Society of Friends, better known as the Quakers.

Out of the religious ferment of Puritan England had come a great leader, George Fox, who founded the Society of Friends. He and his followers were religious anarchists, believing in no church and no priesthood; every man was his own priest and so all were equal. They believed in a literal interpretation of the Biblical injunction, "Thou shalt not kill," a commandment they held should be followed even in time of war. Because they believed that one should quake at the name of God, they soon were popularly called "Quakers." To persecution they offered passive resistance—and they made many converts despite imprisonment and death. Although Fox was the founder, the best-known practitioner was William Penn. Born in 1644, the son of Admiral Sir William Penn, he was converted to Quakerism in 1667, and he sought a place where his fellow religionists would be free from persecution.

There would have been a Quaker colony without Penn. Half of New Jersey was acquired by the Quakers in 1674, and two years later a Quaker commission of four individuals (including Penn) began administering it. West Jersey, their half, was a haven; under the "Laws, Concessions, and Agreements" of the four commissioners, its residents were guaranteed religious liberty, jury trial, and representative government. Then in 1681 Penn and eleven other coreligionists bought East Jersey from Carteret's heirs, and it also became a refuge for Quakers.

William Penn would become the great colonizer of the Quakers, however. In 1681 he was granted the land between forty and forty-three degrees north latitude by Charles II as payment for a debt of £16,000 owed by the monarch to Penn's father. There were many restrictions on the grant: mercantilistic Navigation Acts had to be enforced, laws had to be approved by an assembly, the crown could veto all laws—and the area had to be named Pennsylvania. Penn immediately took steps to colonize, publishing a pamphlet in English, French, German, and Dutch, which, with customary Quaker ethics, understated the attractiveness of the region. Then in July Penn issued his "Conditions and Concessions," which offered a free fifty-acre headright and very liberal purchase of huge estates. The first colonists departed for Pennsylvania in October. Still more came the following year after Penn on May 5 issued his *Frame of Government,* which provided for a governor and a council to be named by the proprietor and an assembly to be elected by the freeholders. The *Frame* also provided for religious toleration and a liberal penal code. Penn himself came over in 1683, and Philadelphia was established as the capital of the colony. German Mennonites came, as well as Quakers, and they founded Germantown under the leadership of Francis Daniel Pastorius. Pennsylvania was such a success that eighteenth-century European philosophers never tired of using it as proof that man could live without monarchy, feudalism, and racial and religious uniformity.

Types of British Colonies

Thus by the 1680s, three types of British colonies had evolved in the New World. The crown (or royal) colony, such as Virginia, was under the jurisdiction of a governor and council appointed in England, but also had a legislative body elected by the freeholders. This lower house alone could initiate fiscal legislation, but all laws were subject to veto by the governor and the crown. A second category was the corporate colony, such as Massachusetts and Rhode Island, where the charter lay with the stockholders (freemen) who elected their governor and both houses of their legislature. Finally, there was the proprietary colony, such as New York, Mary-

37

land, and Pennsylvania, where the owner named the governor and council and the lower house was elected by the freeholders. In all three types of colonies, there was a gradual shifting of power to the lower house of the legislative bodies as these strove to imitate the House of Commons in the British Parliament.

In these governments there was also contention for more equal representation in the lower houses of the legislatures. The apportionment of seats to the legislature generally had occurred shortly after settlement. Then, as pioneers pushed into the back country, they wanted to establish new counties and to be given seats in the legislature. But their cousins along the coast hesitated to share power, and quarrels resulted, quarrels that sometimes became quite violent. In Virginia, for example, back-country residents grew angry when they felt unfairly taxed and underrepresented. Plummeting tobacco prices, caused by the British mercantile law that forced all tobacco to be shipped to England, had brought hard times; this was coupled with a smouldering Indian war on the edge of the frontier, during which Governor William Berkeley refused to send troops to aid the back-country settlers. Led by Nathaniel Bacon, these settlers rallied on May 10, 1676, to revolt. First they defeated the Indians. Then they marched on and conquered Jamestown. Berkeley first was forced to pardon these malcontents and to make Bacon a general in command of militia. The governor intended to crush the rebellion, however, but could not raise troops loyal to him. He fled to Maryland. When Bacon died of a fever in October, 1676, Berkeley returned and hanged twenty-three rebels. Charles II removed Berkeley as governor in April, 1677, but voting reforms instituted by Bacon were repudiated. Thus the smouldering antagonisms between tidewater aristocrats and back-country settlers lingered—and would remain a problem for more than a century thereafter, not only in Virginia but in most other colonies as well.

Spanish Defensive Expansion

Just as England was expanding the area under its jurisdiction, so also were Spain and France. In Florida, the only Spanish settlements were at St. Augustine and St. Mark (at the mouth of the Apalachicola River). Yet Spain regarded land as far north as the thirty-fifth parallel as belonging to it, and was outraged when England colonized the Carolinas. Minor skirmishes along this border would continue for years, with Spaniards and Indian allies raiding north and English farmers retaliating and even initiating forays.

In New Mexico the Spaniards had considerably more success than in Florida. There, led by Franciscan missionaries, their hegemony had been extended north to Taos and beyond by 1621, and as far west as the Hopi country of Arizona by 1629. These missionaries were self-supporting, although they did receive their annual salary of 290 pesos from the royal treasury. Soldiers usually were stationed near these missions; in theory they were there to protect the pueblo Indians and the missionaries from the incursions of hostile natives and to guard the supply caravans. In return they were to receive an annual tribute from the head of each Indian family of one and a half bushels of corn and a piece of cloth. According to law, all other services performed by the Indians were to be paid for. Human nature is all too fallible, however, and the law was generally violated. Consequently, resentment deepened between the Indians and their Spanish conquerors.

The Spanish governors during the period 1610–80 usually considered their office a means of enrichment rather than a public trust. They monopolized commerce, bringing trade goods to the province for sale at exorbitant prices to civilians, soldiers, and Indians, and they appropriated the bounty of nature—piñon nuts and salt —to be sold for personal gain. Indians captured in battle frequently were put to work for the governor weaving woolen goods and preparing hides for export. These burdens, along with those imposed by other Spaniards, widened the gulf between Indian and Spaniard, as did the gradual increase in the tax on heads of native households. This discontent came to a head in 1680 when a resident of San Juan Pueblo named Popé decided to rid New Mexico of the Spanish yoke. On August 10 that year the war began, its goal being to kill all Spaniards and their sympathizers or else drive them from the land. On August 21 the governor led the survivors southward to the site of the present Juaréz, Chihuahua, and founded a settlement known as El Paso del Norte. Twelve years passed before a new governor, Diego de Vargas, was able to return to New Mexico, and not until 1696 was the reconquest completed.

The Pueblo Revolt of 1680 destroyed Spanish settlements in Arizona. But by 1691, even before the reconquest had begun, Father Eusebio Francisco Kino, a Jesuit, was pushing northward from Sonora into southern Arizona to establish missions named Tumacácori and Guevavi and visiting at the site of Tucson. Also, while the refugees from New Mexico were at El Paso, Jumano Indians from West Texas came to seek missionaries, saying they wished to be converted. Franciscan padres already had visited the Jumano villages in 1629, 1632, and 1650. Thus in 1683 the Spaniards were pleased to return to that region. Captain Juan Domínguez de Mendoza and Father Nicolás López, with a large escort of soldiers, journeyed to the site of the present San Angelo, Texas, early in 1684; there they collected numerous buffalo hides, and the padre baptized many Indians. Their report greatly stimulated interest in the region, and doubtless a colony would have been established there soon afterward—had not rumors of a French colony on the Texas coast intervened to divert Spanish attention to that region instead.

The French in Canada

The French indeed were on the Texas coast in 1685, which meant that from the humble beginning at Quebec in 1608 great strides had been made in New France. Samuel de Champlain, founder of the Quebec colony, lived to see many changes before his death in 1635. Recollect Friars had arrived in 1615, to be followed in 1625 by the Jesuits. Meanwhile, Champlain had conducted many journeys of exploration, reaching southward into New York and westward to Lake Ontario and Lake Huron. All the while he was interested in permanent colonization, but his mercantile backers were more interested in the profits to be derived from the fur trade. Champlain did not produce profits sufficient to satisfy his backers, and in 1627 came reorganization. The region of the St. Lawrence was transferred to the Company of New France, composed of the Hundred Associates, named for a group of investors. That year the number of colonists totaled only sixty-five at Quebec, and a war from 1627 to 1632 almost destroyed them; during that conflict, the British captured Quebec and settled French Acadia (which was renamed Nova Scotia). The colony was returned in 1632, and the French put new plans into operation, plans that called for profits from the sale of land as well as from fur. Large estates were granted, provided that settlers were brought to work them. Many of these grants went to speculators who had no intention of bringing settlers, however, and the colony grew slowly. By 1640 there were only 200 residents. The Company of New France learned a historical truth—the French have been notoriously unwilling to emigrate.

However slowly, the colony did grow. In 1641 Montreal was established by the Jesuits, who had interested Frenchmen in winning souls in New France even though worldly profits had proven illusory. Montreal became a commercial and religious center, for its strategic location brought it rich trade—and Iroquois hostility. That Indian hatred culminated in 1648 with the final dissolution of the Hurons, with whom the French had allied themselves, and Montreal fell under full siege thereafter. By 1660 New France was dying from these attacks, and the residents made desperate pleas to the crown for aid. Louis XIV, at the urging of his minister of finance, Jean Baptiste Colbert, decided to expand colonization. The Hundred Associates voluntarily surrendered their charter in February, 1663, and New France became a royal colony (although the Company of the West Indies had a monopoly on the fur trade until 1774).

Louis XIV took vigorous steps to retain the colony. A veteran regiment of more than a thousand troops was sent, and in a winter campaign in 1666–67 they broke the Iroquois grip on Canada. Jean Baptiste Talon was sent as intendant, and he dominated the government until 1772. Government came to be vested in a council consisting of the intendant, the governor, the bishop, and five appointed councilors. Louis XIV did not believe in representative government, either at home or in the colonies, and all such tendencies were suppressed. Talon proved a worthy subject of his sovereign and vigorously pushed growth of the colony. He persuaded the crown to promise 300 colonists a year for ten years, and he encouraged the soldiers who came to defend Canada to stay and make their homes there. Large families and early marriage likewise were encouraged by Talon; thus by 1673 the census showed 6705 residents.

The land system of New France reflected the policies back home—and in France these policies were based on a small amount of land in comparison with the number of inhabitants. Land was parcelled out in large seigniories, a feudalistic device; the seignior, a form of minor noble, in theory was to colonize his land, in return receiving rents from his tenants (peasants). But the seigniors rarely colonized, preferring to dabble in the fur trade rather than trying to collect from unhappy tenants. There were sharp social distinctions between tenant and seignior, even if both lived in rude homes and ate coarse food.

Yet land was too plentiful for peasant lads of ambition to accept peasant status. Many fled to the woods to become *coureurs des bois,* literally "runners of the woods"—unlicensed traders and trappers. Furs were easily sold to provide necessities, and Indian girls became wives. The life was free and easy, filled with adventure, and even advantageous to France; in the process of running the woods, these men extended French influence among the Indians and inclined them toward Catholicism and against foreigners.

The French in Louisiana

French exploration westward had continued, in the tradition of Champlain, from the earliest years. In 1634, Jean Nicolet, one of Champlain's agents, journeyed to Lake Huron, crossed to Lake Michigan, and visited at the Green Bay region of present-day Wisconsin. From Indians in the vicinity he heard of a great river to the south—doubtless the Mississippi—but did not try to reach it. After Champlain's death, the impetus for exploration was provided by the Jesuits, whose exploits rivaled those of the fur traders and trappers. They, too, became agents in the rivalry to win the adherence of the natives to a European power. Each year these missionaries published a report of their activities in New France—the *Jesuit Relations*—which eventually would total seventy-three volumes. These inspired devout, wealthy Frenchmen to contribute funds for the missionary effort; they filled some young French lads with a desire to know the wilderness; and they became the greatest sourcebook for the history of the French in North America. The Jesuits and the *coureurs des bois* became the cutting edge of French penetration of the interior, sometimes separately, sometimes together.

The brothers-in-law Radisson and Groseilliers were south of Lake Superior at mid-seventeenth century, trading with the Sioux in eastern Minnesota. Next came Nicolas Perrot in 1665, who spent five years in that vicinity. It was he who acted as interpreter in 1671 at a council at Sault Ste. Marie (at the passageway between Lakes Superior and Huron). At that council, with all the usual pageantry, Simon Francois Daumont formally claimed the interior of North America for his sovereign, Louis XIV. Fourteen Indian tribes watched this spectacle. The great intendant Talon was determined to do more than lay claim to the region, however. Realizing that more than the reading of a proclamation was necessary, he commissioned Louis Joliet, a French-Canadian, and Father Jacques Marquette, a Jesuit fluent in Indian dialects, to explore the region's river and determine its course.

Marquette and Joliet departed St. Ignace (at the northeast end of Lake Michigan) on May 17, 1673, in birch canoes. Going with them were five other frontiersmen. At Green Bay they began ascending the Fox River to its source. There they carried their canoes a mile and a half to embark on the Wisconsin River, which led them to the Mississippi. Going down the Mississippi proved easy, and they made rapid progress. Past the mouth of the Missouri they swept, past the Ohio, to the Arkansas. There they were convinced that the Mississippi drained into the Gulf of Mexico, not the Pacific Ocean. Satisfied with this knowledge, they began their return trip on July 17. The trip northward was far more difficult than the down-river run; fighting the swift current for every mile, they eventually reached the Illinois River, which they followed to its source. Then they crossed to Lake Michigan, and at the end of September again were at Green Bay. They had traveled more than 2500 miles in just four months—and had exposed the heart of the North American continent.

What Marquette and Joliet had begun was to be finished by a native of Roeun, France, who had been educated to be a teacher. René Robert Cavelier, Sieur de La Salle, born in 1643, had arrived in the New World in 1666 at the age of twenty-three. He was a restless spirit who longed to know the trackless wilderness, and in New France he became legendary as an expert woodsman, a remarkable Indian fighter, and a leader of men. Trading and trapping on the frontier was but a means of furthering his desire to be an explorer, and the exploits of Marquette and Joliet fired his imagination. He became obsessed with a desire to be the discoverer of the mouth of the Mississippi River. In February, 1682, he set out to make that dream a reality. With thirty-one Abenaki and Mohegan Indians, he followed the path of Marquette and Joliet, but did not halt at the mouth of the Arkansas. Instead he pushed on to the Gulf. A short distance from the Gulf, on a point of high ground, he gathered his men on April 9, 1682, to intone the ritual formula of possession:

"In the name of the most high, mighty, invincible, and victorious Prince, Louis the Great, by the grace of God King of France and of Navarre, Fourteenth of that name, I . . . have taken, and do now take . . . possession of this country of Louisiana. . . ."

Knowing that rivers were the natural highways of a wilderness, La Salle saw that a French colony at the mouth of the Mississippi would guarantee French control of the interior of North America. He therefore conceived an even mightier scheme than the one that had driven him to that point: he would colonize the mouth of the Mississippi. Ascending the Mississippi, he sailed for France, where he was granted an audience with Louis XIV. To his sovereign, La Salle stressed that his proposed colony would prove a counterpoise to Spanish power in the Gulf Coast region, that it would serve as a staging area for the conquest of Mexican silver mines, that missionaries would win a rich harvest of converts in the region—all in addition to insuring French control of the interior of North America. The king agreed with La Salle's proposal, and on July 24, 1684, the explorer sailed from La Rochelle with four ships and 400 colonists.

The attempt to plant a French colony at the mouth of the Mississippi proved a series of disasters. La Salle quarreled with the naval commander of the four ships, the Sieur de Beaujeu. Then he fell ill and almost died. One of the ships was captured by a Spanish privateer, thus warning the Spaniards of the French presence. As the remaining ships sailed along the Gulf Coast looking for the mouth of the Mississippi, they were separated. The greatest misfortune, however, was La Salle's failure to find the mouth of the Mississippi. Then, after the French ships had been reunited, Beaujeu threatened to return home. La Salle thereupon stated that Matagorda Bay on the coast of Texas was the mouth of the Mississippi and insisted on being put ashore. One ship was wrecked in navigating the entrance of Matagorda Bay, and Beaujeu quickly departed with almost half the colonists—those too fainthearted to stay with La Salle.

With his 200 colonists, La Salle moved some six miles up Garcitas Creek and erected a post he called Fort Saint Louis. Crops were planted, and forays were mounted to discourage Indian depredations. But disaster continued to plague the colony. The crops failed, and the natives in the vicinity increased their ambushes. La Salle made several attempts by land to find the river mouth he had missed at sea —and failed.

By January, 1687, the colony was in pitiful straits. Only forty-five were still alive; fevers, poor diet, illness, and Indians had accounted for the remainder. Leaving twenty-five wretches at the post, La Salle departed with twenty men, intending to go to Canada for aid and promising soon to return. That promise was never fulfilled. A group of conspirators within his small band killed La Salle. Seven of the survivors, led by La Salle's trusted lieutenant, Henri Joutel, did make it to Canada; Joutel even went to Paris to plead with Louis XIV to send a ship for those at Fort Saint Louis, but the Sun King had lost interest—and nothing was done.

Spanish Texas

If Louis XIV was not interested in the little French outpost, the Spaniards were. In fact, they were in a virtual frenzy to discover and obliterate the French threat to their claims along the Gulf Coast. Four expeditions by sea and four by land failed to find the colony, for it was well hidden. Then in May, 1688, an Indian came to a

Spanish outpost near the Rio Grande and reported that he had wandered into a village ruled by a Frenchman. Alonso de León, captain of the Spanish outpost, took a detachment of troops to investigate and found the story true. Jean Henri was ruling a tribe of Indians as their king; he was a survivor of Fort Saint Louis. Taken to Mexico City to visit the viceroy, Henri agreed to lead a Spanish expedition to the site of Fort Saint Louis.

In March, 1689, Captain de León set out for Texas with eighty-eight soldiers, two priests, and several attendants. Guided by Henri, they arrived at Fort Saint Louis in April. There were no survivors at the site; all the French either had been killed by the Indians or had managed to be adopted into some tribe. While de León conducted his military business, one of the Franciscan priests, Damián Massanet, tried to win the friendship of the nearby Tejas Indians, and upon the Spanish departure, Massanet promised the Tejas he would soon return. The viceroy agreed with this proposal when he received de León's report; he ordered the captain to return to the site and destroy all evidence of French settlement on the Texas coast and to erect a Spanish mission among the Tejas Indians.

Thus in the spring of 1690 Captain de León made yet another trip to Texas. Fort Saint Louis was burned, and Mission San Francisco de los Tejas was erected. This advance of the Spanish frontier therefore was made not for gold or silver—or even particularly to convert the heathen—so much as to keep out the French. It was a case of defensive expansion. But the attempt to settle Texas proved abortive. A supply expedition to the mission in the spring of 1693 found the natives hostile after a drought and an epidemic had sadly reduced their numbers. Even Father Massanet thought the situation hopeless, for when the supply column departed he sent with it a letter to the viceroy asking permission to abandon the site. A council convened by the viceroy concurred, but even before the order could reach Texas the Franciscans had obeyed it. In October, 1693, fearing an uprising, the priests had buried their religious articles and fled toward Mexico under cover of darkness. Texas was left to the Indians once again, with neither Frenchman nor Spaniard to contest for possession.

Between 1610 and 1690 European colonists had spread across much of North America. Spaniards were in Florida, New Mexico, and Arizona, and had moved temporarily into Texas. Frenchmen were living along the St. Lawrence Valley and were moving across the Great Lakes region regularly, spreading out into Minnesota and the Mississippi River Valley. And Englishmen had colonies from Maine to the Carolinas, reaching into the interior almost to the Allegheny Mountains. The methods of colonization had been perfected by each of the three nations, just as each had transferred many of its social institutions to the New World. The actual number of settlers within the present limits of the United States, excluding Indians, was still quite small in 1690; but, as demonstrated in Texas, the three nationalities already were coming into contact and conflict. The stage had been set for colonial wars that would settle the ownership of a continent.

Chapter Three

The War for the New World

Causes of Colonial Wars

CURIOSITY has been a powerful force in human destiny. It has impelled men to seek answers to the unanswerable, to try to learn the unknowable—in short, to quest for they knew not what. Curiosity made the quest as important as the answers, if not more so. It drove men from older, more comfortable ways of life to new and untried methods and places. It caused tears at family partings, but those who cried upon departure often did so hypocritically; their hearts were beating more with excitement for what was to come than for what they were leaving behind. Curiosity forced men from colonies to the frontier. It impelled them to see the far side of mountains and the sources of rivers. And it drove them into conflict with foreigners equally curious—and equally nationalistic.

The period 1689–1763 was one of almost continual warfare in Europe and in North America, for reasons both American and European. There had been strife between the three major colonial powers in North America almost from the start of settlement. Protestant England fought Catholic France and Spain, but the two Catholic powers had battled each other more than they had England. Each of the three powers had Indian allies. Each protested lofty motives. But the early battles had been mere skirmishes. Between 1689 and 1763 would come four major wars—declared wars—and these in large measure were for mastery of North America.

King William's War

The first of these conflicts grew out of an English revolution against the Stuart dynasty. In 1685 Charles II died, leaving the throne to his brother, the Duke of York, who became James II. In just three years the English people grew tired of James, believing that he intended to rule autocratically and that he wished to lead England back into Catholicism. In 1688 they rose up in revolution and drove him from the country; because the victors wrote the histories of the event, it became known as the Glorious Revolution. William of Orange and his wife Mary were invited to assume the English throne as joint monarchs. James fled to France where he appealed to Louis XIV for aid. Louis responded in 1689 by threatening the invasion of William's homeland, the Netherlands. William retaliated by organizing an

44

alliance and making war on France. Known in Europe as the War of the League of Augsburg, in England's American colonies this conflict was labeled King William's War.

In Europe the French and Dutch armies won as often as they lost and acquitted themselves well. In the New World, it was French arms that proved equal to the challenge. Under the capable and energetic governor, the Count de Frontenac, a French force moved northward to capture a Hudson's Bay Company trading post on the bay of that name, and in 1690 a few French troops and large numbers of Indian allies swept southward in a ferocious raid on Schenectady, New York, Falmouth (now Portland), Maine, and the New Hampshire frontier. Likewise, French ships harassed the Massachusetts fishing fleet. These threats—mainly economic—stirred New Englanders to retaliate, although England could offer no real aid.

Massachusetts especially was interested in an English victory, for its citizens were very anxious that James II not return to the throne. In 1684 the charter of Massachusetts had been annulled. Then in 1686, after James became king, he created the Dominion of New England and sent Sir Edmund Andros as governor with authority over the entire region. Andros had angered the Puritans by decreeing that Congregationalists had to share their churches with Anglicans, by trying to appropriate town lands for the crown, and by limiting town meetings to one a year. When news of the Glorious Revolution reached Massachusetts in April, 1689, a mob forced Andros to surrender, and he was sent to England for trial on charges of misgovernment. New York likewise had felt the heavy hand of James II. In 1686 he had disallowed acts of the New York assembly and had given the governor full legislative powers. The following year he had dissolved the assembly, and in 1688 Francis Nicholson was sent as lieutenant governor for New York, which had become part of the Dominion of New England. News of the Glorious Revolution reached New York in May, 1689, and immediately Jacob Leisler and the militia took command of the city of New York. Nicholson was forced to flee. Leisler refused in February, 1691, to surrender to Major Robert Ingoldesby, who had just arrived from England with a regiment. The contest proved unequal, and Leisler was hanged for treason. Henry Sloughter, named the new governor, immediately called an assembly and thereby restored representative government to the colony. New Yorkers therefore did not want a return of James and were ready to fight against him and his French allies.

Thus forces were quickly assembled when the governor of Massachusetts, Sir William Phips, issued a call for volunteers. Phips announced his intention to take Port Royal and Quebec despite the British inability to aid him and the colonists. In the spring of 1690, Phips and his soldiers captured Port Royal, which had only seventy defenders, but which was the source of many of the raids on the Massachusetts fishing fleet. Governor Frontenac so inspired the defenders of Quebec that Phips' assault there came to naught, and he and his army returned to Massachusetts. In 1692 Phips made plans for another assault on Quebec, but again British help was unavailable and Phips' plans failed to materialize. When in 1693 the British did offer help, Phips was too disgusted to try to take Quebec again. French soldiers and their Abenaki Indian allies continued to terrorize the frontier during the remainder of the war, striking at Wells, Maine, and Haverhill, Massachusetts, especially. Also, these French raids so disheartened the Iroquois, who had been allied with the British, that in 1701 they signed a peace agreement with the French.

Peace came in 1697 with the Treaty of Ryswick. To the disgust of New Englanders, this restored Port Royal to the French; in fact, it restored the status quo in both Europe and the New World. The war had settled nothing, and the peace would prove only a breathing spell before another conflict began.

Queen Anne's War

In 1700 the Spanish king, Carlos II, died without an heir. The uneasy truce that began with the Treaty of Ryswick was broken two years later, beginning the War of the Spanish Succession. Louis XIV claimed the Spanish throne for his grandson, Philip of Anjou. England and Austria allied to prevent this, for they feared France would grow too strong if its ruling family also controlled Spain. In England the ruler was Queen Anne; Mary had died in 1694 and William in 1702. Thus in the British colonies, the conflict was labeled Queen Anne's War.

The War of the Spanish Succession lasted eleven long, bloody years. In Europe in the first years of the war, French arms prevailed, but as the years passed, the British army and its allies came to dominate the fighting. In the New World the results were mixed. In 1702 a group of volunteers from South Carolina moved southward and destroyed St. Augustine. But the northern frontier of the British colonies was as exposed as ever to ravages by French-inspired Indian raiders; for example, Deerfield, Massachusetts, was attacked by Abenakis. New Englanders repeatedly begged troops and ships from England, but the Mother Country had none to spare from its European commitments. Finally, in 1710, six warships and a regiment of marines arrived in Boston; these had been intended for an attack on Quebec, but were diverted to Massachusetts in answer to the repeated colonial requests for aid. Four regiments were raised locally, and these, along with the British, moved on Port Royal, the season being too advanced for an assault on Quebec. The French forces at Port Royal, consisting of 300 men, were prevented from deserting by the local governor only by his seizing all canoes in which they might escape. He forced his men to hold out a week under heavy bombardment before surrendering with full honors. Port Royal was renamed Annapolis Royal and would remain permanently British thereafter.

Attempts to capture Quebec in 1711 were humiliating failures, however. Part of the fleet ran aground while ascending the St. Lawrence, and the ground troops, going north by way of Lake Champlain, abandoned their efforts when they learned of the naval disaster. Before another expedition could be launched, the war ended in 1713 with the Treaty of Utrecht. By the terms of this agreement, Philip of Anjou became Philip V of Spain, but the treaty stipulated that one person could not be monarch of both Spain and France simultaneously. Other than this, the French received little for their eleven years of war. England secured title to Newfoundland, Acadia (Port Royal), and Hudson Bay in the New World and Gibraltar in the Old. Also, the French were forced to recognize the Iroquois as British subjects, which eventually gave England a claim to Iroquois lands. Finally, Britain won commercial concessions that included the right to take one ship of 500 tons burden in to the Spanish colonies each year. In return for the loss of valuable and strategic lands in the New World, France had won a throne of doubtful value.

This loss stimulated the French to repair their defenses in New France, and even to expand their holdings. The British acquisition of Acadia was especially dangerous for the French because of its strategic location. To offset the loss of Port Royal, the construction of the fortress of Louisbourg was begun in 1720 on the eastern tip of Cape Breton Island. A naval base, it signaled the French determination to

46

recover Port Royal as soon as possible. Other French military installations included Vincennes (about 1724), Kaskaskia (1720), and Crown Point on Lake Champlain (1731). The English reaction included the erection of forts at Columbia and Port Royal, both in South Carolina (1718), and Oswego on Lake Ontario (1725).

Louisiana and Texas

The major area of expansion during this period, however, was in the Gulf Coast region. In fact, while the War of the Spanish Succession raged in Europe, French colonization on the Gulf Coast had proceeded rapidly. In 1699 an expedition under the command of Pierre le Moyne came by sea from Canada, and in that year he established Biloxi (in present Mississippi) along with a small outpost forty miles above the mouth of the Mississippi. In 1702 came the founding of Mobile (Alabama). From these two major posts the French spread in that vicinity, building trading posts where the Indians were exhorted to loyalty to France. Spain responded to this threat by regarrisoning Pensacola, Florida, which had first been colonized in 1559 but later abandoned.

In 1712, Louis XIV took Louisiana out of the French public domain by granting it as a private monopoly to Antoine Crozat. He sent Antoine de la Mothe Cadillac to govern the area under instructions to increase trade with the Indians and, if possible, to establish commercial relations with the nearby Spaniards in Mexico. Cadillac was under great pressure to produce high profits; the canny Scotsman, John Law, was selling stock in the Louisiana Company in France, using proceeds from sales to announce high dividends; the result was the infamous Louisiana Bubble in 1720. Cadillac found that the Indian trade was not rapidly expandable, and therefore he sought a method of reaching the Spaniards. However, Spanish mercantile regulations forbade such trade with a foreign power.

In 1713 Cadillac sent Louis Juchereau de St. Denis, a Canadian-born Frenchman fluent in Spanish, with a load of trade goods to test the Spanish reaction. On this trip, St. Denis established the outpost of Natchitoches, the first French settlement in present Louisiana, in 1714. He then proceeded to the nearest Spanish outpost, which was San Juan Bautista (on the south side of the Rio Grande opposite the present Eagle Pass). There St. Denis was arrested, his goods were confiscated, and he was sent to Mexico City for questioning. Spanish officials were so alarmed at this French intrusion that the viceroy ordered eastern Texas colonized again. This was accomplished in 1716 by Captain Domingo Ramón. Two years later, San Antonio was established as a halfway station between eastern Texas and the Rio Grande fort of San Juan Bautista. That same year, 1718, the French began the city of New Orleans. These two cities, San Antonio and New Orleans, would become the respective centers of Spanish and French power in the Gulf Coast area. Civilians were brought to both areas, along with soldiers and missionaries, so that flourishing, if small, centers of population resulted.

Georgia Colonized

England likewise was establishing a major colony in the New World during this period between wars. In 1729 the crown had reclaimed the southern part of the Carolinas from the original proprietors, and in 1732 this region was granted by George II to a group of British philanthropists. The spokesman for this group, James Oglethorpe, stated that the projected colony would be a haven for Englishmen imprisoned for debt—good men whose only crime was financial improvidence. Oglethorpe envisioned a colony of yeomen farmers, and therefore the rules of government for Georgia (named in honor of George II) stipulated that no one could own more than 500 acres and no slaves would be permitted. Also included was a ban on the importation of brandy and rum. Georgia's humanitarian proprietors envisioned an economy based on the production of wine and silk. What to Oglethorpe and his group was a haven for convicts, was to George II a military outpost, a means of confining Spaniards south of the Altamaha River; to the Spaniards this same colony seemed a military threat to their possessions.

Oglethorpe arrived in Georgia with the first hundred colonists in 1733, and in February he founded Savannah. With royal and private financing, more needy British colonists were brought, along with persecuted German Protestants. Soon the settlers were grumbling unhappily at Oglethorpe's despotism, for he was ruling without an assembly. South Carolinians gradually infiltrated the colony, gaining wide influence and increasing the number of complaints going to England. In 1742 the ban on importing rum was removed, and in 1749 slavery was permitted. Georgia thereafter based its economy on the growing of rice and indigo, and it became a facsimile of South Carolina. In 1752 the philanthropists relinquished their charter, and Georgia became a royal colony. By that time yet another war had been fought and a second was imminent.

The third imperial war began as an outgrowth of commercial rivalries. The English were abusing the privilege they had won in 1713 of introducing one ship of 500 tons burden into the Spanish colonies each year. A fleet of ships would cross the Atlantic to discharge their goods into the one merchantman that legally could land; in this manner many hundreds of tons of merchandise beyond the 500 tons allowed by treaty were being sold in the Spanish colonies. The Spaniards responded by organizing a special Caribbean coast guard composed largely of ex-pirates. Quarrels resulted between the English and the Spaniards, quarrels that erupted into war when a British officer, one Captain Jenkins, appeared before Parliament carrying a preserved ear that he claimed had been cut from his head by a Spanish officer as a warning to the British. The "War of Jenkins' Ear" lasted some three years, with inconclusive fighting in Florida and on the Pacific Coast, before merging into a general conflict known in European history as the War of the Austrian Succession, in the British colonies as King George's War.

This war began when a woman, Maria Theresa, inherited the Austrian throne. Her father, Charles VI, had foreseen that a war might result from his having no male heirs in a nation which had never been ruled by a female. He had attempted to prevent this by means of the Pragmatic Sanction. Issued in 1713 and signed by the major European powers, this guaranteed the throne to his daughter. But when Charles died, those same European powers made a concerted assault on Austrian possessions, intent upon the dismemberment of the country. With only England as an ally, Maria Theresa conducted an eight-year war with such skill that she kept the throne and most of her empire.

Changes in the British Colonies

In the New World the English colonies were in a much better position to fight than they had been during the previous war, because they had matured considerably. Massachusetts had become a royal colony in 1691, with Plymouth Bay absorbed into it. New York likewise had become a royal colony during the era of the Glorious

Revolution; New Hampshire had become a royal colony in 1679, but had the same governor as Massachusetts until 1741. And the Carolinas, North and South, had become royal colonies in 1729. Thus Connecticut and Rhode Island were the only corporate colonies left, while Pennsylvania and Delaware remained in the hands of the Penn family. New Jersey, which had been a Quaker colony, became a royal colony in 1702 when East and West Jersey were reunited; it had to share the same governor with New York until 1738, when it received its own chief executive. Thus the tendency was toward the abrogation of charters to both proprietors and to corporations, and by 1752 Georgia, South Carolina, North Carolina, Virginia, New Jersey, New York, Massachusetts, and New Hampshire were royal colonies.

Other dramatic changes had been taking place. Before 1680 most immigrants from Europe had been from England. During the next six decades, England ceased to be the major source of new settlers. Germans came in large numbers to the Hudson and Mohawk valleys and to eastern and central Pennsylvania, fleeing the religious and political wars that would decimate their homeland for a century. Even more numerous were the Irish, the greater part of whom were Protestants from Ulster—the so-called Scotch-Irish so famous in American history. Finding the coastlands taken by earlier settlers, they moved to the frontier and became the vanguard of the march toward the Pacific. Other settlers came from France, Scotland, Switzerland, and—unwillingly—Africa. By 1760 non-Englishmen probably represented a third of the colonial population. Intermarriage between these different nationalities started the "Melting Pot." The influx of these foreigners caused the population, which stood at approximately 250,000 in 1690, to double almost every twenty-five to thirty years thereafter. By 1750 it stood at well over a million.

Social Changes

In America the class structure of Europe—nobles, clergy, and peasant—had fallen by the wayside during these same years. There was an aristocracy of sorts, consisting of the largest landowners, the wealthy merchants, and the highest royal or proprietary officials. But these three categories had little in common. Northern merchants did not understand Southern plantation owners, while both disliked governmental officials who represented authority and collected taxes. The middle class consisted, at the upper end of its spectrum, of moderately well-to-do farmers, master artisans, and professionals, such as lawyers, the clergy, and physicians. They were striving hard to improve their standing and thereby win membership in the upper class. The largest class in the colonies stood midway in the middle class: yeomen farmers owning small farms and artisans who had mastered a craft but did not own a shop. Often both were in debt (although they could vote) and thus they developed a debtor psychology. They also had a conscious spirit of independence, hating to be bossed. At the bottom end of the middle class were the tenant farmers, the traveling artisans, and day laborers such as dockhands and farm workers; usually they could not vote and owned little property. The lower class consisted of two groups: indentured servants, whose way had been paid to the New World in return for several years' work (after which they moved up to lower middle class), and slaves who had little hope or ambition because they had no chance of rising. By 1700 slaves numbered 20,000 to 25,000, about a tenth of the population.

The colonial economy likewise was maturing slowly. Private enterprise was the mainspring of British developments in the New World. Because class lines were fluid, ambition and hard work enabled a man to rise on his own merits; conversely a man fell on his demerits—and most of the Protestant denominations emphasized that the heavenly "elect" were rewarded on this earth as well as beyond, giving a double incentive for work and thrift. Some 90 to 95 percent of the colonial population was engaged in agriculture: one-crop farming in the Southern colonies, subsistence farming in the northern colonies. Most industry was still at the household or artisan stage, with commerce occupying the remainder of the working class.

An intellectual maturity also was manifest during the first half of the eighteenth century. This in Europe was the Age of Enlightenment, which was marked by hubristic rationalism. One tenet of this movement held that God had made the world and then had left it to run itself by natural law. This belief in God as a "skilled engineer" who had formulated natural laws—which man could learn through his ability to reason and then use to better himself—was not a formal religion, although it was labeled Deism. God, according to the Deists, was remote and indifferent, not fierce and wrathful as the Puritans believed. Most leading American businessmen and intellectuals, such as Benjamin Franklin, Thomas Jefferson, and Philip Freneau, were Deists, while theologians such as Cotton Mather bridged the gap between the old Calvinistic theory of the elect and salvation by faith, and the new age of reason.

Deistic beliefs, as well as the attack on older religious attitudes, can be seen in the literary hoax that Franklin perpetrated and published anonymously in 1747. In this "Speech of Polly Baker," Franklin used reason and wit to ridicule the punishment of certain kinds of sin. Miss Baker, according to Franklin's account, was brought before a court of magistrates near Boston on charges of having produced a fifth illegitimate child; in her own defense she said:

> Can it be a crime (in the nature of things, I mean) to add to the king's subjects, in a new country, that really wants people? I own it, I should think it rather a praiseworthy than a punishable action. I have debauched no other woman's husband, nor enticed any other youth; these things I never was charg'd with; nor has any one the least cause of complaint against me, unless, perhaps, the ministers of justice, by which they have missed a wedding fee. . . .
> I readily consented to the only proposal of marriage that ever was made me, which was when I was a virgin, but too easily confiding in the person's sincerity that made it, I unhappily lost my honour by trusting to his; for he got me with child, and then forsook me.
> That very person, you all know, he is now become a magistrate of this country; and I had hopes he would have appeared this day on the bench, and have endeavoured to moderate the Court in my favor. . . . What must poor young women do, whom customs and nature forbid to solicit the men, and who cannot force themselves upon husbands, when the laws take no care to provide them any, and yet severely punish them if they do their duty without them; the duty of the first and great command of nature and nature's God, *encrease and multiply*; a duty, from the steady performance of which nothing has been able to deter me, but for its sake I have hazarded the loss of the publick esteem, and have frequently endured publick disgrace and punishment; and therefore ought, in my humble opinion, instead of a whipping, to have a statue erected to my memory.

Fundamentalist Reaction

Puritanism and other fundamentalist sects found themselves battling hard to retain members in the face of such logic during the Age of Enlightenment. Likewise they had been weakened by growing prosperity and the abandonment of religious qualifications for voting. Theologians of the early seventeenth century, such as Jonathan Edwards, were disturbed by this trend toward secularism. Edwards used the thought of the Enlightenment to construct a theological paradox to the new ideas, just as he opposed the concept that man's salvation depended on human moral effort as well as divine grace; instead he reaffirmed God's power to elect or condemn as he chose. He described conversion and redemption as a supernatural illumination of the soul, an effusion of God's beauty in the mind and an intuitive vision of the holiness that is in God and Christ. With dazzling skill Edwards defended the basic Calvinistic position that God was omnipotent and that before God man was impotent. By preaching pietism and election by faith alone, he and others stressed emotionalism and revivalism.

The Great Awakening thus was born in the 1730s with fiery oratory and revivals that soon became emotional orgies. Old denominations split over the issues involved, with small, dissenting sects gaining membership rapidly among the less sophisticated part of the population. The Great Awakening had political and economic as well as religious consequences: it weakened the Anglican Church and thereby the English hold on the colonies; it served as a leveling movement that hastened the separation of church and state; and where religious liberties were won, political liberty soon would follow. Moreover, provincialism declined, morals and manners improved, many schools were founded, and the humanitarian spirit of the age was given considerable impetus.

The school systems being established in the colonies were mainly patterned after the educational methods of England. At first they were closely tied to the churches, with reading materials heavily religious in content, but during the Age of Enlightenment secular subjects were introduced. As in England the type of schooling a student received was based on his "station" in life. Only in Massachusetts and Connecticut was education a public concern; elsewhere the children who were educated were those whose parents were persons of means. Generally, such education, especially in the South, was by the tutorial method. One family or a few usually banded together to hire a tutor to instruct the children. Philip V. Fithian in December, 1773, confided to his journal what being a tutor was like in Virginia at that time:

In the morning so soon as it is light a Boy knocks at my Door to make a fire; after the Fire is kindled, I rise which now in the winter is commonly by Seven, or a little after, By the time I am drest the Children commonly enter the School-Room, which is under the Room I sleep in; I hear them round one lesson, when the Bell rings for eight o'Clock (for Mr Carter has a large good Bell of upwards of 60 Lb. which may be heard some miles, & this is always rung at meal Times;) the Children then go out; and at half after eight the Bell rings for Breakfast, we then repair to the Dining-Room; after Breakfast, which is generally about half after nine, we go into School, and sit til twelve, when the Bell rings, & they go out for noon; the dinner-Bell rings commonly about half after two, often at three, but never before two.—After dinner is over, which in common, when we have no Company, is about half after three we go into School, & sit til the Bell rings at five, when they separate til the next morning; I have to myself in the Evening, a neat Chamber, a large Fire, Books, & Candle & my Liberty, either to continue in the school room, in my own Room or to sit over at the great House with Mr & Mrs Carter—We go into Supper commonly about half after eight or at nine & usually I go to Bed between ten and Eleven. . . .

National Cyclopedia of Biography

Benjamin Franklin

ON August 22, 1772, Benjamin Franklin took pen in hand to attend his correspondence, writing that day thirteen letters in all—on such subjects as the establishment of a nailery, canals, the Pennsylvania Hospital's investments in England, oath taking, silk culture, post office accounts, obtaining workers for a glass factory, the condition of business, the selection of books for a library, and the evils of slavery. Each reflected a different mood; one might be warm and humorous, another angry and indignant, and a third confident and condescending. Yet all revealed something of the character of the man whom David Hume asserted was the first man of letters for whom Europe was indebted to the New World.

Born January 17, 1706, the fifteenth child—and tenth son—of a Boston candlemaker, Franklin received only a brief schooling before being apprenticed to his halfbrother James, a printer. After repeated quarrels with James, young Franklin moved to Philadelphia, arriving there at age seventeen. Dedicated to hard work, reading, writing, and self-improvement, along with careful thought, he first worked as a printer there and for two years in London. In 1728 he formed a partnership and established his own printery. Two years later he acquired sole ownership of the shop, along with a wife. During the next eighteen years he applied himself to his business: "In order to secure my credit and character as a tradesman, . . . I drest plainly: I was seen at no place of idle diversion. I never went out a fishing or shooting; a book, indeed, sometimes debauch'd me from my work, but that was seldom, snug, and gave no scandal. . . ."

Wealthy at forty-two, thanks principally to the great sales of *Poor Richard's Almanack,* he retired to devote himself to his experiments, his studies, and public service. In all areas he won wide recognition and respect. Thereafter, until his death on April 17, 1790, he belonged to America—and the world.

The first American college, Harvard, opened in 1636. By 1764 seven colonial colleges were operating, training men for the professions. Closely related to the amount of education available were the newspapers, and by 1765 some twenty-five were being published. Freedom of the press was established early; the trial of Peter Zenger in 1735 saw this principle widely accepted as part of the law. For the mass of readers, however, it was the almanac that was most popular. *Poor Richard's Almanack*, Benjamin Franklin's creation, had the greatest circulation, for it mixed homilies with weather predictions and information on how and when to plant crops.

Meanwhile, the French colony along the St. Lawrence had not kept pace with developments in the English settlements. There had been virtually no immigration since 1675. There was little room for economic, religious, or social deviation unless the dissenter ran away to live with the Indians. Only in the woods could he escape his "station" in life. The population thus was small; by 1750 it numbered perhaps 60,000.

King George's War

The outbreak of the War of the Austrian Succession—or King George's War—therefore found the Americans in a strong position. On the Continent, England and Austria were pitted against France, Spain, and Prussia; in North America the war mainly was between English and French colonists. New Englanders were most fearful of the French fortress at Louisbourg, which was called the Gibraltar of the New World by its builders. As if showing that New England's fears of Louisbourg were well grounded, an expedition left that bastion in 1744 to destroy the English fisheries at Canso and to threaten Annapolis Royal. Governor William Shirley of Massachusetts was determined to destroy the menace of Louisbourg before privateers from the French fortress swarmed out to destroy English shipping. So in 1745 he prepared an amphibious force of 4000 men under the command of William Pepperell. England supplied a naval squadron for transport and support, and the expedition set sail to storm the most formidable fortress in North America.

With naval protection during the landing, the New England militiamen swarmed ashore on Cape Breton Island, hopes of booty in their hearts. They manhandled cannon through swamps and over cliffs to establish a siege line on three sides of the fort, inside which huddled 2000 regulars and militia plus an equal number of civilians. For six weeks cannon shot rained on the fort, wrecking all but one house inside and battering the inhabitants into submission. On June 29, as much to the surprise of the Americans as the French, the surrender occurred. The remainder of the war consisted of Canadian threats to retake Louisbourg that, without French aid, came to naught, and American threats to invade Canada that, without English support, likewise never materialized. In 1748 the Treaty of Aix-la-Chapelle ended the conflict and, to the great disgust of New Englanders, gave Louisbourg back to France in return for Madras, India. The lesson for Americans was that English imperial considerations were far more important than colonial blood, money, and defensive needs.

The Treaty of Aix-la-Chapelle proved more a truce than a settlement of European differences. Preparations, both diplomatic and military, for yet another war began almost at once. England's major move was the expulsion of the Acadians. By terms of the Treaty of Utrecht, the ill-fated residents of Acadia colony were to move within a year or become British citizens. The majority had remained, but England still doubted their loyalty. By 1750 they numbered some 10,000, quietly working their fertile farms. Then with the end of King George's War, the French at Louisbourg began appealing to the Acadians on the basis of race and religion to throw out the English and to stir the local Indians to war. When in 1755 conflict again came, the British moved immediately to remove this threat. Those Acadians who would not take an oath of loyalty to England were deported. Some were sent to other English colonies, some to French Louisiana, and some scattered far and wide. Within eight years, between 6000 and 10,000 Acadians were deported. And England had strengthened its hold in that region by constructing Halifax in 1749.

The French needed little provocation to respond in kind. In fact, they were as anxious as the British to strengthen their position for the next war, which all were certain would soon begin. Between 1749 and 1753 the French established forts Niagara and Venango, and in 1749 the governor of Canada sent his personal representative, Jean Baptiste Le Moyne, to occupy the Ohio Valley. To protect this occupation, the French built Fort Duquesne (on the site of Pittsburgh) at the forks of the Ohio in 1754.

Attempts to Settle the Ohio Valley

As early as 1747, however, the British had been interested in the Ohio Valley. That year several different companies in Virginia organized to file claims to land along the Ohio River (now western Pennsylvania). England encouraged these colonial speculators as a counterforce to French encroachments. It was this British interest that caused the governor of Canada to build forts, for the Ohio Valley was the route of communication between the St. Lawrence area and the French colonies of the Gulf Coast region. Lieutenant Governor Robert Dinwiddie of Virginia, an investor in this land speculation, therefore in 1753 ordered twenty-one-year-old George Washington to travel west with a protest. Washington, a surveyor, had been working with the Ohio Company, one of the speculative land concerns. The young Virginian arrived at Fort le Boeuf in 1753 with a message demanding French withdrawal, only to be met by a firm refusal. Dinwiddie thereupon determined on stronger action. His call for volunteers was not enthusiastically met by Virginians, who saw little reason to fight for Ohio Company profits, but finally 300 men were raised. With this force, George Washington departed to expel the French from the Ohio Valley.

The expedition was a complete failure. A French advance force came to meet Washington with orders for the Virginians to retire. A clash between this advance party of Frenchmen and an advance party of Virginians led to the death of the French leader, causing angry French charges of murder. Washington halted at Great Meadows and threw up hasty fortifications, calling his emplacement Fort Necessity. In July a French attack obliged Washington to surrender. He retreated ingloriously to report to Governor Dinwiddie that fighting had begun. There had been no declaration of war between England and France. Yet this incident at Great Meadows was the spark that would ignite a world war for mastery of North America.

In England the Privy Council met to discuss the events of the Ohio Valley. The result was a close look at British defenses in the New World colonies, a defense that rested in large measure on the Iroquois Indians. And the Iroquois were discontented—even angry—at the activities of the Virginia land speculators, whose claims threatened their homeland. To restore Indian confidence in the British, the Privy Council called for a meeting in Albany, New York, to take place in June 1754.

Delegates from the northern colonies were to meet with the Iroquois chieftains as well as other native leaders. The Iroquois came, they accepted the lavish British gifts, but they made no promises in return. Their loyalty to England had been weakened by their awareness of superior French might in the Ohio Valley.

Another object of the "Albany Congress" was to formulate a plan for closer cooperation between the colonies. Benjamin Franklin, representing Pennsylvania, presented a bold proposal to the commissioners from the other colonies represented: New England, Maryland, and New York. His "Plan of Union" called for uniting the colonies under a president-general appointed by the king. A council of delegates from the colonies would have the power to legislate on matters of intercolonial interest, to tax, to raise armies, and to negotiate with the Indians, with veto power reserved to the president-general and the crown. Matters of intercolonial interest, as envisioned by Franklin, included the administration and disposal of western lands, the right to declare war and make peace, and to govern frontier regions beyond the boundaries of the colonies. Local matters would be reserved to the individual colonies. The colonial legislatures rejected Franklin's bold proposal because they were loathe to relinquish their powers and because the land speculators opposed it, while the English Parliament rejected it because the members feared rising colonial democratic tendencies.

Another move to strengthen the English position in the New World was the dispatch to Virginia of General Edward Braddock and 1400 regulars in April, 1755. Braddock was ordered to level Fort Duquesne with the assistance of 450 colonial militia under the command of Lieutenant Colonel George Washington. At a military conference in Virginia that summer, Governor Shirley of Massachusetts proposed a strategy: break the circle of French fortresses around the English colonies. Braddock was to lead his force against Fort Duquesne, Shirley was to attack Niagara, Sir William Johnson was to strike at Crown Point, and another force was to move against Beauséjour on the northeastern flank. This strategy was well conceived but poorly executed. Shirley never reached Niagara, while Johnson had to turn back before reaching Crown Point. Only Fort Beauséjour was taken, but this small victory was overshadowed by Braddock's spectacular defeat.

Braddock marched with his force, totaling almost 1900, in July. On the Monongahela River, some eight miles short of Fort Duquesne, he was ambushed by a force of French soldiers and their Indian allies. Braddock was killed along with hundreds of his men. Only the clear-headedness of George Washington and his militiamen saved part of the British force, thereby increasing Washington's estimate of his own ability. This defeat, however, almost destroyed British prestige among the western tribes of Indians, thereby inclining them toward the French. The whole western frontier of Pennsylvania, Virginia, and Maryland thereby was exposed to raids, encouraged by the French, and massacres became almost commonplace. Finally, Braddock's defeat awakened the colonists to their common danger and made them realize that serious common effort would be necessary to win victory.

The French and Indian Wars

Then in 1756 came formal declarations of war in Europe, beginning what was subsequently called by Europeans the Seven Years' War and by the English colonists the French and Indian Wars. This conflict saw England, Portugal, and Prussia pitted against France, Austria, Sweden, Russia, several of the Germanic states, and (later)

Spain. It saw battles occurring on the Continent, in India, the West Indies, and the Philippines, as well as in North America. It clearly was a war for colonial supremacy.

In the early stages of this war, the British suffered badly in Europe as well as in America. The commander of the French forces in Canada, the Marquis de Montcalm, led highly confident troops, emboldened by their early victories, to the conquest of forts Oswego and George in August, 1756. A year later he led another force to victory at Fort William Henry on Lake George; his Indian allies got out of hand at this battle and massacred those who surrendered. That same year, British plans to capture Louisbourg came to naught. Lord Loudon, commander of this effort, saw his ships failing to make the appointed rendezvous and the massing of a superior French naval force at the post.

Such disasters for England brought a change of ministers at home. In June, 1757, William Pitt became prime minister as well as secretary of state, and he reorganized the British concept of fighting the war in an effort to bring victory. He discharged incompetent officers and promoted young ones who showed merit and promise; he subsidized the Prussians to fight on the Continent in order to free British troops for other duties; he used the British fleet to blockade French ports in order to insure English control of the seas; and he concentrated on the conquest of Canada. These tactics paid quick dividends.

On July 26, 1758, Generals Jeffrey Amherst and James Wolfe, with 10,000 troops, conquered Louisbourg. Bonfires of celebration were lighted in New York, Philadelphia, and Boston, as well as London, at this news. Washington served on the staff of General John Forbes in the conquest of Fort Duquesne that same year, and Fort Frontenac likewise was taken. The next year saw even more spectacular victories, as the British took Fort Niagara and the French blew up forts Ticonderoga and Crown Point rather than allow them to fall into English hands. In early September that year General Wolfe brought an army up the St. Lawrence from Louisbourg and with 4500 men slipped up the cliffs west of Quebec; on the Plains of Abraham his men defeated the French and captured the city in a battle that saw both Montcalm and Wolfe killed. On September 18 the French surrendered Quebec, as they did Montreal a year later. These British victories were matched on the sea, in India, and even in the Philippines. Peace came when the French were convinced their cause was lost—and great territorial realignments resulted.

In 1762, by the secret Treaty of Fontainebleau, France ceded to Spain all its holdings west of the Mississippi River as compensation for the Spanish loss of Cuba and Manila to England. Then in the Peace of Paris, signed on February 10, 1763, England received Canada as well as the Louisiana Territory east of the Mississippi. England also gained title to several islands in the West Indies, much of India, and other small bits of territory. Spain ceded East and West Florida to England in exchange for the return of Cuba and Manila. For a time the British government debated taking the sugar islands of Martinique and Guadeloupe instead of Canada. The decision to take Canada clearly showed that England had turned to a policy of territorial imperialism rather than commercial imperialism.

Conditions in 1763

The Treaty of Paris marked the high-water point of England's empire, In the race for North America that began with Columbus' discovery 271 years earlier, only Spain and England remained as claimants (with the exception of Russia, which was

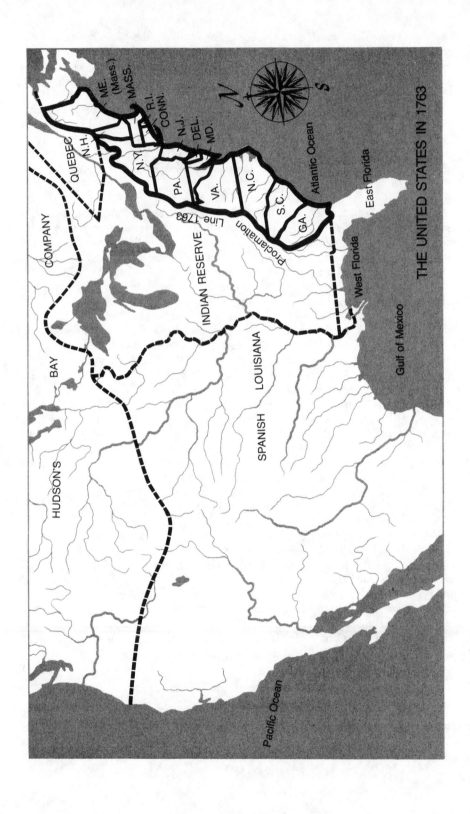

THE UNITED STATES IN 1763

establishing a claim to Alaska). But victory in war often brings more problems than it solves. For England the fruits of victory in the Seven Years' War were bitter indeed. The royal treasury was virtually empty, the national debt was astronomical, taxes were outrageously high, and thousands of young men were dead—for which the American colonies were not grateful. In fact, with the French threat removed, the colonies suddenly found they no longer needed England.

Chapter Four

The World Turned Upside Down

End of the Seven Years' War

IN 1839 most European powers signed a treaty guaranteeing the neutrality of Belgium. In 1914, however, the German army invaded and quickly overran that little country. When other nations reacted against this violation of treaty-rights, Theobald Bethmann-Hollweg, chancellor of Germany, justified his nation's actions by describing the treaty as a mere "scrap of paper."

In one sense a treaty is a mere scrap of paper—but treaties can have far-reaching consequences. And in the long history of human events, few scraps of paper have presaged such changes as the Treaty of Paris of 1763, which brought the Seven Years' War to a close. It influenced the destinies of India, Western Europe, North America, and islands in the Caribbean and the Pacific. More specifically, it postured great changes for American history. While men of good will celebrated the Treaty of Paris in the belief that it had restored world peace, that same treaty was in large measure responsible for revolutionary changes that would bring another war and a new nation into being in just two short decades.

The Spanish Colonies

In the Spanish colonies, the foremost consideration was retrenchment, for the royal treasury had been severely strained in the recent conflict. Changes were in order for the northern Spanish colonies as a result of the war: the French had been eliminated from the colonial race and had ceded the Louisiana Territory west of the Mississippi to Spain as compensation for the loss of Florida; the Spanish boundary had moved eastward, bringing a new enemy, the English. The Spanish monarch therefore determined upon a complete overhaul of colonial policy on the northern frontier. To accomplish this, the Marqués de Rubí was commissioned in 1766 to make an inspection tour from the Gulf of California to the Gulf of Mexico with an eye to accomplishing economies while at the same time reducing the number of Indian raids.

Between 1766 and 1768 the Marqués made his tour. Then in 1769 he presented his report in Mexico City. True enough, the Rubí report stated, the foreign menace was gone, but the Indian menace was greater than ever. Thus the frontier provinces of Texas, New Mexico, and Sonora (Arizona) should be maintained as a buffer, not against the French, but against the natives. Rubí proposed a cordon of forts some 104 miles apart stretching from gulf to gulf. East Texas could be abandoned entirely, the settlers there to be moved to San Antonio to strengthen it. Rubí also recommended an alliance with the Comanches against the Apaches, whom he saw as the principal threat to Spanish settlements. He also recommended fomenting inter-tribal wars everywhere along the frontier, keeping all tribes friendly with Spain.

While Rubí was inspecting the northern provinces, another official, José de Gálvez, was on a tour to recommend changes of an administrative nature. His report stressed that the northern regions, called the Interior Provinces, were far removed from Mexico City and the viceroy's close personal attention, yet were the provinces that most needed a strong administrator. He therefore suggested that the Interior Provinces be separated from the viceroyalty of New Spain and placed under the command of a commandant-general responsible only to the king and with civil, military, and judicial authority for the region.

In 1772 the king agreed to part of the Gálvez-Rubí recommendations when he issued the Royal Regulations. These placed the Interior Provinces under the supervision of a commandant-inspector, but not separate from the viceroyalty. Yet in the next four years there was continued deterioration as the Indians raided almost at will. There were changes, such as the creation of Tucson, Arizona (1776), but these did not have the desired effect. Therefore, in 1776 the king fully implemented the Rubí-Gálvez recommendations, making the Interior Provinces separate from the viceroyalty of New Spain and placing them under the command of a commandant-general. First to occupy this post was Teodoro de Croix, an able, energetic, and knowledgeable brigadier general. In the late 1770s Croix carried out campaigns against the Apaches with Comanche aid, bringing a measure of peace to the north.

Another event of importance in the Spanish colonies was the colonization of California. Diplomatic agents reported to the royal court at Madrid that the Russians were interested in California, that they intended an agricultural colony there to supply food to Russian-American Fur Company trading posts in Alaska. Fearful of the loss of land they claimed, the Spaniards moved quickly. Under the administrative direction of José de Gálvez, an expedition was readied early in 1769 under the command of Captain Gaspár de Portolá and Franciscan Father Junípero Serra. Their orders were to found colonies at San Diego, which had a natural harbor, and at Monterey; in fact, Monterey was the main goal. Sebastián Vizcaíno, a merchant, had sailed up the California coast in 1602 and had reached Monterey. His report described it as "the best port that could be desired, for besides being sheltered from all the winds, it has many pines for masts and yards, and live oaks and white oaks, and water in great quantity, all near the shore."

Serra and Portolá arrived at San Diego on July 1 and held a formal ceremony of taking possession. The captain then took part of the available men north to Monterey—which proved to be a severe disappointment; there was no fine harbor. Thinking he had not yet found Monterey, Portolá continued northward overland until he discovered San Francisco Bay. The following year, on June 3, 1770, a fort and mission were constructed at Monterey, and California had been settled peacefully.

The local Indians were so low on the scale of civilization that they offered no deterrent to Spanish settlement. Life proved very precarious in California, however. The only method of supply was by ship, and wind and waves along the California coast made this a tenuous lifeline. By 1773 there were five missions and two forts in existence, but there were only sixty-one soldiers and a few Franciscan padres in all of California.

At this crucial moment in California's history, Father Francisco Garcés and Captain Juan Bautista de Anza came to the rescue. Garcés was the Franciscan missionary at Mission San Xavier del Bac (Tucson), and Captain Anza the military commander of northern Sonora (Arizona). The two men proposed to the viceroy that they be allowed to lead an expedition in search of an overland route to California. The viceroy gladly agreed. Leaving Tubac, Arizona, on January 8, 1773, Anza, Garcés, and thirty-four soldiers walked westward across what they called *El Camino del Diablo* ("The Devil's Highway"). After terrible suffering, they arrived at Yuma Crossing, where they made friends with the Yuma Indians, crossed the Colorado River, and made their way to Mission San Gabriel (Los Angeles). They then returned to Mission San Xavier in Arizona, arriving there in July, 1774.

The viceroy immediately ordered Anza to demonstrate the useability of this route by taking civilians and cattle across it to California. This Anza did in the fall and winter of 1775–76—transporting 242 people and more than 1000 horses and cattle. In April, 1776, these colonists established the city of San Francisco. The Yuma Indians rose in revolt in 1781, permanently closing the Anza-Garcés road to California, but by that time the colony had become self-sufficient, with several missions in existence and thousands of horses and cattle grazing the rolling hills.

Louisiana proved much more difficult for Spain. Not until 1766 did a Spanish governor arrive to assume charge of Louisiana, which stretched northward as far as St. Louis, established in 1764 as a fur-trading post. Antonio de Ulloa, the first Spanish governor, was a distinguished scholar but an inept governor. He arrived with but few soldiers, expecting no trouble—then made his own. His haughtiness offended the proud French settlers, but they endured his rule until 1768, when he attempted to enforce Spanish mercantile laws. These prohibited trade with France, and in October, 1768, they brought insurrection. Ulloa was unceremoniously expelled. Spanish officials reacted strongly to this threat to their rule.

In August, 1769, General Alejandro O'Reilly, an Irish mercenary in Spanish employ, arrived at New Orleans with twenty-one ships loaded with soldiers. The French insurrectionists immediately begged O'Reilly for leniency. He responded by hanging six of them, sentencing another six to prison, and expelling twenty-one; the property of all thirty-three was confiscated. O'Reilly was merely following his orders, but their execution earned him the name "Bloody O'Reilly." With Spanish authority reestablished, O'Reilly departed, leaving Luis de Unzaga as governor. Unzaga proved quite popular, for he winked at Spanish mercantile laws and allowed smuggling to flourish. Prosperity brought an end to all thoughts of revolt in Louisiana, prosperity generated by fur, sugar, and smuggling. In 1775, when Bernardo de Gálvez assumed the governorship, he was intelligent enough to allow the smuggling to continue. Thus when the American Revolution began, this colony was in a good position to aid the insurrectionists, for Spanish rule had been established and accepted.

The English Colonies

Just as the Treaty of Paris had wrought great changes in the Spanish colonies, so also it brought startling events to pass in the English colonies. British acquisition of Canada and Florida posed difficulties, as did the Ohio Valley, now uncontested British territory. There was an Indian problem in this region that needed a solution. But most pressing of all was the British need for funds. The royal treasury had been sadly depleted by the Seven Years' War, and the debt was astronomical.

Because this war in large measure was for the benefit of the American colonies, members of Parliament thought the Americans should contribute for imperial defense and other imperial needs.

First and most pressing among these problems was the Indian question. Influential merchants in Canada and the American colonies were interested in reserving the western lands for trappers and traders; fur was their main consideration. Equally influential were the land speculators, especially in Pennsylvania and Virginia, who wanted these lands thrown open to their development—which meant removing the Indian menace. While the future of these lands was being discussed in Parliament and elsewhere, the Indians seized the initiative. Led by an Ottawa chief named Pontiac, the tribes of the Ohio Valley went on the warpath in May, 1763, intending to obliterate British forts and drive the white settlers from their region. Reactions to Pontiac's conspiracy varied. In Pennsylvania, the Paxton Boys—men from Paxton and Donegal townships—retaliated by attacking the peaceful Conestoga tribe. After killing many of these Indians, the Paxton Boys marched on Philadelphia to force the legislature to come to the aid of the frontiersmen. Benjamin Franklin and other influential colonial leaders talked them out of a fight. Another method of combating the Indians was to send them blankets from hospital smallpox wards; such blankets spread the infectious disease and killed thousands of Indians, so that by September, 1764, the West had been pacified.

The Parliamentary reaction to Pontiac's conspiracy was an attempt to buy time. The government issued the Proclamation of 1763, which excluded settlers from the trans-Allegheny country until the Indians were pacified and a definite land policy determined. Further, the Proclamation divided the newly acquired territory into four governments—Quebec (Canada), East Florida, West Florida, and Granada (islands in the West Indies). All land west of the Alleghenies to the Mississippi and north from Florida to fifty degrees north latitude was reserved for the use of the Indians: "We do strictly forbid, on pain of our displeasure, all our loving subjects from making any purchase or settlements whatever in that region." This proclamation line swept away the western land claims for all thirteen colonies, and it angered speculators greatly. George Washington and others moved into the Ohio Valley in violation of the line and began staking claims. England therefore was forced to send agents to negotiate treaties with the Indians to legalize such speculative ventures. Choctaws, Chickasaws, Cherokees, and Iroquois in turn were forced to cede more land. So the Proclamation of 1763 pleased neither colonists nor Indians.

To keep speculators out of the western lands, the British crown announced a chain of forts along the Alleghenies, to be manned by 10,000 soldiers. As these soldiers were to be stationed there to "protect" the American colonists, leaders in Parliament and the ministry thought the colonists should pay a large share of the costs. Thus was raised the question of taxation. England had been imposing taxes on Americans since shortly after colonization had become a reality—but always for the purpose of regulating trade, not generating revenues. The first of these navigation acts had come in 1651, and stated that goods imported into England from America had to be carried in ships of which the proprietor, master, and the major portion of the crew were British. In 1660 another act required that ships carrying goods to England or the colonies must have been built in England or in the colonies, and it enumerated certain goods from the colonies that could be sold only to England: sugar, tobacco, cotton, wool, and certain spices. The Act of 1663 placed a heavy duty on European goods bound for the colonies, unless those goods first were brought to England on English or colonial ships. Finally, the Act of 1696 integrated and tightened this system.

The Board of Trade and Plantations operated this system between 1696 and 1768, and had the additional responsibility of examining all laws passed by colonial legislatures with the power of vetoing those laws adversely affecting British interests. Members of the Board of Trade and Plantations generally were from old English merchant families, and they used their influence to increase British profits, not aid the colonies. For example, in 1733 came the Molasses Act, which placed a prohibitive duty on molasses and rum going to the colonies from anywhere except England; these products had been imported directly from the West Indies for far less than they could come from England. By such methods, British merchants were making an estimated annual profit of £2 million on the colonial trade.

Taxes on the Colonies

Americans argued that such a handsome profit was tax enough. Parliament and the ministry thought differently, however, for taxes in North America were very light when compared with those paid by Englishmen at home. Therefore, in April, 1764, Prime Minister George Grenville imposed a tax on the colonies that came to be known as the Sugar Act. This reduced the tax per gallon of molasses (used in the colonies to make rum) from six pence to three, but levied additional duties on sugar and many luxury items such as wine, coffee, silk, and linen. The Molasses Act of 1733 had imposed the original tax of six pence, but this had rarely been collected; the Sugar Act of 1764 clearly implied a British determination to collect the three pence per gallon levy. The act also created a vice-admiralty court at Halifax with jurisdiction over revenue cases; previously, sympathetic juries in the colonies had freed smugglers. Moreover, it specified that customs officials could not be sued for false arrest, and to aid them in their hunt for violators they were authorized to use writs of assistance (general search warrants). Finally, the Sugar Act stipulated that all customs officers had to take up their posts in the colonies, not remain in England and collect their salaries as many had done previously. Grenville and his ministers hoped to raise £45,000 of the £300,000 annual cost of the colonial military establishment through the Sugar Act.

Two additional measures, passed in 1765, caused an even more violent reaction in the colonies: the Quartering Act and the Stamp Act. The first of these required local civil authorities to provide quarters and supplies for British troops at local expense when military barracks proved inadequate; also, part of the cost of transporting the troops within a colony had to be paid by that colony. The Stamp Act called for stamps, costing from a halfpenny to twenty shillings, to be affixed to all newspapers, broadsides, pamphlets, licenses, commercial bills, advertisements, almanacs, leases, playing cards, dice, and legal documents. The act did provide that all revenue thereby raised would be spent in the colonies, but all offenses were to be tried in the admiralty courts, not by civil juries. This measure was designed to raise £60,000 annually in the colonies.

The Colonial Reaction

The Stamp Act caused an immediate and violent reaction in America, for by no stretch of the imagination could it be termed a means of regulating trade. Its sole and obvious purpose was to raise revenue—and it hit the most articulate class: merchants, lawyers, clergymen, and newspapermen. Its consequence was to crystalize constitutional opposition. In July, 1764, James Otis, a lawyer from Cape Cod, issued his *Rights of the British Colonies*, arguing that there could be no taxation of the colonies without their representation in Parliament. Others, such as Daniel Dulany of Maryland, urged the same thoughts, while Patrick Henry introduced a bill in the Virginia House of Burgesses denying the British right to tax and suggested that George III might suffer the same fate as Julius Caesar.

On a more practical level, radical colonists took direct action by forming Sons of Liberty groups in Boston, New York, and other major cities to oppose the Stamp Act. The Sons quickly gained notoriety for such violent acts as destroying the Boston home of stamp agent Andrew Oliver, burning the records of the Boston admiralty court, and ransacking the home of Massachusetts Chief Justice Thomas Hutchinson. Soon the British revenue agents in every colony were so intimidated that many resigned.

Less radical but equally adamant were members of the Stamp Act Congress, held in New York City, October 7–25, 1765. Representatives from nine colonies gathered there at the suggestion of the Massachusetts legislature to consider the menace to the colonies. This congress passed John Dickinson's *Declaration of Rights and Grievances*, which conceded that Americans owed allegiance to the crown but claimed for them all rights of Englishmen, including freedom from taxation without their "own consent, given personally, or by their representatives." It also urged repeal of the Stamp Act. This congress was significant both because of its declarations and because it was the first intercolonial meeting summoned at colonial initiative.

More to the point than the violence of the Sons of Liberty or the lofty declarations of the Stamp Act Congress was the agreement signed by merchants throughout the colonies not to purchase any British goods. Private citizens also agreed with this principle, stating their willingness not to consume any British products. The nonimportation, nonconsumption agreements brought business to a virtual standstill and hit British merchants where it most hurt—in the pocketbook. When the Stamp Act actually became effective on November 1, 1765, it was greeted not by a shower of revenue into the royal treasury but by a howl of protest from British merchants. On December 6 they petitioned London to repeal the Stamp Act.

By this time the Grenville ministry had fallen. It was replaced by the Marquis of Rockingham and his cabinet, and they had to contend with American opposition plus the howls of British merchants. Then in January, 1776, William Pitt rose in Parliament to demand that the Stamp Act "be repealed absolutely, totally, and immediately." The Rockingham ministry acquiesced. On March 18 the act was repealed. However, Parliament simultaneously passed the Declaration Act stating that it and the crown had the right to make "laws" binding on the colonies "in all cases whatsoever." Americans were too busy rejoicing to notice this ominous note— which deliberately avoided use of the word "tax."

The British need to raise revenues was still as pressing as it had been earlier. New duties had to be found, just as some method of persuading the colonies to contribute to royal needs had to be put into effect. And the colonists were resisting. On August 10, 1766, the New York Assembly refused to appropriate money for the support of British troops. The next day there was a clash between the Sons of Liberty and British troops in New York City. On December 19 the New York Assembly was disbanded, and the following year Parliament suspended its legislative powers. Clearly the British government had to find some method of mollifying the colonists. Deft measures were needed—at a time when the government fell, by default, into the hands of an aggressive man of only superficial brilliance.

The Townshend Ministry

In July, 1766, William Pitt, Earl of Chatham, became prime minister. He fell ill shortly thereafter, however, and control of the ministry passed to Charles Townshend. Pitt might have avoided bloodshed and revolution. Townshend lacked the ability to avoid conflict. He was determined to relieve the British taxpayer through colonial taxes, and his method was revenues to be raised in the guise of regulating trade. Parliament complied with his request, and on July 2, 1767, passed the Townshend Revenue Act and the Customs Collecting Act. The latter created four new vice-admiralty courts in the colonies and revised the methods of enforcing the revenue acts. The Townshend duties consisted of taxes on lead, paint, glass, and tea. These were low—but they were attached to articles of common use and tended to raise the cost of living generally. This was intended to raise £40,000 annually, money to be used to pay the salaries of colonial judges and other officials, freeing them of their dependence on colonial legislatures. The Townshend duties seemed almost deliberately designed to anger the colonists: writs of assistance, long a sore point, were included; admiralty courts, not civil juries, were to try offenders; and the use of these funds to pay royal officials' salaries struck at the colonists' only hold over these agents of the crown.

Resistance was quickly forthcoming on several levels. On October 28 in Boston a nonimportation, nonconsumption agreement was drafted by merchants, an idea that quickly spread to other colonies. As a result, imports from England dropped drastically, from £1,363,000 in 1768 to £504,000 in 1769. This had the desired effect on British merchants, who vented their anger on members of Parliament. On a more philosophical level, John Dickinson, a Philadelphia lawyer, published his *Letters of a Pennsylvania Farmer* between December, 1767, and February, 1768. In these essays he conceded that Parliament had the authority to regulate trade but not for the purpose of raising revenue, and declared, therefore, that the Townshend duties were unconstitutional and that Parliament's suspension of the New York Assembly threatened the liberties of all the colonies.

On February 11, 1768, Samuel Adams drafted the Massachusetts Circular Letter, in which he restated the arguments of Dickinson. Sent to other colonial legislatures as a statement of feelings in Massachusetts, Adams' circular letter urged united colonial action to resist unconstitutional taxation, insisted that American representation in Parliament was impossible, and opposed the British efforts to pay colonial officials' salaries from the royal treasury. The newly appointed secretary of state for the colonies, Lord Hillsborough, called Adams' letter a flagrant attempt "to disturb the public peace." Moreover, the royal governor of Massachusetts dissolved the legislature of the colony because of the letter, while customs agents asked for military support. Two regiments under General Thomas Gage arrived in Boston in September, while seven colonial legislatures recorded their agreement with the Circular Letter. For example, in Virginia George Washington introduced a measure known as the Virginia Resolves, which stated that the colonists could be taxed only by their own legislatures. Virginia's governor dissolved the House of Burgesses in response to the Resolves, while in England the House of Lords recommended that the colonial rebels be tried for treason. By January, 1770, insurrection was a definite threat.

On January 31, Frederick Lord North became prime minister. He heeded the plea of British merchants—as well as common sense, which dictated that the Townshend duties were bringing in less money than they were costing—and asked Parliament to repeal all of these taxes except the one on tea. This latter was retained, as a symbol of the crown's power to tax the colonies. This measure passed on April 12, while the Quartering Act was allowed to expire. Peace seemed about to return. Yet while Parliament was debating repeal of the Townshend duties, blood was being shed in Boston. British troops in that city were attacked by a mob on March 5 and, in self-defense, fired into the crowd, killing five and wounding six. The troops' defense of themselves was recognized as legal, and they were defended at their trial by John Adams and Josiah Quincy, both prominent leaders of the Patriot group. The soldiers were acquitted of murder, but among the Sons of Liberty the incident was played up as the "Boston Massacre."

The year 1771 was one of comparative peace. Colonial merchants had turned conservative as a result of their rising fear of acts of violence on the part of the Sons of Liberty. Riots such as the Boston Massacre and the one in January, 1770, in New York City, the so-called Battle of Golden Hill in which there had been a few casualties on both sides, had appalled the merchants and caused them to fear property damage. Samuel Adams and his party were defeated in elections in Massachusetts in 1770. He and his like-minded fellows tried to keep alive the spirit of resistance by creating Committees of Correspondence, the first of which Adams formed in Boston in 1772. The idea spread to other colonies, and they wrote to each other to report "outrages." One incident over which they could gloat was the burning of the *Gaspé,* a British revenue cutter that ran aground in Rhode Island on June 9, 1772, at Narragansett Bay; Rhode Islanders swarmed aboard and set it afire, and no witnesses could be found to identify the culprits.

The Drift to Revolution

The course toward revolution yet might have been changed by men of good will on both sides. Such was not to be the case, however. Americans had begun to believe their own arguments that they could not be taxed without representation in Parliament—such was their traditional right as Englishmen. To rejoinders that they were "virtually" represented in Parliament, they replied that while this might satisfy legal arguments at home it did nothing for them. In short, they were arguing that they were united to England only by loyalty to the crown and that only their own legislative bodies could tax them; they had evolved the commonwealth or dominion concept, and they saw themselves as conservators of traditional British liberties and freedoms. In England, however, such arguments carried little weight. Both the Tory and the Whig parties asserted the right of Parliament to legislate for the colonies in every way, including taxation, and they believed in the right of the crown to veto any colonial laws. The crux of the matter, therefore, was taxation and representation—the Americans opposed British-imposed taxes; the English government opposed the representative governments in the colonies.

The argument came to a head over the Tea Act, passed by Parliament on May 10, 1773, to save the East India Company from bankruptcy. The company had no money, but it did have 17 million pounds of tea. It was granted the right to sell tea directly to the colonies without introducing it first into England, and the company was granted a share of all taxes paid on the commodity in the colonies. New York and Philadelphia merchants protested that the tax on tea should not be paid, although it was far less than Englishmen themselves were paying on tea. The Massachusetts Committee of Correspondence advised that all East India Company tea should not be allowed to land. On December 16, after a town meeting in Boston at which Samuel Adams had declared, "This meeting can do nothing more to save the country," a group of Patriots disguised as Indians boarded three ships in the harbor and dumped their cargoes of tea into the sea. The Boston Tea Party brought to a head the question of home rule, it committed the Patriots to violent action, it inflamed British public opinion against Americans, and it strengthened the hand of conservatives in Parliament. The Boston Tea Party set colonials and Englishmen on a collision course that could be resolved only with sword and musket.

The king, the North ministry, Parliament—the whole structure of English control over the colonies—could not disregard the Boston Tea Party. On March 4, 1774, Parliament was summoned to punish Massachusetts for the defiance of its citizens. Between March 31 and June 2, four measures were passed. The first of these was the Boston Port Bill, which closed Boston harbor and moved the capital of the colony, along with the customs office, to Salem; no ships could call there after June 1 until the East India Company and the customs officers had been paid for their losses, estimated at £15,000. The Massachusetts Government Act came next, lessening the powers of the people by providing that the upper chamber of the legislature be appointed, not elected as previously; the governor would appoint lesser judges and nominate for royal appointment the superior judges; juries would be chosen by the sheriff instead of by election; and town meetings could not be called without the consent of the governor. The third measure, called the Administration of Justice Act, stated that anyone charged with a capital offense would be tried in England if the governor thought he could not get a fair trial in the colony. Finally, the Quartering Act of 1765 was revived, and the royal governor was replaced by General Thomas Gage, who became the colony's chief executive.

These four measures, known in England as the Coercive Acts, promptly were labeled the Intolerable Acts in America. Samuel Adams, through his Committee of Correspondence, was prompt to remind residents of other colonies that what happened to Massachusetts could just as readily happen to them. Then, just as word of the Intolerable Acts was spreading, news came of passage by Parliament of the Quebec Act. Passed on June 22, 1774, the Quebec Act annexed to the province of Quebec (Canada) all territory north of the Ohio River, thereby nullifying the western land claims of four colonies and threatening the profits of many speculative land companies; further, the act stipulated that all fur be shipped from Montreal rather than through New Orleans or any other port, and it recognized Catholicism and allowed Catholics to sit in the provincial assembly. Finally, it provided for French civil law, rather than English common law, to be used in Quebec. This act caused widespread opposition and even more widespread fear. New Englanders resented the benefits granted Catholics, which they felt was contrary to English law. The use of French civil law meant trials without jury, a practice abhorrent to Englishmen. And the loss of land and fur to Canada meant lost profits for New Englanders.

The reaction to the events of the spring of 1774 was a plethora of pamphlets. Thomas Jefferson's *A Summary View of Rights of British America* rejected the power of Parliament, claiming that the colonies need only obey the king. James Wilson of Pennsylvania wrote in a similar vein, as did others. Even Edmund Burke, the great British writer, philosopher, and statesman, wrote the New York Assembly from London that the purpose of the Quebec Act was to circumscribe the growth of the American colonies and to deprive them of their traditional English liberties. The Massachusetts House of Representatives was more direct: it asked all colonies to send delegates to Philadelphia to an intercolonial congress, to meet the first week in September.

The First Continental Congress

On September 5, delegates from twelve colonies were on hand for the First Continental Congress. Only Georgia was unrepresented. The stated purpose of the meeting was to "consult upon the present unhappy state of the colonies." Delegates to this Congress had been chosen by the Committees of Correspondence, and consisted of such radicals as John and Samuel Adams of Massachusetts, Patrick Henry and Richard Henry Lee of Virginia, and Christopher Gadsden of South Carolina; moderates such as Peyton Randolph and George Washington of Virginia, John Jay of New York, and John Dickinson of Pennsylvania; and conservatives such as Joseph Galloway of Pennsylvania. This extralegal body faced a dilemma; it was expected to ward off parliamentary wrath, restore imperial relations to a happy keel, and yet assert colonial rights. The members had to put forward a firm and forceful front to gain the concessions they desired, yet they could not leave themselves open to accusations of radicalism from either American conservatives or British friends. In short, they had to brandish the sword, yet simultaneously extend the olive branch.

Two plans were advocated, one conservative and one radical. Joseph Galloway proposed to the body a Plan of Union, which called for a separate American government consisting of a president-general appointed by the king and a legislative council chosen by the colonial legislatures; no act of Parliament would apply to America unless approved by this body, itself an inferior branch of Parliament, and it would control Indian affairs, western lands, and men and money in time of war. Probably because of false rumors that General Gage had bombarded Boston, Galloway's Plan of Union (so similar to the dominion status conceded Canada in 1867) was defeated. Instead, the Congress voted endorsement of the Suffolk Resolves (taken from a convention in Suffolk County, Massachusetts). These stated that the Intolerable Acts should be resisted "as the attempts of a wicked administration to enslave America," that the colonies should raise troops, and that all join in nonimportation and nonexportation with England, Ireland, and the British West Indies.

On October 14 the Congress issued a more philosophical statement, the Declaration of Rights and Resolves. This condemned the Intolerable Acts, taxation of the colonies, and the large British army in America; it listed the rights of the colonists, among which were "life, liberty, and property" (a phrase borrowed from John Locke's justification of the British Glorious Revolution of 1688); and it asserted that England had only the power to regulate external trade and legislate for imperial affairs. The Declaration was addressed to the king and to the people of England, as much as to Parliament, and was conciliatory in tone, although it limited the king's prerogatives.

Just before adjourning, the Congress established a Continental Association—a system of committees of inspection in towns and counties to supervise nonimportation, nonexportation. The association was charged to inspect customs entries, publish the names of violators, and to confiscate British goods. Thus a Congress

George III

MOST Americans know George III as a power-mad tyrant bent on forcing his royal will on liberty-loving colonists. But in the Great Britain of 1776 he was popular with a majority of Englishmen, who saw him as strongly moral and a bulwark against the hated French. Even his war against America had public support—until it went against England.

Born George William Frederick in 1738, he was descended from the Hanoverian kings of England who had come to the throne in 1714. His great-grandfather, George I, and his grandfather, George II, had paraded their mistresses pubicly and had never shown any great love for the country they ruled. When George III came to the throne in 1760, he was widely loved for his strict attachment to his family (which would number nine sons and six daughters), for his parsimony, and for his self-discipline.

Unfortunately for England, he tried to follow the advice of his mother, who said to him, "George, be king." Through complaisant ministers he tried to rule England absolutely. His dictatorial policies—and the ineptitude of his ministers—led to the American Revolution, while his meddling in local politics caused a reassertion of parliamentary independence later in his reign.

George III ruled England for sixty years (1760–1820), a span that included the American Revolution, the French Revolution, the Napoleonic Wars, and the War of 1812. However, prior to 1810 he underwent five bouts of what then was judged to be temporary insanity, and he gradually went blind. After 1810 he was permanently unable to reign because of his affliction (modern doctors believe he was suffering from porphyria, a disorder of the metabolism). During his last ten years he lived in seclusion while his son (George IV) served as regent.

called to protest against parliamentary usurpation of rights ended by creating powerful extralegal machinery for supervision of American life. As the Congress adjourned, it agreed that unless its demands had been met, it would reconvene on May 10, 1775.

During the fall of 1774, the choices for many Americans became few in number: submission to the authority of Parliament or submission to the vigilance committees in America. Opinion was polarized into two positions: Patriot and Loyalist. Attacks on Loyalists increased in the autumn months of 1774; their property was confiscated, and tar and feathers were liberally applied. "Minutemen" began drilling openly on village greens, while the Continental Association published names of those who imported or consumed British goods under the heading "enemies of *American* liberty." Arms and ammunition were stored, especially in New England, as men prepared to fight for their rights as Englishmen against the usurpations of king, Parliament, or anyone else. The clouds of war were darkening—and ominous with thunder.

The War Begins

On January 19, 1775, the petition of the Continental Congress was laid before Parliament. A majority of the members of that body supported their king, unaware that his intention of suppressing the colonies actually threatened their own liberties and freedoms. Thus on February 9 Parliament voted that Massachusetts was in a state of rebellion. Lord North did make one last try to avoid the bloodshed he foresaw. On February 27 in Parliament he pushed through a resolution, the Plan of Conciliation, stating that Parliament would tax no colony that would tax itself for the cost of its government and its share of imperial defense needs. Yet the time for conciliation had already passed. On March 23 in Virginia Patrick Henry asserted—according to his biographer, William Wirt—a truth so bitter as to be easily forgotten: life, he said, was not so sweet as to be bought at the price of chains and slavery. His "liberty or death" speech set the mood and tone for Americans.

The British response was to order General Gage on April 14 to use force to end the rebellion in New England. Five days later Gage sent 700 troops to seize arms and supplies at Concord, twenty miles north of Boston. Boston Patriots managed to send Paul Revere, William Dawes, and Dr. Samuel Prescott to spread the alarm. The Minutemen gathered along the route of march. At Lexington Green the British troops fired on them, killing eight, then proceeded to Concord. Failing to find the supplies, which had been moved, the British troops began a long and bloody return march to Boston. Minutemen fired upon them, killing or wounding 247 redcoats while sustaining only ninety-five casualties themselves. Thus by the time the Second Continental Congress met in Philadelphia on May 10, 1775, the war was one of bullets, not words, of sword and musket, not pamphlet and petition.

British and American Advantages

At the outbreak of fighting, England seemingly had the edge. It had a centralized administration with great financial and political power. It boasted a large professional army and the world's best navy. It had the industrial capacity to provide the materials of war. It controlled Canada and Florida, both flanks of the rebellious colonies, and it commanded the loyalty of the majority of American Indians and about a third of all American colonists. However, there were many British who opposed the war, while others were indifferent; thus enlistments were slow and foreign mercenaries had to be employed. Furthermore, the British army had to take the offensive 3000 miles from home—a long, difficult line of communication and supply in that age.

Americans had distinct disadvantages also. There was no firm central administrative control of the American effort; the Continental Congress assumed the powers of a central government, but had no way to enforce its decisions. Its army was small and largely ineffective in 1775; few men enlisted for the duration of the war, while colonial militias frequently refused to fight outside their own boundaries. Never did Washington have more than one present-day division, while at one time he had fewer than 2000 men. His officers, usually elected by the troops, underrated cohesion and military discipline. Nor could the United States supply weapons and equipment, for the country had little industrial capacity. Moreover, there was a constant shortage of funds; Congress was afraid to tax—for the war was against that— and thus had to depend on gifts, loans both domestic and foreign, and printing paper money.

On the positive side, however, the Americans did control 99 percent of the territory for which they were fighting. To win, all they had to do was hold out until England grew tired. They had the support of many Englishmen, who realized that Americans were fighting for British rights, as well as for their own, against the usurpations of a would-be tyrant. Also, they could play on centuries-old hatreds in Europe to gain the aid of France and Spain. Finally, the Americans had George Washington as commander-in-chief. Washington was more than just one man: he embodied the American aspiration. He contributed more than just military ability and statesmanship; he contributed his character and charisma to the cause—and by force of personality dragged the country along with him to victory.

Washington was appointed commander-in-chief of the Continental Army by the Second Continental Congress on June 15 and went north to take command of the troops then converging on Boston. As he traveled, battles were occurring. On the night of June 16–17, a Patriot force of 1200 men was sent to seize Bunker Hill, one of the heights surrounding Boston, in anticipation that General Gage would try to occupy it. The Americans occupied and fortified Breed's Hill nearer to Boston, however, and on the morning of June 17 were attacked by 3000 British troops. Twice the Americans repulsed charges, but a third attempt carried the day for England. In the effort, however, they lost 1054 men to American losses of 449. Despite the loss of Breed's Hill, Americans were inspired by their showing for the fight to come. Also inspiring the troops was word that Ethan Allen and Benedict Arnold, with only eighty-three men, had, on May 10, taken Fort Ticonderoga on Lake Champlain. Thus when Washington arrived and took command on July 3, his 14,500 men were in high spirits.

Meanwhile, the Second Continental Congress had been meeting in Philadelphia since May 10. Its composition was distinguished, for among its members were John and Samuel Adams of Massachusetts, Benjamin Franklin of Pennsylvania, John Jay of New York, and Thomas Jefferson and Richard Henry Lee of Virginia. Elected president of the Congress was John Hancock of Massachusetts. The Congress moved to exercise the powers of sovereignty. It authorized an army and created a navy; it appointed Washington commander-in-chief; it commissioned merchant vessels as privateers; it established a postal system and a treasury; it issued paper money and floated loans; it negotiated treaties with Indian tribes; and it tried to provide for defense of the frontier. At the same time, the Congress made attempts to conciliate England. On July 5 it adopted the Olive Branch Petition, authored by John Dickinson, which was an appeal to George III to restrain Parliament from passing further tyrannical measures. The next day, however, the Congress adopted the Declaration of Causes and Necessities of Taking Up Arms, written by Thomas Jefferson and John Dickinson. This statement was intended to aid the American cause in England, for it asserted: "We have not raised armies with ambitious designs of separating from Great Britain, and establishing independence"; yet at the same time it hinted that foreign assistance was available to aid them, and it stated that Americans were "resolved to die free men rather than live slaves." This work done, the Congress adjourned on August 2.

George III dashed any hopes that colonists might have had that their grievances were all at the hands of Parliament, not the crown. His reaction to the Olive Branch Petition and the Declaration of Causes and Necessities of Taking Up Arms came on August 23, when he proclaimed that Americans were rebels and warned loyal subjects to refrain from giving them assistance. Yet in his attempts to suppress the rebellion, he found little popular support from his subjects at home. So few were willing to fight that 30,000 foreign mercenaries had to be employed. (These were commonly called Hessians because so many of them came from the German landgraviate of Hesse.) This move, along with George III's other measures, helped widen the gulf between colonies and England—and drove Americans toward an open declaration of independence.

When the Continental Congress reconvened in Philadelphia on September 12, 1775, all thirteen colonies were represented. The mood of this group was more radical, more inclined toward separation from England than had been the earlier gatherings. In this, the members represented their constituents, who likewise were moving toward a total break with England. Such a shift in attitude reflected many causes. The radicals, through the Committees of Correspondence, had been doing their work well, especially making use of colonial offices vacated by Britishers and occupied by staunch Patriots. Every effort England made to suppress the rebellion caused converts to the Patriot side, as did the British employment of mercenaries. Also, there was a growing awareness that a declaration of independence was necessary in order to secure foreign aid; France and Spain had little desire to anger England solely in the name of "the rights of Englishmen."

Then in January, 1776, came Thomas Paine's *Common Sense,* a pamphlet that asserted England was not necessary for protection of the colonies; France and Spain, Paine argued, were enemies of England, not the colonies. Furthermore, he said it was absurd for an island to govern a continent, and he insisted that American goods would insure prosperity without English connections, for Europeans had to eat. Paine's pamphlet sold an astounding 120,000 copies in just three months. That same month of January, 1776, General Washington publicly declared himself in favor of colonial independence—which carried considerable weight.

Congress responded on April 6 by opening American ports to commerce from all nations except England—a virtual declaration of independence. Then on May 10 the Congress went another step by recommending that the colonies should form their own governments "such as shall best conduce to the happiness and safety of their constituents." Four colonies already had done so; by 1777 all except Massachusetts, Connecticut, and Rhode Island had written new constitutions. The next step came on June 7, when Richard Henry Lee of Virginia introduced a Resolution of Independence in Congress declaring "that these United Colonies are, and of right ought to be, free and independent States, that they are absolved of all allegiance to the British Crown. . . . " Four days later Congress appointed Jefferson, Franklin, John Adams, Roger Sherman, and Robert Livingston to prepare a draft of a formal resolution. The vote on Lee's resolution came on July 2 and was unanimous—twelve to nothing (with New York abstaining, for there was a heavy concentration of Loyalists in New York).

The Declaration of Independence

The Declaration of Independence came largely from the pen of Thomas Jefferson, while the ideas were drawn mainly from John Locke's defense of the Glorious Revolution of 1688. Ironically, the colonists employed British arguments to justify their own revolution: that all men are endowed by nature with inalienable rights, including life, liberty, and the pursuit of happiness; that governments rested on the consent of the governed; that governments were created to guarantee man's natural rights; that a government so failing could be overthrown; and that, specifically, Parliament had no control over the colonies. Again the vote, which came on July 4, was twelve to nothing in favor (with New York abstaining; on July 9 it also endorsed the Declaration).

For the Loyalists, the Declaration of Independence created real problems. The country was committed—and its citizens had to take sides. Loyalty to the king had become treason. And in most colonies the Patriots organized committees to force everyone to take an oath of allegiance to the United States on pain of imprisonment and confiscation of property for failure to do so. The Loyalists were numerous—estimates of their numbers run as high as a third of all colonists; also, they were impressive in quality. In some colonies, such as New York, New Jersey, and Georgia, they possibly were in the majority. Royal officials, Anglican clergy, and the great landowners (except in Virginia) tended toward loyalty, while merchants were about evenly divided. Most Loyalists took the oath and paid their taxes—while praying for defeat. Others fled behind British lines or to Florida, Canada, or England. Some enlisted and fought on the British side; there were several Tory companies in the Southern colonies, while an estimated 15,000 New Yorkers became British troops.

The Revolutionary War

The course of the war was strange—Americans tended to lose the battles, but in the end they triumphed. At the outbreak of fighting, a principal objective was Canada. The Continental Congress on May 29, 1775, had issued an address to "fellow-sufferers" in Canada, inviting them to join the rebellion—which Canadians largely failed to heed, for the Quebec Act had pacified them. On November 8 Benedict Arnold with 600 men reached Quebec and laid siege. Five days later General Richard Montgomery captured Montreal, then moved immediately to join Arnold at Quebec. On December 31 the two forces together assaulted Quebec; Montgomery was killed, the attack failed, and the following spring, Arnold was forced to retreat to Fort Ticonderoga. These moves alarmed England sufficiently for its military strategists to send a large force to Canada.

JOHN ADAMS

Bureau of Printing and Engraving

76

John Adams

BORN on October 19, 1735, at Braintree, Massachusetts, John Adams belonged to a distinguished New England family. Graduating from Harvard at the age of twenty, he taught school briefly, then deeply considered becoming a minister; however, "frigid John Calvin" and "disputed points" of doctrine changed his mind. At last he chose to study law under James Putnam because, as he wrote, "the study and practice of law ... does not dissolve the obligations of morality or of religion."

Married to Abigail Smith in 1764, Adams was a man of great strength and vigor— and a highly developed sense of moral right. He could push the colonial cause because he felt acts of the British Parliament and king were wrong, yet he also could defend the conduct of the British soldiers involved in the so-called Boston Massacre in 1770 because he believed their actions were legal.

By the time of the drafting of the Declaration of Independence, Adams was of medium stature and of stout, well-knit frame (which would tend more and more to corpulence as he aged). His head was "large and round, with a wide forehead and expanded brows. His eye was mild and benignant, perhaps even humorous, when he was free from emotion." When Adams became excited, his eyes would express "the vehemence of the spirit that stirred within."

After the Revolution, Adams went to the Court of St. James as American ambassador, returning to serve as George Washington's vice president—and a figure around whom the Federalists could rally. In 1796 he won the presidency in a bitterly contested election that saw Thomas Jefferson chosen vice president; these two men, with their opposing philosophies of government, became severe critics of one another. However, late in life, after both had retired from public affairs, they began corresponding—and then warmed to the point of friendship. Ironically, the two died the same day, July 4, 1826, the fiftieth anniversary of American independence.

Washington's siege of Boston ended more happily for the American cause. On March 17, Sir William Howe (who had succeeded Gage) abandoned the city by sailing for Halifax; he intended to move on New York City from Halifax. Washington anticipated this move, and between April and August, 1776, moved from Boston to New York. There he had troops numbering approximately 33,000. Howe arrived with 34,000 men, and on August 27 the two forces fought the Battle of Long Island. The Americans were defeated and Washington retreated, evacuating Long Island for Manhattan on August 29–30. Defeated again, Washington retreated to Hackensack, New Jersey, intent on Fabian tactics—no major battle in which his army might be defeated, but retreat, fight small actions, and retreat until the British army was worn down.

On December 11, Washington was forced by Lord Cornwallis to cross the Delaware River into Pennsylvania, whereupon the British troops went into winter quarters. The American general knew that his situation was desperate; his supplies were low, and his troops were dwindling away. To the Continental Congress, Washington wrote of his needs, stating that he must have more men and more material aid or "the game will be pretty much up." Even the ringing words of Nathan Hale as he went to the gallows as a spy—"I regret that I have but one life to give for my country"—did not electrify the young nation. Nor did Thomas Paine's pamphlet *The American Crisis* stimulate a wave of enlistments; his sentence, "These are the times that try men's souls," was most appropriate. A time of trial was ahead. Aiding the American cause far more than words was Washington's brilliant counterattack late that year. On Christmas night, 1776, he recrossed the Delaware to attack the Hessian garrison at Trenton on December 26, killing many of the enemy troops and capturing 2000. Then on January 3, 1777, he fought the Battle of Princeton in New Jersey, defeating Lord Cornwallis, before going into winter quarters near Morristown, New Jersey.

In March, 1777, the British secretary of state, Lord Germain, approved an overall strategy for the war—a three-pronged attack to divide the colonies. One British column was to invade New York from Canada by way of Lake Champlain; another column was to slash into New York from Lake Ontario by way of the Mohawk Valley; and Lord Howe was to seize Philadelphia. Only one aspect of this plan succeeded, however. Lord Howe landed 15,000 troops at the head of Chesapeake Bay to find Washington and 10,500 men blocking the road to Philadelphia. On September 11, Howe defeated Washington at the Battle of Brandywine Creek in Pennsylvania, then slipped around the Americans and occupied Philadelphia at the end of the month.

Elsewhere the master plan failed. Colonel Barry St. Leger, leading the British force from Lake Ontario, was forced to retire by the timely actions of Benedict Arnold in late August. General John Burgoyne, moving down the Lake Champlain route from Canada, fought a series of engagements collectively known as the Battle of Saratoga (between September 19 and October 17). Near Freeman's Farm at Bemis Heights, Burgoyne suffered heavy losses, first to General Horatio Gates and then to Benedict Arnold. On October 17, Burgoyne surrendered 5700 men to General Gates. Meanwhile, Washington was moving into winter quarters at Valley Forge, there to suffer from shortages of food and supplies during the bitter cold. Although to the men with Washington at Valley Forge it seemed that the American cause was ill-fated, the Battle of Saratoga had changed the course of the war; the news of that victory, when it arrived on the Continent, led French and Spanish generals to think the Americans had a chance of victory—and therefore merited French and Spanish aid. In 1778 France declared war on England and Spain made a similar decision. French volunteers, the French fleet, Spanish supplies, and the diversion of war in Europe took enough pressure off the Americans to enable them to continue the struggle.

This European aid was secured through the diplomatic efforts of Silas Deane, Arthur Lee, and Benjamin Franklin. On March 4, 1778, Congress ratified the result of their efforts, a treaty with France establishing an alliance between the two nations and providing that neither nation would make peace without consulting the other. The American navy profited greatly from this arrangement; soon ships outfitted in France were attacking British coastal towns, while John Paul Jones used French ports as bases for his battles with British men-of-war. French noblemen, such as the Marquis de Lafayette, gave prestige to the colonial army by their presence with Washington, as did Baron Friedrich Wilhelm von Steuben and Thaddeus Kosciusko.

Equally noteworthy was the Spanish contribution from Louisiana. Governor Bernardo de Gálvez seized eleven English vessels at New Orleans. He also sold needed supplies to the Americans at Fort Pitt and other frontier posts. From New Orleans came the weapons and ammunition that enabled George Rogers Clark to fight the British and the Indians in the Illinois country. Gálvez invaded East and West Florida, capturing Mobile in March, 1780, and the following year secured Pensacola, Florida, thereby making Florida Spanish once again. The British grew tired of this Spanish bother and determined on an expedition down the Mississippi from Canada; it was to take St. Louis, reconquer Illinois, and make contact with British troops in Florida. Captain Emmanuel Hesse gathered some 1000 soldiers and Indian allies and moved on St. Louis. However, Captain Fernando de Leyba, commanding at St. Louis, frustrated the plan; with only 300 soldiers and militia he fought so vigorously on May 26, 1780, that the attackers grew discouraged and retired northward. Thus, Spanish aid diverted British soldiers to Florida, enabled George Rogers Clark to hold the Northwest Territory for America, and frustrated British plans to link Canada and Florida by way of the Mississippi River.

Meanwhile, in May, 1778, Lord Howe was supplanted as commander of British forces by General Henry Clinton. His orders were to evacuate Philadelphia and move to New York City. When Clinton began this move, Washington followed him across New Jersey, and on June 28 they fought the inconclusive Battle of Monmouth, which ended in a draw that allowed Clinton to enter New York City. Washington followed and encamped at White Plains to keep watch.

The major thrust of the war then swung southward. British strategists felt they could count on heavy Loyalist support to conquer the Southern colonies. Under Clinton's planning, Savannah, Georgia, was taken in December, 1778, and Georgia was soon overrun. Clinton personally led a force, going by ship from New York, that on May 12, 1780, took Charleston, South Carolina, along with 5000 American prisoners. Clinton then departed for New York, leaving Cornwallis in charge. In July, Cornwallis moved northward, and on August 16 he inflicted a crushing defeat on the Americans under General Gates at Camden, South Carolina. However, as Cornwallis' army marched into North Carolina, it suffered a defeat at King's Mountain on October 7, 1780, forcing Cornwallis back into South Carolina. Then on January 16, 1781, Cornwallis was defeated again at Cowpens, South Carolina, by an American force led by General Daniel Morgan. Cornwallis thereupon decided to

Joseph Brant

JOSEPH BRANT was born in the Ohio Valley, the son of a chief of the League of the Iroquois. Inasmuch as descent in this tribe was matrilineal and his mother was not a Mohawk, he could never rise to the rank of chief, but he did become a war chief. At nineteen he was sent to Moor's Charity School at Lebanon, Connecticut, and there he was converted to the Anglican Church, after which he left this religious endeavor to join the Iroquois contingent fighting under Chief Pontiac. Always he was caught between his desire to convert his tribe to white ways and to lead them in war against the whites.

In 1774 Brant became secretary to Guy Johnson, the British Indian superintendent. At the outbreak of the American Revolution he used his influence to persuade the Iroquois to join the British side and to discredit the Reverend Samuel Kirkland, a missionary who had succeeded in persuading the Oneida and Tuscarora (tribes in the League of the Iroquois) to join the Americans. As a war chief of the Mohawks, Brant was commissioned a British captain and sent to England to be presented at court as an Indian ally of the crown. Returning to the New World, he fought as commander of an Indian contingent at the Battle of Long Island in 1776 and was with St. Leger's expedition at the Battle of Oriskany in 1777.

Between 1778 and 1780 Brant led his Indian followers on raids in the Mohawk Valley, southern New York, and northern Pennsylvania. Constantly he exhorted his followers that an American victory would mean destruction of all the Indian nations. He and his followers were accused of perpetrating massacres such as those at Cherry Valley in 1778 and at Wyoming in 1779. Brant later claimed that he did not join in these events, but his troops were responsible for reprehensible killings.

At the end of the American Revolution, Brant frustrated an attempt by Red Jacket, a rival Mohawk chief, to negotiate a peace treaty with the United States. Later he tried, unsuccessfully, to do the same thing so that he and his people could remain in their traditional homeland. Failing to come to terms with the United States, Brant persuaded Governor Haldimaud of Canada to assign the Mohawks a reservation on the Grand River in upper Canada. And on a journey to England in 1785 he was successful in attaining an indemnification for the Mohawks for their losses during the war.

Brant's later years were spent in translating the New Testament and other religious documents into the Mohawk language and in promoting Indian acceptance of the white man's ways. He died on November 24, 1807, at the Grand River Reservation, far from the valley he had known as a youth and to which his people never could return. For him and the Mohawks the war did not end successfully; no treaty could be made that would return their homes to them.

move northward into Virginia; he marched, raiding villages and farms along the way, to take up a position at Yorktown on August 1, 1781. He believed that the British navy could evacuate him should that become necessary.

George Washington learned that a French fleet of twenty vessels under Admiral de Grasse would be at Yorktown, not the British fleet. Therefore he and the French commander, the Comte de Rochambeau, gave up their plan to attack New York City and led their troops southward. With the aid of the French fleet, they assembled an army of 16,000 troops at Williamsburg and on September 28 began the Siege of Yorktown. Three weeks later, on October 19, Cornwallis surrendered 7000 troops to Washington. Lord North, upon hearing the news, cried out, "Oh God! It is all over!" He resigned the ministry in March, 1782, and the Marquis of Rockingham formed the government that would negotiate a treaty of peace.

Attempts to settle the war diplomatically were the province of the Continental Congress, which had remained in session throughout the war. It had established a Committee for Foreign Affairs on April 17, 1777, which was responsible for sending agents to Europe to secure aid from other nations. By April of the next year, England had responded to the prodding of prominent citizens by naming a British Peace Commission. This commission spent the summer and fall in America, but was unsuccessful. Then, on November 3, 1779, Congress appointed John Adams to negotiate peace with England. In June, 1781, Benjamin Franklin and John Jay became part of a peace commission with Adams; Thomas Jefferson also was named to the committee, but refused to serve. The commission made little headway until 1782, when on March 4 the House of Commons voted to end the war in America and on March 22 the Rockingham ministry assumed office. On April 12 the British dispatched Richard Oswald to Paris to begin negotiations with Franklin. After seven years of warfare, serious negotiating began.

The Peace Treaty

The treaty that resulted a year and a half later was favorable to the United States largely through Franklin's efforts. Strangely, the American enemies at the conference were the French and Spanish diplomats, not the English. Spain had never recognized American independence, and it did not want the Americans to gain the Mississippi River as a western boundary; instead the Spanish envoys were seeking to have the Northwest Territory retained by England and to have Alabama, Mississippi, and parts of Kentucky and Tennessee ceded to Spain. Franklin, in separate negotiations with England, pointed out the British advantages to an amicable parting with the former colonies, and thus separate treaties resulted. On January 20, 1783, England signed treaties with France and Spain that gave Florida to Spain. Then on September 3 came the Peace of Paris between England and the United States.

The Peace of Paris recognized American independence. The United States renounced all claims to Canada, and in return received the Mississippi as its western limit. Other boundaries included the St. Croix River in Maine, the St. Lawrence-Atlantic divide, and the forty-ninth parallel in the north; and the thirty-first parallel and the Apalachicola and St. Mary's rivers in the south. Furthermore, the United States retained fishing rights off Newfoundland and Nova Scotia and in the St. Lawrence. Both sides agreed that creditors of either nation would not be hampered in collecting debts, while the Continental Congress agreed to recommend earnestly to the states that they restore confiscated Loyalist property. The British agreed to return the slaves they had captured during the war, while the Americans stipulated there would be no further confiscation of Loyalist property. And the United States received right of transit on the Mississippi River.

The Peace of Paris settled the major issues between the participatory nations, but it could not and did not solve the problems for some of the major pawns and victims of the war, namely, the American Indians who were involved. Chief among these tribes were the Mohawks of upstate New York, led by Joseph Brant.

The Impact of the Revolution

The war for American independence was more than an isolated case of incipient nationalism. It was a war of principle, a battle over ideas, a cry of the human spirit that would turn the world upside down. The ideas of the American Revolution—the natural rights of man, the transcendent worth of the individual, and the concept of government resting on the "consent of the governed"—were in themselves not new. What was new was that these ideas precipitated a war that brought forth a nation dedicated to these principles. Thus the new nation, by the simple fact of its existence, stirred men's minds and hearts as the ideas never had—and in the next fifty years would spark more revolutions than any other ideology ever would. The world *had* been turned upside down.

Chapter Five

A Practical Republic

The Responsibility of Freedom

AMERICANS in 1783 could celebrate their freedom from England. Yet within just four short years they learned that freedom brought responsibilities and the need for self-discipline, a concept that seemingly must be relearned by each generation. They had fought against taxation—and then had to tax themselves. They had fought against the burdens of government—and then had to govern themselves. They had fought against invasion of their individual rights—and then in the name of the "general good" had to place restrictions on the exercise of individual rights. They quickly were made to realize that the world is one of reality, not of theory, that freedom belongs only to the strong, not the weak, and that freedom is costly, not free. Yet the nation survived this time of trial—though not without turmoil—because of one difference between the old order and the new: their taxes, their governmental burdens, and their restrictions on individual liberties were self-imposed.

The immediate tendency following the Revolution was toward fragmentation. Hatred of the English central government had not inclined the revolutionists to sympathy toward an American central government. Even the words of the pamphleteer Thomas Paine had little immediate effect. The last issue of his *American Crisis* stated, "Sovereignty must have power to protect all the parts that compose and constitute it; and as UNITED STATES we are equal to the importance of the title, but otherwise we are not. Our Union, well and wisely regulated and cemented, is the cheapest way of being great—the easiest way of being powerful, and the happiest invention in government which the circumstances of America can admit of." Yet the consent was lacking.

The State Constitutions

The war itself had not provided the spark of unity. In fact, almost the opposite had occurred. During the years of conflict, the various states had been drafting constitutions as recommended by the Continental Congress. There they had put into practice the theory that government is of the people, for the people, and by the people, resting on the consent of the governed, and given solid form in a written constitution. During the war the "compact theory" had been poorly practiced; the difficulties of war made it almost impossible for the people to ratify the constitutions thus written. In some states, such as New Hampshire, Georgia, Delaware, New York, and Vermont, the legislatures had ratified the constitutions. In others, such as Pennsylvania, Maryland, and North Carolina, the constitutions were framed by constitutional conventions, but not ratified by the people. Only Massachusetts followed what would be called the modern process—a constitutional convention wrote the document in 1780 and then it was ratified by the people. New Hampshire's constitution would be ratified this way in 1784.

These state constitutions, so diverse in origin, did have remarkable similarities. They showed the impact of the principles that had motivated the war. They contained bills of rights, provided for elected legislatures (bicameral except in Pennsylvania) with power over the purse strings, allowed little real executive power, and designated frequent elections. Yet despite the "rights of man" concept, there were property qualifications for voting in every state except one, and in most there were religious qualifications (or oaths) designed to prevent Roman Catholics from holding office; in short, the framers of these constitutions subscribed to the theory that the body politic was constituted by those with a stake in society.

None of the new state constitutions broke radically with the past. They were conservative in mixing their colonial experiences with previous English practices. There were genuine social and economic gains manifest in these documents, however. Virginia in 1776 had passed a call for "free exercise of religon," and everywhere the established church lost political power. Another change was the abolition of slavery through gradual emancipation in Pennsylvania, Connecticut, Rhode Island, New Jersey, and New York by 1786, while the importation of slaves had ended in all states save South Carolina and Georgia by the same year. Primogeniture and entailed estates were abolished. And debtors and prisoners generally were better treated by the states than they had been under English common law. Yet the American experience was not a revolution in the sense that France would undergo a few years later (or Russia in the twentieth century). The basic structure of society was not altered—the revolution was principally political, not social. True, many Loyalists had been impoverished, but the Patriots who were enriched became just as socially and politically conservative as the Loyalists had been.

The Articles of Confederation

During the war there had been an attempt to create a national government of sorts, one capable of conducting the revolution. On June 12, 1776, Congress had appointed a thirteen-man committee to draft the Articles of Confederation; this committee consisted of one member from each state. Largely the work of John Dickinson, the Articles were submitted to Congress exactly one month later, and called for a central government with an executive council of state, reserving only the police power to the states. More than a year later, on November 15, 1777, the Continental Congress approved the Articles. These provided for a unicameral Congress with no executive; there would be an executive committee but no chief executive. Each state was to have one vote in Congress. The unanimous consent of all states was needed to amend the Articles, while the vote of nine was necessary to pass most legislation. The states were restricted in that they could not make treaties or raise armies or navies without permission of Congress. Further, each state was required to extend its privileges and immunities to free citizens of other states, and each had to give "full faith and credit" to acts of other states. The central government was granted the power to wage war, conduct foreign affairs, settle interstate quarrels, issue money, manage Indian affairs, deliver the mail, and establish the value of coins. Yet it could not raise a national army, tax, or regulate commerce; funds and troops were to come from the states by quota (according to population) as voted by Congress.

Ratifying the Articles of Confederation moved smoothly at first. By July, 1778, eight states had agreed to them. The stumbling block proved to be the western land claims of the various states, many of which overlapped. New Jersey, Delaware, and Maryland refused to agree to the Articles until all states ceded these claims to the central government. Maryland summed up the feeling in these three states: the war was a common effort and western lands should be a common heritage "subject to be parcelled by Congress into free, convenient, and independent governments." In September, 1780, Congress asked those states with western land claims to surrender them to the central government. New York led the way with such a cession in 1780, and Virginia (which had the best claim) followed in January, 1781. Thereupon Maryland ratified the Articles in February, the last state to do so, and on March 1, 1781, the Articles were proclaimed in effect. Robert Livingston became secretary of foreign affairs and Robert Morris superintendent of finance. Government under the Articles of Confederation had begun.

The Financial Crisis

The most pressing problem facing the new government in 1783—as during all its existence—was money. On January 25 that year, Congress proved unable to satisfy the claims of the officers of the Continental Army for back pay. Only the firm action of George Washington, who denounced Major John Armstrong, leader of the dissident officers, prevented a mutiny. Then in April, when Congress proposed to raise funds by collecting an import duty and taxing on the basis of population, both measures, which were in the form of amendments to the Articles of Confederation, failed to win passage. Therefore on June 24, Congress had to move from Philadelphia to Princeton and later to Annapolis to escape mutinous Pennsylvania regiments demanding their pay. Even the interest on the public debt could not be paid. Financier Robert Morris urged passage of land taxes, excise taxes, and a poll tax—but the recalcitrant congressmen failed to act. Washington did prevail on the army to disband in June because Congress did promise to pay soldiers in warrants good for western land. And Congress secured a loan from Holland that enabled it to meet its obligations for a time. The central government finally came to rest in New York City, which was declared the temporary national capital on December 23, 1784.

The government under the Articles of Confederation had as much difficulty in the field of foreign affairs. During the war, the colonies had experienced a certain commercial prosperity owing to trade with France, the French West Indies, and Spain. After the conflict terminated, these trading concessions largely were revoked by Spain and France. Likewise, British Orders in Council closed the British West Indies to American shipping in May, 1783, thereby cutting off another profitable source of trade. Because the United States presented the spectacle of a nation virtually without a central government, the British refused to abandon their posts in the Northwest Territory; thereby they protected the valuable fur trade until, as they thought, the United States would collapse into anarchy. Attempts to negotiate commercial treaties with foreign powers failed (except with Sweden and Prussia); the reasons for such failure were manifested to John Adams in England, when he was told, "One treaty, or thirteen?" The central government's inability to secure commercial concessions from foreign powers led the states to commercial warfare with one another, each erecting tariff barriers against the others and engaging in petty boundary disputes that led to a condition of thirteen virtually independent states rather than "United States."

The impotence of the central government led Spain to dabble in sedition on the American frontier. Spanish officials hoped to secure the territory between the Appalachians and the Mississippi River and between the Ohio River and the Gulf of Mexico. Therefore, from its forts in East and West Florida, Spain urged the local Indians to war on American frontiersmen, and the American treaty rights of transit on the Mississippi River were flouted openly. Moreover, Spanish money went to selected individuals in the Southwest for the purpose of financing secession from the United States and annexation to Spain. John Jay, secretary for foreign affairs, negotiated with the Spanish ambassador, Diego de Gardoquí, and produced a proposed treaty that would have surrendered the American claim to navigation of the Mississippi for twenty-five years in return for favorable reception of American ships in Spanish ports; however, the treaty failed passage in Congress because Southern states interested in the river voted against it.

The Western Lands

Congress did have one major success—its handling of the western lands. In 1785 came the Land Ordinance, recommended by George Washington the year before and largely written by Thomas Jefferson. This ordinance applied to the Northwest Territory and provided for orderly survey and purchase. It provided for a rectangular survey of the land into townships each six miles square (thus consisting of thirty-six sections of land). Four sections in every township were reserved for the government and another to maintain public schools. The others were to be sold at auctions, to be held at convenient spots, with the minimum price one dollar per acre in cash. Yet the basic price of $640 discouraged actual settlers, while the dollar-per-acre price discouraged speculators. Therefore Congress passed a special act allowing the purchase of a million and a half acres at nine cents per acre by a group that organized as the Ohio Company. At the urging of that company, Congress in 1787 provided for the government of the region by adoption of the Northwest Ordinance, which became the basis of political organization for all western lands. By terms of this ordinance, there were to be no slaves in the region north of the Ohio, which would be divided into not less than three nor more than five states. A governor and three judges, appointed by Congress (later the president) would rule until 5000 free male inhabitants had settled there; then they could elect a legislative body and send a nonvoting member to Congress. When a proposed state had 60,000 inhabitants, it would be admitted to the Union "on an equal footing with the original States in all respects whatever." Thus Congress early dedicated itself to an anticolonial policy; the territory owned by the United States eventually was to be given equal standing with the original states, not held as colonial dependencies to be exploited. Such a progressive measure was almost without precedent in world history. Under this ordinance of 1787, the orderly settlement of Ohio proceeded rapidly. Marietta was established in 1788, as was Cincinnati.

In the Southwest, however, settlement was much more disorderly. Two specula-

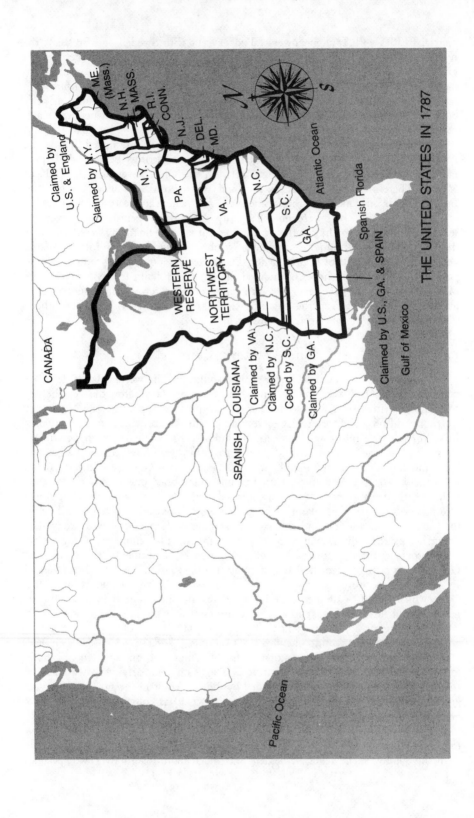

THE UNITED STATES IN 1787

CANADA

Claimed by
U.S. & England

Claimed by N.Y.

ME.
(Mass.)

N.H.

MASS.

R.I.

CONN.

N.Y.

PA.

N.J.

DEL.

MD.

VA.

N.C.

S.C.

GA.

WESTERN
RESERVE

NORTHWEST
TERRITORY

SPANISH
LOUISIANA

Claimed by VA.

Claimed by N.C.

Ceded by S.C.

Claimed by GA.

Atlantic Ocean

Spanish Florida

Claimed by U.S., GA. & SPAIN

Gulf of Mexico

Pacific Ocean

N

S

tors from Virginia, John Sevier and James Robertson, had taken frontiersmen into the Watauga and Holston rivers region in the 1770s, while Daniel Boone had blazed the Wilderness Road into Kentucky for the Transylvania Company in January, 1775. Settlement of this region continued during the revolutionary war. By 1784 there were some 10,000 settlers, periodically fighting the Cherokees, and on August 23, 1784, they organized the state of Franklin (in present Tennessee). Other would-be states were organized in Kentucky by the Transylvania Company and in the Cumberland Valley by James Robertson. Internal strife, Indian wars, and conflicts for leadership disrupted all three projected states to the extent that George Washington on a visit to the region in 1784 was appalled and urged Congress to provide for orderly settlement of the West.

Sad as was the central government's record in foreign affairs, disorganized as was the southwestern frontier, and fumbling as were the central government's efforts to run the country, it was largely economic discontent that led to the formation of a "more perfect Union." During the Revolutionary War, there had been a certain amount of prosperity. Smuggling, trade with France and Spain, the high profits from privateering and the sale of foodstuffs had enabled most Americans to enjoy a rising standard of living. This happy state of affairs did not continue when the war ended. Spain and France closed their ports to American goods. Pirates harassed American shipping in the Mediterranean. England imposed the navigation acts against American goods. Attempts by the central government to negotiate commercial treaties with foreign nations were ridiculed, while the states enacted stiff tariffs against each other. Such conditions generated a depression—which naturally hit the debtor class in America hard. Creditors pressed for payment of debts that the small farmers—and this category included a large percentage of the population—could not pay. The obvious answer, cried the farmer and the small retailer, was for the states to print more money. Paper money became the panacea, in the eyes of the debtor class, that would solve the postwar depression.

In seven states this demand became reality, but in Virginia, Connecticut, Delaware, and Maryland the legislatures refused. Where the demand was met, the paper currency quickly depreciated. In Rhode Island, for example, paper money declined in value so rapidly that merchants avoided debtors for fear of payment! The Rhode Island legislature responded by passing a law that made refusal to accept paper money a crime punishable by fine and imprisonment without a jury trial. A butcher, John Weeden, appealed conviction under this law to the state Supreme Court. On September 25, 1786, in *Trevett* v. *Weeden,* the Supreme Court refused to hear the case on the grounds that it had no jurisdiction, then declared the law repugnant to the provisions of the state charter (and therefore unconstitutional). This action set a precedent for the process of judicial review.

Elsewhere the debtor class, not content with laws and judicial process, used more direct action. In New Hampshire, for example, the militia was called out in 1786 to disperse a mob of debtors demanding passage of a paper money law. The Massachusetts legislature refused to pass such a law, then had to adjourn for six months to avoid the farmers' demands.

Farm foreclosures increased in number to such an extent that in August a rebellion occurred. Led by Daniel Shays, a former army officer and an impoverished farmer from the western part of Massachusetts, distressed citizens gathered in county conventions to draft resolutions to the legislature, resolutions that declared they were underrepresented in the state legislature, which was true, and that they were victims of rich men in Boston, which was partly true. Conventions soon gave way to armed mobs that prevented civil courts (where foreclosure proceedings were heard) from sitting, and then moved to prevent criminal courts (where rioters were tried) from sitting. From there they moved toward the state Supreme Court at Springfield and even threatened Confederation arsenals to secure weapons. Governor James Bowdoin sent 600 militiamen to protect the Supreme Court, but Shays and his followers nonetheless forced the court to adjourn on September 26. Then on January 25, 1787, Shays attacked the arsenal at Springfield, but was beaten off by the militia. Two days later a large army of 4000 arrived, and Shays fled through wintery cold to a refuge in Vermont. "Shays' Rebellion" deeply shocked conservatives, not only in Massachusetts but also in other states. Washington wrote James Madison about the rebellion and suggested that the United States was "verging to anarchy." Madison replied that a new government was needed, a thought shared by many responsible members of American society.

Toward a New Government

The present Constitution appropriately had its beginnings in the home of George Washington. On March 28, 1785, a convention of delegates from Virginia and Maryland met there to discuss commercial problems. They decided that perhaps Congress needed additional powers and suggested a convention be held at Annapolis the following year. The Annapolis Convention met September 11–14, 1786, with delegates attending from New York, Pennsylvania, New Jersey, Delaware, and Virginia. The delegates adopted an invitation written by Alexander Hamilton. This called for all thirteen states to send delegates to a convention to meet in Philadelphia in the spring of 1787 for the purpose of discussing commercial matters and to draw up proposed changes in the Articles of Confederation. The impotent Congress, which rarely had a quorum, endorsed this call on February 21, 1787, for the "sole and express purpose of revising the articles of Confederation."

This gathering, which would be the Constitutional Convention, met on May 25, 1787, at the Pennsylvania State House (Independence Hall), with delegates eventually present from all states save Rhode Island. These fifty-five delegates were among the most distinguished men in America. They averaged forty-two years in age, thirty-one had college educations, and half were lawyers. George Washington was chosen president of the assembly. Other leading figures included James Madison, who contributed so much he has been called Father of the Constitution; William Paterson of New Jersey, who championed the interests of small states; Alexander Hamilton of New York, who worked for a national government with a strong chief executive; Gouverneur Morris of Pennsylvania, who aided in forming the language of the Constitution; and Benjamin Franklin, who effected some of the important compromises of the convention. Other prominent members of the convention included James Wilson of Pennsylvania, Roger Sherman and Oliver Ellsworth of Connecticut, Rufus King and Elbridge Gerry of Massachusetts, John Dickinson of Delaware, Luther Martin of Maryland, and Charles Pinckney, Charles Cotesworth Pinckney, and John Rutledge of South Carolina. The two best-known Americans absent from the meeting were John Adams and Thomas Jefferson, both of whom were abroad on diplomatic missions.

At the outset two arguments were advanced. The first held that the delegates should comply with their instructions and prepare amendments to the Articles. The second held that the Articles should be discarded entirely and a new plan of government drafted. Only a short while was needed for the second argument to prevail. Then, fearing that the news of this decision would cause a sensation, the members of the convention voted to hold their sessions in secret. Next came introduction of various plans for the projected government. The first of these came on May 29; written by Madison and presented by Edmund Randolph, it was labeled the Virginia Plan (also, the "large-state plan"). This proposed a congress with representation based on population; the lower house would be elected by direct popular vote and the upper house named by the lower. The executive would be chosen by the legislative branch, with state officials bound to support the national government, which would have a veto power over state laws. Finally, a "council of revision," composed of the executive and members of the judiciary could veto acts of the legislature.

For two weeks the convention discussed the Virginia Plan, making minor revisions in it. Then on June 15 came the New Jersey Plan (or "small-state plan"), presented by William Paterson. This proposed, in essence, a continuation of the Articles of Confederation, but with the Congress having power to tax imports, regulate trade, and tax; Congress would name a plural chief executive and appoint a supreme court; acts of Congress and its treaties would be the "supreme law" of the land; and the executive branch would be responsible for enforcing the laws.

Three days after Paterson's plan was introduced, Hamilton submitted a plan. He proposed that the congress contain two houses—the lower house to be elected by the people and the upper to be named by electors chosen by the people—and a very strong chief executive; the president and senators would serve for life, and the president would name state governors.

Thus the delegates had several alternatives as they strove to fashion the final form of government. The basic dilemma was the question of what type of government the nation should have: was it to be a weak central government and strong states or a strong central government and weak states? The ideal of local self-government was attractive to all, yet the national government had to have real powers if the nation was to survive. The result was "federalism"—a division of powers—whereby the national government was to have specified powers in matters of concern to all Americans, such as national defense, while local matters were left to local governments. The large state–small state feud was settled by terms of the "Great Compromise" of July 5. Proposed by Robert Sherman of Connecticut, this called for a House of Representatives, elected on the basis of population, and a Senate, elected on the basis of two per state. Bills to raise money would originate in the House. Also, in determining representation in the House, five slaves would count as three free men.

The major deficiencies of the government under the Articles of Confederation were then remedied by the delegates. Congress was given the power to tax, to declare war and suppress insurrections, to regulate commerce, to coin money, and to make treaties binding on the states. Moreover, it could make "all laws which shall be necessary and proper for carrying into execution the foregoing," as well as all laws necessary for the "general welfare of the United States." These clauses were inserted to make certain that the new government would never be as restricted—and impotent—as had been the government under the Confederation, although the framers of the Constitution doubtless never foresaw just how the "general welfare" and "necessary and proper" clauses would be abused in the twentieth century.

The other major flaw in the Articles of Confederation, the lack of a chief executive, was remedied by providing for a president who would serve four years, not for life as Hamilton had advocated and not for a year as others had advocated. The chief executive would be elected, not directly by the people and not by the states, but by an electoral college; the framers of the Constitution did not trust the people sufficiently to entrust them with this function. The president could appoint his administrators, with senatorial consent; would be commander-in-chief of the army and navy; and could veto acts of Congress (subject to their passage over the veto by a two-thirds vote in both houses). Finally, the Constitution provided for an independent judiciary system. The chief court of the land would be the Supreme Court of the United States to hear cases on appeal from the lower courts (as established by Congress) and from state courts in cases involving the Constitution, and under treaties with foreign powers and the laws of the nation. There was no specific mention of judicial review; however, the Constitution did specify that state laws repugnant to the Constitution and to federal law must give way to federal law.

Ratifying the Constitution

When the Constitutional Convention adjourned in September, 1787, a woman hurried up to Benjamin Franklin and asked, "Well, Doctor, what have we got? A republic or a monarchy?" Franklin answered, "A republic—if you can keep it!" The inventor's reply was correct, both for his day and for our own. What Franklin did not say was that the republic as structured by the Constitution was, in reality, another revolution. The delegates to the Constitutional Convention had met with specific instructions to revise the Articles of Confederation, but had drawn up a document that abolished the old government and substituted a new one. Some historians have labeled the Constitution and the federal government instituted under it "The Revolution of 1789," and so it was: a peaceful revolution, a welcome revolution, a revolution without bloodshed—but a revolution nonetheless.

The heart of the revolution was the method of adoption for the new Constitution. In concluding their work, the delegates at the Constitutional Convention decided that their handiwork should be ratified, not by Congress or by the state legislatures, but by special ratification conventions. Another revolutionary feature was that the Constitution would become effective when ratified by conventions in only nine of the thirteen states. Under the Articles of Confederation, the votes of all thirteen states were necessary for amendment; now the Articles were being abolished by roughly a two-thirds vote of the states.

The final signing occurred on September 17. As George Washington arose from the chair from which he had presided, which was inscribed with a gilded half-sun, Benjamin Franklin observed: "I have often and often in the course of this session . . . looked at that . . . without being able to tell whether it was rising or setting; but now at length I have the happiness to know that it is a rising and not a setting sun."

Yet before that sun could rise, the Constitution had to be ratified, a process that proved quite difficult. Opposition sprang from many sources. Some Americans believed the new government would be too weak; others thought it would be too powerful. Some people feared the president would be a dictator; others feared the court system. Many were concerned because the original document contained no bill of individual rights. Still others opposed it because there was no ban on slavery. In short, ratification was not to be easy, although five states accepted it with deceptive speed.

In Pennsylvania there was an immediate call for a convention. Those opposed to the strong national government, called anti-Federalists, were so surprised by such rapidity that, to prevent a vote, they absented themselves so no quorum could be established. Delaware meanwhile called a convention, and on December 7, by a unanimous vote, passed its resolution of acceptance. Then in Pennsylvania, where Philadelphia artisans wanted a strong government, those who wanted the Constitution, called Federalists, physically carried two anti-Federalists to the convention, held them in their seats so a quorum could be established, and voted acceptance of the Constitution. Next came New Jersey, where there was almost unanimous acceptance on December 18. In Georgia, where help was needed from a strong government to subdue the Creek Indians, the Constitution was ratified on January 2, 1788. The Connecticut session lasted only five days, with overwhelming acceptance coming on January 9.

The first note of discontent with the finished Constitution came in Massachusetts, where the convention met on January 9. The delegates were strongly Federalist in sentiment, although backcountry delegates were opposed. Yet even the Federalists were unhappy with the documents because it contained no bill of rights guaranteeing individual liberties. The debate lasted almost a month. The Federalists finally won there by persuading state leaders such as John Adams and John Hancock that a bill of rights would be added to the Constitution by way of amendments. The vote on February 6 was 187 for to 168 against. Maryland was easily under Federalist control, and the vote there, on April 26, was 63 to 11 in favor of the Constitution. Likewise, South Carolina favored the document on May 28 by a strong majority. The ninth state to ratify was New Hampshire, which did so on June 21 by a vote of 57 to 47. Technically the Constitution became effective then. However, in Rhode Island, where the debtor class was strongly in control, the Constitution was rejected; the vote there, held on March 24 by referendum, was negative.

Even with nine states ratifying the Constitution, the new government could not function effectively without Virginia and New York. In Virginia, Patrick Henry, the fiery orator, and George Mason, a respected scholar and statesman, opposed adoption. The Federalist promise of a bill of rights softened opposition, as did the spreading knowledge that George Washington would consent to serve as the first president. Thus on June 25 Virginia ratified the Constitution by a vote of 89 to 79.

Rejection seemed certain in New York, however. There the anti-Federalists had a wide majority when the convention met on June 17. Public opinion gradually was shifting, however, because of a series of essays, signed "Publius," which appeared in New York newspapers; written by Alexander Hamilton, James Madison, and John Jay, these eighty-five essays were published as *The Federalist* and constituted a strong exposition (and explanation) of the Constitution. The tide turned in New York, moreover, when word arrived that both Virginia and New Hampshire had ratified. That, along with a promised bill of rights, caused the vote, taken on July 26, to be favorable, although by the uncomfortable margin of 30 to 27.

North Carolina, like Rhode Island, was largely under the control of debtors, and it, too, rejected the Constitution. The vote there in July, 1788, was 185 against to 84 for. Neither state joined the Union until after the new government was in actual operation. Only after Congress threatened the two recalcitrant states with trade duties and treatment as foreign nations did they consent to join. North Carolina ratified the Constitution on November 21, 1789, after the Bill of Rights had been proposed in Congress, and Rhode Island surrendered on May 29, 1790, by the narrow margin of only two votes.

The new Union had been forged—but the government created on paper had to be transferred to the realm of reality. The visionary schemes of the Founding Fathers had to be put into practice. The Congress of the Articles of Confederation agreed with the will of the people in one last act; on September 13 it set New York City as the site of the new government and March 4, 1789, as the date for the first meeting of the new Congress. It further provided that presidential electors were to be chosen on the first Wednesday in January and were to vote on the first Wednesday in February, 1789. On October 10, 1788, the Congress of the Confederation transacted its last business and expired.

On March 4, 1789, the guns of the Battery on Manhattan Island saluted the new government, which was supposed to convene that day. Not until April 1, however, did the House of Representatives have a quorum, and five more days passed before the Senate had enough members present to do business. That day the two houses examined the ballots of the electoral college and declared Washington (sixty-nine votes) president and John Adams (thirty-four votes) vice president.

The man who had won the war now would guide the destiny of the young Republic through its critical first years as a nation. His would be a large and burdensome task, with many causes for worry. The Republic was small, stretching from the Atlantic to the Mississippi and from Florida to Canada. It numbered less than four million citizens, 95 percent of whom lived on farms. There was little manufacturing, with most such goods being imported from Europe. The Army was small, the Navy almost nonexistent. Political disunity was rife: in the South, in Kentucky and Tennessee, talk of secession was common; in the North, Vermonters were openly negotiating with England for recognition as a separate republic. Neither Rhode Island nor North Carolina had as yet ratified the Constitution. And even in the eleven states that had ratified the Constitution, there was distrust of the new government. Many people feared a government that could tax them directly. State and local politicians were jealous that the federal structure would encroach on the power and prestige that previously had been theirs. Finally, there was no money in the federal treasury, no machinery of government existed, and no precedents had been set to guide the actions of the new federal officials.

The First President

George Washington left his home of Mount Vernon for New York City on the morning of April 16, 1789. To his diary he confided his thoughts: "I bade adieu to Mount Vernon, to private life, and to domestic felicity, and with a mind oppressed with more anxious and painful sensations than I have words to express, set out for New York. . . ." His ten-day journey to the capital was a triumphal parade, with dinners and fireworks and little girls dressed in white strewing flowers in the path of his carriage. Then, on April 30, came the inauguration. At the old New York City Hall, serving temporarily as the Capitol, Washington at noon took the oath of office, dressed in a brown suit and white stockings and with a sword hanging at his side: "I do solemnly swear that I will faithfully execute the office of President of the United States and will, to the best of my ability, preserve, protect and defend the Constitution of the United States."

Washington's administration began at a time of rising prosperity—which certainly helped. The painful adjustments following the Revolution had been made, and depression was ended. Also, the great wars of the Napoleonic era were beginning in 1789, so that in the next several years American goods were in demand overseas. Many citizens equated returning prosperity with the new government. Also, the new government had the backing of a favorable press and hopeful public opinion. Even its opponents, such as Patrick Henry, Samuel Adams, and Thomas Jefferson, were determined to give it a try. Finally, the new government was largely in the hands of its friends. In the first Congress was only one man who had opposed ratification of the Constitution, and Washington's first appointees were, with few exceptions, strong Federalists.

Washington was aware that his first acts would set the tenor of the Republic for years to come: ". . . my station is new," he confided to his diary, "and, if I may use the expression, I walk on untrodden ground. There is scarcely an action, the motive of which may not be subject to a double interpretation. There is scarcely any part of my conduct which may not hereafter be drawn into precedent." Especially was this true of the cabinet system of government, for which there was no constitutional basis. Washington was unwilling to come to vital decisions without asking advice from men in whom he had confidence. From this quirk of personality came the cabinet, a body entirely different in origin and function from the British cabinet. There had been talk in the Constitutional Convention of providing the president with a privy council, but this had failed. Washington turned to his administrative heads of departments for advice, and they became the cabinet. During his administration there were five such heads: between July 27 and September 24, Congress created the departments of State, War, Treasury, Post Office, and Attorney General. Heading these were Jefferson (State), Henry Knox (War), Hamilton (Treasury), Samuel Osgood (Post Office), and John Jay (Attorney General). At the same time Congress gave the president power to remove his appointees without the consent of the Senate (which approved their appointment).

Another quirk of Washington's personality that shaped American government was his impatience. On August 22, Washington asked the Senate for advice and consent on a treaty with the Creek Indians. The Senate's sense of its dignity defeated its ambitions in this case, however, for that body referred the matter to a committee. Washington thereupon decided henceforth to submit only the signed treaties to the Senate for acceptance or rejection, but not to ask its advice during the treaty-making process. Since that summer of 1789, foreign affairs have been conducted solely by the president through the Department of State.

In terms of a legislative program in that first Congress, several matters of great importance were passed. On September 24, 1789, came the Judiciary Act, which provided for a Supreme Court, consisting of a chief justice and five associate justices (the Constitution does not specify the number); three circuit courts, with two Supreme Court justices per circuit; and thirteen district courts. Congress also submitted a Bill of Rights, in the form of twelve constitutional amendments, to the states for ratification; ten of these were accepted and became part of the Constitution on December 15, 1791. Congress also attacked the government's most pressing problem, money. On July 4, 1789, at the suggestion of James Madison, Congress approved a tariff that taxed imports an average of about 8.5 percent. Although this act was designed to raise revenue, it nevertheless had protectionist features; goods arriving on American ships paid 10 percent less duty than goods arriving in foreign ships.

George Washington

As first president of the newly established United States, George Washington faced a great challenge, but his life had been filled with challenges he had met and overcome. Born on February 22, 1732, at Wakefield, his father's plantation in Westmoreland County, Virginia, he lived, after the death of his father, with his elder half-brother Lawrence at Mount Vernon. Educated by his father and half-brother, he excelled in mathematics and surveying, although he did gain an appreciation for music and drama, and he read many books about history and military campaigns. As a member of one of the better families of Virginia, he moved in a society that stressed courtly manners, poise, and dignity, and these qualities became a part of his nature.

Arriving at manhood, he worked for a time as a surveyor, a task which took him into the wild back country. There followed a voyage to Barbados in the West Indies with Lawrence Washington; on this trip he was infected with smallpox, but survived to become immune thereafter (and thus was in no danger when this disease broke out among his troops during the Revolution). When Lawrence died in 1752, Mount Vernon passed into Washington's hands, and he undertook its management. That same year he was appointed a district adjutant in the colonial militia, and in the French and Indian Wars that followed he acquitted himself with distinction as a lieutenant colonel; to his diary in that period he confided, "I have heard the bullets whistle, and, believe me, there is something charming in the sound." Indeed he had, for in the attack on Fort Duquesne in 1755 he had four bullets through his coat and two horses shot from beneath him, but he escaped untouched. By the end of that war he was commander-in-chief of Virginia's militia forces defending the western frontier from Indian attack.

In 1758 Washington married Martha Custis and returned to Mount Vernon as a gentleman farmer, serving from 1759 to 1774 as a member of the Virginia House of Burgesses. And his fellow Virginians elected him to the First and Second Continental Congresses, by which time he was widely known and respected. He was not quick-witted and schooled in political theory, as were Jefferson and Hamilton; he was no deep scholar, as was Madison; nor was he a brilliant orator like Patrick Henry or the man of words like Thomas Paine. Rather Washington had that indefinable quality of leadership and the ability to inspire confidence that came from his solemn and dignified bearing, his good judgment, and, as one contemporary said, his "common sense lifted to the level of genius." Captain George Mercer, who served as his aide in 1760 in the colonial militia, described him as more than six feet in height, 190 to 200 pounds, and large framed: "His bones and joints are large as are his hands and feet. . . . In conversation he looks you full in the face, is deliberate, deferential and engaging. His voice is agreeable." His friends stated that in private he was charming and personable, even "chatty" and on rare occasions "impudent." In public, however, he was reserved and solemn, a man of grave dignity.

On June 15, 1775, the Continental Congress asked him to assume command of the Continental Army. He accepted with reluctance, writing, "It is an honor I wished to avoid. . . . I can answer but for three things: a firm belief in the justice of our cause, close attention in the prosecution of it, and the strictest integrity." For some time his goal was reconciliation with England; gradually, however, he realized the necessity of the Declaration of Independence. During the war, saddled with raw troops, hampered by shortages of supplies and weapons, and criticized by bureaucrats who little appreciated his problems, he nevertheless achieved brilliant victories amid many reverses. In everything he gave credit to his soldiers: "Posterity will bestow on their labors the epithet and marks of fiction; for it will not be believed that such a force as Great Britain has employed for eight years in this country, could be baffled in their plan of subjugating it. . . ." Only Washington's leadership, his courage, his confidence, and his military genius achieved the triumph that ended at Yorktown.

The war over, he returned to Mount Vernon, stoutly resisting popular moves to proclaim him a dictator or king. When restive officers in the army talked of military revolt, he reproved them and ended the threat. During the next five years he enlarged his home at Mount Vernon, enjoyed his adopted children, served as an Episcopalian vestryman, and practiced scientific farming. But, also, he corresponded widely about the defects of the government under the Articles of Confederation, welcomed distinguished visitors at Mount Vernon, and hosted various gatherings. When the constitutional convention met in Philadelphia in 1787, he reluctantly agreed to be a delegate from Virginia—and served as president of the meeting. The result, he felt, was "the best that could be obtained at this time," for it approached "nearer to perfection than any government hitherto instituted among men."

With the Constitution ratified, the public demand that Washington serve as the first president was so strong that everyone knew he would be elected. When informed that the presidency has been thrust upon him—and he had not sought the office—he accepted at "the greatest sacrifice of my personal feeling and wishes." He added, "Integrity and firmness are all I can promise." Privately, however, he had his doubts that he could administer the government as successfully as he had commanded the army, and, above all, he did not want to appear in public as incompetent. "My movements to the chair of government will be accompanied by feelings not unlike those of a culprit, who is going to the place of his execution," he wrote.

Then in September, 1789, the Treasury Department was organized, and Alexander Hamilton was appointed to head it. One of his first tasks was the drafting of a fiscal report to guide Congress in its deliberations. This he did in a series of reports which he used to advance his own theories of government. His intent was to favor the merchant, the creditor, and the monied class and thereby win their support for the federal government. His opposition came from Thomas Jefferson and those who favored the farmer, the state governments, and the debtor class. In foreign policy, Hamilton favored England, while Jefferson favored France. From this contest over internal and foreign policies were born the two political parties that would grow in strength during Washington's term and then fight for supremacy in the following two decades.

Hamilton's "Report on the Public Credit" was delivered to Congress on January 14, 1790. In it he proposed funding the national debt ($12 million foreign; $44 million domestic) at face value. "If all the public creditors receive their dues from one source distributed with an equal hand," Hamilton reasoned, ". . . they will unite in support of the fiscal arrangements of the government." He suggested that all creditors exchange their old notes for new bonds which, in time, would be paid at full value. Madison strongly opposed paying the domestic debt at face value, for this would work to the benefit of speculators who had bought up Continental bonds at a fraction of their value. Southerners opposed Hamilton's plan, for it called for the federal government to pay off state debts incurred on behalf of the Revolution; most Southern states had already paid these, leaving the Northern states to benefit most from this proposal. This fight over federal fiscal policy was settled at a dinner at Jefferson's home. Hamilton and the Northerners agreed to locating the permanent capital of the United States on the Potomac in return for Southern support for the funding bill. Thus on August 4 the Funding Act was passed, and Congress could adjourn with positive action taken.

The Second Congress convened for its first session in Philadelphia on December 6, 1790. Philadelphia would remain the capital until 1800, when the city established in the District of Columbia was ready to receive the government. A week after Congress convened, Hamilton presented his second report, a call for a national bank. This recommendation proposed a Bank of the United States capitalized at $10 million, the federal government providing 20 percent of the money and private sources contributing the remaining 80 percent. The bank would serve as depository for federal funds, its notes would be the nation's principal currency, and it would assist the government in funding the debt. In addition, it would perform other normal banking functions. Despite heavy Southern opposition, led by Madison, the House passed the bill on February 8 by a vote of thirty-nine to twenty; thirty-three of the positive votes came from Northerners, whose region stood to profit most. During debate on the measure in the Senate, Jefferson made known his opposition, arguing the doctrine of strict interpretation of the Constitution: nothing in the Constitution specifically authorized the government founding a bank, and therefore to create one would be unconstitutional. Hamilton replied on February 23, arguing a loose construction of the Constitution: under the "necessary and proper" clause, Hamilton reasoned, the government had the authority to create a bank. The Senate agreed with Hamilton, and on February 25 Washington signed the bank bill, which chartered the bank for twenty years, to be headquartered in Philadelphia.

This debate had long-lasting consequences. The Bank of the United States would be an issue for almost half a century, while the "strict construction" versus "loose construction" of the Constitution would be a rallying cry for those who believed in states' rights against those favoring a large federal government—an issue yet much alive in the United States. In the immediate aftermath of passage of the bank bill in 1791, the issues raised would serve to polarize opinions and divide Americans into two political camps: Hamiltonians (or Federalists, as they were better known) and Jeffersonians (or Democrat-Republicans, as they came to be known). In short, political parties were born from this debate.

Hamilton's third recommendation was passage of an act to collect excise taxes on various commodities, especially distilled liquors. Congress agreed, passing the measure on March 3, 1791, with little debate. When stock in the Bank of the United States was offered to the public on July 4, 1791, it was sold entirely within an hour. Faith in the credit of the United States was high. Hamilton presented his final recommendation on American fiscal policies on December 5, 1791, a "Report on Manufactures," in which he urged a protective tariff to encourage American manufacturing, bounties to farmers growing specified crops, and federal spending for internal improvements. Hamilton's program in its entirety—a bank, funding the public debt to be paid at face value by the federal government, excise taxes, a protective tariff, bounties to help agriculture, and publicly funded internal improvements—committed his followers, the Federalists, to these goals; Hamilton had written the platform for the Federalists. Also, these were the goals of New Englanders committed to manufacturing and commerce.

Resistance to the excise tax on whiskey began in August, 1792, in North Carolina and western Pennsylvania. Farmers found corn bulky and hard to transport, so they converted it into whiskey for easy shipment to market. This practice was so standard that whiskey had become a medium of exchange in several parts of the nation. Thus a tax on whiskey seemed a tax on money itself, and objections led to shooting of tax collectors. Another feature of the law very objectionable to farmers was that violators were to be tried in federal court. In Pennsylvania the federal court sat at Philadelphia, 350 miles from Pittsburgh, the scene of whiskey-making. The trip itself was a costly fine, even though an accused man might be found innocent. Despite the unrest created by the excise tax, Washington was easily reelected president on December 5, 1792, by 132 electors. Adams was reelected vice president with 77 electoral votes, while George Clinton, a supporter of Jefferson, received 50 votes.

Foreign Entanglements

Early in Washington's second term, the major concern of the nation became foreign, not domestic, affairs. Inspired in part by the American example, revolution swept France beginning in 1789 and ending on September 21, 1792, with the proclamation of a republic. At first Americans warmly supported their French cousins in what seemed a parallel experience. However, early in 1793 Louis XVI was executed, and there followed the infamous Reign of Terror that saw the guillotine stifling dissent. Conservative Americans, especially the Hamiltonians, turned against the French Revolution, while the Jeffersonians still maintained sympathy for it while deploring its excesses. On February 1, 1793, France declared war on England, Spain, and Holland in an attempt to extend its boundaries and its doctrines. Because the United States was exporting goods to France and to England, the government was faced with making a choice between them. Hamilton exerted his influ-

National Cyclopedia of Biography

Alexander Hamilton

BORN illegitimate in 1757 in the Leeward Islands at the British colony of Nevis, Alexander Hamilton knew poverty as a youth. At the age of twelve he began working in a general store, but because of his obvious brilliance some of his wealthier relatives provided the money for his education. Arriving in New York City in 1772, he went to a grammar school for a year, then entered King's College (Columbia University). However, his education was interrupted by the Revolution. A staunch Patriot as early as 1774, he wrote pamphlets which, although he was only seventeen, showed a remarkable grasp of the issues and a great mind.

Commissioned an officer of artillery in 1776, he came to the attention of General George Washington, and on March 1, 1777, he became secretary and aide-de-camp to that great man. His duties were arduous, for Washington was serving virtually as secretary of war as well as commanding general, and Hamilton handled the correspondence and provided administrative organization.

By the end of the war Hamilton was known in the best circles of American society, and he had married Elizabeth Schuyler of the prominent Schuyler family of New York. Admitted to the New York bar in 1781, he was small of stature and slight of build, had a fair complexion and feminine softness about his face, but bore himself with great dignity. Elected to Congress in November, 1781, he showed himself a believer in a strong central government; this he continued after he retired from Congress in 1783, fighting for his concepts at the Annapolis Trade Convention and in the Constitutional Convention and as secretary of the treasury in Washington's administration. Until his untimely death in 1804, a result of his duel with Aaron Burr, Hamilton was a major leader of the Federalists.

ence on Washington to favor Great Britain, while Jefferson used his persuasive powers in favor of France. The dispute came to a head on April 8, 1793, when Edmond Charles Genêt, the French minister to the United States, arrived at Charleston, South Carolina, to a tumultuous welcome by its pro-French citizens. As he made his way north to present his credentials to Washington, Genêt intrigued with Americans to attack Spanish Florida and Louisiana and he issued letters commissioning American privateers to attack British shipping. Meanwhile, in Philadelphia, Jefferson argued to the president that the American treaty of 1778 with France obligated the United States to defend the French West Indies and to receive prize ships captured on the high seas. Hamilton countered with the argument that the treaty of 1778 was with the royalist government and that the United States should side with England to defeat the Republicans. Washington responded to these arguments with a Neutrality Proclamation on April 22, and he received Genêt with distinct coldness and a statement that he would tolerate no violations of neutrality. Genêt persisted in his activities, believing that the majority of Americans were with him, whereupon Washington, on August 23, demanded that he be recalled by his government. By this time, however, Genêt's group was in disfavor in France, and he asked to be allowed to stay in the United States, a request that was granted.

America profited greatly from the European conflict, as its exports of food and other materials commanded premium prices. With the French fleet at the mercy of England's naval superiority, the French government threw the West Indies open to American shipping. England retaliated by declaring food to be contraband (as materiel of war) and began seizing American ships. The American government reiterated its declaration of neutrality and asserted that neutral ships made neutral goods, especially in the case of food. By the spring of 1794 some 300 American ships had been seized by England, and even the Federalists, who favored conciliation with England, believed war was imminent. Moreover, the British had refused to return many of their northwestern posts on American soil to American control, and the Canadian governor-general, Lord Dorchester, chose that time to incite the Indians of the Northwest to raid in the Ohio country. The Jeffersonian Republicans demanded that Congress pass commercial retaliatory laws against England—that British ships be embargoed from American ports and that American ships be kept from trading with England. In April, by a razor-thin vote, the measure passed Congress, to be in effect for one month (subsequently it was extended two months).

President Washington favored diplomacy to settle the growing problems with England, and on April 16, 1794, he named Chief Justice John Jay as special envoy to Great Britain to negotiate points of difference between the two nations. That fall Jay found his position somewhat strengthened by General Anthony Wayne's defeat of the Indians in the Ohio country at the Battle of Fallen Timbers. Jay began negotiating to secure British surrender of the posts in the Northwest Territory, British indemnity for American ships they had captured, and British recognition of the rights of neutrals. There was talk that if England failed to agree to these demands, Jay was to proceed to Sweden and Denmark to discuss with them a combined assault on Britain's failure to respect neutrality. However, Alexander Hamilton was so pro-British that he informed them of Washington's secret decision not to join the Swedes and Danes in armed neutrality against England, and thus Jay failed to gain concessions that might have resulted.

On November 19 the Treaty of London was signed between the United States and

England. Known in America as Jay's Treaty, this instrument provided for the British evacuation of the Northwest posts, although it stipulated that Canadians could still trap furs south of the border and trade with the Indians; a joint commission was created to discuss payment for captured American ships; and Americans could trade with England on a most-favored-nation basis, as well as trade without discrimination in the British West Indies. Jay failed to get the British to recognize the rights of neutrals on the high seas, however, and the British continued to stop and search American ships, just as they continued to force many crewmen on American vessels into British naval service (a practice known as impressment).

Jay's Treaty was greeted in America with a loud outcry of public indignation. Washington, after long hesitation, sent it to the Senate with his endorsement, and that body ratified it on June 25 by a bare two-thirds majority. Even Hamilton's series of newspaper articles (signed "Camillus") in defense of the treaty did not allay public indignation, and Jay was hanged in effigy in many places around the country.

Spain, meanwhile, had reconsidered its alliance with England against France and made peace with the revolutionary government of its northern neighbor. Fearful of attacks by American frontiersmen on its New World colonies, Spanish officials determined to make concessions to the United States in return for friendship and peace. Thomas Pinckney, American minister to England, went to Spain, and there, on October 27, 1795, signed the Treaty of San Lorenzo. This instrument, known as Pinckney's Treaty, stipulated the thirty-first parallel as the boundary between Florida and Georgia, and it granted Americans free navigation of the Mississippi "in its whole length" and free use of the port of New Orleans for three years (with provisions for extending the time period). Pinckney's Treaty was enthusiastically received in America, especially by frontiersmen who found it much easier to transport their goods to the Eastern seaboard by way of the Mississippi than overland.

Internal and external policies of the Washington administration coincided during his second term on the matter of excise taxes. Despite the opposition to this tax which had arisen during Washington's first term, Hamilton as secretary of the treasury argued that collections should continue to convince foreign powers that a republic could make its citizens show financial responsibility; otherwise the public credit of the United States might collapse. By 1794 opposition to the excise tax on whiskey had risen to such heights that receipts from it had fallen below the cost of collection. That summer, when federal marshals attempted to arrest violators, they were attacked by irate farmers and distillers. Hamilton persuaded Washington that such attacks were rebellion against the United States, and on August 7 the president issued a proclamation ordering the rebels to return to their homes and calling out 13,000 militiamen from four states to suppress the uprising against federal authority. Washington himself accompanied the troops as far west as Carlisle, Pennsylvania, while Hamilton—who had dreams of martial glory—rode all the way with them. The show of force caused the "Whiskey Rebellion" to collapse. About a hundred men were arrested by the militia, and two were convicted of treason. They were sentenced to death, but Washington pardoned them. This show of force did much to advance the standing of the federal government, both at home and abroad. Internally it demonstrated the effectiveness of the national government, for it showed that the laws would be enforced. And abroad it demonstrated that the government could make its citizens pay taxes, and thereby strengthened the credit of the United States.

George Washington had seriously considered retiring at the end of his first term in office and had asked Madison and others to draft suggestions for a farewell address. In 1796 he used these suggestions to prepare such a paper, which was not delivered in person but published in the newspapers on September 17, 1796. In this valedictory to the nation, Washington warned against political parties, especially those based on geographical grounds *"Northern* and *Southern, Atlantic* and *Western."* Instead, he urged a "unity of government which constitutes you one people." On foreign policy, he stressed "extending our commercial relations . . . with . . . as little political connection as possible," for "temporary alliances for extraordinary emergencies" could always be established. "As a very important source of strength and security," he wrote, "cherish public credit. One method of preserving it is to use it as sparingly as possible, avoiding occasions of expense by cultivating peace, but remembering also that timely disbursements to prepare for danger frequently prevent much greater disbursements to repel it."

He thus did not argue against "entangling alliances," but for commercial ties. His advice on this score would not be remembered, just as was forgotten his wisdom on public credit. His retirement after two terms did establish a precedent that would be broken only once in American history, and his years in office had set the pattern for the presidency and for the government of the United States for the next two centuries. At last he could retire to his plantation of Mount Vernon secure in the knowledge that the government of the nation had been established on a firm foundation. His years of retirement were few, however, for he died in 1799. For seven weeks after his death, a torrent of tribute flowed in state legislatures, Congress, and town hall meetings, as well as in taverns and ordinary conversations. Funeral enactments occurred in more than 200 towns, as Americans vied to express their grief at the passing of the hero "first in war, first in peace, and first in the hearts of his countrymen." That phrase, so often repeated, reveals facts about Washington not usually remembered. He was, first and foremost, the soldier who won the American Revolution. Yet as president much of his time was consumed in keeping the infant nation out of the European vortex of conflict stirred by the French Revolution. He was probably the most popular American, within his own time, who ever lived—friends and enemies alike agreed on this score. He was a great man, a good man, and a human man—one still worthy of imitation, one whose precepts for government still bear heeding.

Chapter Six

The Republic Redefined

The Second President

THE men commonly known as the Founding Fathers of the United States were not gods or even giants. They were exceptional, without doubt, in that they had read extensively, had thought much, and, in many cases, had written considerably on the subject of government and political affairs. But the one word that best characterizes them is *practical*. They were men who understood reality, who faced the world as it was, not as they wished it to be. To better understand the influence of this practicality, one should compare the American and French constitutions, one written in 1787, the other in 1791. One details a government that works; the other is filled with flowing rhetoric and fanciful ideas—and impractical. The Americans of the Constitutional Convention did not believe they were producing a finished document that would never need correction. They foresaw that events and the passage of time would make corrections necessary, just as a ship's course can be charted in general but requires small changes as wind and waves demand. Therefore the Americans who drafted the Constitution provided for amendments, and many of them were in the First Congress, which enacted the first ten amendments (the Bill of Rights). They knew that they had created a practical republic, but that occasionally it would need course corrections and redefinition.

Built into the original Constitution was a method of orderly change of head of government, a process requiring revolution in many nations. Under provisions of the Constitution, presidential electors gathered on December 7, 1796, to choose a successor to George Washington, who was retiring voluntarily. The first president had deplored the rise of party politics, and the Constitution did not provide for political parties, but partisan effort was important in the selection of the second president. The Federalists at first wished to name John Jay their candidate, but the furor over his treaty ruined his chance of election. Therefore the Federalists named John Adams of Massachusetts for president and Thomas Pinckney (who had wide support because of the popularity of his treaty with Spain) for vice president. The Republicans responded by naming Thomas Jefferson for president and Aaron Burr of New York for vice president. Hamilton, who disliked Adams, worked for the election of Pinckney, a scheme that caused Adams to win election to the presidency with but seventy-one electoral votes to Jefferson's sixty-eight. Thus, as stipulated by the Constitution, Adams became president and Jefferson vice president.

The election of 1796 resulted in increased partisan rivalry. Republicans characterized Adams as a "three-vote president," a phrase that infuriated him. Adams was
tactless, unattractive, and cold; he also was intelligent, well-educated, widely read,
master of four languages, experienced in foreign affairs and diplomacy, and owned
perhaps the largest private library in America during his time. Yet for all his
wisdom, he was a poor judge of character, a fact reflected by his inept cabinet—and
rendered doubly devastating by Adams' frequent absence from his post, leaving the
government in the hands of men essentially Hamiltonian. And while Adams bent
his energies toward keeping America out of war, his anti-French cabinet officers
brought the country to the brink of conflict.

Problems with France

The difficulties in foreign affairs stemmed from vagueness of the unfortunate Jay
Treaty. To the French, Jay's treaty seemed an alliance between America and England (although in America it was bitterly denounced as pro-British). Locked in a
life-and-death struggle with England, France began attacking American ships
bound for England. By Adams' inauguration, the French already had captured some
300 American ships. They also had refused to receive Charles C. Pinckney, who had
been sent as ambassador to France; in fact, French police informed him that unless
he obtained a permit allowing him, as a foreigner, to be in France he would be
arrested. When news of this high-handed treatment reached America, Federalists
demanded war with France. Adams determined to negotiate, however.

On March 31 the president named Pinckney, John Marshall, and Elbridge Gerry
as commissioners to France to seek an end to French harassment of American shipping and to settle points of difference between the two nations. Talleyrand, the
French foreign minister, refused to receive the three officially, but through three
subordinates he demanded that Adams apologize for his anti-French remarks to
Congress, that the United States loan money to France, and that a bribe of
$250,000 be given him. Marshall and Pinckney, both Federalists, left Paris in
anger, while Gerry, a Republican, stayed to negotiate (until Adams angrily ordered
him home). In their reports to Adams, the commissioners referred to the three
French subordinates as X, Y, and Z. These reports became public as the "XYZ
Affair," and caused a strong reaction against France. Adams declared he would not
send another delegation to France until he received assurances of decent conduct.
Congress reacted more strongly; it abrogated the treaty of 1778, created the Navy
Department, ordered the purchase of several naval vessels, and provided for raising
a military force of 10,000. Washington was asked to come from retirement to head
this army on July 2, 1798, with Alexander Hamilton to be his second in command.

The Navy Department acted with dispatch. Three large frigates were finished,
along with some twenty lesser vessels, and privateers were commissioned to prey on
French shipping. The result was an undeclared naval war with France that raged in
1798 and 1799. More than a hundred French ships were captured. Although the
French were able to inflict casualties on the Americans, the loss of these ships and
the forceful actions of the United States Navy caused officials in Paris to assume a
more conciliatory attitude toward Americans. Adams took advantage of this change
when, on February 18, 1799, he named William Vans Murray, Oliver Ellsworth,
and Patrick Henry (who was replaced by William R. Davie) to negotiate a peaceful
settlement. These three agents arrived in France early in 1800 to find Napoleon in

power. With him they negotiated a treaty, which was signed on September 30. This document recognized the abrogation of the treaty of 1778, and it secured recognition of the right of neutral nations on the high seas (that is, the principle that neutral ships made neutral goods). Some Americans were angered because the treaty did not provide an indemnity for ships already captured, but the agreement did end the threat of war with France. Alexander Hamilton in particular led a tirade against the president, seconded by his followers, with the result that the Federalist Party was badly split in the election of 1800—allowing Thomas Jefferson to win election.

Another result of the quarrel with France was the enactment of repressive measures at home. Foreign policy exerted a strong influence on domestic policy. Adams was a man of large ego, and the Republican charge that he was a "three-vote president" angered him mightily. Then came the Republican tirade against his anti-French stand, which made him even angrier. Many of the critics of the Adams administration were recent political refugees from France and Ireland, and they had gravitated to Jefferson's Republican Party. Adams and the Federalists responded to their attacks by passage of the Alien and Sedition Acts, four measures very repressive in intent. The first of these, the Naturalization Act, came on June 18 and increased the residence requirement for citizenship from five to fourteen years. The Alien Act allowed the president to deport any alien suspected of being dangerous or treasonable and provided a jail sentence for any who refused to go or who came back. The Alien Enemies Act allowed deportation or imprisonment of aliens during time of war, at the discretion of the president. Finally, the Sedition Act made it a crime to write or publish "any false, scandalous, and malicious statements" about the president or Congress in order to bring them "into contempt or disrepute" or to "stir up sedition within the United States." Hamilton advised his fellow Federalists that these acts were too severe, but they passed. They passed because of fear of foreigners and war, but mainly because of rabid partisan politics.

John Adams seized on these new laws and, with the exception of the Alien Enemies Act, used them. Editors of newspapers favoring the Republican cause were jailed or fined—or lapsed into silence. Even the outbreak of an epidemic of yellow fever in the summer of 1798 in Philadelphia did not halt the bitter political fighting. One traveler reported that in the capital city that summer all he heard was the moans of the dying, the wails of the living, the hammering of casket-makers; newspapers, he reported, were filled with names of the dead, but they saved ample space to report on the feverish party battles then underway. So far did Adams go that he had Matthew Lyon, an outspoken Republican congressman from Vermont, jailed and fined $1000 for sedition. His fine was paid by a group of leading Republicans, including Jefferson, while his constituents reelected him to Congress.

Although only fifteen indictments and ten convictions came under the Sedition Act, these tended to bring the courts into disrepute. Trials under the Sedition Act were travesties on justice, with Federalist judges and Federalist United States marshals clearly behaving in an unconstitutional manner. That same year the Eleventh Amendment to the Constitution was added to prevent federal courts from hearing a suit against any state by "citizens of another State, or by citizens of any foreign state." Another result of the Alien and Sedition Acts was unification of the Republicans in opposition to them. Jefferson drafted a resolution passed by the Kentucky legislature, as did Madison in Virginia; these two documents, known as the Kentucky and Virginia Resolutions, stipulated that the Constitution was a voluntary compact of equal and sovereign states who retained the right to judge the powers of the central government. If the central government assumed powers not delegated to it, the resolves argued, the individual states could declare such laws of the national government null and void. In effect, then, the Kentucky and Virginia Resolutions defended the states'-rights theory of government and contained the seeds of subsequent efforts to justify secession from the Union. They also followed Jefferson's belief in a strict interpretation of the Constitution, arguing against the Hamiltonian-Federalist belief in a loose construction of the Constitution.

Jefferson Elected

As the nation approached the election of 1800, the Republicans foresaw an excellent chance of victory. The XYZ Affair had cost them popularity, but the Federalists were hurt far more by the Alien and Sedition Acts and by a sharp split in their own ranks. Adams dismissed his secretary of state and secretary of the treasury, both supporters of Hamilton, to name men more responsive to himself. When the Federalists caucused to name their candidates, they chose Adams for President and C. C. Pinckney for vice president, men whom Hamilton and his followers could not support. The Republicans responded by naming Jefferson for president and Aaron Burr for vice president. The campaign was noted for the bitterness of its debate and the virulent hatreds it unleashed. The vote, when announced, was a crushing defeat for the Federalists; neither of their two men had received sufficient ballots to win. The vote was seventy-three for Jefferson, seventy-three for Burr, sixty-five for Adams, and sixty-four for Pinckney. The tie between Jefferson and his running mate Burr did present an opportunity to the Federalists, however. Burr was from New York, a central state; also, he was known as an opponent of the Navy and a friend of the commercial interests of New England. This tie vote was an opportunity for the Federalists because the Constitution provided that in cases of a tie for the presidency, the House of Representatives would decide between the contenders, each state having one vote. The Federalists chose to throw their support to Burr as an affront to Jefferson—and Burr was delighted. Instead of refusing to go along with this maneuver, he allowed it to happen.

As there were sixteen states, and a majority vote was necessary to win, nine votes were needed for victory. As Jefferson foresaw, he won eight votes on the first ballot, with Burr receiving six votes, leaving two tied. Thus it went for a week in February. On the seventeenth, on the thirty-sixth ballot, Hamilton used his influence to throw the election to Jefferson. A president had been chosen, the Republicans had triumphed, and talk of secession died. The next Congress tried to prevent such a deadlock ever occurring again; it passed the Twelfth Amendment, ratified by the states in September, 1804, which stipulated that electors cast their ballots for president and vice president separately.

Before the Republicans could assume office, however, there was a "lame-duck" session of Congress. It convened on November 17 in Washington, D.C., where "only the distances were magnificent," as one critic asserted. Pierre Charles L'Enfant had drawn up the plans for the city, but by November, 1800, few dwellings had been completed. That lame-duck Congress proceeded to pass a Judiciary Act on February 27, 1801, in which it reduced the number of Supreme Court justices to five and created sixteen circuit judgeships. Adams accepted this move as a means of filling the federal judiciary with Federalists, who could be expected to give their own interpretation to the Constitution during the Republican ascendancy. He also had appointed

John Marshall as chief justice of the Supreme Court on January 20, 1801. On the evening of March 3, before Jefferson was inaugurated the next day, Adams appointed his judges, giving rise to cries of a "midnight appointments" to lifetime jobs. Then Adams refused to attend Jefferson's inauguration. He retired to Massachusetts, where later he could write that the one notable achievement of his administration was that he had been able to prevent a civil war—which had never seemed very imminent.

Jefferson and the Federalists

Thomas Jefferson later wrote about his election to the presidency in 1800: "The revolution of 1800 was as real a revolution in the principles of government as that of 1776 was in its form." He viewed the election of himself and his party, which had won control of both houses of Congress, as the triumph of Republicanism over the Federalists, who would have subverted the Constitution. He declared, "The Federalists wished for everything which would approach our new government to a monarchy; the Republicans, to preserve it essentially republican." In his statements during the campaign, he had sounded so democratic that the Federalists feared his administration would be little short of anarchy. Yet in his inaugural address he chose to be conciliatory to his former opponents. This address, delivered in the city of Washington, was a call for unity: "We are all Republicans, we are all Federalists. If there be any among us who would wish to dissolve the Union or to change its republican form, let them stand undisturbed as monuments of the safety with which error of opinion may be tolerated where reason is left free to combat it." He elucidated his firm belief in democratic government: "Sometimes it is said that man cannot be trusted with the government of himself. Can he, then, be trusted with the government of others? Or have we found angels in the form of kings to govern him?"

In his inaugural address, Jefferson also indicated the type of government he intended to administer: equal and exact justice to all men; peace, commerce, honest friendship with all nations, entangling alliances with none; support of state governments in their rights; the right of election by the people; supremacy of civil over military authority; a well-disciplined militia; and economy in public expenditures. At the same time he was trying to apply these principles to the national government, he was introducing simplicity into the social life of the capital.

To aid him in his administration, Jefferson relied heavily on two men: his secretary of state, James Madison, and his secretary of the treasury, Albert Gallatin. Following their advice, as well as the dictates of his own beliefs, he exercised the principles of a strict constructionist of the Constitution. Thus he abolished the whiskey excise tax and he allowed the Alien and Sedition Acts to expire, as well as pardoning those imprisoned for political reasons. He also reduced government expenditures by reducing appropriations, dismissing some federal employees, mainly Federalists, and severely cutting the size of the Army and Navy. His middle-of-the-road policies angered extremists in both Federalist and Republican parties; some Republicans declared he was no better than a Federalist, while some Federalists declared he was ruining the country. But, for the most part, his moderation pleased the majority of Americans, including many Federalists who joined Jefferson's party when they decided he was not going to abolish Hamilton's financial system, declare war on England, or wreck the federal structure in favor of states' rights.

Thomas Jefferson

WHEN the Continental Congress in June, 1776, appointed a committee to draft a declaration of independence, Thomas Jefferson was in his thirty-third year, making him the youngest delegate serving in that body from Virginia. Standing more than six feet tall, a slim and erect aristocrat, he was red haired and given to freckles, so shy with strangers that he found it difficult to make an effective public speech, but warm and amiable with friends. After an early education with private tutors, he had attended Virginia's William and Mary College, graduating in two years to begin a study of law with George Wythe, one of the great lawyers of the day. His education, in its various stages, had brought him fluency in the classical languages, a deep and abiding interest in science, and a thirst to know the thinking of the social philosophers of the day.

"Red Tom," as some would call him, had little faith in organized religion, but formulated for himself a strict code of personal conduct. Married to Martha Skelton, a widow, he built for his family the plantation of Monticello, was active in legislative affairs in Virginia until 1775, and strenuously defended the rights of the colonists during the growing quarrels with England. In the Continental Congress he was silent during debates, but worked effectively on committees. It was his reputation for having a "masterly pen" that brought him an appointment to the committee to draft the Declaration of Independence.

Lawyer, classicist, philosopher, and thinker, as well as musician and poet, Jefferson nevertheless affected rustic dress and a casual pose in public. As president he introduced simplicity into the social life of the capital when it was moved to Washington, D. C. The secretary of the British legation commented that the president looked like a "tall, large-boned farmer." A product of his Virginia background, he idealized agriculture as a way of life; this, he wrote, was what developed moral and political virtue. Big cities, he thought, corrupted men, and neither city men of commerce and capital nor city men who labored could be trusted to preserve democracy. He therefore wanted the United States to be a land of yeoman farmers. Many of his acts as president were based on this assumption.

Few men in American history—or the world—have combined to such a degree his idealism and, simultaneously, his political realism. Also, few presidents have been so adamantly opposed to war that they prevented American entry into one in the face of such provocations as Jefferson faced.

Jefferson and the Courts

The only domestic program followed by Jefferson that caused conflict was his attitude toward the judiciary. Almost every federal judge was a Federalist. The president acted to bring the judiciary more in line with his own Republican principles, especially those judges appointed by Adams in the last moments of the Federalist administration under the Judiciary Act of 1801. One such "midnight" appointee, William Marbury, had yet to receive his commission. Acting through Secretary of State Madison, Jefferson refused to deliver Marbury's commission, whereupon Marbury appealed to the courts for a writ of mandamus that would compel the secretary of state to deliver the commission. In accordance with a section of the Judiciary Act of 1789, he brought his case directly to the Supreme Court. Chief Justice John Marshall wrote the majority decision in the case *Marbury* v. *Madison,* delivered on February 24, 1803. He declared that Marbury was clearly entitled to the commission, but asserted that the Court could not issue a writ of mandamus because it had no constitutional authority to do so. In short, the decision declared unconstitutional Section 13 of the Judiciary Act of 1789, which specifically had given the Supreme Court the power to issue such a writ. This was the first time the Supreme Court declared an act of Congress unconstitutional (a power that would not be exercised again until 1857), and provided a precedent for judicial review—the right of the courts to review acts of Congress for constitutionality. In a nutshell, Marshall made it plain that there were limits to the power of the Republican majority in Congress.

To rid the courts of the Federalist judges, Jefferson and the Republicans resorted to impeachment. One federal district judge, clearly insane, was easily removed, but proceedings against Associate Justice Samuel Chase of the Supreme Court fell short. Chase was a man of brilliant mind but undisciplined tongue. He rarely lost an opportunity in addressing juries to denounce the Republican Party in vile and strong language. The House of Representatives voted a bill of impeachment, but in the Senate Chase was acquitted of all charges and returned to the bench in triumph. Thus impeachment was abandoned as a weapon by the Republicans, and Jefferson left the courts alone thereafter, confident that the popularity of his programs would allow him to name Republicans to the judiciary thereafter. But Federalist judges proved exceptionally long-lived. John Marshall presided over the Supreme Court for thirty-four years, and some of his fellow Federalists outlived him; thus the courts proved to be a center of Federalist thinking and a means of rendering Federalist interpretations to the Constitution for more than three decades after the party itself no longer existed.

Another important feature of Jefferson's domestic policy was legislation about the public domain as contained in the Land Act of 1804. The laws of the federal government relating to the sale of public land had been established through Federalist legislation that specified the sale of land in large blocks—640 acres at two dollars an acre was the minimum purchase under the Land Act of 1796, reduced by the Land Act of 1800 to a minimum of 320 acres with some credit extended. Jefferson's Land Act of 1804 reduced the price of the 320 acres to a dollar an acre, with 25 percent down, the rest to be paid in four years. This meant that for eighty dollars any American could become a land-owning farmer. This act stimulated western settlement and development—clearly in line with Jefferson's principles. Under this stimulus, Ohio was admitted to the Union in 1803, with several other states soon to be carved out of the old Northwest Territory.

Jefferson and Foreign Affairs

In the field of foreign affairs, Jefferson covered himself and his party with popular approval during his first administration. Through Jefferson's policies came the first real assertion of America's sovereign rights on the world scene—the war with the Tripolitan pirates. The outlaw nations of Morocco, Algiers, Tunis, and Tripoli, whose rulers were in league with the Barbary pirates, were preying on vessels in the Mediterranean, demanding tribute from maritime nations. Most nations were paying, even England, which had the world's best navy. In fact, it was widely believed that the British were happy with this situation, which worked to their advantage because it prevented small nations from enlarging their maritime fleets. During the Washington and Adams administrations, the United States had paid these pirates more that $2 million, but still American losses increased. Then in 1801 the Bashaw of Tripoli demanded an increase in American payments. Jefferson decided to fight. He ordered the Navy to send a squadron of ships to blockade the Tripolitan pirates in their home ports, a move that the economy-minded Congress refused to endorse with strong monetary support.

During this undeclared war with the pirates, the Navy conducted itself gallantly. Early in 1804 Lieutenant Stephen Decatur stole into the harbor at Tripoli and burned the frigate *Philadelphia,* an American ship that had run aground and had been captured by the pirates. The Bashaw of Tripoli had increasing domestic problems during that year, and in 1805 he sued for peace. The treaty that was negotiated did not end American payments of tribute, but it did reduce them severely—they were paid until 1816. New England merchants were pleased with Jefferson's actions in this war and gave him increasing support as a result.

The other major item of foreign policy during Jefferson's first administration was the Louisiana Purchase, also intimately connected with events in Europe, especially the Napoleonic Wars. Napoleon had risen to power in the late 1790s in France, and he dreamed of reestablishing the French empire. As a move in this direction, he forced the corrupt and weak Spanish government to retrocede the Louisiana Territory to France by the secret Treaty of San Ildefonso of October 1, 1800. He then sent an army of 27,000 men to occupy Louisiana and, on the way there, to stop in Haiti and suppress a slave insurrection. Unfortunately for Napoleon's dreams of empire, his army was decimated in Haiti by yellow fever and the rebelling slaves. Nor could he send another army to occupy Louisiana because of the press of his European involvements.

Meanwhile, Jefferson had heard of the secret Treaty of San Ildefonso and watched with anxiety. Spain, by 1800 an ally of France, was sharply curtailing American rights of transit on the Mississippi and of deposit of goods at New Orleans. The president therefore in January, 1803, asked the Senate to name James Monroe as minister extraordinary, with authority to work with the American minister in France, to seek the purchase of New Orleans from Napoleon. The Senate concurred with this request, and Congress secretly voted $2 million for such a purchase. When Monroe arrived in France, it was to discover that the French shortage of troops and their war with England had worked to American advantage; Napoleon could not occupy Louisiana, and if he kept title to it the British doubtless would take it. So when the American ministers approached the French government on April 11, 1803, about the purchase of New Orleans, they were offered all of Louisiana. There was no time for consultation with Jefferson and the French government wanted to move quickly. After considerable haggling about price, the treaty was drawn up and signed on April 30, 1803, with a price of $15 million. "We have lived long," stated Robert Livingston, the American minister to France who aided Monroe in these negotiations, "but this is the noblest work of our lives."

That noble work proved a headache to Jefferson when the treaty reached his desk. A strict constitutionalist, he could find nothing in that document that said the government had the authority to acquire new territory. At first he considered a constitutional amendment to authorize the purchase, but that took time—and there was no time, for Napoleon was pushing for ratification of the treaty. With no further ado, Jefferson simply sent the treaty to the Senate, and that body ratified the agreement in October.

There then arose a second obstacle. The Constitution stated that a treaty was the law of the land, yet it also stated that money bills should originate in the lower house. The Louisiana treaty obligated the United States to pay France $15 million. Fortunately the House concurred with the treaty and voted the money, and a crisis was averted. By a stroke of the pen, the United States had doubled in size.

As with all such fortuitous events, the Louisiana Purchase immediately raised new problems, specifically the amount of territory acquired. The treaty was vague on the question of Louisiana's specific boundaries. In fact, Napoleon had commented, "If an obscurity did not already exist, it would, perhaps, be good policy to put one here," meaning that with a vague boundary the United States would be free to take as much territory as it could from Spain. This question about the exact western boundary of Louisiana led Jefferson to ask Congress to authorize funds for the exploration of the newly acquired territory. The president had a long interest in such exploration. When ambassador to France in 1786, he had approached John Ledyard, a Connecticut Yankee then in Europe, with a scheme to explore the American West. Ledyard should, Jefferson suggested, make his way across Europe, through Russia, to the west coast of the American continent and cross to the eastern seaboard. Ledyard had made the attempt, but was turned back in Russia.

Exploring the West

In January, 1803, Jefferson had requested and Congress voted a secret appropriation of $2500 to finance an exploratory party to the American West for the purpose of promoting trade with the Indians. To head this expedition the president chose his private secretary and fellow Virginian, Meriwether Lewis. He in turn invited William Clark, brother of George Rogers Clark of Revolutionary War fame, to be coleader of the expedition. Before the party could prepare for its western journey, the Louisiana Purchase was consummated. Thus the Lewis and Clark expedition, when it set out on May 14, 1804, was exploring the limits of the purchase. In addition, Jefferson gave it other tasks: to ascend the Missouri River, cross the mountains, and descend to the Pacific by the most practicable river. Along the way it was to make records of the soils, minerals, furs, sources and courses of rivers, and promote trade and friendship with the Indians.

Moving up the Missouri from St. Louis by keelboat, the Louis and Clark expedition made slow progress through the summer and fall of 1804, averaging nine miles a day. By late October they were at the site of the present Bismarck, North Dakota, where they went into winter quarters. They named their stockade Fort Mandan after the Mandan Sioux in the vicinity, and spent the winter meeting with Indians and laying in a supply of smoked meat for the following year. During that winter,

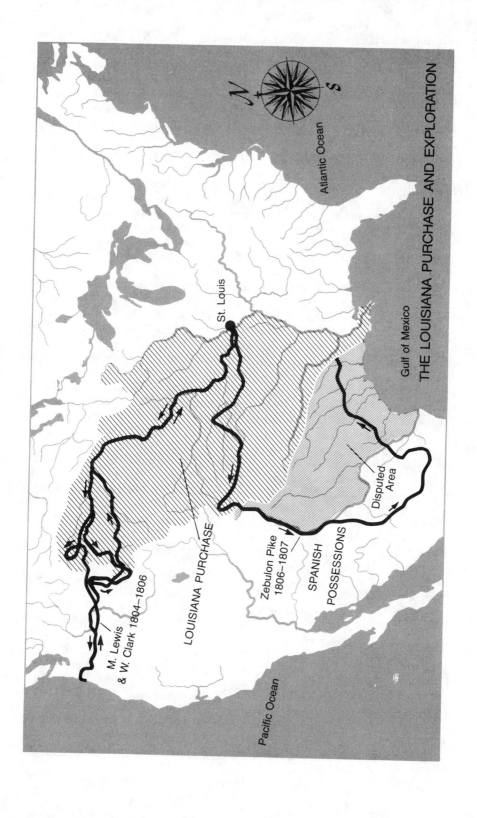

THE LOUISIANA PURCHASE AND EXPLORATION

Atlantic Ocean

St. Louis

Gulf of Mexico

LOUISIANA PURCHASE

M. Lewis & W. Clark 1804–1806

Zebulon Pike 1806–1807

SPANISH POSSESSIONS

Disputed Area

Pacific Ocean

they also were visited by Touissant Charbonneau, a French trader, and his wife Sacajawea, a Shoshone Indian. Lewis and Clark hired Charbonneau and his wife as interpreters and guides. Then, April, 1805, some members of the party were sent downriver to St. Louis with specimens and reports, while the remaining thirty-three members of the party went upriver. "I could not but esteem this moment of my departure as among the most happy of my life," Clark recorded in his journal.

Following the Missouri, they arrived at the Great Falls of the Missouri—the site of today's Great Falls, Montana. There they made carts and hauled their boats around the falls. It took them a month to make the eighteen-mile portage. When they reached the headwaters of the Missouri, they met the Shoshone Indians, and the chief of that tribe proved to be Sacajawea's brother. Through that tie, the expedition secured horses for the mountainous part of their journey. Food became scarce in the mountains, and they were reduced to living on "portable soup"—horse and dog meat. Finally they reached the Clearwater. There they fashioned canoes from hollowed tree trunks, and in these they floated downstream to the Columbia and down it to the Pacific. "Great joy in camp, we are in view of the Ocian," wrote Clark on November 7.

Winter quarters were erected on the north bank of the mouth of the Columbia, a stockade they designated Fort Clatsop in honor of the local Indians. The winter of 1805–06 was a miserable one. It rained constantly, and the explorers were plagued by fleas. To get food from the Indians, the men boiled salt from sea water in great kettles. Hunters killed 150 elk and 38 deer, from which were fashioned 338 pairs of moccasins for the long trek home. And from a whale washed ashore they cut meat; one soldier wrote, "We mix it with our poor elk meat and find it eats very well."

On March 23, 1806, they began the return trip. Their trade goods were exhausted; to get food from the Indians, Lewis and Clark assumed the role of doctors, receiving dogs and other food from the natives in return. Lewis wrote, "In our present situation I think it pardonable to continue this deception for they will not give us any provision. . . . we take care to give them no article which can possibly injure them." The main mishap on the return trip came in the Rockies, where one of the hunters mistook Lewis for a bear and shot him in the leg; he was disabled for a month. Recovering their boats on the eastern slope of the mountains, the expedition went down the Missouri much faster than they had ascended it, making forty to seventy-five miles a day and reaching St. Louis on September 23, 1806. Clark wrote, "We were met by all the village and received a hearty welcome from its inhabitants." They had been given up for dead.

The knowledge gained by Lewis and Clark was valuable, but it did not satisfy Jefferson's curiosity. In fact, he already had been sending out parties for further exploration of the Louisiana Territory. Congress in April, 1804, had appropriated $3000, with which Jefferson financed an expedition in the Southwest. Sir William Dunbar and Dr. George Hunter were chosen to search for the headwaters of the Red and Arkansas rivers. They were blocked in this effort by the hostility of the Spaniards, who feared that such exploration might result in a boundary settlement between American Louisiana and Spanish Texas that would be prejudicial to Spanish interests. Therefore Hunter and Dunbar spent their four months in the Ouachita River Valley of present Arkansas, an area already settled by American frontiersmen. While their expedition made no discoveries of exploration, it did gather valuable scientific information.

In 1805 Congress voted $5000 for exploration, which the president used to finance another attempt to find the source and course of the Red River. Headed by Thomas Freeman, the expedition consisted of twenty-four men, seventeen of them soldiers. That summer, they traveled from the Mississippi up the Red River, but again Spain, fearing the results might prejudice its interests, moved to interfere. A Spanish force of one hundred soldiers under Captain Francisco Viana met Freeman's expedition some 635 miles above the mouth of the Red River (at approximately the site of present Wichita Falls, Texas). Jefferson had ordered Freeman to avoid hostilities with the Spaniards, and he therefore agreed to turn back rather than fight. In his report he stressed that, although he had failed to find the headwaters of the Red, he had held several conferences with the Indians and he had gathered valuable information about the geography of the region.

The question of the boundary between Louisiana and Texas almost precipitated a shooting war between the United States and Spain in 1806. Spaniards claimed the boundary between the two states was the Arroyo Hondo. Some ambitious and land-hungry Americans argued that the boundary was the Rio Grande, but the U.S. government assumed the position that the Sabine River was the boundary. Gradually the number of Spanish troops in Texas was increased to the record number of 1368. In Louisiana the American commander, the enigmatic General James Wilkinson, seemed ready to fight. Then suddenly on October 29 he proposed a compromise— the United States would keep its forces east of the Arroyo Hondo and Spanish troops would stay west of the Sabine until the two governments negotiated a compromise. The result would be a neutral ground. This agreement prevented war and led to thirteen years of negotiation, ending with the Treaty of 1819 that settled the boundary between Louisiana and Spanish possessions.

While Jefferson was sending men west to explore, General Wilkinson likewise was sending soldiers for the same purpose, principally Lieutenant Zebulon M. Pike. In August, 1805, Pike was sent to find the headwaters of the Mississippi River, which he did during the winter of 1805–06. Then in July, 1806, Wilkinson dispatched Pike westward, perhaps as an innocent pawn in the Aaron Burr conspiracy, perhaps for other reasons. Pike's orders were to take twenty-two soldiers west from St. Louis, to meet with the Osage and Pawnee Indians in council, and then to explore for the headwaters of the Arkansas and Red rivers. He departed St. Louis on July 15, 1806, met with the Plains tribes, and ascended the Arkansas. On November 15 he glimpsed the Rocky Mountains, and on the twenty-third was at the site of the present Pueblo, Colorado. There, looking to the north, he saw a mighty peak, later to be named for him. After exploring the Royal Gorge of the Arkansas, he turned south, a foolhardy decision for December in the Rocky Mountains. Because of heavy snowfall, he and his party almost perished before being arrested by Spanish soldiers and taken to Santa Fe. Questioned there and at Chihuahua City by Spanish officials, Pike had all his papers and maps taken from him, then was escorted out of Spanish territory and dumped into Louisiana on July 1, 1807. His report, published in 1810, was quickly translated into French, German, and Dutch, and served immediately to popularize the West (as had published accounts of the Lewis and Clark expedition).

Meanwhile, Jefferson's popularity from the Louisiana Purchase had begun to wane. But as he approached the election of 1804, it was still with wide public support. John Randolph, a Republican from Roanoke, Virginia, could declare, "Never was there an administration more brilliant than that of Mr. Jefferson up to this period. . . . Taxes repealed; the public debt amply provided for; sinecures abolished; Louisiana acquired; public confidence unbounded." By 1804 every state legis-

117

lature except three—Massachusetts, Connecticut, and New Hampshire—was in Republican hands. Jefferson was easily renominated by his party and carried every state of the Union except Connecticut and Delaware, receiving 162 electoral votes. His Federalist opponent, Charles C. Pinckney of South Carolina, got only fourteen. It was a massive victory for Jefferson, a reward from the people for the accomplishments of his first term. His next four years were not so pleasant, however.

The Burr Conspiracy

First, there was the question of the former vice president, Aaron Burr. Because of his failed attempt to win the presidency in 1800, Burr had become a bitter political enemy of Jefferson. He gravitated toward the Federalists, who also hated Jefferson, and he joined them in an attempt to dismember the Union by establishing a "New England Confederacy." To accomplish this, however, the New England secessionists needed the state of New York as a buffer against the might of Virginia. They approached Alexander Hamilton, a leading Federalist, to join them; the New Yorker refused. Thereupon the secessionists asked Burr to run for governor of New York; presumably, if he won, he would then lead New York in joining the New England Confederacy. Hamilton opposed Burr's election, however, and succeeded in thwarting him. Burr in anger challenged Hamilton to a duel. Hamilton accepted, intending to miss his opponent, while Burr came to kill—which he did. At the duel on July 11, 1804, Hamilton was shot in the chest, and he died thirty hours later. With him died the New England Confederacy, especially when Jefferson was so overwhelmingly reelected.

Because Burr was under indictment for participating in the duel with Hamilton, (dueling was illegal in New York), he could not return to New York. Therefore his eyes turned westward. Just before leaving Washington in March, 1805, he approached the British ambassador with a proposal to detach the western states from the Union in return for half a million dollars. Before receiving a reply, he left for the West. There he allied himself with General Wilkinson, the wily military scoundrel whom Jefferson unaccountably had made commander of the department of Louisiana, and with Herman Blennerhassett, an Irish exile who owned an island in the Mississippi River. Burr's plan was to use Blennerhassett's Island as a staging ground for a military force that would possibly take part of the United States and annex it to Spanish territory (for which he had received $10,000 from the Spanish minister in Washington); or possibly take part of the Spanish colonies in the Southwest and annex them to the United States, thereby restoring Burr's national popularity; or possibly take part of Spanish territory and part of American territory and establish an independent republic. Burr's intentions were shadowy and have never been fully exposed.

Before any of his plans could mature however, Burr was double-crossed by General Wilkinson, who rushed away from his agreement with the Spaniards about the boundary between Louisiana and Texas to inform Jefferson that Burr was planning to dismember the Union. Jefferson immediately issued an order for Burr's arrest on grounds of treason. The former vice president almost made good his escape, but was arrested in Alabama in February, 1807. In March he was brought before the federal district court at Richmond, Virginia, where Chief Justice John Marshall presided. Burr was indicted for treason, and on August 3 the trial began. Marshall issued a court order requiring Jefferson's attendance and testimony at the trial, but Jefferson refused to appear, setting a precedent for future presidents. Marshall, who hated his cousin Jefferson, did not want the president to win the case, and in his charge to the jury he insisted on strict adherence to the constitutional provision regarding treason: "Treason against the United States shall consist only in levying war against them, or in adhering to their enemies, giving them aid and comfort." Moreover, the Constitution stipulated that "No person shall be convicted of treason unless on the testimony of two witnesses to the same overt act, or on confession in open court." There was no overt act of treason in Burr's activities, nor were there two witnesses to an overt act. Thus Burr was freed, although he doubtless was guilty of conspiracy to commit treason. He fled to France—and anonymity. Marshall's insistence on a strict definition of treason not only freed Burr, but set a precedent that would hold through American history.

European Entanglements

In Jefferson's second term, the major events were not connected with internal affairs, but with the Napoleonic Wars of Europe. The French emperor had won most of the battles on the Continent, while England dominated the seas. Thus America was caught in a life-and-death struggle between the two nations for mastery of Europe. As a neutral nation, the United States desired to trade with both. Yet the Navy was in no position to enforce American neutrality or to force the European contenders to respect the American flag. During the battles against the Tripolitan pirates, which occurred in shallow waters, the Navy had found that forty-five-foot gunboats were ideal; Congress and President Jefferson thereafter insisted on building these gunboats rather than the large frigates the Navy wanted. By 1807 the Navy had sixty-nine gunboats, the largest of which was only seventy-five-feet long. When one of them, torn from its moorings by a tropical storm, was deposited in a cornfield, a Federalist critic declared, "If our gunboats are no use on the water, may they at least be the best on earth." With a navy of this character, diplomacy with European powers could hardly be favorable to American interests.

The immediate conflict with Britain came precisely because that country ruled the seas. British seamen were constantly deserting because conditions on British ships were deplorable, punishment was severe, and the pay low. Conditions and pay were much better on American vessels, so many deserting British sailors joined the American merchant service. Britain was desperate, owing to the war, and began the practice of impressment, stopping American vessels on the high seas and forcing into British service any sailor who had the slightest trace of an Irish or British accent on the excuse that he was a deserter. Mistakes were inevitable and were impossible to rectify, to say nothing of the slur on American rights. England had been practicing impressment since 1776, but Americans had protested to no avail. Then in 1804 impressment increased considerably, leading to confrontation. In June, 1807, came violence. A new American frigate, the *Chesapeake,* was being completed at Norfolk, Virginia. The commander of a British naval squadron just offshore suspected that a British deserter was serving aboard the *Chesapeake,* but the American Navy Department said it had checked without finding him. When the *Chesapeake* was completed, it put out to sea, without guns, on a trial run. The British frigate *Leopard* followed and signaled that it wished to send dispatches to London, for whence the American ship was bound. But when a boat came alongside the *Chesapeake* it was filled with a boarding party intent on searching for deserters. The American commanding officer unfurled sails and started away, whereupon the *Leopard* opened fire. The American captain was forced to surrender after taking twenty-one casual-

119

ties. The British then boarded, found the "deserter" they wanted, and took him, along with three Americans they impressed into British service.

The *Chesapeake-Leopard* Affair left the United States in an uproar. Jefferson certainly could have had a declaration of war from Congress had he asked. He called Congress into special session, and it voted $850,000 to strengthen the Navy, yet Jefferson did not ask for a declaration of war. Instead he instructed American diplomatic officials in London to demand an apology and a cash indemnity. England not only refused, but instructed its officers to step up impressment. Jefferson then responded by asking Congress to pass an embargo act—no trade whatsoever with Europe. This, he thought, would force respect for the American flag on the high seas. And on December 22, 1807, Congress gave him what he wanted in the Embargo Act. This measure prohibited the exporting of American goods by land or by sea, and it stipulated that most British manufactures were not to be imported. The embargo went into effect immediately, and for fourteen months all American ships stopped legally sailing for foreign ports. In New York City one traveler noted, "Not a box, bale, cask, barrel or package was to be seen. . . . The streets near the waterside were almost deserted; the grass had begun to grow upon the wharves."

The Embargo Act was designed to hurt England and France, but actually did them little damage. In Spanish Texas, officials railed that the embargo was aimed at subverting the loyalty of Plains Indians from Spain to the United States, for the presents annually distributed to the natives were being imported from the United States because of the Napoleonic Wars. In truth, the embargo most hurt Americans engaged in manufacturing, commerce, agriculture, and shipping. There was widespread violation—smuggling—which caused the federal treasury to lose import duties. Many seamen and shipwrights left the United States for Canada. Several small shipping lines were ruined, and many of the smaller seaports, such as New Haven, Connecticut, never really recovered afterward. The price of agricultural commodities fell disastrously, but cotton and tobacco could be stored to await the end of the embargo. Thus New England and New York suffered most, leading to a Federalist suspicion that the Embargo Act was intended as punishment for New England specifically. Jefferson finally realized the futility of the embargo, and three days before leaving office (March 1, 1809) he signed a bill repealing it. This act, passed at his request, opened trade with all nations except England and France, yet provided that the president could order trade resumed with either of them if they ceased violating American neutrality.

Finally, in the field of foreign policy, Jefferson made an abortive attempt to acquire West Florida from Spain. He believed that Napoleon could acquire this from Spain the same way he had acquired Louisiana, and then the United States could purchase it. He asked Congress for a secret appropriation of $2 million for diplomatic purposes. Republicans balked in the belief that the Constitution had been abused when Louisiana was acquired and that there was no justification for a second abuse of it. John Randolph, a distant cousin of Jefferson, bolted the party, declaring that the president was really a Federalist and was not following Republican principles. Nothing came of the effort to acquire Florida.

Madison Elected

As the election of 1808 approached, Jefferson chose to follow the two-term retirement policy of George Washington, reinforcing a tradition that only Franklin

Roosevelt would feel qualified to break. A Republican congressional caucus, all loyal Jeffersonians, nominated James Madison for president and George Clinton for vice president. The Federalists responded by naming Charles C. Pinckney and Rufus King as their candidates. Madison easily won, receiving 122 electoral votes to Pickney's 47. Jefferson retired to his Virginia home, Monticello, to become the senior statesman of his party, which was gradually changing its name to the Democratic Party. For the next seventeen years, until his death on July 4, 1826, Jefferson was the "Sage of Monticello," giving advice to members of his party and to the government.

A man in sympathy with the changing times, James Madison took the oath of office in a suit of cloth of American manufacture. In his inaugural address he spoke of the need to promote American industry and "external as well as internal commerce." He kept as secretary of the treasury Albert Gallatin, who had served Jefferson so well, and the two men developed a firm basis for federal aid to American industry independent from European raw materials, markets, or wars.

The Road to War

Madison came to office when conditions in Europe were deteriorating badly. France and England were locked in a life-and-death struggle. Napoleon had made himself master of the Continent, dominating practically all Europe except Portugal. His rival, England, ruled the seas. In this struggle, Napoleon's strategy, as he expressed it, was "to bring that nation of shopkeepers [England] to its knees" by his "Continental System." By this he meant he would allow no exports from the Continent to England nor any imports to the Continent from England. The British responded with their "Orders in Council," which stated, in effect, that no imports or exports would be allowed to the Continent. The United States, under the leadership of Madison, was caught in the middle of this, fighting for the rights of neutral nations.

Congress did give Madison some direction in December, 1809, when it passed Macon's Bill Number 2, to become effective May 1, 1810. This provided for an end to nontrading with England if it rescinded its Orders in Council, but to retain noncommerce with France; or, if France rescinded the Continental System, trading would be resumed with it but not England. Napoleon, who had nothing to lose since England controlled the seas, repealed his decrees on August 5, to take effect on November 1. Madison therefore allowed trade with France but not England, an action that Congress ratified on March 2, 1811. This series of acts made war with England almost inevitable, for the British were determined to halt trade with France and they had to continue impressment.

Another factor leading to war was a group in the United States actively promoting such a conflict. In the election of 1810 many young and belligerent congressmen had been sent to Washington, a group that quickly became known as the "War Hawks." Henry Clay, who became Speaker of the House, echoed this sentiment when he said in a speech, "Is it nothing to us to extinguish the torch that lights up savage warfare?" referring to the popular belief that the British were encouraging the Indians to attack in the Northwest Territory. "Is it nothing," he continued, "to acquire the entire fur trade connected with that country?" John Randolph, responding to Clay's harangue, said, "Agrarian cupidity not maritime right urges the war. Ever since the report of the Committee on Foreign Relations came into the House,

121

122

James Madison

FIFTY-EIGHT years old when he took office on March 4, 1809, James Madison had won the presidency because of his mental abilities, not because he was a strong, charismatic leader. Born on March 5, 1750, at Port Conwya, Virginia, he began school at age twelve, studying classics as well as French and Spanish. His tutoring completed, he enrolled at the College of New Jersey (now Princeton), excelling in history, government, and debating. Graduating in 1771 after two years of study, he remained on campus another year to pursue his interest in Hebrew and ethics. Possibly he was considering the ministry as a career, but, returning to Virginia, he grew melancholy. A frail young man who stood only five feet four inches tall, he became convinced that he was destined to die young, and gradually he withdrew from society.

Two issues of the day roused him from his lethargy, however: the fight for religious toleration in Virginia and the growing struggle with England. A devout Anglican, Madison nevertheless firmly believed in freedom of conscience. He was elected to the Committee of Safety for Orange County, after which in 1776 his neighbors chose him to represent them in the convention then framing a constitution and declaration of rights for Virginia. It was he who offered the resolution subsequently adopted granting religious freedom in that state. Elected to the state Assembly, he then was chosen in 1780 to represent his state in the Continental Congress. During his three-year service there, he was one of the few delegates in regular attendance; he advocated that the central government should have the power to tax, fought for Virginia's rights to its western lands, and helped arrange the famous "three-fifths compromise" whereby five slaves would count as three free persons when counting the people in a state for purposes of representation in the U.S. House of Representatives. In return for his service, his home state of Virginia often failed to pay him a salary.

After Congress moved to Princeton, New Jersey, Madison gave up his seat and returned to his Virginia home, Montpelier, there taking up the study of law. He was allowed little time for this, however, for his neighbors again chose him to represent them in the state Assembly, where he would serve to 1786. There his ideas were evident in many pieces of legislation: to develop the state's commerce, to allow the free exercise of religion, to keep the currency sound, and to aid the back country. And, because he was a leader in bringing about the series of conferences that would lead to the Constitutional Convention, he was elected one of Virginia's delegates to the gathering in Philadelphia.

Washington Irving wrote in 1812: "As to Jemmy Madison—oh, poor Jemmy! He is but a withered little apple-john." Small of size and frail of constitution, he also was a scholar in politics, a man driven to deep thoughts about government and constitutional law. Despite being gray and bookish, however, he lived to the age of eighty-seven, four years beyond the lifespan of Thomas Jefferson, who exercised two hours every day.

we have heard but one word—like the whip-poor-will, but one eternal monotonous tone—Canada! Canada! Canada!" He meant that the War Hawks were bent on war with England in order to acquire Canada.

The popular belief that the British were fomenting Indian warfare on the frontier had some basis in fact. Indeed, such a belief seemed confirmed in June, 1811, when Tecumseh and a religious mystic known as the Prophet organized an Indian Confederacy in Indiana Territory. The two were capitalizing on Indian discontent over American frontiersmen moving into this area and on Tecumseh's wide popularity among the natives of the region.

According to Shawnee tribal tradition, Tecumseh was born about March, 1768, near what is now Springfield, Ohio. His father was killed at the Battle of Pleasant Point in 1774, yet Tecumseh grew to manhood a distinguished warrior even without a father to guide him. He approached his adult years very unhappy at the encroaching whites who were forcing his tribe farther and farther west. A chief by 1808, he led the Shawnee to a site on the Wabash River near the mouth of the Tippecanoe, where they settled with permission from the Potawatomi and Kickapoo Indians. Angry at the land hunger of the whites, Tecumseh gradually came to believe that no land sales to whites were valid unless all Indian tribes, not just one, assembled and assented to them, for the land did not belong to one tribe alone. Governor William Henry Harrison of Indiana and other American officials rejected this argument, for they realized their government would never again be able to consummate a sale if this became reality.

Tecumseh also believed that if all Indian tribes were to confederate there would be sufficient strength to resist white encroachment. Thus he began working to pull together all tribes from the Great Lakes to the Gulf of Mexico; in this he was aided by his brother (perhaps a twin), Tenskwatawa, who was known as the Prophet. This religious mystic preached with evangelical and revivalistic fervor that the Indians must return to the pure ways of their ancestors, throwing out all white influences. Tecumseh had some success in this venture. When delegates from various tribes visited his village, known as Prophet's Town, he would exhort them to drink no alcoholic beverages, to develop their agricultural skills, and to accept nothing from whites on credit.

In this drive at unification, Tecumseh and the Prophet were aided by the British in Canada, who wanted allies against the Americans. From them the Indians obtained arms, ammunition, and clothes. As Tecumseh traveled up and down the Mississippi Valley, he exhorted the Indians: "Our fathers, from their tombs, reproach us as slaves and cowards." American observers noted that he was tall, straight, and lean—and a great orator. With British advice, he foretold the appearance of a comet in the heavens; when this appeared in 1812 as he had forecast, the Creek Indians were so impressed that they rose against the whites—with disastrous results for their tribe.

Tecumseh met Governor Harrison at Vincennes in August, 1810, for a conference. There he demanded the return of Indian lands with such violence that the conference came to naught. The next year, at another conference, he was overawed by the militia present and asserted his peaceful intentions. Yet that same year he journeyed south to solicit more members for his confederation, warning his brother not to go into battle unprepared in his absence. However, that summer was dry, crops were ruined, game became scarce, and the Prophet allowed himself to be drawn into a battle at Tippecanoe Creek on November 6-7. Governor Harrison and his troops were victorious, and this disaster caused many braves to desert Tecumseh.

Thereafter his confederation began to fall apart. The country hailed this as a victory not only against the Indians but the British as well.

Only President Madison seemed reluctant as the country was led into war. Congress authorized raising the Army to 50,000 men on February 6, 1812, and then on April 4 placed a ninety-day embargo on ships in American harbors. Finally, on June 1 Madison came before Congress to request a declaration of war. He listed four major causes: violation of the American flag, impressment of American sailors, violation of the rights of our status as a neutral nation, and Indian raids instigated by the British. Congress agreed on June 18 with a declaration of war against England, unaware that two days earlier Britain had repealed the hated Orders in Council (mainly because of bad harvests and the need for American foodstuffs). Congress adjourned without voting taxes to support the war, which became the main issue in the election of 1812. Northern Republicans, who opposed the conflict, nominated De Witt Clinton, nephew of the vice president, whereupon the Federalists decided not to run a separate candidate but to support Clinton. The Southern Republicans renominated Madison, who carried the South and the West with 128 electoral votes, while Clinton carried New England and the Middle States with 89 electoral votes. If the election was a referendum, then the country had ratified the declaration of war.

Despite the brave talk of the War Hawks, Madison's grudging support, and the results of the election, the United States was woefully unprepared for war in 1812. American military leadership was old and out-of-date; the generals mainly were aged veterans of the Revolutionary War with little experience. The army was small, just 6700 regulars. The secretary of war, William Eustis, was a hack politician incapable of giving direction to the American effort. The Navy was ineffective—containing only twelve major ships, the largest a forty-four-gun frigate, and 200 gunboats—although it did have some experience and good leaders. And a shortage of funds plagued the country, for the Bank of the United States had expired in 1811, leaving no central agency to fund the war. The British, in comparison, had a large, well-trained army; great wealth; industrial capacity; and a navy of more than 800 vessels, 230 of them larger than any American ship. However, England was engaged in a general war in Europe, making the conflict with the United States a side issue, a minor annoyance; there also were difficulties of supply and transport for a war that had to be fought in America; and hampering British efforts was the American privateer fleet, which was large and effective.

The War of 1812

For the United States the major military objective was Canada. Despite England's inability to spare troops for the New World, however, Americans were unable to achieve their desire to conquer and annex the geographical giant to the north. The few British troops there, aided by Canadian and Indian volunteers, were able to beat back the invading Americans. In 1812 a three-pronged American attack was projected, but in New England, the logical jumping-off point for invasion, there was bitter opposition to the war. In July, 1812, General William Hull led 2000 men from Detroit into Canada; there he allowed his baggage to be captured, retreated, and then on August 16 surrendered Detroit to the brilliant British General Sir Isaac Brock. Hull later was court-martialed for cowardice and neglect of duty, was convicted, and was sentenced to death, but the sentence was not executed because of Hull's good record in the Revolutionary War.

The second part of the attack on Canada in 1812 was conducted by Captain John E. Wool, who crossed at Niagara. He failed because the New York militia refused to cross the state boundary. Similarly, General Henry Dearborn was to invade Canada by way of the Champlain River route. His militia likewise refused to march beyond state boundaries, and he was forced to abandon the campaign. Thus the year 1812 closed on a note of dismal failure.

The one bright aspect of the war was at sea, where the Navy scored brilliant victories. And the 500 American privateers that year and during the remainder of the war captured approximately 1300 British ships with cargoes valued at $40 million.

Little real action could take place along the northern border until the United States gained naval supremacy on the Great Lakes, however. General Dearborn rallied his troops, crossed into Canada, and attacked the capital of the province of Upper Canada; during the battle the city, York (present Toronto), was burned on April 27, 1813, when a powder magazine exploded, killing 300 American soldiers. Dearborn was soon forced to withdraw despite his victory.

Then in September, 1813, Commodore Oliver Hazard Perry, who had supervised the construction of an American fleet on Lake Erie, achieved a brilliant and decisive victory over the British fleet at Put-In Bay. Afterward he sent his famous message, "We have met the enemy and they are ours." This victory on September 10 forced the British to abandon Detroit eight days later.

William Henry Harrison quickly reoccupied this town, then moved across into Ontario, where on October 5 he won the Battle of the Thames River. It was at this engagement that the Shawnee chief Tecumseh was killed. At the outbreak of the War of 1812, Tecumseh had led his followers into the British camp and was given the rank of brigadier general. He had aided Sir Isaac Brock in the capture of Detroit, but simultaneously he had saved the lives of American soldiers about to be massacred there. In fact, his white enemies always commented on his mercy and humanity, noting that he would not torture prisoners and that his word was good. Tecumseh's Indians had fought with the British at Brownstown, Fort Meigs, and Fort Stephenson; this aid later would be cited as one major reason why Americans failed to conquer Canada during the war. And when the British retreated following Perry's victory on the Great Lakes, it was Tecumseh and his Indians who covered the retreat; during this action he was killed.

Other battles in the Northwest went against the United States in the year 1813, however. At the Battle of Chateaugay River on October 25, American troops advancing from Plattsburg, New York, met the British, skirmished, and fell back. On December 30 the British captured Buffalo and burned it.

The campaigns of 1814 promised many more such American defeats. With Napoleon defeated and sent into exile, the British could turn their full attention to the conflict with the United States and mount major attacks. First, they extended a naval blockade along the Atlantic coast and landed troops near Washington. General William H. Winder, commander of the American defenses, proved incompetent and was routed, opening the way to Washington. On August 25 the British set fire to the Capitol and other public buildings in Washington in retaliation, said they, for the burning of York. However, their failure to capture Fort McHenry, which defended the harbor of Baltimore, caused them to withdraw on September 15. (It was during the heroic defense of Fort McHenry that Francis Scott Key was moved to write "The Star-Spangled Banner.")

Another British strategy that year saw them attempting an invasion of the U.S.

by Niagara, Lake Champlain, and New Orleans. The attempt at Niagara failed because a rising U.S. Army leader, Colonel Winfield Scott, and General Jacob Brown managed to turn them back decisively. Similarly, the British force invading by way of Lake Champlain was defeated on September 11 by Captain Thomas Macdonough of the Navy during the Battle of Lake Champlain. However, only in the South could the Americans find real satisfaction with the conduct of the war, and this resulted in the emergence to national prominence of Andrew Jackson.

British influence in Florida had stirred the Creek Indians to the use of tomahawk and arrow in West Florida (present Alabama). On August 30, 1813, the Creeks had attacked Fort Mims, Alabama, and had killed half the defenders. Jackson organized 2000 Tennessee volunteers and in November inflicted decisive defeats on the Creeks. Then on March 27, 1814, he and his troops again defeated the Creeks at the Battle of Horseshoe Bend, so disheartening the Creeks that on August 9, by the Treaty of Fort Jackson, these Indians ceded most of their lands to the United States. These exploits brought Jackson transfer to the regular Army and command of the Southwest. His next move was to attack Pensacola, which he captured on November 7, 1814, thus ending the Spanish-British threat from that quarter. Then Jackson hurried to New Orleans to prepare its defenses against the projected British invasion.

The British troops—7500 regulars under General Sir Edward Pakenham—landed on November 26, 1814, and began maneuvering to attack New Orleans. Jackson gathered a rag-tag army of American militia, sailors, and pirates, such as those led by Jean Lafitte. The battle came on January 8, 1815. Jackson had established his defensive position five miles below New Orleans, and there the British attacked with disastrous results. American losses amounted to fewer than one hundred men, while the British withdrew after losing more than 2000, including Pakenham. This startling victory easily made Jackson the great hero of the war.

Internal opposition to the war had been impressive, both in numbers and quality. Just after the war was declared, fasts and protests were staged in Massachusetts on June 26, 1812, and on July 2 the state of Connecticut refused to call out its militia for federal use. On August 5 came a memorial from Rockingham County, New Hampshire, denouncing the war. It was written by Daniel Webster. Not until 1814, however, did the opposition grow to considerable size, although New Englanders had refused to subscribe to war loans, and their militia often had refused to fight beyond state boundaries. Then on December 15, 1814, at the call of Massachusetts, delegates gathered at Hartford, Connecticut, to discuss "public grievances and concerns." The Hartford Convention, as it was called, was under the leadership of old-line Federalists, and the report from this convention, issued on January 15, 1815, urged the states to resist the unconstitutional acts of Congress; the report also called for seven amendments to the Constitution, which included an end to the three-fifths compromise (counting slaves as three-fifths of a person for representation in Congress), the admission of new states to be by a two-thirds vote of Congress (not a simple majority), no embargo to be imposed for more than sixty days, no declaration of war without a two-thirds vote of Congress, and no president to serve two terms. Moreover, the delegates threatened secession from the Union if their demands went unheeded. The news that peace had been concluded came before their deadline expired, discrediting the convention—and the Federalist Party largely responsible for it.

The Peace Treaty

In fact, the Battle of New Orleans itself had been fought two weeks after a peace treaty had been signed by England and the United States. Both sides had decided by the summer of 1814 that peace was more desirable than war. The British had been fighting since 1792, their taxes were extremely burdensome, their public debt was astronomical, and their citizens were tired of war. The American War Hawks had been sobered by two years of failure, there was great opposition in the country to the war, and the people were tired of war. When Madison learned that the British were ready to discuss terms, he sent Henry Clay to join Albert Gallatin and John Quincy Adams at Ghent, Belgium, where the two sides agreed to meet. The American delegation was one of the ablest in American history. The British team of negotiators were not so able, as their best men were in Vienna, where the fate of Europe was being settled. The British delegates arrived with strong proposals, for they believed their forces in America would be victorious on the battlefield. They wanted the southern boundary of Canada moved southward to include access to the Mississippi River, they wanted part of Maine, and they wanted an Indian buffer state created in the Northwest Territory. American demands included an end to impressment, return of all territory in British hands, indemnities for seized merchant vessels, and a declaration of the rights of neutral nations.

The two sets of demands were so far apart that seemingly no agreement could be reached. Adams even urged breaking negotiations. Meanwhile the British cabinet was questioning the war hero Wellington about pushing the conflict in North America to total victory; Wellington replied that such a course of action would be more costly than England was willing to pay. Therefore the British became more conciliatory, and on December 24, 1814, the Peace of Ghent was signed. It provided *status quo ante bellum*, which meant a restoration of all territory and all conditions to what they had been before the war. There was no talk of neutral rights, impressment, blockades, or buffer nations. The treaty did call for the establishment of certain commissions to adjust the boundary between the United States and Canada. The United States Senate ratified this agreement—which was not victory, but likewise not defeat—on February 15, 1815, and the war was over.

The War of 1812 was not a second war for independence, as some Americans had believed. It ended the difficulties with England, at least the major ones. Yet the war was rationalized into a victory by Americans, a feeling that "we licked the British twice and we can do it again." This transformation in public opinion came because the news of Jackson's victory at New Orleans spread through the country with the news of the Treaty of Ghent; also, the creditable naval victories during the war made it seem that the United States had won. And impressment ceased—there no longer was any need for England to impress—just as did the Indian wars in the Northwest Territory.

The War in Retrospect

The War of 1812 did have beneficial effects in America. It promoted manufacturing and self-reliance to the extent that the United States no longer was so dependent on Europe. And, after two decades of European conflict, the United States was freed at last to turn inward to developing its own resources. Another result of the war came in 1816, when Madison proposed to the British that both nations should keep war vessels off the Great Lakes, something that appealed to both nations on the basis of economy. The British ambassador in Washington, Charles Bagot, met with Richard Rush, and in April 1817, they entered into a pact, the Rush-Bagot Agreement, which provided that each country would maintain no more than four armed vessels on the Great Lakes thereafter. In practice, this agreement has meant that for a century and a half there have been no armaments along the Canadian-American border.

Another effect of the war was the tariff of 1816. At the end of the conflict Americans were anxious to purchase European goods, which had been impossible to procure during the conflict and which were superior to American manufactures. English merchants deliberately dumped goods into America at low prices, even at a loss, to bankrupt American industry. Henry Brougham told Parliament in 1816: "It is well worth while to incur a loss on the first exportation in order, by the glut, to stifle in the cradle those rising manufactures in the United States, which the war has forced into existence." At Madison's urging, Congress moved to prevent the death of American manufacturing by passing a protective tariff. Previous to 1816 all tariffs had been passed to raise revenue; the one that year was designed to aid industry. New Englanders supported the bill heartily, while Southerners worked against it. In the agrarian South most goods were imported either from the North or from England; Southerners thus wanted to keep the tariff as low as possible. The vote in Congress therefore was on sectional lines, and the tariff passed, signaling a growing sectional division in the country.

With heated feelings and growing passions, the nation approached the election of 1816. The Federalist Party was dying, but it did manage to nominate a candidate, Rufus King of New York. He had early opposed the War of 1812, then had changed his mind and had urged vigorous prosecution of the conflict, so he seemed appealing to both sides. Yet King was a minor candidate; the real fight that year was between Southern and Northern Republicans. The Southern faction of the party wanted William Crawford of Georgia; Crawford, however, favored Madison's secretary of state, James Monroe. Monroe narrowly won the vote of the Republican caucus. In fact, he found the election easier to win than the nomination. King carried only Massachusetts, Connecticut, and Delaware with their thirty-four electoral votes. Monroe received 183 electoral votes and carried all the other states.

Changing Political Alliances

The election of 1816 was the last in which the Federalist Party would field a candidate. The party was dead. Despite the passing of the Federalists, the Republicans, or, as they were becoming widely known, Democrats, would begin to split even in their moment of triumph. Jefferson, Madison, and Monroe were from the same state, leading to charges of a "Virginia Dynasty." Yet for almost eight years after the War of 1812 was concluded, there was only one political party—the "Era of Good Feeling," it has been called.

The twenty years following George Washington's exit from national politics had seen the country redefining its republican status. Political parties had emerged, contending for mastery of America's destiny during a time of crisis. Then, when America's independence had been reasserted and the wars were past, the country was united, free at last to turn inward to develop its own resources and its own future. Victory brought unity, but unity produced still further stresses that would lead to the development of new issues, new quarrels, and a new direction for America.

129

Chapter Seven

What Destiny America?

Decades of Change

THE four decades following the close of the War of 1812 saw great and rapid changes in the United States. The Federalist Party died just at the end of that conflict, but another was soon born to replace it; then, in 1852, the new party wrecked itself. But the major political event of these four decades was within the Republican Party, which redefined itself under its new name, the Democratic Party. And, just as the political focus of the nation was changing, so also were the boundaries; the country would double again in size, adding Florida, Texas, Oregon, the Mexican Cession, and the Gadsden Purchase, thereby rounding out its continental limits. In the economic sector, change likewise was dramatic; manufacturing increased, canals were dug, railroads were built. America was becoming a technological nation. These political, geographic, and economic changes were but outward manifestations of changes within the fabric of American society, however, for the people were becoming more democratic, more pragmatic, more vibrantly American.

The first eight years of this period saw the United States ruled by the party of Thomas Jefferson, yet with deep divisions growing within it, divisions revolving around who would succeed President James Monroe. Born in 1758, Monroe was an ardent admirer and follower of Jefferson, and had sought to be his successor. He had been forced to give way to James Madison, however. Yet he had not deserted the party and thus was available for the nomination in 1816. Once in office, he surrounded himself with the strongest cabinet since Washington's first administration —John Calhoun of South Carolina as secretary of war; William H. Crawford of Georgia as secretary of the treasury; William Wirt of Maryland as attorney general; and John Quincy Adams of Massachusetts as secretary of state. These men, each strong in his own section, so pleased the nation that Monroe, making a tour of the country before his inauguration, was cheered everywhere, even in New England. During this tour, the Boston *Columbian Sentinel* published an article that gave the age its name, the Era of Good Feeling. This proved so true that in 1820 Monroe was reelected with only a single electoral vote (from New Hampshire) cast against him.

Monroe's First Administration

The first three years of Monroe's administration proved prosperous. England's textile mills needed Southern cotton; the price of tobacco was high in Europe; and poor harvests in Europe in 1816 and 1817 brought high prices for corn, wheat, and beef. Agricultural prosperity in turn led to a growth of population in the western states as farmers sought to open new, rich soil to cultivation. Between 1810 and 1820, Indiana's population jumped an astonishing 500 percent, Illinois' 268 percent, and Missouri's 237 percent. By 1820 Ohio numbered more residents than Massachusetts, and the West more people than New England.

The young congressmen of the Democratic Party, led by Henry Clay, Speaker of the House of Representatives, gave endorsement to this rapid growth and began demanding economic independence from Europe. Clay's economic system, which he called the American System, needed a high tariff to protect American manufactures, a Second National Bank, and federal money for "internal government"—which meant federal subsidies for roads, canals, and other expensive ventures. Clay saw the South providing the raw materials of industry, the North providing manufacturing, banking, insurance, and shipping, and the West becoming the food-producing center of the nation. Under Clay's vigorous leadership, Congress passed the Tariff of 1816, which set high duties on incoming manufactured goods and which, incidentally, helped bury the declining Federalist Party.

Next, Clay pushed vigorously for the Second Bank of the United States. Hamilton's national bank had expired in 1811. Private banks had leaped to fill the void, some 300 or more state and private banks; these, by 1817, had issued approximately $100 million in paper currency, much of it unnegotiable even in a neighboring community. These "facility notes," as they were called, were fueling the postwar boom and real-estate speculation. To end this threat, the administration early in 1816 secured introduction of a bill creating the Second Bank of the United States, which would serve as a depository for all government funds. The government was to subscribe a fifth ($7 million) of its $35 million capitalization and would appoint five of the twenty-five directors; the remaining four-fifths of the bank's capital would come from stockholders, who would elect the other twenty directors. The Bank Bill passed and was signed, with power to establish branches in different parts of the country.

Although some stabilizing agency was badly needed to supply fiscal sanity, the bank did not provide this. First it outdid the state banks in the lavishness of its loans; then, in 1818, fearing the boom it had created, the bank began to exercise deflationary measures. The result, in part, was the Panic of 1819, a depression of widespread proportions. In retaliation, several states took punitive measures. Maryland, for example, decided to tax the bank out of existence. The local branch manager fought this tax to the Supreme Court, which ruled in the case, *McCulloch* v. *Maryland,* in 1819 and found in favor of the government. Chief Justice John Marshall, speaking for the Court majority, noted that the federal government had two kinds of power: fundamental and derived. Congress by the Constitution had the authority "To coin money, and regulate the value thereof," a fundamental power. If, in doing these, it needed to create a bank, then it could do so—a derived power. "Let the end be legitimate," declared Marshall, "let it be within the scope of the Constitution, and all means which are appropriate, which are plainly adapted to that

James Monroe

end, which are not prohibited, but consistent with the letter and spirit of the Constitution, are constitutional." On the right of a state to tax a federal agency, Marshall wrote that the power to tax was the power to destroy; one level of government therefore could not tax another—and thus Maryland's law taxing the bank was unconstitutional. Bank supporters celebrating this decision by Marshall overlooked the implications of the decision; the Chief Justice clearly implied the subordination of the powers of the states to the federal government.

A happy by-product of the Panic of 1819 was the abolition of imprisonment for debt in many eastern states, which also passed liberal bankruptcy laws. Another by-product was the Land Law of 1820, whereby Congress reduced the minimum amount of land a settler could purchase from the public domain to eighty acres at $1.25 per acre—cash. Thus for $100 any citizen could obtain sufficient land to become a subsistence farmer.

Also during the Monroe administration came the Missouri Compromise, an attempt to settle the question of slavery in the newly acquired Louisiana Territory. Louisiana itself had become a state in 1812 with no thought of ending slavery there; that institution had existed in Louisiana under both French and Spanish governments, and it continued under American rule. Then in 1819 an enabling act was introduced in Congress to admit Missouri as a state. James Tallmadge of New York shocked Southerners on February 13 of that year by introducing an amendment to the bill, the so-called Tallmadge Amendment, which would have prohibited further introduction of slaves into Missouri and would have freed all children of slaves at age twenty-five. The Tallmadge Amendment passed the House by a narrow vote, but failed in the Senate. Nothing more was done until the next session of Congress, which convened in December, 1819. Alabama entered the Union on December 14, 1819—with slavery there unquestioned—making the balance between free and slave states in the Union eleven to eleven. Missouri would unbalance the nation in favor of slavery; Northerners could not abide that thought. Thus began a great debate. Jefferson wrote early in 1820 that this "momentous question, like a fire-bell in the night, awakened and filled me with terror," for it was threatening the foundation of the Union.

At the height of the debate, the northeastern part of Massachusetts applied for admission as a free state. Less fiery members of Congress seized on this application as a means of compromise. Maine would enter as a free state and Missouri as a slave state, thereby preserving the ratio of free and slave states. Some down-easterners from Maine resented this role. One objected to entering the Union as "a mere *pack-horse* to transport the odious, anti-republican principle of slavery into the new State of Missouri." But compromisers, led by Speaker of the House Henry Clay, carried the bill, and both states were admitted. A clause in this act prohibited slavery forever "in all territory ceded by France to the United States . . . which lies north of 36° 30'," however. Monroe hesitated about signing the bill on the ground that the Constitution nowhere sanctioned congressional exclusion of slavery in the Louisiana Territory; yet he overcame his principles and signed the act.

Next came congressional ratification of Missouri's constitution, which contained clauses forbidding the entrance of free Negroes into the state and prohibiting the freeing of any slaves without the consent of their owners. Congress eventually went along, the bills were signed, and the Missouri Compromise became a reality. This compromise averted civil war for a generation, but it left ugly memories. Southerners resented the attacks on their labor system and their social order, as well as the challenge to their ethical standards. Northerners hated the spread of slavery into even one more state. Sectionalism was intensified—sectionalism that would boil up again and again until war spread across the land.

Monroe and Foreign Affairs

In the field of foreign affairs, the Monroe administration fared much better. First was an agreement with England concerning the boundary with Canada. The Treaty of Ghent, which had ended the War of 1812, provided for a commission of experts to meet and determine this boundary. By the Convention of 1818 (which actually consisted of four different commissions' findings), the forty-ninth parallel was extended westward from Lake of the Woods to the crest of the Shining (Rocky) Mountains; beyond this, in the Oregon country, the United States and England agreed on joint occupation for ten years. In 1827 this agreement was extended indefinitely, with either nation desiring to end it to give one year's notice. This, coupled with the Rush-Bagot Agreement concerning armaments along the international boundary, did much to relive tensions between Canada and the United States.

Also contributing to a lessening of tensions with England was the British attitude toward events in Florida. On December 26, 1817, President Monroe empowered General Andrew Jackson to pursue hostile Indians into Florida, where they were being encouraged by British traders. Jackson responded by writing Secretary of War Calhoun for permission to seize Florida; when Monroe failed to answer, Jackson interpreted this to mean Monroe approved. Jackson thereupon invaded, seizing St. Mark's on April 7, 1818, and Pensacola on May 24. He arrested two British traders who were inciting these disorders and hanged them after a preemptory court martial. Finally, he claimed all of Florida for the United States. Englishmen demanded war, as did Spaniards, and Jackson's enemies in Congress and the cabinet, men who aspired to the presidency and who saw Old Hickory as a potential rival, urged that the president punish Jackson and issue an apology to England and Spain. Secretary of State John Quincy Adams refused, instead saying that Spain deserved to have Florida invaded because it had failed to maintain order there—and he demanded that Spain pay for the cost of Jackson's army. Spain was in no condition to fight, owing to internal problems, and yielded to Adams' demands.

Adams quickly moved to take advantage of Spanish weakness to settle several points of difference between the two nations, and on February 22 concluded a treaty with the Spanish minister in Washington, Luis de Onís. This agreement, known both as the Treaty of 1819 and the Adams-Onís Treaty, provided for the American purchase of Florida for $5 million—money mostly owed to Amerian merchants who had lost ships to Spain during the Napoleonic Wars. It also established a boundary between the Louisiana Territory and the Spanish Southwest whereby the United States gave up all claims to Texas; in return Spain ceded to the United States its claims to the Oregon Territory north of the forty-second parallel.

This agreement left only three nations contending for Oregon—the United States, England, and Russia. The region known as the Oregon Territory had first been visited by Captain James Cook, an Englishman, in 1778. Rich in fur, especially sea otter pelts, this region had attracted other Englishmen, Americans, and Russians. Spain, however, had an ancient claim to the entire region and moved to expel the intruders, but was not powerful enough to enforce its claim, and by terms of the Nootka Sound Agreement of 1794 had agreed to the rights of other nations in the region. Then in 1818, when England and the United States had concluded an agreement about the boundary between the United States and Canada, the Oregon Territory had been defined as that region from the crest of the Rockies to the Pacific and between the forty-second parallel and fifty-four degrees, forty minutes north latitude; the Convention of 1818 had provided for joint occupation of this region by Americans and Englishmen. Thus the Treaty of 1819 eliminated Spain from the race for this territory. Russia proved anxious to increase its holdings; by an imperial decree in 1821, the tsar stated that the southern boundary of Russian Alaska thereafter would be the fifty-first parallel. This Russian move angered both England and the United States, and Madison sought some way to combat it.

Another problem in foreign affairs that needed a solution was the American position toward the emerging republics of Latin America, countries that had won their independence from Spain during the Napoleonic Wars. Spain desired to reconquer its lost colonies and appealed to its European neighbors—France, Prussia, Austria, and England—for assistance. The United States was sympathetic to these new republics in the Western Hemisphere, however, and had been quick to extend diplomatic recognition to them. Monroe and his advisers considered the situation and discerned three reasons for wishing to keep the Latin American nations free: first, a victory for republicanism in Latin America was a victory for democracy everywhere; second, keeping the European powers out of Latin America would improve the American defensive posture and would avoid future confrontations with European nations; and third, a return of Spanish control would bring a return of monopolistic trade restrictions that would prevent American commerce with those nations.

While Monroe was deliberating the problem of Latin America and the problem of Russian expansion of Alaska, he received a note from George Canning, the British foreign secretary, that indicated England's policies coincided with American desires. England had even more trade and commerce with the Latin American nations than did the United States and had loaned money to the new governments there; if Spain regained its colonies, both trade and loans would be lost. Likewise England could only lose if Russian expansionism was not checked in the Pacific Northwest. Madison's secretary of state, John Quincy Adams, urged American unilateral action on both problems. The result was a message written largely by Adams and delivered by Monroe in December, 1823, in his annual message to Congress. Known as the Monroe Doctrine, it had two parts. The first part was aimed at Russia and declared: "the American continents, by the free and independent condition which they have assumed and maintain, are henceforth not to be considered as subject for future colonization by any European power." The second part of the doctrine, aimed at Spain and its former colonies, stated that any attempt by European powers to extend their system of government to or reassert their claims in any part of the Western Hemisphere would be considered by the United States "as dangerous to our peace and safety."

Actually, the Monroe Doctrine was a restatement of American foreign policy as implied in George Washington's Farewell Address and practiced in the intervening years. Monroe was merely reaffirming the classic American principles of hemispheric separation and an avoidance of foreign entanglements. Moreover, the doctrine simply articulated what Americans in general had believed since the days of the Revolution: there were two worlds, Old and New, and these should remain separate. This policy had been shaped in the preceding decades by the tension between the American dream of isolation and the reality of the nation's involvement in

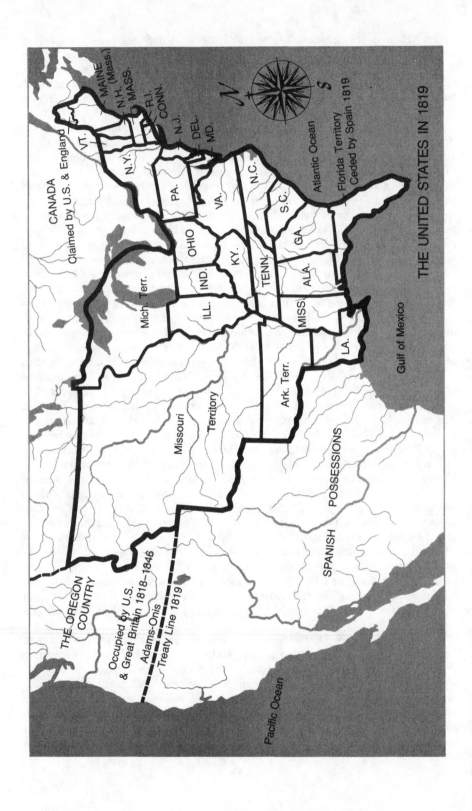

THE UNITED STATES IN 1819

CANADA
Claimed by U.S. & England

MAINE (MASS.)
N.H. (Mass.)
MASS.
R.I.
CONN.
N.Y.
VT.
N.J.
DEL.
MD.
PA.
VA.
OHIO
IND.
ILL.
KY.
TENN.
N.C.
S.C.
GA.
ALA.
MISS.
LA.
Mich. Terr.
Ark. Terr.
Missouri Territory

THE OREGON COUNTRY
Occupied by U.S. & Great Britain 1818–1846
Adams-Onis Treaty Line 1819

SPANISH POSSESSIONS

Atlantic Ocean

Florida Territory Ceded by Spain 1819

Gulf of Mexico

Pacific Ocean

N
S

world affairs; still to be answered were the thorny problems of freedom of the seas, freedom of trade, and neutrality in European disputes.

George Canning publicly pretended to be annoyed with the Monroe Doctrine. However, it was exactly what he wanted. The United States had made a public assertion of policies that would aid England, and the British Navy would enforce these policies; yet England was not embarrassed before its European neighbors by having to back down on commitments it had made at the end of the Napoleonic Wars. And the Monroe Doctrine was effective. In treaties made in 1824 and 1825, signed by Russia, England, and the United States, the Russians recognized that fifty-four degrees, forty minutes, north latitude was the southern boundary of Alaska, leaving only England and the United States in contention for Oregon Territory. Spain likewise desisted from its attempts to retake its former colonies. They remained republics with which the United States enjoyed a brisk commercial trade.

The West Explored and Exploited

The Treaty of 1819, which settled the long boundary dispute between the United States and Spain, triggered still another round of exploration in the West. That boundary was vague: it commenced in the Gulf of Mexico, ran up the west bank of the Sabine River to the thirty-second parallel, thence due north to the Red River, then went up the south bank of the Red River to the one hundreth meridian, thence due north to the Arkansas River, then up the south bank of the Arkansas River to its source, due north to the forty-second parallel, and thence to the Pacific Ocean. Yet the course of the Red River was largely unknown, as were the headwaters of the Arkansas River. President Monroe wished to know the precise locations of these rivers, their courses, and their points of origin. Therefore another major exploratory expedition was sent under the command of Major Stephen H. Long. On July 2, 1820, with nineteen men, Long departed up the Missouri River, followed the Platte to its fork, and went up the South Platte to the site of the present city of Denver. Moving south, the expedition located the Arkansas, ascended it through Royal Gorge, and explored toward its headwaters. Then Long and his men moved southward to a river they thought to be the Red; however, Long was not certain and split his command, one group to descend what was thought to be the Red, the other to go farther south to the next major river and descend it. Neither was on the Red River, however; the northern group was on the Cimarron, the southern group on the Canadian—both of which flow into the Arkansas. The two parties were reunited at Fort Smith, Arkansas.

In his report of his western explorations, Major Long declared, "In regard to this extensive section of country between the Missouri River and the Rocky Mountains we do not hesitate in giving the opinion that it is almost wholly unfit for cultivation, and of course uninhabitable by a people depending upon agriculture for subsistence." On his map of that region, Long labeled it the "Great American Desert," and so it would remain in textbooks for the next four decades. Zebulon Montgomery Pike had come to the same conclusion on his trip of 1806–07 when he had written, "Our citizens . . . will, through necessity, be constrained to limit their extent on the west to the borders of the Missouri and the Mississippi, while they leave the prairies incapable of cultivation to the wandering and uncivilized aborigines of the country."

137

A close reader of both Pike's and Long's reports was John Calhoun, secretary of war in the Monroe administration. In 1823 Calhoun proposed to President Madison that the Great Plains region be set aside as a permanent home for the Indians, a proposal for which he claimed four advantages: it would give the Indians a home, thereby making the government their benefactor; it would minimize racial conflict between Indians and Americans; it would enable the government to regulate trade with the Indians; and there would be no more wars between the two races, thereby saving money for the government.

Monroe agreed to this plan, which called for the removal of all Indians then east of the Mississippi to this region. In a message to Congress on January 27, 1825, Monroe asked that the program be enacted into law, commenting that it would "promote the interests and happiness of those tribes." Congress approved it, and Calhoun's program became official government policy. Under terms of the plan—which, in effect, meant one big reservation for Indians on the Great Plains—the five civilized tribes then living in Georgia, Tennessee, and the Carolinas were forced to move to the Indian Territory (Oklahoma) in the late 1820s; some of the Seminoles resisted, leading to a long war in Florida.

Perhaps best known of all the wars fought in connection with the policy of Indian removal, however, was that against the Sauk and Fox Indians led by Chief Black Hawk. Born at the great Sauk village on the Rock River (near the present Rock Island, Illinois), Black Hawk grew to manhood watching his tribesmen trade furs to Spaniards and Frenchmen at St. Louis for supplies and weapons. When he learned of the American purchase of Louisiana Territory, he conceived a great hatred for them. Then he saw Sauk chiefs in 1804 cede fifteen million acres of land to the United States. Then during the War of 1812 he sided with the British and fought under Tecumseh. After the war he brooded about the loss of Sauk and Fox lands east of the Mississippi River and worked to get British help from Canada for an Indian uprising. Also, he labored with others to create a giant Indian confederation to oppose the westward movement of Americans.

In June, 1831, led by Black Hawk, the Sauk Indians returned to their ancient village on the Rock River, bringing a confrontation with American troops sent to the area at the request of the governor of Illinois. Black Hawk was forced to withdraw to the mouth of the Iowa River on the west side of the Mississippi. However, a year later, in April, he and four or five hundred warriors crossed the river to fight for those lands in Illinois, as well as in Wisconsin and Missouri. In this move Black Hawk believed he would receive help from the British in Canada, and he was joined by warriors from the Winnebago, Potawatomi, and Mascouten tribes. Before this army could arrive at the site of the old village, however, American troops arrived and Black Hawk's army disintegrated.

The conflict known as the Black Hawk War began when Illinois volunteers attacked Indians sent by the Sauk chief under a flag of truce. Two natives were killed in the fighting, whereupon Black Hawk led his warriors northward, pursued by regular Army troops and Illinois volunteers (included in the latter group was young Abraham Lincoln). Hampered by hunger and by their women and children, the Sauk hurried across the Mississippi River in an attempt to end the fighting, but they were attacked at the mouth of the Bad Axe River in Wisconsin, defeated, and forced to surrender. Black Hawk, two of his sons, and other chiefs were taken as prisoners to Fort Armstrong, commanded by General Winfield Scott, and there on September 21, 1832, they signed a new treaty. Called the Black Hawk Purchase,

138

this treaty forced the Sauk to give up more of their land in return for an annuity and a reservation in Iowa. Black Hawk was taken east in the spring of 1833 for a meeting with President Andrew Jackson and afterward was confined for a short time at Fort Monroe, Virginia. Later the Indian was allowed to return to Iowa, where he died in 1838.

There were numerous other small conflicts in the removal of the Indians west of the Mississippi, but by 1840 Calhoun's plan largely had been accomplished. The removal of most Eastern tribes and their concentration in the West was hailed as a great national achievement. But hardly had this been accomplished when technological improvements and advancements made it possible for farmers to move onto the Great Plains, thus triggering yet another round of long, bloody Indian wars.

The Election of 1824

As the election of 1824 approached, there were too many candidates for president. The two-term precedent had been so firmly established that Monroe was stepping aside, leaving this top political prize to no specified heir. New Englanders wanted John Quincy Adams, while Carolinians wanted John Calhoun. Henry Clay had the backing of Kentucky, while Andrew Jackson, hero of New Orleans and Florida, had mass public appeal. Clay and Adams were most alike in attitude: both favored a protective tariff, federal aid for internal improvements, and a centralized banking system to finance the development of the nation. Jackson's policies were unknown, although in 1821 he had said he was unfit to be president. To the astonishment of the public, the Democractic Caucus nominated Secretary of the Treasury William H. Crawford of Georgia, not one of the top four contenders.

Every candidate except Crawford ignored the party caucus. The followers of each candidate became engaged in endless intrigue, trying to get a combination of two of the four as presidential and vice-presidential candidates and thus having a winning slate. In only one instance was this successful—Calhoun agreed to a slate that included Jackson for the top office and himself for the second position. The popular vote in the election of 1824 was difficult to determine, as electors in six states were still chosen by the state legislatures, and in other states not all candidates were listed on the ballot. A rough approximation of the popular vote, however, showed Jackson receiving 153,000 votes, Adams 108,000, Clay 47,000, and Crawford 46,000. In the electoral college—where the vote really counted—Jackson had ninety-nine votes, Adams eighty-four, Crawford forty-one, and Clay thirty-seven. No candidate had received a majority. Thus the election was thrown into the House of Representatives, with the race narrowed to the top three contenders.

Clay, who had run fourth and thus had been eliminated, was in a position of strength. His support would elect the next president—and he was known to disagree with the policies of Crawford; moreover, Crawford had suffered a stroke in 1823 and had experienced a relapse in 1824, leaving him in no condition to sustain the rigors of the office of president. Clay also was known to dislike Jackson; he had stated previously, "I cannot believe that killing 2,500 Englishmen at New Orleans qualifies [him] for the various difficult and complicated duties of the Chief Magistracy." Clay had a private interview with Adams just before the House voted, and afterwards he announced he would support Adams. The result was the election of Adams to the presidency—whereupon Adams named Clay secretary of state. Jackson's bitter followers immediately cried that a "deal" had been made: Clay's sup-

John Quincy Adams

port in return for his being named secretary of state, which then was considered the next step to the presidency. Clay denied the charge of collusion, but it dogged him the rest of his life. He even fought a duel with John Randolph of Virginia over this, the only damage from it a hole in Randolph's white overcoat.

The Adams Administration

Immediately after the election of 1824 ended, the campaign for the presidency in 1828 began. Jackson's followers cried corruption and collusion. Adams, whose four years in office began on a sour note, suffered in this race because of his personality as much as the method of his election. His prior experience had been in foreign, not domestic, policy. In his inaugural address, however, he argued for a strong national government, for internal improvements, a national university, a national observatory, and federal support of literature, agriculture, science, and art. These measures could be undertaken, he said, under the constitutional clause of providing "for the common defense and general welfare." Adams' program went against the overwhelming sentiment of his day, which favored states' rights and a weak central government. Therefore most of his program was rejected by Congress.

In the field of foreign affairs, where he did have knowledge, his critics hampered his efforts to the point of failure. For example, in 1826 the United States was invited to send delegates to a congress of Latin American nations meeting in Panama. Adams was excited by this, believing it might be a first step toward American annexation of Cuba, but he failed to consult the Senate about the appointment of delegates. Only after hard politicking did Adams and Secretary of State Clay persuade a reluctant Congress to vote funds for delegates' expenses, but one of the appointed delegates died en route to the conference and the other arrived too late to participate in its deliberations.

Internally, Adams' policies invoked anger and hostility. For example, he revoked a fraudulent treaty signed by the Creek Indians, which had defrauded them of land, and arranged to restore a million acres to them. The governor of Georgia declared that any attempt by the federal government to restore this land to the Creeks was an unwarranted invasion of states' rights and would be met by force. (This dispute would only be resolved after Jackson became president.) Adams also supported Henry Clay's "American System" of internal improvements, which Jackson's backers likewise called an invasion of states' rights.

Finally, Adams hurt his chances for reelection in 1828 by refusing to use the presidency for political purposes. During his four years in office he removed only twelve men from office, all for fraud or malfeasance, rather than using the patronage power to build a political machine. As late as 1828 he appointed a Jacksonian as postmaster at Philadelphia. Thus in the election that year, Adams was running from a position of weakness.

The Election of 1828

During the immediate campaign in 1828, Jackson's backers, masterminded by Martin Van Buren of New York, introduced a carnival spirit into the proceedings. They charged Adams with extravagance and aristocratic leanings, picturing Jackson as a man of the people. They charged Adams with thwarting the will of the people by stealing the election of 1824, which he had won by a shady deal with Clay. They paraded with hickory sticks to symbolize their support of Old Hickory, and they distributed hickory brooms to show the need of sweeping the "rascals" out of Washington. Adams' men responded by calling Jackson a ruffian, a butcher, and—worst—that he and his wife had lived together in sin. (Jackson had married Rachel Robards thinking her divorce was legal; later they learned that it was not and had remarried. Rachel suffered tremendously during the campaign—and died in December after the election. Jackson was convinced that the vicious story during the election had killed her, and he never forgave it.)

In the heat of the election, Jackson supporters in Congress decided to push a bill calling for a tariff so high it would have no chance of passing Congress. The intent was to claim in the North that Jackson stood for a high tariff, yet when the bill died Jackson could pose in the South as opposed to a high tariff. To the suprise of all, the bill passed and became law—the "Tariff of Abominations." Jackson was unhurt when the scheme backfired and was swept into office by 647,000 popular votes to Adams' 508,000 and 178 electoral votes to Adams' 83. The South and West had elected Jackson.

Jackson Inaugurated

Jackson's inauguration attracted a motley army of office seekers, personal friends, and sightseers to the number of ten to fifteen thousand. Webster wrote, "I never saw anything like it before. Persons have come five hundred miles to see General Jackson, and they really seem to think that the country is rescued from some dreadful danger." Another anti-Jackson man declared, "To us, who had witnessed the quiet and orderly period of the Adams Administration, it seemed as if half the nation had rushed at once into the capital. It was like the inundation of the northern barbarians into Rome. . . . " During the inaugural ceremony these people were sufficiently impressed to remain quiet, but afterward they thronged forward toward their leader. Jackson reached his horse and rode for the White House, followed by the mob. Police control proved ineffective, and the crowd pushed into the executive mansion by both doors and windows. Waiters emerging with refreshment-laden trays were thrown to the floor by the crush; china and glassware were smashed; gallons of punch were spilled on the carpets; in their eagerness to be served, men with muddy boots leaped upon damask-covered chairs, overturned tables, and brushed bric-a-brac from mantles. Finally punch and whiskey in tubs were placed on the lawn and the mob moved outdoors. After the inaugural party ended, several thousand dollars' worth of broken china and cut glass made the White House look like a pig sty. Jackson had taken office.

His cabinet was not especially distinguished. Martin Van Buren became secretary of state, while John Calhoun as vice president thought he would be the power behind the throne. For advice Jackson turned not to his cabinet nor to his vice president, however, but to old friends and cronies, men mainly from Tennessee, all able politicians who looked to building a political machine. Since these unofficial advisors usually gathered in the White House kitchen to talk, drink, and play poker, they became known as the Kitchen Cabinet.

And move they did to build a political machine. First came a "housecleaning" during which the spoils system was instituted with a vengeance. Previous office holders were dismissed wholesale, to be replaced by Jackson men expected to contribute 10 percent of their government salaries to party coffers, as well as work directly for the party. Jackson also used the veto as a political weapon; in fact, he vetoed more legislation in his two terms of office than had all previous presidents combined. Jackson was a firm believer in removing the Indians westward—as stipulated in the Calhoun-Monroe legislation—and used the powers of his office to effect it. When John Marshall, in the case *Worcester* v. *Georgia,* ruled in 1832 that the Cherokees could not be removed from Georgia, Jackson allegedly made his famous comment: "John Marshall has made his decision; now let him enforce it." Jackson did act on that philosophy, even if he did not make the decision; the Cherokees were removed, which proved very popular with Westerners.

Jackson was willing to sacrifice some of his popularity, however. On May 27, 1830, he vetoed the Maysville Road Bill, which had authorized the use of federal funds to construct a road from Lexington to Maysville, Kentucky. He stated that Northeastern states had built their roads at their own expense, that the road was entirely within one state, and that he did not believe federal funds should be used for that purpose. (That the road was in Henry Clay's state probably aided Jackson in reaching such a decision.) The veto message, drafted with the help of Martin Van Buren, was a strong blow to Clay's economic program of internal improvements, although it did cost Jackson much support in the West. By the end of 1830 the president had vetoed three other internal-improvement measures, which Clay's followers declared were proof of Jackson's anti-internal-improvement stance; nevertheless, his administration spent more money on such improvements than had any previous administration.

Jackson also hurt his support in the South by an open break with Calhoun. The alliance between the two men had been instrumental in Jackson's election in 1828. Martin Van Buren, however, worked to drive a wedge between the two men by calling Jackson's attention to letters written by Calhoun in 1818 which condemned the general's activities in Florida. The real break between the two men came as a result of the Peggy Eaton scandal. Secretary of War John H. Eaton had married Peggy O'Neale Timberlake, daughter of a boarding-house keeper. Peggy Eaton was young, vivacious, charming, lovely, and slightly unconventional—and hated by the other cabinet members' wives. Led by Mrs. Calhoun, the Cabinet wives ostracized Peggy Eaton. This angered Jackson, who remembered how such snubs had wounded his Rachel. He therefore instructed the cabinet members to be nice to Mrs. Eaton. Only Van Buren could comply, for he was a widower. The other cabinet members resigned. This did not displease Jackson, for it left him free to appoint men more in sympathy with his own aims and thereby build the Democratic Party into his own organization. The Peggy Eaton scandal also saw Martin Van Buren selected as Jackson's running mate in the election of 1832 and Calhoun losing his chance for that position and subsequent nomination for president in 1836.

Public Lands and Tariff

The real fights of Jackson's first administration came over the issue of the sale of public lands and the tariff. Westerners generally favored cheap public land and the rapid sale of the public domain to actual settlers. Easterners, however, feared that quick sale of land would bring in so much money that the government no longer could justify a high tariff. Southerners seized on this fight between West and Northeast to try for a lower tariff. John Calhoun provided the philosophical framework for this battle in his *South Carolina Exposition and Protest.* In this he

Andrew Jackson

declared that the protective tariffs of the 1820s were unconstitutional, and he asserted that any state had a right to nullify or prevent the enforcement within its boundaries of an unconstitutional act of Congress. This doctrine of nullification later was called South Carolina Exposition, but inasmuch as Calhoun's pamphlet was published anonymously he did not receive credit for the doctrine. This went to Senator Robert Y. Hayne of South Carolina.

On January 19, 1830, when the Senate was debating a limitation on public land sales in the West, Hayne argued the doctrine of nullification and asserted that the Eastern states had been "selfish and unprincipled" in attempting to arrest the development of the West. Daniel Webster replied that the East had always favored Western development. What followed was labeled the Webster-Hayne Debate, during which Hayne enunciated the theory that each state had the right to decide what laws of Congress were just and to be obeyed while nullifying the others. Webster's reply, a four-hour speech, was that the federal government had been created by the people, not the states, and that there was no middle ground between obedience to the federal government and open rebellion: "Liberty *and* Union, now and for ever, one and inseparable!" cried Webster. A month later, Jackson gave a toast in which he stated, "Our Union, it must be preserved," indicating he sided with Webster.

As the election of 1832 approached, Congress passed the Tariff of 1832, which lowered duties on imported goods substantially. However, the lowered duties were not enough to satisfy the South, and South Carolina decided to put the doctrine of nullification to the test. In local elections in the state, nullifiers won. They immediately called a convention, which met in Columbia on November 19, 1832. The convention adopted an ordinance "to nullify certain acts of Congress of the United States, purporting to be laws, laying duties and imposts on the importation of foreign commodities." The tariffs, the resolution stated, were null and void in South Carolina, the state would not pay the duties, and if the United States attempted to use force South Carolina would secede. Jackson responded by increasing the number of federal troops in South Carolina. He sent General Winfield Scott, the nation's best military figure and a polished peacemaker, to the state, and publicly denied the right of secession. Jackson vowed to meet what he called treason with force. Henry Clay thereupon quickly readied a compromise bill calling for a gradual lowering of duties, which became the Tariff of 1833. This law led South Carolina to repeal its Nullification Ordinance—and averted the crisis. Neither side had won a clear-cut victory, but the president had asserted the power of the federal government.

Finally, as the election of 1832 approached, internal improvements at federal expense were called into question, especially the Bank of the United States. This bank was the heart of Clay's American System, which included a protective tariff to aid infant industries, federal aid for internal improvements, a federal bank to provide stable currency and credit, and sectional economies.

The American System

On the last point the "Great Compromise" was merely putting into words what already had happened to the economy of the United States. Each of the three sections—North, South, and West—had developed certain specialties. A one-crop economy based on cotton production through slave-labor characterized the South. Slavery in the cotton fields had been uneconomic until 1793 and Ely Whitney's

145

invention of the cotton gin. After this event the institution of slavery fastened upon the South, and cotton became king. J. M. Peck, who traveled and then wrote guides about the areas he had visited, commented in 1837 about cotton and sugar planters:

> These people, found chiefly in Mississippi, Louisiana, and the southern part of Arkansas, have a great degree of similarity. They are noted for their high-mindedness, generosity, liberality, hospitality, sociability, quick sense of honor, resentment of injuries, indolence, and, in too many cases, dissipation. They are much addicted to the sports of the turf and the vices of the gaming tables. Still there are many planters of strictly moral and even religious habits. They are excessively jealous of their political rights, yet frank and open-hearted in their dispositions, and carry the duties of hospitality to a great extent. Having over-seers on most of their plantations, the labor being performed by slaves, they have much leisure, and are averse to much personal attention to business. They dislike care, profound thinking and deep impressions. The young men are vola-tile, gay, dashing and reckless spirits, fond of excitement and high life.

Yet for the slaves life was not filled with "excitement and high life." Theodore Weld in 1839 published *American Slavery As It Is,* a work that soon became almost a bible for the antislavery movement. In it Weld sought to prove

> that the slaves in the United States are treated with barbarous inhumanity; that they are overworked, underfed, wretchedly clad and lodged, and have insufficient sleep; that they are made to wear round their necks iron collars armed with prongs, to drag heavy chains and weights at their feet while work-ing in the field, and to wear yokes, and bells, and iron horns; that they are often kept confined in the stocks day and night for weeks together, made to wear gags in their mouths for hours or days, have some of their front teeth torn out or broken off, that they may be easily detected when they run away; that they are frequently flogged with terrible severity, have red pepper rubbed into their lacerated flesh, and hot brine, spirits of turpentine, &c., poured over the gashes to increase the torture; that they are often stripped naked, their backs and limbs cut with knives, bruised and mangled by scores and hundreds of blows with the paddle. . . .

Most of the cotton produced by this planter class and slave labor, as well as by yeoman farmers employing only their own families, at first went to England and the Continent, but the growing tendency was for it to go to the industrializing North-east. The first full-time factories in America to prove economically feasible were cotton-spinning plants. There were a few in New England before the Napoleonic Wars, but when that conflict prevented importation of European goods, American factories increased rapidly in number. The War of 1812 drove capital from ship-ping, which was dangerous and costly, to manufacturing. In 1813 Francis Cabot Lowell and other New England merchants joined to use $600,000 for building an integrated cotton manufacturing plant. Under one roof, cotton moved from the bale to spinning, weaving, dyeing, and the printing of cotton cloth. These same mer-chants then established their own sales agency instead of depending on local job-bers. Then they introduced power looms and power spindles—and made such prof-its that they soon were imitated by other manufacturers. The result was a gradual industrialization of the Northeast. Between 1813 and 1816 Massachusetts chartered more than eighty textile manufacturing concerns.

To insure a steady labor supply, many of these factory owners hired young women, eighteen to twenty-two years of age, sheltering and feeding them in company houses. This method produced a 12.5 percent annual return for Lowell and his fellow merchants, but this did not satisfy them. Soon they were employing a growing number of children in their factories. Seth Luther in 1832 published "An Address to the Working-Men of New-England," in which he characterized labor in these factories as little better—possibly worse—than slavery in the South. He advised anyone wanting to see what a real cotton mill was like to visit it incognito:

> In that case we could show him some of the prisons in New England, called cotton mills, instead of rosy cheeks, the *pale, sickly, haggard* countenance of the ragged child. Haggard from the *worse* than *slavish* confinement in the cotton mill. He might see that child driven up to the 'clockwork' by the cowskin [whip], in some cases; he might see in some instances, the child taken from his bed at four in the morning, and plunged into cold water to drive away his slumbers, and prepare him for the labors in the mill. After all this he might see that child *robbed,* yes, *robbed* of a part of his time allowed for meals by moving the hands of the clock backwards, or forwards, as would best accomplish that purpose. . . .

Luther claimed that even physical torture was used on children in these mills to get more work out of them. The normal workday was fourteen hours, for which the pay was seventy-five cents to one dollar. Luther claimed that in twelve states of the United States there were 57,000 persons employed in cotton mills, and that two-fifths of this number were below sixteen years in age. Naturally, such children could not go to school, and thus they would remain illiterate, chained to the mills for the rest of their lives.

Industrialization of the North

The Panic of 1819 slowed the industrial pace in the North somewhat, but then in 1821 came the Latin American revolutions, opening new markets and bringing a revival in business. New Englanders then expanded not only in manufacturing, but also in banking and commerce, in real estate and water-power companies. The corporation was employed to raise money through the sale of stock, and also provided limited liability to investors.

This industrialization had produced efforts at labor unionization. The first labor movement in America came not in factories but among urban handicraftsmen, however. These workers were protesting the lengthened working day made possible by the introduction of gas lamps; previously they had worked from sunup to sundown, but with gas lamps the work day was lengthened to a uniform twelve-hour day. Yet when workingmen organized, as they did in Philadelphia in 1828—the Workingmen's Party—the platform had little to do with wages and everything to do with status. They wanted free public education for their children, abolition of imprisonment for debt, and mechanics' lien laws. These unions fared poorly, however, for the obstacles to labor organization were powerful: democracy itself, along with federal laws. The opportunity to better oneself was so prevalent that few workers were class-conscious. And, owing to the federal nature of the government, the "workies" had to gain control of many state governments to attain their ends. No party organized solely at the state level could expect to win. Despite such handicaps, the workingmen's organization polled 30 percent of the vote in New York City in the election of 1829. These gains soon evaporated when prosperity returned about 1833, causing workers to forsake social goals to move in the direction of trade organization, the closed shop, and the strike. By 1837 the movement was sufficiently strong for delegates from twelve northern cities to gather to form the National Trades Union. Strikes became frequent, and in many places the ten-hour day was realized. Then came the Panic of 1837, widespread unemployment, and lower wages. The trade union movement collapsed in the fight to retain jobs at whatever wage and whatever hours.

Western Farming

The sectionalized economy needed a food-producing region to survive, a role the West assumed. The new states carved from the old Northwest Territory, along with the newer states south of that region—Missouri, Tennessee, and Kentucky—concentrated on production of corn, hogs, wheat, and other foodstuffs. The major route of transportation at this time, however, was by water—and the Mississippi River and its tributaries all flowed to New Orleans and the South. Thus the economic connections of the West and South had forged a political alliance that angered Northerners, and which led to a search for better methods of communication and transportation to link the Northeast and West together. Eastern manufacturers likewise wanted a better system of transportation in order to distribute their goods.

Rivers had been the natural highways of America since the earliest colonial days. Shallow-draft keelboats were the primary cargo-carriers—until the advent of Robert Fulton's steamboat. His *Clermont* made the run from New York City to Albany in 1807, demonstrating the practical potential of his new craft. Four years later the *New Orleans*, also constructed by Fulton, was plying the Mississippi and bringing a transportation revolution. Before the arrival of steamboats on this artery of commerce, the cost of shipping a hundred pounds of freight from Louisville to New Orleans was five dollars; by 1820, steamboats had cut this cost to two dollars; and by 1840 the rate was twenty-five cents. Yet the steamboat still meant that the West was linked even more firmly with the South, both economically and politically. Northerners still needed more direct connections.

Highways at first seemed an answer to Northern needs. These had been built to the West, generally following Indian trails. Yet in spring and fall, during the rainy season, these became quagmires, and in winter they were frozen and blocked by snow. Federal funds were used for road construction beginning in 1806 with passage of an act creating a "National Highway." Five years later work began on the road running from Cumberland, Maryland, to Wheeling, Virginia, on the Ohio River; this was completed by 1818. Later the road was lengthened to Vandalia, Illinois, a point reached by mid-nineteenth century. Turnpike construction under state charters was another method whereby good roads were built, and by 1824 there were some 10,000 miles of turnpikes. Yet these were inadequate. Generally they were short, and they did little to improve the sorry country roads.

The answer to Northern needs for better transportation links with the West came with the canal. Governor De Witt Clinton of New York (1816–22 and 1824–28) was a prime mover of canal construction, for he wanted New York City to share in the bonanza of shipping business that New Orleans was monopolizing. State funding enabled the Erie Canal to be constructed between the Hudson River and Lake Erie in the years 1817–25; when opened, the canal was 363 miles long,

148

had eighty-three locks, and cost $7 million. In its first year of operation, it returned half a million dollars, and it paid for itself in just seven years. In the process it reduced freight costs between Buffalo and Albany from one hundred dollars to ten dollars a ton, and it reduced travel time from twenty to eight days. The Erie Canal largely was responsible for New York City rising to preeminence as a port city; by 1850 nearly half of all American foreign trade was passing through it.

The Erie's success was so dramatic that other states jumped into the canal building race. Seaboard states, as well as those in the interior, initiated ambitious, costly plans and began construction. Philadelphia hoped to tap the western market by means of a combined railroad-canal system; completed to Pittsburgh in 1834 at a cost of $10 million, it was financed entirely by the state. Baltimore initiated construction of the Chesapeake and Ohio Canal without great foresight; work halted when the canal reached the southern mountains, and it never was completed. Western states likewise sought to build canals. Ohio, for example, financed the Ohio and Erie Canal between 1825 and 1833, a 308-mile, $8 million project that connected Portsmouth on the Ohio River with Lake Erie. Most such work was economically unsound and would contribute to the Panic of 1837, when the bubble burst.

Yet these canals did what Easterners wanted. They connected the food-growing West with the industrializing Northeast—and Westerners turned gradually to the Northeast for political, as well as economic, alliances. This move was strengthened by railroads, which would supplant the canal in the 1840s as the prime method of moving freight and cement such an alliance between West and Northeast that the two would fight side-by-side when the Civil War began.

The Bank War

Financing much of the canal, turnpike, and railroad construction was the Second Bank of the United States. This bank had been chartered in 1816 for twenty years. At first it had proven unsuccessful. Then it came under the management of Nicholas Biddle, who made it profitable—if conservative and Eastern-dominated. In the West the bank was hated for dominating the economy of the nation and for restricting the free-wheeling policies of the newer banks of the West. Jackson, when he became president, was convinced the bank was unconstitutional. A strict constructionist, he found nothing in the Constitution giving the government power to charter a bank. Biddle also was a political foe of Jackson, another reason for the president to oppose the bank and to seek to bury it. Biddle chose to precipitate the issue by asking that the bank's charter be renewed in 1832, although its original charter had four more years before expiring. With Henry Clay's aid, a bank bill cleared both houses of Congress in 1832. Jackson promptly vetoed it, calling the bank a harmful monopoly and unconstitutional. His veto message was good politics. The Second Bank of the United States became a prime issue in the election of 1832 as a symbol of Henry Clay's American System, as opposed to Jackson's strict construction of the Constitution.

Jackson was easily renominated by his Democratic Party. His opponents, who labeled themselves the National-Republicans, chose Henry Clay as their standard bearer. A third candidate, William Wirt of Maryland, was selected by the Anti-Masonic Party. Wirt himself was a member of the Masonic Order, while the party's platform called for destruction of that fraternal group. The Anti-Masonic Party selected its candidate by the convention process rather than by the party-boss caucus,

Martin Van Buren

a method other parties would quickly adopt. The election was a Jacksonian landslide. Old Hickory received 219 electoral votes, Clay 49, and Wirt 7.

Overwhelmingly chosen for a second term, Jackson moved to kill the bank, although it still had four years before its old charter expired. Jackson did this by removing federal funds from it in 1833; without this money the bank died quietly. Also during his second term, Jackson moved rapidly on westward removal of the Indians; which caused several Indian wars. Finally the president became alarmed over the large volume of public-land sales on credit and the wildcat speculation this had engendered. To halt this he issued his Specie Circular, an executive order stipulating that all land sales had to be paid for in hard money (gold or silver). The Specie Circular collapsed the inflationary pyramid of paper credit that existed in the country—and thereby helped bring on the Panic of 1837 and a depression that would last six years.

Jackson was a strong president who made warm friends and bitter enemies. He angered Southern planters during the Nullification Controversy; he angered Easterners by killing the bank and vetoing internal improvement bills; and he angered Westerners with his Specie Circular. But he dominated the Democratic Party; he instituted political methods that persist to this day; and he easily named his successor. In 1836 the Democratic Party named Martin Van Buren of New York as its candidate. Opposition that year was provided by a loose group, united only by hatred of Andrew Jackson, who called themselves Whigs because, they said, they were opposing monarchical tyranny. Included in this party were Clay, Calhoun, Webster, their followers, the probank crowd, the nullifiers, the anti-Masons, and other assorted anti-Jacksonians. They had money, intelligence, prestige, control of newspapers, and great leaders. But they could not agree on a single presidential candidate in the election of 1836. Therefore they chose to run several sectional candidates: Webster in New England, William Henry Harrison in the West, Judge Hugh L. White in Tennessee, and Willie P. Mangum in South Carolina. This strategy was intended to split the vote so the election would be thrown into the House, as in 1824. The plan failed, however. Van Buren won a narrow victory, receiving 762,000 popular votes to 735,000 for his combined opponents; in the electoral college he had 170 votes to Harrison's 73, White's 26, Webster's 14, and Mangum's 11. The Whigs did manage to throw the election of the vice president into the Senate, and Richard M. Johnson, a Whig, was elected. Also, Harrison's strong showing made him the most likely Whig candidate for president in 1840.

The Van Buren Administration

Van Buren's term of office was most unpopular, despite his good intentions and his intelligent efforts. Within weeks of his taking office, the Panic of 1837 began, and misery gripped the nation. Van Buren thought the solution to the depression was the creation of an independent subtreasury system to supplant the defunct bank. All federal funds, under his plan, would be deposited in subtreasuries located in all parts of the nation. Congress gave the president what he wanted, but the subtreasuries failed to end the depression. Farmers were bitter at the low prices prevailing for their produce; workingmen in the cities were unemployed; and the creditor class saw profits fall disastrously. Van Buren also continued Jackson's wars against the Indians, particularly against the Seminoles of Florida; however, the Seminoles, aided by fugitive slaves who had taken refuge among them, could not be defeated.

151

William Henry Harrison

As the election of 1840 approached, the Whigs used the Indian wars to picture the abolitionist Van Buren as fighting in order to aid the slaveholders of the South. Unenthusiastically the Democrats renominated Van Buren, but they sensed defeat. The Whigs met in a mood of victory at Harrisburg, Pennsylvania, in December, 1839. Henry Clay thought the nomination was his, but Webster threw his support to William Henry Harrison of Ohio and that elderly gentleman was picked. Harrison was a military hero of the War of 1812 and of the wars against Tecumseh. Yet he knew little of politics, was almost seventy years old, and had little knowledge of the issues confronting the country. His running mate was John Tyler of Virginia, a renegade Democrat who hated Jackson and who, it was thought, would appeal to Southerners. However, the Whigs were so diversified a group that they could agree on nothing except candidates and so issued no platform.

The Election of 1840

The campaign of 1840 saw the introduction of circus techniques that still prevail in electioneering in America. The Whigs used parades, demonstrations, songs, and showmanship. Because Harrison had once worn a coonskin cap, lived in a log cabin, and drank hard cider, coonskins, cabins, and cider became the campaign symbols of the Whigs. Their slogan was a chant:

> Little Van's policy, fifty cents a day and French soup;
> Harrison's policy, two dollars a day and roast beef.

Whig orators told the public that Van Buren lived in the White House like a perfumed Oriental potentate, sampling French cookery from golden plates, that he ate turtle soup and then rested on a Turkish divan. Old Tippecanoe, stated the Whig orators, was satisfied with stern simplicity.

The Democrats responded that such tactics were undignified. They made fun of the Whigs' antics. But the public did not. On election day the simple hero of Tippecanoe received 234 electoral votes to Van Buren's 60.

Once installed as president, Harrison turned to Clay for advice—just as Clay had thought he would. Clay named the cabinet, and he issued a call for a special session of Congress to provide for federal aid to internal improvements. Harrison spent most of his time fighting off would-be office holders. Then, a month after taking office, April 4, 1841, he died suddenly, leaving John Tyler president. Tyler proved to be a Democrat in everything except name, turned solidly against Clay, and followed Democratic policies. The tariff was raised, and he vetoed a bill to create still another bank of the United States, although he did allow the subtreasury system to lapse. Tyler vetoed so many acts providing for federal aid to internal improvements that the Whigs read him out of the party, and his entire cabinet, except Secretary of State Daniel Webster, resigned. (Webster was negotiating a settlement with England of the boundary between Maine and New Brunswick.) Tyler then proceeded to name his own cabinet, all Democrats, and by the end of his term had openly changed parties.

As his administration progressed, Tyler more and more became aware that the majority of his decisions had to do with the Southwest and the far West. For twenty years and more, Americans had been moving westward, seething with a restless energy and little concern for national boundaries. Politicians had paid little attention to that section of the continent, for the frontiersmen had no vote in

John Tyler

national affairs. Yet in the process of their westward migrations, they had raised several issues that would come into sharp focus in the mid-1840s, issues such as New Mexico, California, Texas, and Oregon.

The Fur Trade

The Pacific Northwest and the Mexican Southwest had first come into prominence because of the fur trade. Mountain men, as they were called, had been stimulated to journey to the upper Missouri River country by the reports of Lewis and Clark, which told of fortunes to be made in the fur trade. These hardy frontiersmen soon were visiting the Missouri, the Yellowstone, the Green, and other northwestern rivers—as well as the Gila and Colorado rivers of the Southwest—in search particularly of the beaver, whose pelt was used to make hats and coats. St. Louis became the headquarters of this trade, and the city prospered from it. Because of the dangers posed by hostile Indian tribes, only large, well-armed expeditions could operate in safety, and in 1809 a group of St. Louis merchants formed the Missouri Fur Company to finance such parties. The directors of this company included William Clark, Manuel Lisa, and the Chouteau brothers. John Jacob Astor's American Fur Company likewise operated from St. Louis, averaging approximately half a million dollars a year in profits. Then in 1834, on a trip to Europe, Astor noted a change in styles: "It appears that they make hats of silk in place of beaver," he commented. The fickle god of fashion killed the beaver trade. During its heyday, however, the quest for beaver pelts had opened vast stretches of the West, brought Indians into contact with Americans, and produced a class of men familiar with the paths through the region. "The map of the West was drawn on beaver skins," one historian truthfully would write later. Mountain men left their names imbedded in American geography on mountains, rivers, and towns; and when other, less venturesome individuals moved West, the mountain men were there to serve as guides. And the fur trade made John Jacob Astor the first American millionaire. His American Fur Company was the first integrated corporation in the country, rich in capital, strong in management, aggressive in competition, and active in politics. This company gave a new direction to American business and set the pattern for the future.

The Santa Fe Trade

At the same time some Americans were seeking profits from the beaver, others were trading for profits with the Mexican territory of New Mexico. During the Mexican Revolution of 1810–21, New Mexico was isolated from the interior and could not receive goods. Wealth and a desire for merchandise built up during this eleven-year struggle. Then, in 1821, with the coming of Mexican independence, Spanish restrictions on trading with foreigners fell. Late in 1821, William Becknell, a mountain man trading for furs in what is now Colorado, first heard the news that New Mexico was open to foreign trade. He took his goods to Santa Fe, traded openly, and returned to Missouri with 600 percent profit! In the spring of 1822, on borrowed capital, he made a second trip using wagons. He journeyed from Independence, Missouri, to Santa Fe, opening a wagon road that would be called the Santa Fe Trail and returning again with a 600 percent profit. Becknell's road and his profits encouraged others to enter this trade, and it increased greatly in a few

155

short years. The Santa Fe trade never involved large numbers of individuals, but it did open a major route across the West. It also lured Americans to a new section of the continent, some of whom would stay to live in New Mexico. And it led to political and territorial ambitions that would be realized at the first opportunity.

The Settlement of Texas

Another area of growing American involvement, also leading to territorial expansion, was Texas. Like New Mexico it belonged to Spain until 1821 and the Mexican Revolution. It had been colonized for more than a century by the time it became part of the Republic of Mexico, but numbered less than 3500 settlers (other than Indians) at the time of Mexican independence. Then in 1820 to the dusty streets of the capital at San Antonio came Moses Austin, a former Connecticut Yankee who had moved to Missouri in 1796, when that area yet belonged to Spain, to mine lead. In Missouri, Austin had prospered until the Panic of 1819 bankrupted him; then, seeking a place to recoup his fortune, he turned to Texas. On December 23, 1820, he petitioned Governor Antonio María Martínez for permission to colonize 300 American families in the province. This project finally received approval in January, 1821, but Moses Austin died of pneumonia late that spring, long before he could carry out his dream.

Taking over the project was Austin's son, Stephen Fuller, then just twenty-eight years old. Receiving approval first from the Spanish government, then from the Mexican government after it gained independence, Austin advertised for colonists. He found many Americans anxious to settle Texas even though they had to become Mexican citizens. They came because the Panic of 1819 had bankrupted many people; because of geography—the frontier had reached the edge of the Great Plains, the Great American Desert, where there was scant rainfall, few trees, and a climate unsuited to the crops they had grown in the East, while Texas had the rainfall, the trees, and a climate similar to that in the East; and because of the Land Law of 1820, which provided that eighty acres was the minimum purchase at $1.25 per acre, all in cash. During the Panic of 1819, few frontiersmen had one hundred dollars cash. In Texas, under terms of Austin's grant, a man could get 4428 acres, if a rancher, or 177 acres, if a farmer (and most claimed to be *both*, thereby qualifying for some 4600 acres) at a cost of eleven dollars down and eleven dollars a year for three years.

Other colonizers followed Austin's lead, and by 1830 Americans were far in the majority in Texas. That year Mexican officials, alarmed at the rapid influx, moved to halt the immigration by stipulating that no more Americans could move to Texas, by raising the import duties on American goods, and by sending more soldiers to Texas, many of them convict soldiers. Then in the summer of 1835, Antonio López de Santa Anna, an ambitious, unscrupulous, cruel, vindictive tyrant, overthrew the constitution of 1824, which provided for a federal republic, and established himself as dictator of Mexico. Texas was but one of seven Mexican states to rise against such usurpations. In the fall of 1835 the Texans drove all Mexican troops from the province, but voted in convention that they were fighting to remain a state in Mexico under the constitution of 1824, not for independence.

Santa Anna arrived at San Antonio on February 23, 1836, with an army of more than 5000, determined to crush the revolt. Defending San Antonio was a small army that would total only 187 men, commanded by Davy Crockett, William Barret

156

Travis, and James Bowie. Travis was representative of the many men who participated in the Texas Revolution—and symbolic of those who died. Born in 1809 in what is now Saluda County, South Carolina, he moved to Alabama with his family when he was nine. There he grew to manhood on a farm, but he aspired to more. Before his twentieth birthday he was admitted to the bar after reading law. Then, unable to support himself from the practice of law, he taught school for a time. Standing six feet tall, weighing 175 pounds, red-headed and blue-eyed, he married one of his students. However, this union proved most unhappy to both participants, and in 1831 he left for Texas, where he established a law practice at Anahuac (on Galveston Bay).

In Texas, Travis quickly conceived an intense dislike for the Mexican government and became a leader of the militant faction. In 1832 he participated in disputes with the Mexican commanding officer at Anahuac and was arrested briefly. Later that year, in October, he moved to San Felipe, the center of the American colonists in Texas. There he practiced law, was secretary of the city council, and courted a young lady whom he intended to marry. His divorce from his first wife was approved in 1835, and he was awarded custody of his son. The outbreak of the revolution prevented his second marriage, however.

During the early fighting Travis commanded a scouting company at the Battle of San Antonio. Next he was a recruiter and then was named a major of artillery. Transferring to the cavalry as a lieutenant colonel, he arrived at San Antonio on February 3, 1836, at the head of twenty-five men. Commanding the volunteers there was James Bowie. Both men received orders from the Texan government to abandon San Antonio, but chose to disregard the order. On February 23, when Santa Anna and his army arrived at the city, the men withdrew into the mission chapel known as the Alamo. When Bowie fell ill, Travis assumed total command of the tiny Texan force. Desperately he wrote for aid: "I call on you in the name of liberty, of patriotism & everything dear to the American character to come to our aid. . . . If this call is neglected, I am determined to sustain myself as long as possible & die like a soldier." In the last message smuggled from the Alamo he included a note to the friend caring for his son: "Take care of my little boy. . . . If this country should be lost, and I should perish, he will have nothing but the proud recollection that he is the son of a man who died for his country."

The final Mexican assault came on March 6 after thirteen days of fighting. The Alamo fell and all Texan defenders died—at a cost of 1500 Mexican soldiers—without their ever knowing that Texas had declared its independence. At a convention, starting March 1, independence was declared, San Houston was elected commander-in-chief of the army, and a constitution was written that provided a temporary government for the republic. Houston quickly organized his troops, trained and supplied them as best he could, and on April 21 met Santa Anna in battle at San Jacinto. Joining battle at three-thirty in the afternoon, while an improvised band played the popular tune "Will You Come to the Bower I Have Shaded for You," the 783 Texans charged, shouting "Remember the Alamo." Eighteen minutes later the battle was over. Six hundred and thirty Mexicans were dead, and 730 had been captured, including President Santa Anna. Texan casualties were only eight killed and seventeen wounded. The Battle of San Jacinto had established, de facto, the independence of Texas.

In October, 1836, the voters of the Republic of Texas approved the constitution that had been drafted, voted to seek annexation to the United States, and elected

National Cyclopedia of Biography

Sam Houston

SAM HOUSTON's life was colorful and controversial, exemplifying the opportunities of the American frontier. He rose from humble origins to become governor of two states, a representative of both in Congress, and president of a republic. He was born in 1793 in Rockbridge County, Virginia, but moved, after the death of his father, to Tennessee in 1807. With less than a year and a half of formal education, he ran away in 1809, when farming and clerking proved distasteful, to live with the Cherokee Indians for three years. Returning to white society in 1812, he founded a subscription school that he taught for a year.

During the War of 1812 Houston enlisted as a private and rose to the rank of second lieutenant, winning a commendation from General Andrew Jackson for his coolness and courage. After the war he applied for and received a commission in the Army; this he held until his resignation in 1818, serving at Nashville. Afterward he studied law and was quickly admitted to the bar, then established a practice at Lebanon, Tennessee.

Entering politics in 1819, he proved a colorful and magnetic orator and was elected attorney general of Tennessee. After two terms in Congress, to which he was elected in 1823, he was elected governor in 1827. He married Eliza Allen in January that year, but in April she left him. Houston thereupon resigned his governorship and fled to the Indian Territory (Oklahoma) to live with the Cherokees. Twice he represented this tribe in dealings with the federal government. On the second trip in 1832, Ohio representative William Stansberry charged him with misdealings with the Indians. Enraged, Houston beat the Congressman with a cane, for which he was tried before the House of Representatives, which then reprimanded him.

Late in 1832 President Andrew Jackson sent Houston to deliver peace medals to western Indians and to negotiate with them. Afterward he moved to Texas, establishing a law practice at Nacogdoches. There he aligned himself with the militant faction, and when the revolution began in October of 1835 he was elected commander-in-chief of the army. When the volunteers refused to follow his orders, he spent the winter of 1835–36 with the Cherokees—only to be named commander-in-chief again on March 6, 1836. Immediately he rallied a small army, drilled it briefly, then led it into battle. On April 21 he met the Mexican force commanded by President Antonio López de Santa Anna at San Jacinto Bayou. In the battle, which lasted only eighteen minutes, Houston's 783 men decisively defeated 1500 Mexicans and captured Santa Anna.

That autumn Houston was elected president of the Republic of Texas, a position he won again in 1841. During his two terms he worked to secure annexation of Texas to the United States, which became a reality on December 29, 1845. Afterward Houston became one of the state's first U.S. senators, an office he held until 1859. He was the only Southern Democrat to vote for the Compromise of 1850, and frequently he spoke out on behalf of the Indians.

Married again to Margaret Lea of Alabama, he fathered eight children, maintaining a home at Huntsville, Texas. Proud to the point of being vain, Houston in later years signed his first name with an I instead of an S, so that his signature read, "I am Houston."

In 1859, fearing the Southern drift toward secession, he returned to Texas to campaign for the office of governor. Despite charges against him of cowardice and treason, he won. In office he opposed secession and was able to force a statewide vote on the issue early in 1861. When this vote went against him, he refused President Abraham Lincoln's offer of federal troops to help him remain in office. In March of 1861 he was deposed from office because he refused to take an oath of allegiance to the Confederacy, but prophetically he stated to rabid Southern partisans: "You may, after the sacrifice of countless millions of treasure and hundreds of thousands of lives, as a bare possibility win Southern independence, if God is not against you, but I doubt it." Retiring to his home in Huntsville, he died on July 26, 1863, having seen most of his predictions borne out.

Sam Houston their president. Houston favored peace with the Indians and with Mexico, and he followed conservative fiscal policies. During his two-year term, he did not arrange annexation to the United States. Abolitionists in the United States Congress prevented this, charging that the Texas Revolution had been a "slaveocracy conspiracy"—that is, colonization and the subsequent revolution had been a conspiracy by slave-owning Southerners in order to gain more slave territory for the Union. Although annexation failed, Houston did secure diplomatic recognition by the United States; just before Jackson retired from office in March, 1837, he named an American minister to Texas, thereby giving it diplomatic recognition. In 1838, Texans elected Mirabeau Bonaparte Lamar to a three-year term as president. Lamar believed in war against the Indians and against Mexico, as well as expansion of Texas to the Pacific Ocean. He drove the Cherokee Indians from the Lone Star Republic in a long, costly series of Indian wars. Moreover, he believed in deficit financing, and bundles of paper money were printed. In foreign affairs, he secured recognition from England, France, Belgium, the Netherlands, and several Germanic states. But during his term of office, the value of Texas money fell to fifteen cents on the dollar.

In the fall of 1841 Sam Houston was reelected president, and skillfully he began playing on American hatred of England to reopen talks on annexation. He indicated to Americans that if the United States did not take Texas into the Union he would have to forge closer ties with Great Britain—and England was interested in keeping Texas out of the Union to prevent an increase in American strength. Secretary of State John C. Calhoun in the Tyler administration negotiated a treaty of annexation, which was submitted to the Senate in April, 1844. This treaty called for annexation of Texas as a territory, with the United States taking control of Texas' public land and paying off the Texas public debt (which amounted to approximately $10 million). Again the slavery issue was raised, and the treaty was defeated by a vote of thirty-six to sixteen.

The Election of 1844

The Texas question became a major issue in the American election of 1844. The Democratic candidate, James Knox Polk, declared strongly for annexation, while the Whig candidate, Henry Clay, tried to straddle the issue. Polk had served fourteen years in Congress, four of them as Speaker of the House, but he was little known when he was nominated. The Whigs used the slogan "Who is James K. Polk?" On election day the voters knew who he was; he received 1,337,000 popular votes to Clay's 1,299,000 and 170 electoral votes to Clay's 105.

Polk's victory caused President Tyler to push for the annexation of Texas. In the early months of 1845, at the behest of the lame-duck president, a joint resolution of annexation passed Congress, and Tyler signed it on March 1, 1845. Its terms provided that Texas would enter the Union as a state, would retain its public land and its public debt, and would be allowed to divide into five states at any time it chose in the future. Texans subsequently voted to accept this offer, drafted a state constitution, and submitted it to Congress. Polk signed the bill making Texas the twenty-eighth state on December 29, 1845. However, Mexico had never officially ratified the independence of Texas—nor was it ready to yield to the United States without war. On March 6, 1845—five days after Tyler signed the joint resolution of annexation—the Mexican ambassador in Washington demanded his passport and departed, thereby severing diplomatic relations between the two countries. However, his motive was Mexican politics, not nationalistic indignation. The ambassador, Juan N. Almonte, was a member of the Centralist Party, which had just been deposed in a coup by the Federalists; thus his action was designed to embarrass the new regime and to rally Mexicans around the Centralists. When Polk came into office, he inherited an incipient war with our neighbor to the south. To be free to devote his full attention to this situation, however, he had to settle yet another dispute, one with England over the Oregon Territory.

The Oregon Question

Spain had been eliminated from the race for ownership of Oregon by terms of the Treaty of 1819, and Russia by treaties in 1824 and 1825 with England and the United States. These agreements left only America and Great Britain in contention for a vast territory stretching from forty-two to fifty-four-forty north latitude and from the crest of the Rocky Mountains to the Pacific. By terms of the Convention of 1818, both nations would occupy this area for ten years; then, in 1827, joint occupation was extended indefinitely with the proviso that either nation wishing to end the arrangement had to give one year's notice.

During the early years of this agreement, England clearly dominated the region. The Hudson's Bay Company, a joint stock enterprise, was given control of the territory, and it established a major "factory" at Fort Vancouver, sending Dr. John McLoughlin as "factor" with orders to make profits. It was McLoughlin more than any other man who would open Oregon to permanent settlement by proving its agricultural potential. McLoughlin was born in Quebec and studied medicine there and then in Scotland, returning to Canada as a licensed physician. In 1814 he became a partner in the North West Company, a fur trading firm, and was assigned to the Rainy Lake District in Ontario.

In 1821, when the North West Company merged with the Hudson's Bay Company, McLoughlin was assigned to the Columbia District as factor. His orders to monopolize the fur trade and to make maximum profits coincided with British interests in Oregon, for to do one he would accomplish the other. Establishing Fort Vancouver (today's Vancouver, Washington) as the capital of his empire, McLoughlin set up farms, orchards, and a dairy to supply food to his trappers; this increased profits for the company, because food thereafter did not have to be shipped in from England. He even built a mill and shipyards to accomplish the same purpose, just as he promoted peace among the Indians so they could spend their time trapping instead of fighting. Ships from England annually arrived with merchandise and departed with furs valued as high as $150,000 a year.

McLoughlin tried to persuade the Indians in Oregon not to trade with Americans, but he never allowed his obligations to England and the company to override his humanitarian impulses. He told the Indians not to murder Americans, and he lavishly entertained American travelers. The natives referred to him as "White Eagle" because of his long white hair; American travelers described the six-foot, four-inch McLoughlin as dignified and imposing. And in the 1830s, when American missionaries and settlers did begin arriving in Oregon, McLoughlin extended them credit until their crops could be harvested. The Hudson's Bay Company chided him about losses owing to the many loans never repaid, but he replied that on humanitarian grounds he could not refuse help to the newcomers.

161

Bureau of Printing and Engraving

James K. Polk

The start of American settlement in Oregon originated with the visit in 1831 of Nez Perce Indians to St. Louis; there they requested missionaries and indicated a desire to become Christians. In 1834, Jason Lee and a party of Methodists answered this call; they went to Oregon to minister to the Indians, and there they were joined in 1835 by Marcus Whitman and his Presbyterians. To raise money these missionaries wrote long descriptions of the country, its beauty, and fertility, letters widely printed in religious newspapers and magazines. When the Panic of 1837 hit, pioneers looking for a place to start over again chose Oregon, and the overland migration began.

By 1841 the Oregon Trail was well established. It began at Independence, Missouri, followed the Missouri River to its junction with the Platte, followed up the Platte and its North Fork to Fort Laramie, crossed the Continental Divide at South Pass, went to Fort Hall and on to the Snake River, and descended the Snake to the Columbia, which brought pilgrims to Oregon. The trek was 2000 miles and six months long, went across plains, deserts, mountains, and rivers, and averaged two graves to the mile during the twenty-five years of its major usage.

By 1843 there were so many Americans in Oregon that they gathered in convention and petitioned for the United States to extend jurisdiction over the territory. Congress ignored this request, and in 1844 it became yet another election issue. Polk, the Democrat, championed the annexation of Oregon; Henry Clay, the Whig, was indecisive, just as he was on the Texas question. The voters were not indecisive, however, and Polk was swept into office.

Talks had started with England about Oregon as early as 1842. That year Secretary of State Daniel Webster had been inclined to accept the Columbia River as the northern boundary of American territory. England then had demanded all of Oregon, so no settlement had been reached. Then in the 1845–46 session of Congress, Polk asked that the required one-year notice be given England. Congress complied, and England was notified, whereupon negotiations began. The Oregon Treaty of June, 1846, provided that the forty-ninth parallel boundary would be extended westward from the Rockies to the Pacific, but that all of Vancouver Island would go to England. In August, 1848, Oregon was voted territorial status by Congress. The Oregon Treaty of 1846 thus freed the United States to give full attention to the crisis that would be labeled the Mexican War.

Causes of the Mexican War

Many reasons have been advanced for the war between the United States and Mexico, some of them valid and some of them not so valid. For example, historians of the post–Civil War period stated that the war was caused by a slaveocracy conspiracy, when, in truth, New England's congressmen voted steadfastly for it while John C. Calhoun and other leading Southerners voted against it. Other "traditional" causes include (1) a cultural conflict—that a difference in cultures produced a hatred between Mexicans and Americans (there were hatreds, but these persisted long after the war, just as they had before, and never caused another conflict), (2) the vacuum theory—that the Southwest was scantily populated and that Nature abhors a vacuum and thus Americans moved into it (most of northern Mexico is still thinly populated, yet Americans have not moved into it), and (3) "Manifest Destiny"—that Americans believed themselves God's chosen people with a divine mandate to extend their enlightened system of government, economy, and social

Jesse Applegate

ONE man who made the Oregon Trail trek and then wrote about his experiences was Jesse Applegate, born in Kentucky in 1811. Ten years later his family followed the tide of westering pioneers by moving to Missouri, and there Applegate grew to thin, wiry manhood. He attended Rock Spring Seminary (later Shurtleff College) at Shiloh, Illinois, studying mathematics and surveying. He then taught school and studied to perfect his skills as a surveyor. His education finally completed, he became a clerk in the surveyor general's office in St. Louis, then worked in western Missouri as deputy surveyor general while farming in the Osage Valley.

In 1843, because of economic hard times and the growing slavery controversy, Applegate joined a wagon train bound for Oregon, taking with him a large herd of cattle; in fact, he was placed in charge of the train's cattle, and out of this came a book, *A Day with the Cow-Column in 1843*. In this he traced a typical day on the Oregon Trail. At four o'clock each morning the sentinels fired their rifles to awaken everyone. Men immediately began rounding up the animals, while the women prepared breakfast. By seven o'clock everyone had eaten, the wagons were hitched, and the train began to roll: "The clear notes of the trumpet sound in the front; the pilot and his guards mount their horses, the leading division of wagons moves out of the encampment, and takes up the line of march, the rest fall into their places with the precision of clock work. . . ." At noon the train halted, but the oxen were not unhitched as they grazed; an hour later, a cold meal eaten, the wagons rolled again, although teamsters drowsed at their perches. Always there was the unexpected: "An emigrant's wife whose state of health has caused Dr. Whitman to travel near the wagon for the day, is now taken with violent illness. The doctor has had the wagon driven out of line, a tent pitched and a fire kindled. Many conjectures are hazarded in regard to this mysterious proceeding, and as to why this lone wagon is to be left behind." At dusk the wagons were circled, the oxen turned out to graze, and fires lighted for cooking the evening meal. Fortunately the ill woman recovered: "as the sun goes down, the absent wagon rolls into camp, the bright, speaking face and cheery look of the doctor, who rides in advance declares without words that all is well, and both mother and child are comfortable."

In 1849 Applegate moved to southern Oregon to establish a ranch in the Umpqua Valley. He built a large home, which he called the Yoncalla, raised beef for sale to miners, and dispensed liberal hospitality to visitors. He was known to neighbors as a man who could walk sixty miles in a day, and they said he looked like a classical Roman and possessed Roman virtues. In later years he was called the Sage of Yoncalla, and to his home came such prominent visitors as Schuyler Colfax and Samuel Bowles. He helped throw Oregon's vote to Lincoln in the Republican convention of 1860 and promoted unionist sentiment during the Civil War. He also promoted the Oregon and California Railroad but refused to be subservient to railroad interests. He died on April 22, 1888.

order to the entire North American continent (most frontiersmen never thought in such terms and probably would have dismissed them had they heard them). The real causes of the Mexican War were far less theoretical and much more realistic. First, there was the claims question. Americans whose property had been destroyed in Mexico had filed claims with their government, hoping to be paid. The United States had first attempted to collect these claims in 1829, but Mexico had refused to discuss them. Then in 1837, just before leaving office, President Andrew Jackson had attempted to collect the claims without success. Finally in 1839 Mexico agreed to binding arbitration, the King of Prussia acting as arbiter. But the Mexicans stalled eighteen months before coming to the conference table, then walked out with less than a third of the claims settled. One payment was made on the amount settled; then Mexican officials refused to pay more. The claims question alone justified war by all international usages of that day. For example, France went to war with Mexico in 1838—the Pastry War—to collect claims owed French citizens, and England sent its fleet to Mexican waters to enforce payment of claims owed Englishmen.

Another cause of the war was the American desire for California. Businessmen were anxious to acquire the ports of San Francisco and San Diego to facilitate trade with the Orient. England likewise coveted California, and its agents were active in a state with only tenuous ties with Mexico City, one that already had declared its independence once and might do so again with slight provocation. The American desire for California had been amply demonstrated in 1842 when the commodore of the American Pacific Naval Squadron, Thomas Ap Catsby Jones, incorrectly believing that a war had begun between his country and Mexico, sailed into Monterey, the capital of California, and captured it—only to learn there was no war. His apology did not appease Mexican honor.

When James K. Polk became president, he moved to acquire California. He tried to do this by offering to trade the Texas claims for California, an offer Mexico spurned. Polk then made inquiries if the government of Mexico would receive an American diplomat empowered to discuss all issues in dispute between the two nations. The Mexican government indicated it would meet with such an ambassador, and Polk sent John Slidell. But when Slidell arrived, the Mexican government refused to talk with him. Polk then sent Captain John Charles Frémont and a party of sixty soldiers westward, ostensibly to explore. When Frémont arrived in California, however, he was ordered out of the state by its governor; he led his men north across the forty-second parallel into Oregon and waited.

Much of the blame for the war rests with Mexican politicians—as well as American ones. Mexican demagogues had so inflamed their people that no diplomatic solution to the problems between the two nations could be reached. The administration that indicated it would talk to Slidell was overthrown by revolution just for agreeing to see him, although it had refused to do so when he arrived, to be replaced by the militant regime of General Mariano Paredes. Mexican officials were intransigent because they felt they could win a war with the United States. They based this belief on the premise that the United States and England were going to war, and thus the United States would be faced with two enemies. Also, French military advisors, then training the Mexican army and then thought to be the best military tacticians in the world, said that Mexico would win a war with the United States, despite the American population of 17 million to Mexico's 7 million. The United States had a regular Army of only 7200 men, while Mexico's regular army numbered 27,000—and in a defensive war, said the French advisors, regular troops could easily defeat militiamen and volunteers, while the American Army would be drawn deep into Mexico where its supply lines could be interdicted and the army cut to pieces. Thus Mexican politicians were emboldened to make statements to the effect that they would see "the Eagle and Serpent flying over the White House" before they would negotiate any settlement with the United States.

The final and explicit cause of the Mexican War was the Texas boundary question. When Texas won its independence from Mexico, the government of the new republic signed treaties with the captured dictator Santa Anna stipulating the Rio Grande as the southern boundary of Texas, but those treaties had never been ratified in Mexico. Subsequently, the Republic of Texas asserted by congressional decree that the Rio Grande was its boundary, and the Republic had been recognized by the United States, England, France, Holland, Belgium, and several Germanic states. In 1845, when Texas was about to join the Union, Mexico had offered a treaty of recognition to Texas with the Rio Grande as boundary if Texas did not join the Union. When Texas spurned the offer by joining the Union, Mexico began asserting that the Sabine River, not the Rio Grande, was the boundary. (No responsible Mexican official ever claimed the Nueces River was the boundary, contrary to what some Americans later asserted.)

While Texas was still negotiating its annexation to the United States, Polk ordered General Zachary Taylor to move to a position to defend Texas. This he did in July, 1845, bringing his 4000 troops to the mouth of the Nueces River, there establishing an encampment that later became the city of Corpus Christi. Taylor, born in Virginia in 1784, had served in the army since 1808, gaining distinction in the War of 1812 and the Indian wars, and rising to the rank of brigadier general. Muscular and stocky, rarely in full uniform, he was dubbed "Old Rough and Ready" by his troops. At Corpus Christi he waited for further orders, which came in January, 1846; Polk, when notified of the failure of the Slidell mission, ordered Taylor to the mouth of the Rio Grande. There on April 24, a detachment of his dragoons were attacked by Mexican soldiers, and sixteen of them were wounded or killed. Taylor immediately sent word of this attack to Washington.

Meanwhile, Polk had been considering the situation, and on May 8 he convened his cabinet. Slidell, who had just returned from Mexico, urged immediate action. The president then told the cabinet that war was inevitable and asked their advice. Only the secretary of the navy urged against a declaration of war, asserting that the United States should wait for a warlike act by Mexico. The next day Polk received word of the attack on Taylor's troops, and this time the cabinet vote was unanimously in favor of war. Polk went before Congress on May 11 to deliver his war message: "After repeated menaces, Mexico has passed the boundary of the United States, has invaded our territory and shed American blood on American soil. . . . As war exists, and notwithstanding all our efforts to avoid it, exists by act of Mexico itself, we are called upon by every consideration of duty and patriotism to vindicate with decision the honor, the rights, and the interests of our country." On May 12 the House voted for war 174 to 14 and the Senate 40 to 2, simultaneously authorizing the enlistment of 50,000 volunteers and appropriating $10 million for the effort.

Polk was a lean, angular man with long grizzled hair, cold gray eyes, and somber face—but he was not the international plotter he has been pictured as being. Cold rather than passionate, sly rather than bold, methodical rather than dashing, he

National Cyclopedia of Biography

John Charles Frémont

BORN in Savannah, Georgia, in 1813, the son of a French emigré, handsome John Charles Frémont proved precocious, especially in mathematics and natural sciences. After he was expelled from Charleston College in 1831 for irregular attendance, he obtained a position teaching mathematics on an American warship, following which he helped survey a railroad route between Charleston and Cincinnati. In 1838, when the Army's Corps of Topographical Engineers was organized, he secured a commission as a second lieutenant and began active duty, working first on an expedition surveying in Minnesota and the Dakotas.

While in Washington, D. C., Frémont met and fell in love with Jessie Benton, daughter of the powerful senator from Missouri, Thomas Hart Benton. After their marriage, Frémont was given several choice appointments thanks to the influence of his new father-in-law: surveying the Wind River chain of the Rockies (1842) and exploring South Pass and the Oregon country (1843). His wife helped write his reports, which then were printed as government documents; these brought him wide popular acclaim as "The Great Pathfinder," when in reality he was employing mountain men, such as Kit Carson, as guides and merely following their trails through the West.

Following his adventures in California during the Mexican War, Frémont acquired the Mariposa estate, a large land grant in the Sierra foothills, and grew wealthy from mining there. He bought real estate in San Francisco and lived lavishly, winning election as a U.S. senator from California. However, he drew the short term for the new state and served only a few months, after which he visited Paris and London, raising funds for ambitious schemes on the Mariposa. In 1856, the newly formed Republican Party chose him as its first presidential candidate because of his strong stands against slavery in Kansas and against enforcement of the Fugitive Slave Law. His campaign suffered from a shortage of funds, and he lost.

Frémont's subsequent career was disappointing. His overspeculation at the Mariposa led to loss of that property. Then in 1861, at the outbreak of the Civil War, he performed disastrously as a Union major general in St. Louis and in western Virginia. In 1864 Radical Republicans approached him about running for president in opposition to Abraham Lincoln; Frémont first accepted, then declined ungraciously. After the war he was involved in promoting the Kansas and Pacific and the Memphis and Little Rock railroads, both of which went bankrupt in 1870, leaving him almost penniless. In 1878, through the Republican Party, he was appointed governor of Arizona Territory, a position he held until 1881, when angry protests from settlers in that territory led to his removal. His old age was filled with frustrating schemes to recoup his fortune, during which time he was supported by his wife's writing. In 1890 he was pensioned at $6000 a year as a major general, but he died three months later in New York.

Zachary Taylor

"never dreamed of any other war than a war upon the Whigs," as one contemporary phrased it. Polk wanted California, and he intended to settle the Texas boundary question—but by legal means, not war. It is slanderous to state that he deliberately provoked a war to acquire California; he preferred diplomacy to sword and musket, but politicians in Mexico left him no choice. Given the scant Mexican hold on California and the British interest there, Polk would have been derelict in duty to do other than he did.

The Mexican War

Zachary Taylor needed no declaration of war by Congress to tell him that a conflict had started. On May 7 at Palo Alto (north of the Rio Grande) he defeated a Mexican force three times the size of his own, largely through the accuracy of his artillery. The next day he won the Battle of Resaca de la Palma. Then on May 18 he occupied Matamoros south of the Rio Grande without firing a shot. Polk thereupon named him commander of the "Army of the Rio Grande" and promoted him to brevet major general, while a grateful Congress voted him its thanks and two gold medals. Polk preferred Taylor to Commanding General of the Army Winfield Scott, a known Whig aspirant to the presidency.

Taylor, his army now grown to 6000 men through volunteers, marched to Monterrey, Mexico, which he captured in battle September 20–24. However, he angered Polk by granting the Mexicans an eight-week armistice at the end of this engagement—and he was emerging as the hero of the war, with Whigs starting to mention his name as a presidential contender. Polk thereupon ordered him to hold at Monterrey and remain on the defensive. Taylor ignored the order, advancing southward along a line 400 miles long. This advance brought him into contact with Antonio López de Santa Anna and a Mexican army of 20,000 men. Santa Anna, an exiled Mexican dictator living in Cuba, had approached the American consul and asked to be allowed through the American naval blockade of Mexico, promising an end to the war if his request was granted. Landing on August 16, he was elevated to the presidency, raised an army, and marched north to expel Taylor. On February 22–23, 1847, they fought the Battle of Buena Vista. Many of Taylor's force, the volunteers, broke and fled, but his artillery proved so effective that the Mexicans were forced to retreat, Santa Anna withdrawing to Mexico City to regroup. Again Congress voted Taylor a gold medal of thanks, but Polk demeaned him, and the president transferred half his troops to the command of Winfield Scott, who was preparing to invade Mexico at a different point. (Scott was also a Whig, and Polk hoped to dimish Taylor's popular appeal.)

On March 9 Scott's army landed at Vera Cruz in the largest amphibious assault of the nineteenth century, conquering the city on March 27 in a brilliant victory that saw only twenty Americans killed. This triumph was followed by equally brilliant victories: on April 17–18 his men scaled the plateau on the road leading to Mexico City and defeated Santa Anna in the Battle of Cerro Gordo; on August 19–20 his troops triumphed at the battles of Contreras and Churubusco, suffering heavy casualties, but opening the way into Mexico City; then, when negotiations proved fruitless, Scott and his men on September 8–14 were victorious at Molino del Rey, Chapultepec, and Mexico City. Fighting ceased on October 12. Scott then turned his troops into an army of occupation, restoring order so effectively that a delegation of high Mexican officials asked him to become dictator of that nation.

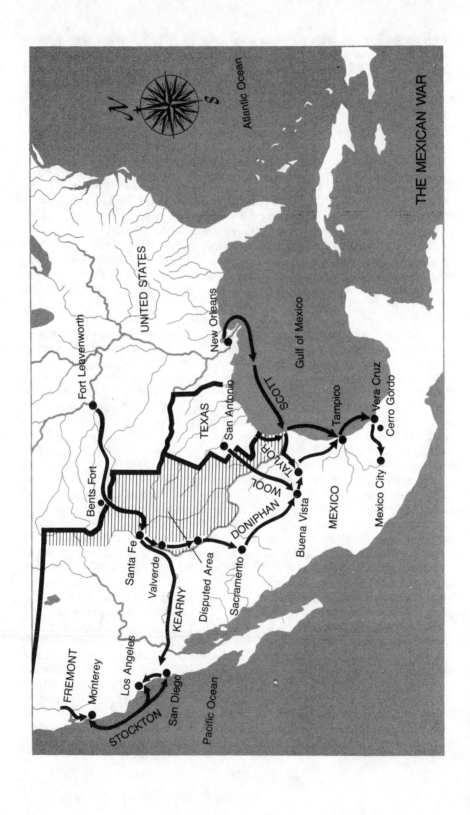

THE MEXICAN WAR

Polk threatened to court-martial Scott on spurious grounds, hoping thereby to discredit a Whig rival, but Congress voted Scott another gold medal and its thanks for his conduct of the war. Polk's charges were withdrawn.

A third major army in this conflict was the "Army of the West," organized at Fort Leavenworth, Kansas, under the command of Brigadier General Stephen Watts Kearny. With a rag-tag army of 2700 men, he marched toward Santa Fe on June 26, 1846. Advance agents persuaded the Mexican governor of New Mexico to surrender the province without a fight—after a satchel of gold reportedly changed hands—and Kearny took over peacefully. At Santa Fe on August 19 he guaranteed the citizens freedom of religion, recognition of their land titles, and full rights of American citizenship. Then he divided his army into four parts: the first to remain in New Mexico as an army of occupation, the second to march southward under Colonel Alexander W. Doniphan to Chihuahua City and then link up with Taylor, the third to be led to California by Kearny, and the fourth, the Mormon Battalion, to open a wagon road from Santa Fe to San Diego under the direction of Lieutenant Colonel Philip St. George Cooke.

Doniphan performed his task brilliantly. His troops, volunteers from Missouri, fought a battle on December 25–28 at El Brazito that opened El Paso to conquest, and then on February 28 they fought the Battle of Sacramento, thereby gaining control of Chihuahua City. Afterward Doniphan linked up with Taylor, completing his task. Kearny set out for California with 300 dragoons. While on the Gila River in New Mexico, he met Kit Carson returning from California with dispatches that told of a successful American takeover there. John Charles Frémont, waiting in Oregon, had received orders from the president by special courier and had reentered California in May, 1846. Joining with discontented Americans in California—and supplied with guns brought by American naval vessels—he had proclaimed the Bear Flag Republic. By July 9 the American flag was flying at the principal northern California settlements of San Francisco, Monterey, and Sonoma. With the help of Commodore Robert F. Stockton, naval commander in the region, the American forces were moved southward to San Diego and Los Angeles, which also were conquered, and on August 13 the war seemed over. Kit Carson then was sent east with this news, meeting Kearny coming west.

General Kearny, upon receipt of Carson's news, sent 200 of his dragoons back to Santa Fe, proceeding west with the other one hundred—guided by Kit Carson, who was persuaded to return to California. At the Colorado River, Kearny began to hear disturbing rumors of a Mexican counterrevolution, rumors that proved true on December 6 when the Americans met Mexican insurgents, led by Andres Pico, near Los Angeles. At the Battle of San Pascual, Mexican lancers wreaked havoc on Kearny's force, which had allowed its powder to get wet. Kit Carson slipped through the lines to secure aid from Frémont's force and lift the siege. Shortly all resistance collapsed in Mexican California—whereupon Frémont and Kearny began quarreling over who was to govern California. When officials in Washington sustained Kearny, the general had Frémont arrested and court-martialed for disobedience. He was found guilty and sentenced to dismissal from the Army, but the sentence was remitted by President Polk for Frémont's contributions in the war. In disgust, Frémont resigned his commission.

Meanwhile, Philip St. George Cooke was leading the Mormon Battalion westward and, in the process, opening a wagon road. The Mormons arrived at San Diego on January 29, 1847, after performing their task satisfactorily. Their road,

National Cyclopedia of Biography

Winfield Scott

A soldier in an age when the U.S. Army largely was ineffective, Winfield Scott by study and hard work made himself the best military man in the country, wrote manuals on tactics and infantry, and tried to upgrade the Army. Simultaneously he was a negotiator who avoided war on several occasions and a moralistic man who helped found the national temperance movement.

Scott was born near Petersburg, Virginia, on June 13, 1786. Failing to inherit the family wealth through legal technicalities, he attended William and Mary College, but quit because he disapproved of the irreligious attitude of the students there. After reading law, he was admitted to the bar in 1806, but after practicing only two years, he was appointed a captain in the Army. Sent to New Orleans, he quickly got into trouble by asserting that the commanding general of his department, James Wilkinson, was as great a traitor as Aaron Burr; for this he was court-martialed and suspended from the Army for a year.

By the outbreak of the War of 1812 Scott was a lieutenant colonel. During the conflict, the six-foot, five-inch, 230-pound Scott was wounded several times, but showed such judgment and courage that he was promoted to brigadier general, was breveted a major general, was voted the thanks of Congress and a gold medal, and was offered —but declined—the position of secretary of war in James Madison's cabinet.

After the war concluded, he remained in the Army as commander of the Eastern Division. Twice (1815 and 1829) he went to Europe to study foreign military tactics, and he sought to upgrade the officers and men under him by authoring training manuals and conducting military institutes for his officers. In 1828 he participated in the Black Hawk War, and four years later President Andrew Jackson sent him to South Carolina during the nullification controversy; his tact during this confrontation probably averted civil war. In 1835 Jackson sent him to fight the Seminole and Creek Indians in Florida, but he was deprived of materials and moved slowly; Old Hickory, who disliked Scott and who had prevented him from becoming commanding general of the Army, thereupon removed him from his command to face a board of inquiry. The board promptly exonerated him with praise for his "energy, steadiness and ability."

Following the abortive Canadian revolt of 1837, President Martin Van Buren sent Scott to bring peace to the troubled Niagara region. A year later Scott convinced 16,000 outraged Cherokees that they should move peacefully from Tennessee and South Carolina to the Indian Territory, and also he persuaded these natives to be vaccinated. His tact and skill as a negotiator in 1839 brought peace in the "Lumberjack War" over the boundary between Maine and New Brunswick. In reward for these activities, he at last was named general-in-chief of the Army (1841), a position he held for twenty years.

Scott's insistence on maintaining strict standards of dress and discipline in the Army caused the troops to refer to him as "Old Fuss and Feathers." Opposed to the use of strong alcoholic beverages, he once ordered that any soldier found intoxicated had to dig a grave his own size and then contemplate, for soon he would fill it if he persisted in drinking. His arguments against alcoholic beverages led to the founding of the first temperance societies in the United States.

Following the Mexican War, Scott was nominated for the presidency by the Whigs, but he was defeated easily in a pompous and lackluster campaign. Congress three years later recognized his accomplishments by naming him a lieutenant general, the first American to hold that rank since George Washington. On November 1, 1861, he retired from the Army at his own request, dying on May 29, 1866, at West Point, New York.

known as Cooke's Wagon Road, later would be used by gold seekers bound for California. Thus in every engagement the American volunteers had outfought Mexican regulars, and the battles had been won. There followed a diplomatic search for peace.

Polk's efforts to conduct the war—and to end it through diplomacy—were hampered by critics in Congress and the public. Even as Americans were winning battles and carrying the American standard onto Mexican soil, debates about the possible fruits of the war raged. On August 8, 1846, David Wilmot, a Democrat congressman from Pennsylvania, introduced an amendment to a bill appropriating $2 million to be used in negotiations with Mexico to secure territory; known as the Wilmot Proviso, this proposed that "neither slavery nor involuntary servitude shall ever exist" in any territory so acquired from Mexico. The House adopted the Wilmot Proviso, but two days later the Senate rejected it. Wilmot refused to quit, however; time after time to bill after bill he tried to attach his proviso, so that Congress—and the nation—continued to debate the question of slavery in the territories. On February 19–20, John C. Calhoun tried to answer the question by introducing—and advocating passage of—the Calhoun Resolutions; in these he argued that since the territories belonged to all the states, Congress could not abolish slavery in them nor could Congress dictate to any state regarding its constitution. The issue was compromised somewhat during the course of debate on creation of the Territory of Oregon; between January and August of 1848, Senators Lewis Cass of Michigan and Stephen A. Douglas of Illinois urged the doctrine of "Popular Sovereignty"—which meant that each territory would be created with no stipulations about slavery and that as it entered the Union it could vote for itself on the question. These men argued that American history was filled with the doctrine of allowing local communities to judge such questions for themselves. The Oregon bill was passed and signed by Polk on August 14, but there was no decision about territory gained from Mexico during the war.

The Treaty of Guadalupe Hidalgo

Negotiating the peace treaty with Mexico was Nicholas P. Trist, a clerk in the State Department who accompanied General Scott during his campaign. Trist had quarreled with Scott to such an extent that "Old Fuss and Feathers" had demanded his recall. Just after this letter of recall arrived, the Mexican government indicated a willingness to negotiate. By this time Trist and Scott had become fast friends, a fact that further alarmed Polk. Also, by the summer of 1847 the president and his cabinet were considering a lengthy occupation of Mexico to make that country pay the cost of the war, which was mounting toward a final total of $100 million. And some Americans were talking of annexation of all Mexico to the United States, a goal known as the "All of Mexico" movement. Even Polk was attracted to this idea. But Trist, without any authorization, proceeded to negotiate, and on February 2, 1848, he concluded the Treaty of Guadalupe Hidalgo. It provided for Mexican recognition of the Rio Grande as the boundary of Texas, and the "Mexican Cession," which included all of Upper California and New Mexico; in return for these concessions, the United States agreed to pay $15 million and the claims, which totaled another $3¼ million. Added to this cost were the American war casualties of 1548 dead, 4102 wounded, and 10,790 dead of disease.

Polk, upon receiving Trist's treaty, was in a quandary. He regarded the former

State Department clerk as "an impudent and unqualified scoundrel," but the treaty contained everything he wanted: recognition of the Rio Grande as the boundary of Texas and the acquisition of California (including the port of San Diego). Polk therefore sent the treaty to the Senate, where it passed with only minor changes and was proclaimed in force on July 4, 1848. The United States was increased in size by half a million square miles of territory—and again at peace.

The Boundary Survey

The new boundary had yet to be surveyed, however. Just before going out of office, Polk named Democrat John B. Weller of Ohio the commissioner and Andrew B. Gray of Texas the surveyor of the Joint Boundary Commission. These two men met with their Mexican counterparts at San Diego on July 6, 1849, and proceeded to survey the southern boundary of California. However, by this time the Whig Party had taken office, and in a political maneuver, Weller was fired. In his place the Whigs appointed a Rhode Island literary figure, John Russell Bartlett. The new commissioner met the Mexican boundary commissioner in El Paso early in December, 1850, there to discover that the map used by the treaty-makers at Guadalupe Hidalgo was sadly in error. The Mexican commissioner, Pedro García Conde, used this error to get Bartlett to agree to a boundary forty miles north of El Paso rather than the eight miles the map showed. The Bartlett-Conde Agreement, as this was known, thereby gave away 6000 square miles of territory to Mexico, territory rightly belonging to the United States and territory vitally necessary for a southern transcontinental railroad route. When Gray, the surveyor, protested this giveaway, the Whig administration in Washington fired him. Congress responded by withholding money for the boundary survey. The result was a near-second Mexican War. The governor of New Mexico insisted that the land in dispute belonged to the United States and said he would exercise jurisdiction over it; the governor of the Mexican state of Chihuahua responded that the Bartlett-Conde Agreement was irreversible and said he would exercise jurisdiction over it. Both sides began massing troops. War clouds hung heavily over the Southwest in early 1853.

The Gadsden Purchase

The Democratic administration that took office in March, 1853, did not want another war, however. The Mexican War had cost the Democratic Party much prestige and possibly the election of 1848; party leaders failed to see how a second war could do anything other than provide a repetition. And in Mexico, Antonio López de Santa Anna was back in power as dictator; his first need was money, and so he preferred negotiations. Thus James Gadsden was sent to Mexico to negotiate a settlement, and from this emerged a treaty, signed on December 30, 1853, and known as the Gadsden Purchase. This drew the final boundary between the United States and Mexico, originally calling for payment of $15 million in return. Certain senators objected to the price, however, one saying that as a private citizen he could have bought the land for $7000. The Senate reduced the amount of the payment to $10 million and the treaty became effective on June 30, 1854.

The Treaty of Guadalupe Hidalgo and the Gadsden Purchase brought to a close the period of American expansion, although there was talk of further acquisitions

177

during the decade of the 1850s. For example, on February 28, 1854, Spaniards in Cuba seized an American vessel, whereupon Pierre Soulé, the American minister to Spain, demanded satisfaction and almost triggered war. Subsequently, on October 18 of that year, Soulé, John Y. Mason, American minister to France, and James Buchanan, American minister to England, met at Ostend, Belgium, and issued what became known as the Ostend Manifesto, in which they recommended that the United States buy Cuba or consider "wresting it from Spain." Also in 1854 Commodore Matthew C. Perry returned to announce that he had succeeded in opening Japan to trade with the United States.

Considering the problems caused by the territorial acquisitions from Mexico, it seemed strange that Americans had not been cured of their expansionist tendencies. James K. Polk left office before the real problems surfaced. He retired confident that he had accomplished the annexation of Texas, had settled the Oregon question, had reduced the tariff, and had doubled American territory. He was so tired by his efforts that he died only months after leaving the White House. His successor, who had to contend with the problems Polk left unsolved, did not live to complete his term.

The Election of 1848

The election of 1848 was fought within the heat generated by recent debates in Congress over slavery in the territories. This fight between abolitionists and proslavery factions had grown so extreme that both Whig and Democratic parties avoided the issue in their platforms. The election generated little public interest; the only real question in the minds of the public was which party General Taylor would head. Taylor, who in June, 1846, had written that he would decline the presidency if it was offered to him, gradually had changed his mind, and by early 1848 actually believed both parties would nominate him and that he would be elected by acclamation—as Washington had been (Taylor greatly admired Washington and liked his sycophants to compare him, not unfavorably, with the first president). The Democrats met at Baltimore on May 22, but chose Lewis Cass of Michigan and William O. Butler of Kentucky to head their ticket. The platform endorsed popular sovereignty.

Taylor had returned to the United States from northern Mexico in November, 1847, to campaign in his own peculiar fashion. The Whigs responded on June 7 by naming him their candidate in their convention at Philadelphia, with Millard Fillmore of New York as his running mate. There also was a third-party candidate, Martin Van Buren, who headed the slate of the Free Soil Party, a radical abolitionist grouping. On election day General Taylor won a narrow victory, carrying seven northern states and eight southern ones; he won only because the Free Soilers split the vote so badly in New York that Taylor carried the state. The vote in the electoral college was Taylor 163, Cass 127, Van Buren zero. In his inaugural address, Taylor advocated military and naval preparedness, friendly relations with all foreign powers, federal encouragement of agriculture, commerce, and manufacturing, and congressional conciliation of the sectional controversy. Four of his seven cabinet members were Southerners, but it contained no men of real ability. Because of his political naiveté, Taylor suffered in his relations with Congress, and he almost ruined the Whig Party because he believed himself above politics: "*I am a Whig,*"

178

he stated, *"but not an Ultra Whig."* The result was discord and dissension within party ranks.

The Compromise of 1850

Taylor's major problem was the issue of slavery in the territory just acquired from Mexico. To the surprise of Southerners, as well as Northerners, Taylor supported provisions of the Wilmot Proviso. When Texans tried to organize what they called Santa Fe County in eastern New Mexico—claiming all territory east of the Rio Grande and arguing that American blood could not have been shed on American soil if that region did not belong to Texas—Taylor issued orders to the Army to stop them. He also sent word to New Mexicans to organize their own government, write a constitution, and apply for admission to the Union as a free state. He followed the same course with California, where the gold rush of 1848–49 had brought so many tens of thousands of Americans that it also was asking for statehood. Still another problem facing Congress was the question of Utah. The Great Basin region around the Great Salt Lake had been settled in 1847–49 by members of the Church of Jesus Christ of Latter Day Saints—the Mormons—under the leadership of Brigham Young. Young had succeeded to the mantle of church leadership —and five wives—upon the death of the sect's founder, Joseph Smith, and he led the Mormons west seeking a place free from persecution. With the Treaty of Guadalupe Hidalgo, the Mormons found themselves again in the United States; statehood, they thought, would allow them to control their own destiny, so they held a constitutional convention, wrote a constitution, and in 1849 were applying for admission as the state of Deseret.

Two other problems were convulsing the nation in 1849–50. Southerners were angry at the effects of the underground railroad, the name given the efforts of abolitionists to spirit runaway slaves northward; they wanted the federal government made responsible for returning such slaves to their owners and were demanding passage of a fugitive slave law. Northern abolitionists were angry that in a nation whose credo was "all men are created equal," slaves were being openly bought and sold in the shadows of the Capitol; they wanted the slave trade abolished in Washington, D.C.

Of all these questions, the most volatile was the Texas boundary problem. Southerners were so incensed over this that they were threatening to join Texas in secession if New Mexico east of the Rio Grande was not given to the Lone Star State. Alexander Stephens of Georgia declared in a speech before the House of Representatives that the first federal gun fired on Texas officials would be a signal for Southerners from the Delaware to the Rio Grande to rise up against the Union. President Taylor answered such talk with a forthright declaration: "Disunion is treason."

Fortunately for the nation, the "Old Giants" were still active in Congress: Clay, Calhoun, and Webster. They moved to stop dismemberment of the Union. Clay called for compromise in a speech on January 29, 1850: California would enter as a free state; New Mexico would be given separate territorial status; Texas would be paid $10 million for ceding its claim to New Mexico, thereby giving it sufficient funds to pay its debts as a republic; Utah would be given territorial status (not statehood because of opposition to the Mormon practice of polygamy); a fugitive slave law would be passed; and the slave trade in Washington, D.C., would be abol-

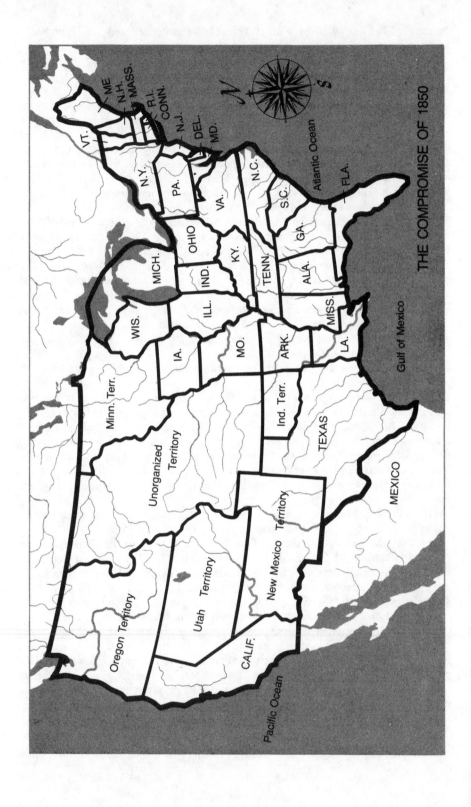

THE COMPROMISE OF 1850

ished. Southerners, who opposed the entry of California as a free state, were appeased by the application of the doctrine of popular sovereignty to New Mexico and Utah.

Clay's proposal met bitter debate, perhaps the most bitter in the history of Congress. On March 7, 1850, Daniel Webster addressed the Senate "not as a Massachusetts man, not as a Northern man, but as an American." Slavery, he said, was forever excluded from New Mexico and Utah by the law of geography; the arid Southwest would not admit cotton culture. Thus, he asserted, there was no reason needlessly to anger the South—allow popular sovereignty in these territories. In the midst of this debate, President Taylor died suddenly. On July 4, 1850, he attended the laying of the cornerstone for the Washington Monument. He sat too long in the hot sun, then drank cold water and ate cold cherries, washed down with iced milk. That night he developed what his doctors called "cholera morbus"—but which probably was a heat stroke—and died on July 9, to be succeeded by his vice president, Millard Fillmore, a moderate who favored compromise.

By September 5 all the measures proposed by Clay had been passed. Lumped together, they were called the "Compromise of 1850." Without doubt they preserved the Union and postponed civil war a decade. But they killed the Whig Party. Northern and southern branches of the party were so alienated they could never unite again. They did rally in 1852 to nominate military hero Winfield Scott; Southerners found him acceptable, but they repudiated the Whig platform, while Northerners liked the platform but repudiated Scott. The Democrats in their convention that year deadlocked between support for Lewis Cass and support for Stephen A. Douglas of Illinois. The result was selection of Franklin K. Pierce of New Hampshire. Too new to politics to have made many enemies, he was acceptable to all factions of the Democratic Party and proceeded to win the election handily; he received 254 electoral votes to Scott's 42. With the solid defeat of Scott and the deaths of Clay and Webster in 1852, the Whig Party likewise was dead.

Beginnings of Disunion

As the Whig Party fell to pieces, the abolitionist wing began talking of founding a new party, one radical in nature and totally dedicated to ending slavery. The proslavery faction of the party chose to join the Democrats, with whom they felt more at home. Meanwhile, Franklin Pierce was offering little leadership to the troubled nation. He was good-natured, affable, and well-liked, but the country was in desperate need of a dynamic leader who could unite it. Pierce was not that man.

Into this volatile situation came publication of a volume that inflamed tempers still more, Harriet Beecher Stowe's *Uncle Tom's Cabin*. A New England abolitionist living in Cincinnati, Miss Stowe wrote with deep passion about the evils of slavery, and her book sold an incredible 300,000 copies. Northerners, after reading the book, tended to disregard the Fugitive Slave Law, which Southerners saw as proof that they could not get justice within the Union.

The inward look that began in 1815 saw the nation expanding to the Pacific shore within the next four decades—but it did not see unity coming to the Union. Manufacturing secured a firm foothold, but so did high tempers and an unwillingness to compromise. Sectional economies brought sectional outlooks that were incompatible. Men who thought the War of 1812 or the Mexican War was the testing period of American democracy were dismayed in the 1850s to realize that the greatest test was yet ahead.

Bureau of Printing and Engraving

Millard Fillmore

FEW men holding high public office have had their reputations so wrongly vilified as the thirteenth president of the United States, Millard Fillmore, a staunch constitution-alist who followed the law even when it conflicted with his conscience. Born in 1799 on a farm four miles from Summer Hill, New York, he early showed a strong love for books, but because of family poverty he was apprenticed to a carder and cloth finisher in order to contribute to the family income. Later, his apprenticeship com-pleted, he determined to study law and was admitted to the bar in Buffalo at age twenty-three.

While building a practice, he taught school and did manual labor. Then in 1829 he was elected to the state legislature as a Whig, where he earned a reputation as a man of high moral principle. In the legislature one of his goals was the abolition of imprisonment for debt, which he finally accomplished. During his years in Albany he had several opportunities to profit from his position, but his was a rugged honesty that prevented accumulating wealth by wrongful means. Also during this period he showed an unfaltering trust in the truthfulness and goodness of his fellow men. These same traits he carried to Washington as a congressman in 1832. There he opposed slavery and worked to abolish the slave trade. In addition, as chairman of the House Committee on Ways and Means, he opposed the United States Bank, wanting a bank-ing system based on government bonds.

In 1848 his integrity and honesty caused the Whig Party to name him as the run-ning mate for Zachary Taylor, hero of the Mexican War, and when "Old Rough and Ready" died on July 9, 1850, he became president. As chief executive he upheld the Fugitive Slave Laws, despite his hatred for the institution.

Few other controversies marred his administration, which was marked by prosper-ity and tranquility. Retiring from office in 1853, he lived quietly until his death in 1874. John Quincy Adams, who observed Fillmore as a congressman, once commented that the New Yorker was "one of the ablest, most faithful and fairest-minded men" with whom he had ever served.

Chapter Eight

A House Divided

The United States at Mid-Century

By the mid-1850s the United States had undergone—and survived—great trials. Europeans who had predicted a short life for the small, fifth-rate power created by revolution and dedicated to republican democracy would have been astounded to discover, just three-quarters of a century later, a two-ocean nation of more than twenty million citizens with a growing network of transportation facilities, rising factories, and a flourishing economy. Wars had brought death to many of its young men. Opinions had been sharply divided on controversial questions. Sectionalism had reared its head to preach and threaten disunion. But the democratic process had been strengthened, not destroyed, by wars, sectionalism, and other problems.

Yet in the mid-1850s there was a new threat to democracy and union, lending weight to the cliché that every generation had to win freedom anew—sectionalism was growing more rampant; abolitionists were becoming more militant in their demands for an end to the "peculiar institution" of the South; and representatives of all factions and all sections were moving in the direction of no compromise. The nation would soon discover anew the price of freedom—and of union.

The Kansas-Nebraska Act

By the 1850s there was growing talk of a transcontinental railroad, one that would weld California and the Pacific Coast to the rest of the Union by rails of iron. Yet the eastern terminus of such a railroad would profit so greatly that the sectional controversy was injected into the discussion. Debate on the specific route of a transcontinental railroad centered in Congress, for the federal government was to subsidize the undertaking. Senator Stephen A. Douglas of Illinois intended that the railroad be built from his state westward. New England-born, Douglas had invested heavily in railroads and land speculation, and he realized that to persuade Congress to agree with him to subsidize the railroad through his section of the country it would be necessary to get settlers into the region west of Illinois.

Congress attempted to resolve the question of the railroad route by providing for a series of surveys. The Army Appropriations Act of March, 1853, provided funds for surveys "to ascertain the most practicable and economical route for a railroad

184

from the Mississippi River to the Pacific Ocean." The Corps of Topographical Engineers, the map-making branch of the Army, carried out the project in 1853–54 and found four practical routes: a thirty-second parallel route, a thirty-fifth parallel route, one between the thirty-eighth and thirty-ninth parallels, and one between the forty-seventh and forty-ninth. Essentially, nothing was solved by the survey.

Douglas thereupon used his position as chairman of the Senate Committee on Territories to introduce the Nebraska Act, providing for the organization of the Territory of Nebraska "with or without slavery" on January 4, 1854. His intent was settlement of the region, thus strengthening his argument for a route westward from Illinois. Two weeks later came an amendment to his bill to repeal the Missouri Compromise of 1820; this was done to get Southern support for the measure. Then on January 23 Douglas offered a new bill, the Kansas-Nebraska Act, which would create two new territories, divided along the fortieth parallel, with or without slavery. The act specifically called for repeal of the Missouri Compromise. Douglas predicted that his bill would produce a "storm," and he was right.

Northerners charged that Douglas was making a bid for Southern support in order to win the presidency in 1856. Senator Salmon P. Chase of Ohio on January 24 published an "Appeal of the Independent Democrats," which attacked the Kansas-Nebraska Act as a plot to keep free laborers out of the two territories. In truth, Douglas' motives were more economic than political. Also, he believed that free-soilers would so dominate the region that slavery would be excluded. Northern Democrats split with their Southern cousins on the bill, while the Whigs voted against it by fifty-seven to seven. Yet the bill passed the Senate by a vote of thirty-seven to fourteen and, on May 22, the House by a vote of 113 to 100. President Pierce signed it into law on May 30.

Bleeding Kansas

Neither North nor South was content to allow local settlers to decide so important a question as free state versus slave. Both Northerners and Southerners organized emigrant aid societies to "assist" the "right kind" of settlers to go to Kansas; Nebraska was never much in doubt, for the normal flow of settlers westward insured that it would be free soil. Pierce's appointee as governor of Kansas, Pennsylvanian Andrew H. Reeder, arrived to organize local government and called for an election to be held on November 29. In that first election of a territorial legislature, some 1700 Missourians crossed the boundary to vote their principles—the result was a strongly proslavery legislature which overrode Governor Reeder's vetoes to prescribe the death penalty for anyone who helped a slave escape or who incited a slave conspiracy. Even to question the legality or the morality of slavery would bring two years at hard labor.

The abolitionist faction in Kansas responded by electing their own government. It met at Topeka and drafted a free-state constitution, which was submitted to Congress with the request that it be accepted. They also elected their own slate of state officials. The result was two governors and two legislatures, both claiming to represent Kansas. Both sides began arming themselves, and bloodshed was not long in coming. In May, 1856, a group of proslavery men from Missouri, led by a United States marshal, raided the free-soil town of Lawrence, burned the hotel, and destroyed homes and printing presses. Only two lives were lost in the celebrated "sacking of Lawrence," but it inspired retaliation. John Brown of Osawatomie, a

Franklin Pierce

fanatical and demented abolitionist, responded by gathering six like-minded follow-ers, riding to Pottawatomie Creek, and wantonly hacking five men to death. Such events triggered fighting that would eventually take 200 lives in the territory that came to be called "Bleeding Kansas."

The violence then spread to Congress. In the Senate, Charles Sumner of Massachusetts rose on May 19, 1856, to speak about the border ruffians of Missouri. During his speech he referred to Senator Andrew P. Butler of South Carolina so insultingly that two days later Congressman Preston Brooks, a representative from South Carolina and a nephew of Butler, attacked Sumner with a cane, beating the senator so severely that Sumner was an invalid for three and one-half years. Again sectional tension increased.

The Republican Party

Within this context, new political parties arose to replace the old Whig Party. Antislavery Democrats, old-line Whigs, and disgruntled men in general were looking for a new political home. Two would-be replacements rose. The American Party, whose platform was strongly anti-Catholic and antiforeign, was formed in 1852. Because its meetings were secret, as were its leaders, it was popularly known as the "Know Nothing Party," its members, when questioned, replying, "I know nothing." Mysterious passwords and secret handclasps increased the popularity of the party, but it split on the issue of the Kansas-Nebraska Act, as well as suffering from its secrecy; with unknown leaders, it found it difficult to win elections.

The other possible replacement for the Whig Party was formed between February and July, 1854. Its first gathering was at Ripon, Wisconsin, on February 28, and it called itself the Republican Party. Other meetings were held in the North, with cohesion achieved on July 6 at Jackson, Michigan. In general the party stood for a high tariff—and thus it attracted businessmen; it supported abolition—so it attracted the free-soilers; it was committed to a homestead law that would provide 160 acres free to any head of family—so it had the support of the poor. Thus the election of 1856 was decisive, for it would determine which of the two new parties would survive to supplant the moribund Whigs as the second major political organization in the country.

In the election of 1856 the first party to gather in convention was the American Party. At Philadelphia the delegates proceeded to name Millard Fillmore of New York and Andrew J. Donelson of Tennessee to head their ticket, although Northern delegates were so incensed at the choice that they walked out in protest. The Democrats gathered at Cincinnati on June 2, where they passed over Stephen A. Douglas to name James Buchanan of Pennsylvania, who had forty years of political experience behind him. Cautious and narrowly constitutional in his thinking, Buchanan was an honest man who loved the Union. He had been minister to England during the Pierce administration squabbles, and thus his views on most issues were unknown—which made him attractive as a candidate. John C. Breckinridge of Kentucky was selected to run for the vice presidency, a choice that attracted Southern votes without the taint of extremism. The Republicans gathered at Philadelphia on June 17 to nominate John Charles Frémont, the Great Pathfinder, on a platform of "Free men, free land, and Frémont." His running mate was William L. Dayton of New Jersey. In the general election on November 4, Buchanan won handily, with 174 electoral votes to Frémont's 114 and Fillmore's 8. Yet it was a sectional victory

187

for Buchanan; he won in the South and West, while the North went solidly Republican.

Hardly had Buchanan been inaugurated when his first crisis arrived—the *Dred Scott* decision by the Supreme Court. Dred Scott, a slave, was taken by his master in 1834 from Missouri to Illinois and then to Wisconsin. Later he was returned to Missouri where his owner died. He eventually became the property of John F. A. Sanford of New York. Encouraged by free-soilers, Scott sued for his freedom on the basis of his residence in the free-soil state of Illinois (no slavery by terms of the Northwest Ordinance of 1787) and in Wisconsin (no slavery on the basis of the Missouri Compromise of 1820). The case finally reached the Supreme Court in May, 1856, and was decided on March 6, 1857—just two days after Buchanan became chief executive. Chief Justice Roger B. Taney wrote the majority decision in *Dred Scott* v. *Sanford.* In it, he said slaves were not citizens and therefore Scott could not sue in court and, further, that Scott was not free by virtue of the Missouri Compromise because the compromise was unconstitutional. Thus, said Taney, Scott's fate would have to be decided by the state of Missouri. Taney ruled the Missouri Compromise unconstitutional under terms of the Fifth Amendment: "No person shall be . . . deprived of life, liberty, or property without due process of law."

The *Dred Scott* case caused great public controversy, for it threw open all United States territory to slaveowners and rendered meaningless congressional debate on the subject. Furthermore, it rendered all territorial legislative rulings on slavery unconstitutional, as territorial legislation existed by virtue of congressional legislation. In short, the *Dred Scott* decision left Americans no room for neutralism on the slavery question, and it fanned the fires of sectionalism.

Buchanan and Kansas

Buchanan's administration also was confronted with the question of Kansas. The president chose Robert J. Walker of Mississippi as governor of the territory. Walker arrived to find the proslavery legislature would not submit its work to popular election, for its members knew that the majority of the voters were antislavery. Walker found only 200 slaves still in the territory—owners realized the institution was doomed there—and determined to bring Kansas into the Union as a free state. However, the proslavery faction rigged an election in June, 1857, at which a state constitutional convention was selected. This convened at Lecompton on October 19; by November 8 it had drafted a constitution guaranteeing the right to own slaves —and the delegates voted not to submit their work to popular ratification. Instead the people could vote only to accept the constitution with or without slavery; regardless of the vote, slaves already in Kansas would remain. Governor Reeder opposed the Lecompton Constitution, for he realized it did not represent popular opinion; this he knew because on October 5–6 an all-Kansas election had been held, with the free-soilers winning easily. The abolitionists subsequently gathered at Topeka and drafted a free-soil constitution, which also was sent to Congress.

With two constitutions before Congress, President Buchanan chose to support the Lecompton Constitution out of fear of Southern secession. He urged admission of Kansas under the proslavery document—whereupon Governor Reeder resigned in disgust. Buchanan's decision also angered Stephen A. Douglas because it violated popular sovereignty and thereby developed a growing split in the Democratic Party. The bill to admit Kansas under the Lecompton Constitution passed the Senate, but

James Buchanan

on April 1 failed in the House of Representatives. Representative William D. English of Indiana, a Democrat, proposed a compromise on April 23. The English Bill, as the measure was known, proposed admitting Kansas under the Lecompton Constitution, plus land grants to the new state, if Kansas' voters accepted the Lecompton Constitution. If the voters rejected the constitution, then Kansas would continue as a territory. Reject it the voters did, by the wide margin of 11,812 against to 1926 for. There the matter rested.

James Buchanan thus was not providing strong leadership at a time when the nation was badly divided along sectional lines. Talk of secession and civil war became common—just as economic hard times gripped the nation. The Panic of 1857 started that year, a short-lived but severe depression resulting from overspeculation in railroads and land, poor banking practices, and European wars. The misery generated by the panic caused a rising demand for free land in the West and for a high protective tariff, both of which the Republican Party had already espoused. Party leaders realized they could win in 1860, and the race for the Republican nomination began as early as 1858.

Douglas and Lincoln

An obscure race in the congressional election of 1858—the contest for a Senate seat from Illinois—brought to national attention the man whose name would be forever linked with events of the next few years—Abraham Lincoln. In a self-description written at the time, Lincoln stated, "It may be said I am, in height, six feet four inches, nearly; lean in flesh, weighing on an average of one hundred and eighty pounds; dark complexion, with coarse black hair and gray eyes. No other marks or brands recollected." At this time he was clean-shaven and, as later, quite gaunt. Born in Kentucky, he had lived for a time in Indiana before arriving in Illinois. There he somehow managed to gain an education and was admitted to the bar as a practicing attorney. Despite his lack of formal schooling, he had a remarkable command of the English language and had become well known locally. He was elected to the state legislature, and he served a term in Congress during the Mexican War; During the two years in Washington he had gained some fame for his "spot resolutions"—he wanted President Polk to show the exact spot where American blood had been shed on American soil. He was a Whig, then a Republican, and in 1858 that party had nominated him for the Illinois Senate seat—no real honor as the Democrat incumbent was one of the best-known politicians at the national level, Stephen A. Douglas, the "Little Giant" whose name was being prominently mentioned for the presidency in 1860.

On June 16, 1858, at the Republican convention in Springfield, Lincoln in his acceptance speech made his famous remark that "a house divided against itself cannot stand. I believe this government cannot endure permanently half slave and half free." Senator Douglas carefully studied this speech, which had received national attention, and used it to attack Lincoln. The Republican responded by challenging Douglas to debates in the seven districts where each man had not already spoken. Douglas accepted.

Between August 21 and October 15 came the Lincoln-Douglas debates, seven of them in all. The trend of each was approximately the same. Each man would try to pick flaws in the previous statements of the other in order to force some damaging statement from him. At Freeport, Lincoln asked Douglas: "Can the people of the

190

Abraham Lincoln

United States territory, in any lawful way, against the wish of any citizen of the United States, exclude slavery from its limits prior to the formation of a state constitution?" To answer this, Douglas either had to abandon popular sovereignty or else defy the *Dred Scott* decision. Douglas cleared Lincoln's trap with his "Freeport Doctrine"; he said that, regardless of Supreme Court decisions, the people of a territory could encourage or discourage slavery if they so chose, for slavery could not exist without certain essential police regulations that could be provided only by territorial legislation. By passing the necessary laws, that body could make the existence of slavery possible; by refusing, it could keep slavery out. The Freeport Doctrine satisfied Douglas' Illinois constituents, but it angered Southerners and further increased the split in the Democratic Party at the national level. In the election for the senate seat, Lincoln won the popular vote, but Douglas was elected by the state legislature. Yet newspapers in different sections of the nation had carried full accounts of the debates—debates that had reduced to concrete form many hazy notions about slavery, debates that showed the power of Lincoln's mind, debates that gave Lincoln national stature.

John Brown's Raid

A year later came an event further dividing the Democratic Party and further exposing the paucity of leadership in the Buchanan administration—John Brown's raid. A demented veteran of Bleeding Kansas who thought killing done in the name of abolitionism was righteousness for the Lord, John Brown conceived a scheme of attacking a federal arsenal and using the captured weapons to arm slaves, who, in turn, would kill their masters and win their freedom. Prominent Northern leaders—including ministers such as Dr. Thomas Wentworth Higginson—knew of this projected raid and provided Brown with the necessary funds and weapons to execute his plan. With eighteen dependable followers, Brown rented two houses on a farm in Maryland just four miles from Harper's Ferry, Virginia, a federal arsenal. The attack came on October 16, 1859. First, the abolitionists cut the telegraph wires to prevent word of their attack from spreading, then they seized the bridge over the Potomac, and finally they captured the arsenal. By midnight Brown was in full control and sending out parties with weapons to free slaves and arm them. This projected chain reaction of freeing slaves, arming them, and their growing revolt—until every slave was free and every slaveowner dead—failed when slaves refused to be armed or to kill their masters. By noon, October 17, a Monday, Brown and his remaining followers were besieged at Harper's Ferry. Army Colonel Robert E. Lee arrived that evening with a company of Marines, and the next morning Brown was captured. He was tried for conspiracy, murder, and treason, found guilty, and sentenced to the gallows.

Men from every political party, including Lincoln and Douglas, condemned Brown's raid. Yet Brown's bravery on the scaffold touched millions. As he stood there on December 2 at Charles Town, Virginia, he declared, "Now, if it is deemed necessary that I should forfeit my life for the furtherance of the ends of justice, and mingle my blood further with the blood of my children and the blood of millions in this slave country whose rights are disregarded by wicked, cruel, and unjust enactments, I say, let it be done." Six of his followers later met a similar fate. Ralph Waldo Emerson, a famous essayist, declared that Brown had made the "gallows glorious like the cross."

Interestingly, Brown's backers took no part in the general mourning among abolitionists and liberals over his death. They were busy fleeing. Some went to Canada. One, Gerritt Smith, had a nervous breakdown, but he thought to destroy all evidence of his participation before his collapse. A Senate investigating committee was appointed on December 14, 1859, to ascertain if the attack was the work of an organized group, and it worked until June, 1860. Yet it obviously did not wish to probe too deeply for fear of the effect on the nation; if it did prove a conspiracy, then it would confirm Southern charges to that effect. No federal grand jury proceedings ever were instituted, although the committee found enough documentary evidence to warrant them. Times definitely were extraordinary when clergymen, businessmen, and professional reformers could participate in murder and treason with complete impunity. Times were extraordinary when Emerson and Henry David Thoreau could proclaim a murderous monomaniac like John Brown an "angel of light" and made him a martyr whose deeds others were asked to emulate. Southerners knew of the conspiracy and reacted bitterly. A North Carolinian declared, "I have always been a fervid Union man, but I confess the endorsement of the Harper's Ferry outrage . . . has shaken my fidelity. . . . I am willing to take the chances of every probable evil that may arise from disunion, sooner than submit any longer to Northern insolence and Northern outrage."

The Election of 1860

Thus dawned the election year of 1860. Some Americans were thoughtfully reading Charles Darwin's *Origin of Species,* while others were absorbed by news of the visit by a delegation from Japan. But the big news was the sectional controversy. Jefferson Davis fired the first political salvo by introducing resolutions in the Senate on February 2. These "Davis Resolutions" stated that attacks on slavery violated the Constitution, that the national government was obliged to protect slavery in the territories, and that state laws interfering with the recovery of runaway slaves were unconstitutional. These resolutions triggered bitter debate about slavery until their passage on May 24. Lincoln, in a speaking tour, declared in his "Cooper Union Speech" at New York City on February 27 that moderation was needed, and he defended the Republican Party against charges of radicalism. Congressional Republicans pressed sectional economic legislation, however. They pushed a free-homestead bill through Congress by a sectional vote, only to have Buchanan veto it because of Southern pressure. On May 10 a Northern-backed tariff bill passed the House, intended to protect manufacturing but costly to Southerners. And in May Republicans pressed for a bill to fund a transcontinental railroad along the forty-first parallel.

Amidst such heated debate, the Democratic Party met in convention on April 23 at Charleston, South Carolina. Buchanan was discredited and unable to control the convention. Southern delegates wanted in the platform a proslavery plank that stated that no one—not Congress, not a territorial legislature—could abolish slavery or interfere with the American right to own slaves. In short, the South had abandoned popular sovereignty in favor of the *Dred Scott* decision. Northern delegates wanted Stephen A. Douglas nominated on a platform of popular sovereignty. The committee on resolutions had to choose between popular sovereignty and congressional protection for slavery; it chose the latter. But when the issue came before the convention as a whole, it voted for *Dred Scott*—and the party split. Delegate

193

Yancey of Alabama shouted, "The Democratic Party must take the position that slavery is right." Delegate Pugh of Ohio responded, "Gentleman of the South, you mistake us. We will not do it." The result was a deadlock in which no candidate could be nominated, and the delegates knew it. They adjourned to meet later.

On May 7 a group of former Whigs, Know-Nothings, and older politicians who looked with horror at the approach of civil war met at Baltimore to form the Constitutional Union Party. Their platform, they declared, was the Constitution, the Union of the states, and the enforcement of all laws. They nominated John Bell of Tennessee for president and Edward Everett of Massachusetts for vice president. Their hope was to win the border states and to awaken Union sentiment in the others.

The Republicans met in Chicago on May 16 with great enthusiasm. The splintering of the Democratic Party was a guarantee of almost certain victory for them. The preconvention favorite was William H. Seward of New York, but he had a reputation as a radical, and he was backed by the unsavory political boss, Thurlow Weed. After an all-night bargaining session, Lincoln's managers secured the support of delegates from Ohio and Pennsylvania, enough to give him the nomination, along with Hannibal Hamlin of Maine for the second spot on the ticket. The platform denounced John Brown's raid as the work of "border ruffians," but it denounced the Southern doctrine that Congress should protect slavery in the territories; as an alternative, it asserted that there should be no further extension of slavery. It also called for continuance of the Union, yet stated that states' rights should be upheld. On economic issues, it stated that Republicans stood for a high tariff, a homestead law to provide free land, and federal aid for a railroad to the Pacific, and it called for admitting Kansas to statehood. Yet it emphatically declared that each state should "control its own domestic institutions," a provision clearly aimed at appeasing Southerners.

When the Democrats reconvened, it was in Baltimore on June 13, with Northerners clearly in the majority. Southern delegates promptly walked out, whereupon the Northern wing of the party nominated Stephen A. Douglas for president and Herschel V. Johnson of Georgia for vice president. The platform promised that the Dred Scott decision would be upheld. Southern Democrats subsequently met on June 28, also in Baltimore, and nominated John C. Breckinridge of Kentucky and Joseph Lane of Oregon to head their ticket. Every ballot for Breckinridge seemed a vote for Southern rights and Southern independence. The platform called for equal rights for slaveowners to settle in the territories and for a lowering of the tariff.

In this four-way race a totally sectional candidate won the presidency. Lincoln had 1,866,452 popular votes, Douglas 1,376,781, Breckinridge 847,953, and Bell 590,631. But in the electoral college Lincoln received 180 votes, Breckinridge 72, Bell 39, and Douglas 12. Douglas had carried only Missouri and half of New Jersey. Breckinridge carried all of Dixie, along with Delaware and Maryland; Bell received the vote of the three border states of Tennessee, Kentucky, and Virginia. Lincoln, who got not a single recorded vote in ten Southern states, carried the Northeast, the Northwest, and the Far West; thereby he became a minority president with 39.87 percent of the popular vote, and he had antiadministration majorities in both houses of Congress. For the first time in American history, the president represented a truly sectional party—and for the first time in American history the democratic process broke down. Southerners believed the election of Lincoln was a deathblow to Southern prestige and to the Southern way of life. As the governor of South Carolina phrased it, the election of Lincoln would "inevitably destroy our equality in the Union, and ultimately reduce the Southern states to mere provinces of a consolidated despotism, to be governed by a fixed majority in Congress hostile to our institutions and fatally bent on ruin." A Republican victory meant to the South more runaway slaves, more raids by men like John Brown, more aggressive abolitionists. Many arguments were advanced to support such fears—some constitutional, some economic, some strategic, some sociological—but in reality the Southern reaction to Lincoln's election was the result of fear, anger, and hysteria.

Alexander Stephens of Georgia clearly stated the folly of secession, even for the purpose of protecting slavery. He pointed out that Southerners and Democrats controlled both houses of Congress, at least until 1863. Lincoln could do nothing without congressional consent; he might outlaw slavery in the territories, but with secession the territories would be lost to the South. Stephens said that Northern states might not be enforcing the Fugitive Slave Law, but with secession it would become a dead letter. Abolitionists might not be pleasant fellow countrymen, he said, but an international boundary would not stop their propaganda. Republicans had promised no interference with slavery in Southern states and, according to Lincoln, stood ready to show their sincerity by a constitutional amendment to that effect. And, he said, the only way the slaves could be freed in unwilling states was by constitutional amendment or by act of war; in 1861 the first way was impossible because there were sufficient slave states to block a constitutional amendment, while the second method was courted by secession.

Southerners did not want cold reason in their beds, however. They reacted emotionally. They believed they could survive in happier fashion as an independent nation than as part of the United States. They believed that world demand for cotton would save them. (In reality, the world supply of raw and manufactured cotton had exceeded demand; Europe was far more interested in wheat than in cotton.) Southerners also felt they had historical precedent on their side. The doctrine of seccession had long been honored in theory and in practice. The United States had begun by seceding from England. Vermont had seceded from New York. And Northerners had threatened secession during the War of 1812, as South Carolina had threatened during the nullification controversy. Nowhere had the doctrine of secession been specifically repudiated, while the doctrine of states' rights was widely held and generally popular in all the United States.

On December 20, 1860, South Carolina led the way for the South. A convention at Columbia formally repealed the state's ratification of the Constitution by a unanimous vote; a "Declaration of Causes" listed repeated Northern attacks on slavery and the victory of the sectional Republican Party. By February 1, 1861, six other states had followed: Georgia, Florida, Alabama, Mississippi, Louisiana, and Texas. In the Lone Star State, Governor Sam Houston steadfastly opposed secession and managed to force a popular vote on the issue—the only Southern state where the people voted on it. Texans overwhelmingly approved secession, whereupon Houston refused Lincoln's offer of troops to hold him in office. He also refused to take the oath of secession and was forced from office. To an audience at Galveston he sadly commented, "You may, after the sacrifice of countless thousands of treasure and hundreds of thousands of precious lives, as a bare possibility, win Southern independence, if God be not against you; but I doubt it." He was right—but it would be billions of dollars and more than a million lives later that the proof came.

On February 4 delegates from six Southern states (Texans were absent) met at Montgomery, Alabama, and there organized a Confederate government. Four days later they published a provisional constitution, followed on March 11 by the permanent constitution of the South; this constitution was never submitted to popular vote. These delegates also adopted a flag, the "Stars and Bars," and they elected Jefferson Davis their president and Alexander Stephens their vice president. Davis was a graduate of West Point, a veteran of the Mexican War, and had served in both houses of Congress, as well as in the cabinet (secretary of war) of Franklin Pierce.

Attempts at Compromise

There were last-minute attempts at compromise to avoid a civil war. President James Buchanan declared that secession was unconstitutional, but he argued that he and Congress had no authority to prevent it. He urged compromise—but on Southern terms. When Southerners began seizing federal property in the South, such as forts and arsenals, Buchanan chose to ignore such moves. He would let the Union crumble rather than use force. Lincoln, meanwhile, had no constitutional authority until he was inaugurated. Both law and custom forbade his interfering. Buchanan lacked the imagination to put forward a plan to forestall secession, but others did not. On December 18, 1860, two days before South Carolina left the Union, Senator John J. Crittenden of Kentucky proposed a plan that bore his name; he suggested that slavery be banned in all territory north of thirty-six degrees thirty minutes north latitude, that slavery be maintained by federal protection south of that line, that future states enter the Union as free or slave as they voted at the time of entry, that Congress agree not to abolish slavery in any area under its jurisdiction where that area was surrounded by slave territory (as, for example, in the District of Columbia), that the Fugitive Slave Law be enforced, that where the law was not enforced the federal government compensate the slaveowner, that Congress earnestly recommend the repeal of all state laws designed to aid fugitive slaves, and that no further constitutional amendments ever be made that would allow Congress to touch slavery in any state.

The Crittenden Plan was introduced in Congress, but extremists on both sides refused to accept compromise. The old, great leaders in Congress of the previous half century—Clay, Calhoun, Webster—were gone; the new leaders were extremists determined to prevail or destroy. Lincoln was approached by Republicans in Congress for advice about the Crittenden Plan. He replied that the plan was inconsistent with Republican principles of no advance of slavery in the territories and therefore they should not support it. The resolution failed passage.

On February 4, 1861, the same day that delegates were meeting at Montgomery to form the Confederacy, a convention gathered in Washington. Called by the torn state of Virginia, the peace convention was attended by delegates from twenty-one states, both free and slave, but no one had the potential of leadership to save the Union. The proposals made there were similar to those in the Crittenden resolution —and failed for much the same reasons. This peace commission proposed constitutional amendments to allay Southern fears, but the amendments were rejected in the Senate.

Secession

Lincoln arrived secretly in Washington on February 23, afraid of an assassination plot. On March 4 he was inaugurated president. In his inaugural address, he stated that he had no intention of interfering with the institution of slavery in those states

196

where it existed, but he did insist upon preserving the Union by denying the right of secession. The main thrust of the speech was conciliatory, however: "We are not enemies, but friends. We must not be enemies. Though passion may have strained, it must not break our bonds of affection." He proceeded to name his cabinet—William H. Seward as secretary of state, Salmon P. Chase as secretary of the treasury, and Gideon Welles as secretary of the navy were the only illustrious names in it— and to wait for the South to indicate what the future held. That indication came at Fort Sumter, South Carolina, in the harbor at Charleston. It was one of the few remaining federal posts in the South still in Union hands when Lincoln was inaugurated. Southerners announced their intention to take it. Lincoln's cabinet, including Seward, its most influential member, recommended that it be surrendered. At 4:30 A.M. on April 12, General Pierre G. T. Beauregard ordered Southern batteries to open fire, impatient for Lincoln to act. Thirty-four hours later the post surrendered. Remarkably not a man had been killed.

The response to Sumter was dramatic. Virginia, Tennessee, North Carolina, and Arkansas seceded to join the Confederacy, bringing the number of its states to eleven. The western part of Virginia refused to accept this action, however, and on June 11 it organized a Union government that would bring it separate statehood as West Virginia on June 20, 1863. On April 15 Lincoln called for 75,000 volunteers to suppress the rebellion, and he took forceful steps to hold Missouri, Kentucky, Maryland, and Delaware in the Union despite their being slave states. On May 8 the Confederate Congress voted to move the Southern capital from Montgomery to Richmond, and it authorized President Davis to raise 400,000 volunteers for Southern defense. The war had begun, a war that would claim lives, destroy property, and create problems as intractable as those it solved.

North and South in 1861

The war pitted a loose agrarian confederacy of eleven states with a population of about 9 million (including 3.7 million slaves) against twenty-three states with a population of 22,700,000. The North had 110,000 manufacturing establishments as compared with the South's 18,000. Northerners likewise had more capital resources; they retained the regular Army, most of which stayed loyal; they had $2,270,000 worth of firearms to Southerners' $73,000; and they enjoyed numerous other advantages. Yet the War Department had no plans for conducting the conflict, for it largely was in incompetent hands. Winfield Scott, the commanding general of the Army, was a brilliant tactician and commanded the respect of his junior officers to such an extent that many of his former subordinates, such as Robert E. Lee, probably would not have fought against him. Yet Scott was seventy-five years old, and Lincoln refused his advice (although later in the war he would return to it).

Southerners were beginning their experiment under severe disadvantages. Yet, apart from slavery, they were fighting for those things men hold most dear, liberty, self-government, and home, while Northerners had little more than the abstract concept of the Union to fight for. To win, the South had only to hold its own territory until Northerners grew weary of the fight. For Northerners to win, its sons had to conquer the South and crush its spirit. A negotiated peace settlement of any sort would be a Southern victory, for anything less than unconditional surrender would result in special privilege for the South. As Lincoln sought a replacement for General Scott, he personally evolved Northern strategy: to blockade Southern ports from

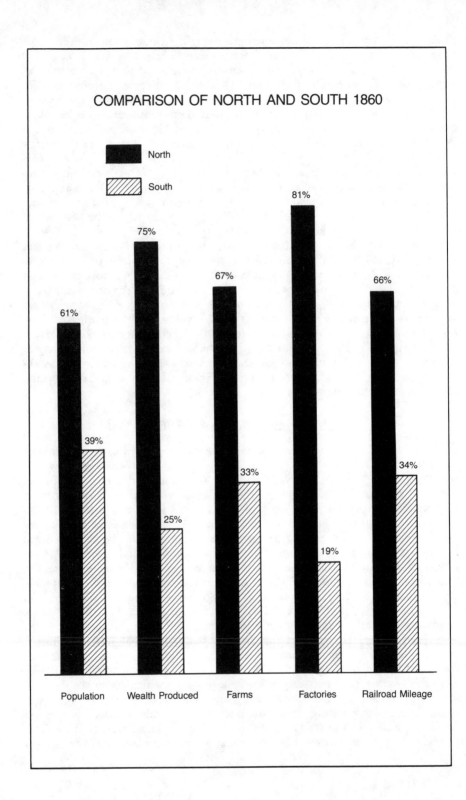

COMPARISON OF NORTH AND SOUTH 1860

North

South

the Chesapeake to the Rio Grande, to capture the principal Southern port cities, to seize Richmond, and to divide the South through capture of the Mississippi, Red, and Tennessee rivers. The blockade was intended to prevent the Confederacy from procuring the manufactured goods it so desperately needed, while the divide-and-conquer tactic would allow Northern strength to overcome resistance piecemeal. Southern strategy, largely determined by Jefferson Davis, was to capture Washington, move into central Pennsylvania, and force Union recognition of Southern independence.

Battles and Leaders

On July 21, 1861, came the first real test of arms, the Battle of First Manassas (Bull Run). General Scott sent General Irvin McDowell and 30,000 troops against 31,000 Confederates commanded by Beauregard and General Joseph E. Johnston; Scott sent his men into Virginia at the president's orders and contrary to his own advice. They clashed at Manassas Junction. By 3:00 P.M. it seemed that McDowell had won a brilliant victory, but Jackson made a heroic stand (which gave him his nickname "Stonewall") and turned the battle for the South. The Union troops broke and ran in disgraceful flight, stampeding the thousands of spectators from Washington who had journeyed down to see the "victory." Some of McDowell's troops did not stop running until they reached New York and even Maine. Stonewall Jackson asked Jefferson Davis for 10,000 men, stating that with them "I will be in Washington tomorrow." He likely would have been, but Davis had determined upon a defensive posture and refused the troops—thereby losing the Southern chance for a quick victory.

If there were thoughts of a quick end to the war in the North, the Battle of First Manassas ended them. On July 26 Lincoln replaced McDowell with General George B. McClellan, then just thirty-four years old. And on November 1, when Scott retired at his own request, McClellan became commanding general of the Army. Yet McClellan was too slow and cautious to be a good soldier, and too vainglorious to be a good tactician. He was good at training the raw recruits that Lincoln's call for volunteers produced, however, and he proceeded to mold the Army of the Potomac into an effective force.

By January, 1862, Republican leaders in Congress were demanding more than recruit training, however; they wanted action. On every front the war was going badly for the United States. Confederate forces from Texas, under command of Lieutenant Colonel John Robert Baylor, had captured the southern half of the Territory of New Mexico; called Arizona, this region was officially admitted as a territory of the Confederacy on February 14, 1862. And a Southern force under command of Brigadier General Henry Hopkins Sibley was marching into New Mexico to conquer the rest of it for the Confederacy. On the diplomatic front, England was wavering toward diplomatic recognition of the South, while the rest of Europe waited to take its cue from the British. In disgust, congressmen pressured Lincoln for a war to the finish.

On January 27 the president acceded to congressional demands for action by issuing his General Order No. 1 in which he called for "a general movement of the land and naval forces of the United States against the insurgent forces" to begin on February 22; Lincoln was committing himself to full-scale war. But McClellan was hesitant. He boasted that he would be in Richmond, the Confederate capital, by

Washington's birthday, but he made no move until March 17, when he began the Peninsula Campaign. With 130,000 men, he went down the Potomac to the peninsula between the York and James rivers; this was done to avoid the marshes between Washington and Richmond. McClellan advanced cautiously, but by May 21 he had his troops along the Chickahominy River—in places only seven miles from Richmond. General Joseph E. Johnston counterattacked at Seven Pines on May 31 and at Fair Oaks Station on June 1, inflicting great casualties on McClellan and causing him to decide to wait for reinforcements before assaulting Richmond. Meanwhile, Stonewall Jackson was making a brilliant maneuver up the Shenandoah Valley, a diversionary tactic between March 23 and June 9 that forced 54,000 Union troops to move to protect Washington—while Jackson returned to Richmond to unite with Robert E. Lee, who on June 1 had become commander of the Confederate Army of Northern Virginia.

Lee then moved his troops to attack McClellan's force in what became known as the Seven Days' Battle. Between June 26 and July 2, Lee forced McClellan to retreat to Harrison's Landing. Lincoln visited McClellan there and vetoed McClellan's suggestion that the Richmond campaign be renewed; the president ordered the troops back to Washington, named Henry W. Halleck general-in-chief of the Union Army, and all returned to the federal capital. The Peninsula Campaign was ended.

McClellan's blunders in Virginia were offset somewhat by Union victories elsewhere. In 1862 New Mexico and Arizona were cleared of the Confederate troops commanded by Sibley and Baylor through the efforts of volunteers from California and Colorado, while Missouri and Kansas were forcibly prevented from seceding and brought under nominal Union control. John C. Frémont was sent to St. Louis to command the Western Department, but his disastrous policies caused his removal in November, 1861; his replacement proved more adept, although he was unable to prevent guerrilla bands from roaming the countryside.

The most heartening victories in 1862 came at sea, however, for there federal arms totally prevailed. The blockade of Confederate ports was tightening to almost total Union control. Southerners, desperately in want of arms, munitions, medical supplies, food, clothing, and even the most common items, attempted to break the blockade. Confederate engineers transformed the wrecked frigate *Merrimac* into an iron-plated monster they called the *Virginia;* it was unable to operate on the high seas but in the calm waters off Hampton Roads, Virginia, it could engage the Union ships on blockade duty. On March 8 the *Virginia* sank the wooden *Cumberland* and burned the *Congress.* The next day, when it came out to attack the *Minnesota,* it met a Union counterpart, an ironclad "cheese-box on a raft" named the *Monitor,* the brainchild of Swedish inventor John Ericson. They fought an indecisive five-hour battle that saw both ships retreat; the *Monitor* was swamped in high seas on its way to port, while the *Virginia* was forced to withdraw for repairs and was burned on May 10 to keep it out of federal hands.

And in April, 1862, federal forces captured New Orleans, thanks to the Navy. Twenty-seven vessels under the command of Captain David Farragut, with an army of 15,000 men under General Benjamin F. Butler, sailed up the Mississippi to the Crescent City. After a bombardment that saw city fathers unwilling to surrender—indeed, setting fire to everything that might help the federals—the troops came ashore on May 1 to take control. New Orleans remained in federal hands throughout the rest of the war, a severe loss to the Confederacy.

Meanwhile, other engagements were tightening the Union hold on the entire Mississippi. Confederate General Leonidas Polk had seized the river terminals of the Mobile and Ohio Railroad at Columbus, Kentucky, at the outbreak of the war and had established Forts Henry and Donelson to protect this strategic stance. In the spring of 1862 Union General John Pope drove the rebels from southeastern Missouri in the vicinity of New Madrid on March 13. Then on April 17 he took the heavily fortified Island No. 10 in the Mississippi, thereby opening the river all the way to Memphis for the Union forces. At Cairo, Illinois, was General Ulysses S. Grant, to whom on February 1, 1862, came Halleck's permission to attack Forts Henry and Donelson. Grant had his troops moving the next day, and on February 6 was in command of Fort Henry. Nine days later his men faced Fort Donelson, expecting a long siege. Contrary to Union expectations, however, the Confederates stormed out to attack and almost won. Grant staved off the defeat, and on February 16 that fort also surrendered.

Grant pressed his advantage, although briefly relieved of command in March by Halleck. When he resumed command on March 17, he found most of his men at Pittsburgh Landing on the Tennessee River (just opposite Corinth, Mississippi, on Tennessee's southern boundary). Confederate Albert Sidney Johnston attacked Grant's position on April 6. There followed the Battle of Shiloh, during which Johnston was killed. Grant might have won a decisive engagement had General Halleck not arrived to take personal command; he procrastinated until the Confederates withdrew, their army still intact. The Battle of Shiloh might have been indecisive, but Grant was emerging as one of the few Union generals willing to take responsibility.

In the late summer of 1862 the Confederates regained the initiative they had lost at sea and in the West. Halleck, now the commanding general of the Army, sent General John Pope, a rash, boastful incompetent, with 75,000 men to invade Virginia. As he neared Gordonsville, he met Stonewall Jackson and a Confederate army that defeated him and sent him retreating toward Manassas. There on August 29–30 Lee and Jackson fought Pope in the Battle of Second Manassas, inflicting severe defeat on the out-generaled Pope. Following up this advantage, Lee and Jackson entered Maryland, only to come into contact with Pope's successor, General McClellan, to whom Lincoln had turned in his desperate search for a fighting general. The two forces met on September 17 on the hills near Antietam Creek (close to Sharpsburg, Maryland). The battle was a draw in that neither side won a clear victory—but Lee was forced to withdraw into Virginia. This battle confirmed British opinion that the South could never win, and thereafter they gave scant support to the Confederacy.

Just as Lee was turned back from his attempt on Maryland, so also were other Confederate thrusts unsuccessful. General Van Dorn led troops against the federal forces in the Memphis-Corinth region, but accomplished nothing of importance. Likewise, Braxton Bragg and Kirby Smith, who sallied into Kentucky with a Confederate army to win that state, reached to within a few miles of Cincinnati but then were forced out. Neither North nor South could gain an advantage—but the South could only lose in a war of attrition.

Politicians on both sides preached the necessity of sacrifice. Levies of men followed earlier levies, with both Union and Confederacy relying on conscription laws. Both had to suspend the writ of habeas corpus to stifle dissent. Ironically, the war being fought to preserve freedom (as both sides declared they were doing) resulted in less freedom. Both sides suffered in other ways, but especially was there hardship in the South. Both printed inflationary paper money that was not backed up by specie and thus deteriorated in value, yet it was Southerners who found themselves short of food and medicine, with coffee and other near-essentials nonexistent.

Another measure was being readied that would sorely hurt the South. Lincoln was gradually yielding to pressures to deprive Southerners of property valued at between two and four billion dollars—their slaves. Congress was moving rapidly in that direction, and the president was forced to follow. On August 6, 1861, Congress had passed a Confiscation Act, stating that all slaves working or fighting with the Confederate Army were free. Then on April 16, 1862, Congress had abolished slavery in the District of Columbia, with compensation to owners averaging $300 per slave. Next, on June 19, came uncompensated abolition of slavery in the territories. Lincoln decided to join this movement and used the occasion of the Battle of Antietam, a partial federal victory, to promulgate his preliminary Emancipation Proclamation. Dated September 22, but officially in effect on January 1, 1863, it stipulated that slaves in the areas still in rebellion were free. This was a war measure, one hopefully that would cause insurrections in the South.

In another move of more direct consequence for the prosecution of the war, Lincoln, on November 5, 1862, removed McClellan for his hesitancy in battle and replaced him with General Ambrose E. Burnside. With 125,000 men, Burnside invaded Virginia, bent on reaching Richmond by way of Fredericksburg. Lee had anticipated the move and had his men spend a month fortifying the heights around the latter. Six times Burnside sent his force storming up the hills against Lee's 70,000 men. Federal losses mounted to 13,000, while Lee lost 5000. The federals thereupon recrossed the Rappahannock and withdrew. On January 25, 1863, Lincoln replaced Burnside with General Joseph Hooker.

"Fighting Joe" Hooker started the Army of the Potomac in Virginia in the spring of 1863, declaring, ". . . may God have mercy on General Lee, for I will have none." Hooker knew he could not take Fredericksburg by frontal assault and so tried to encircle Lee and attack from the rear. The result, on May 2–4, was the Battle of Chancellorsville. Lee split his troops, with his men striking the center of Hooker's force while Stonewall Jackson and his men attacked Hooker's right flank. Hooker lost heart and, instead of counterattacking while the Confederates were divided, decided to withdraw toward Washington. Yet the victory for the South was a costly one—17,000 men dead, including Stonewall Jackson. Lee decided on a desperate gamble as a result of the Battle of Chancellorsville. The South, he saw, would lose a war of attrition. Therefore he believed the only way to victory was a strike northward, a dash into Pennsylvania, even Ohio, demoralizing Northerners into recognition of the Confederacy or at least negotiating a settlement. Jefferson Davis would allow him no more men than he already had, and on June 23 he started up the Shenandoah Valley toward Pennsylvania. Five days later Lincoln replaced Hooker with General George G. Meade, who led troops north after Lee and took a position at Frederick, Maryland.

The two armies met by accident on June 20 at Gettysburg, Pennsylvania, where the fight began on July 1 and lasted three days. The Confederates drove the Union troops back to high ground at Cemetery Hill and Culp's Hill, taking up facing positions on Seminary Ridge. On the final day came a suicidal charge into Union lines in an attempt by the Southerners to take the high ground. General James Longstreet sent the divisions of Pickett, Pettigrew, and Trimble toward the center of the Union lines, only to have them slaughtered. Meade thereupon called a council of war, despite a telegram from Halleck (at Lincoln's insistence) that said, "Call no council of war." While the Union officers talked, Lee withdrew his army in orderly fashion. Lincoln later declared in sorrow, "Our army held the war in the hollow of its hand and let it escape." Had Meade been decisive, the war might have ended at Gettysburg.

Almost simultaneously in the West, Union troops were gaining other momentous victories. "The Gibraltar of the Mississippi," Vicksburg, fell into Union hands after a lengthy siege. Vicksburg was on a ridge of high bluffs overlooking the river, protected by long stretches of marshy land to the north. Grant had tried various schemes to get near the city but had failed. He had by-passed it to take Jackson, Mississippi, on May 14; then he returned to take possession of the heights on the river north of Vicksburg. Unable to take it by storm, he laid siege to the city and starved it into surrender on July 4. With Vicksburg gone, the South had to yield Port Hudson on July 9—and the Mississippi was entirely in Union hands, separating Texas, Louisiana, and Arkansas from the rest of the Confederacy.

One other Confederate force, commanded by General Braxton Bragg, was operating in Tennessee and endangering Union control of that region. In June, 1863, after months of delay, General William Rosecrans left Murfreesboro to pursue Bragg. On September 19–20 the two met at the Battle of Chickamauga. Bragg's troops broke through Rosecrans' lines and would have won an overwhelming victory had General George H. Thomas not held, earning for himself the nickname "The Rock of Chickamauga." Bragg next drove Rosecrans back into Chattanooga, whereupon Grant took command of the West, brought up reinforcements, and defeated Bragg at Lookout Mountain on November 24 and at Missionary Ridge the next day. Bragg thus was forced out of Tennessee into Georgia, where William Tecumseh Sherman would pursue him in 1864. Grant had made such a reputation for himself in the West that Lincoln was willing to give him a chance as commander, not only in the East but as commanding general of the Army. Certainly he could fare no worse than had his predecessors in that position. He assumed command on March 9.

A nonbraggart—in contrast to the men who preceded him—a shabby dresser, shy, quiet—Grant seemed hardly a general at all. He had served in the Army prior to the war, but had resigned in the mid-1850s to farm. Yet once in command, he moved vigorously to pursue his tactic: "Find out where your enemy is. Get him as soon as you can. Strike at him as hard as you can and keep moving." In May he sent General Sherman marching from Tennessee into Georgia bound for the Atlantic, thereby further dividing the South. Between May and December, Sherman carried out those orders. By July, after eight weeks of relentless pushing, he had forced the Confederates across the Chattahoochee River, and on September 2 he was in Atlanta. Continuing eastward, he pursued a "scorched earth" policy in his march to the sea, destroying everything along a sixty-mile front. By the time he reached the coast on December 13, he and his men had done an estimated one billion dollars in damage—and more than that in Southern morale.

Sherman's march did much to reelect Lincoln in 1864. The Republican Party gathered that year on June 7 in Baltimore to nominate Lincoln for president and Andrew Johnson of Tennessee for vice president on what was called a Union ticket. The Democrats gathered on August 29 to nominate General George B. McClellan and George H. Pendleton of Ohio as their ticket. Their platform called for an

Bureau of Printing and Engraving

Ulysses S. Grant

immediate end to the war. McClellan in his speeches repudiated the peace plank, thus trying to appeal to both supporters and opponents of the war. Lincoln, meanwhile, anticipated a close vote and so hurried Nevada into the Union to secure three more Republican electoral votes. Sherman's victory at Atlanta greatly aided Lincoln, however, and he did not need the three votes Nevada gave him. Lincoln was reelected with 2,206,938 popular votes and 212 electoral votes to McClellan's 1,803,787 popular votes and 21 electoral votes.

It was well that Sherman won at Atlanta, for Grant was not faring so well against Lee in Virginia. The Wilderness Campaign began early in May, 1864, as Grant led his Army of the Potomac across the Rapidan. On May 5-6 the Union force of 100,000 men met Lee's army halfway through a heavy forest near Chancellorsville. The two-way battle resulted in a draw—but Grant kept advancing. On May 10 the armies met again at Spotsylvania Court House. Again there was heavy fighting and heavy losses, and again Lee withdrew—to be followed by Grant. On June 1-3 Grant attacked Lee's entrenched forces at Cold Harbor in suicidal assaults. This battle, like those that preceded it, ended indecisively. By this time Grant had suffered an incredible 55,000 casualties, and Northern newspapers were calling him "the butcher."

Grant next moved south of Richmond to Petersburg, which he took on June 15-18 at the cost of 8000 more men. There he settled down to besiege Richmond, to starve it out, for it now was cut off from the South. Nine months later the seige was still underway. Lee tried a diversionary invasion of the North to lift the siege. General Jubal Early was sent down the Shenandoah Valley toward Washington and entered Maryland, getting as far as Chambersburg, Pennsylvania. However, he was stopped by General Philip Sheridan on October 19 at the Battle of Cedar Creek and forced back into Virginia.

By early 1865 the end was in sight for the South. In February, Sherman began moving north from Georgia into the Carolinas, devastating the countryside, while Grant held tenaciously to his position near Richmond. Lee attempted to maneuver southward to link up with Confederate troops in North Carolina, but his path was sealed before him by April 7. On April 9 the two great commanders met at Appomattox Court House, Virginia, and Lee surrendered. Grant proved as generous in peace as he had been inexorable in war. Southern troops were allowed to keep their horses and mules for plowing, while officers were allowed to retain their sidearms. Soon afterward, other Southern commands likewise surrendered, and the long, cruel war came to an end. Jefferson Davis was pursued to Georgia where he was captured on May 10, to be imprisoned at Fort Monroe, Virginia, for two years.

Diplomacy During the War

The one way the Confederacy might have won its fight for independence was not on the battlefield but on the diplomatic front—and there it was quite unsuccessful. The Union blockade isolated the South to such an extent that its agents largely were prevented from accomplishing their missions. Yet the blockade did tacitly tender Union recognition that the South was in a state of belligerency, although Lincoln steadfastly refused to recognize the existence of the Confederacy. Secretary of State William Seward, who for some two months after assuming office had difficulty recognizing that he was not president, suggested that Lincoln send notes to England, France, Spain, Russia, and other European powers, stating that those powers were not to interfere in what was totally an American affair.

In England the upper classes favored the South because of Southern aristocratic tendencies; the middle and lower classes detested slavery, although they had little love for the North. The British attitude was important to the United States, for the rest of Europe took its ideas about America from England. Lord Palmerston, the prime minister, suggested a state of neutrality, which Queen Victoria proclaimed on May 13, 1861. This British proclamation of neutrality recognized Confederate belligerency but not Southern independence. Fortunately for the United States, England moved quickly on this; had the British waited until the summer, when the Confederates won the Battle of First Manassas, they might well have recognized the South. That England refused to interfere in the imbroglio was largely a credit to Charles Francis Adams, the Union's minister to Great Britain. Adams had ability, was clear-headed, even-tempered, and an excellent diplomat.

Jefferson Davis recognized the advantage to the South if it could secure diplomatic recognition from England, and he sent two agents, James M. Mason and John Slidell, as commissioners to that country. They went to Havana, where they took passage aboard the British mail steamer *Trent*. On November 8, 1861, the American warship *San Jacinto* stopped the *Trent*, American sailors and Marines boarded the English vessel, and Mason and Slidell were removed. News of the *Trent* affair caused wild rejoicing among Northerners, but Britishers considered it an insult to their flag, a seizure in violation of international law. British officials demanded the release of Mason and Slidell, with a "suitable apology for the aggression." Secretary of State Seward, fearing war with England, announced on December 26 that the American naval captain had acted without orders, that Mason and Slidell were being released, and that they would be allowed to continue to England.

Another source of friction between the United States and England was the building of Confederate warships in British shipyards. Several raiders were constructed in England, equipped for war in British ports, and sailed from England to attack American shipping. The *Florida*, the *Shenandoah*, and the *Alabama* were among these vessels, with the *Alabama* inflicting considerable damage on the American Navy during the course of its career at sea. Adams protested so vehemently that British officials ordered a halt to such practices; especially did the British change their attitude toward Southerners after the Union victory at Antietam and the issuance of the Emancipation Proclamation. Thereafter British policy was definitely pro-Union.

Without foreign aid, Southern independence was doomed. Southerners fought gallantly, but without the manufacturing capacity to sustain their soldiers they could only meet defeat through attrition. The war thus drew to a close in the spring of 1865.. Casualties—North and South combined—totaled a staggering one million men, almost 40 percent of the men under arms. The Union had been tried and sustained, but at a heavy price in blood and treasure.

Chapter Nine

A Restructured Republic

Results of the War

REUNIFICATION of the Union saw the South changed by the victorious North, but in the process the North also evolved into something different than it had been before the war. What emerged was a new nation. The North during the Civil War had sacrificed much; it had gone deeply into debt, had surrendered many traditional American freedoms, and had seen its young men killed and wounded. The only tangible product of this sacrifice was Southern acceptance of the fact that the Union was indissoluble, that slavery was ended, and that the old Southern leadership in national politics was terminated. To many Northerners, however, these attainments were insufficient. Especially were these insufficient to Northerners who realized that each point proven had merely raised still more problems: the Union had been preserved but with frightful tensions within it; the Negro had been freed but his new status had not been defined; and Southern leadership at the national level was ended, but who would take its place in the South? During the war, Northern ministers had urged and preached that God was on the Union side. If the South had sinned—and sinned knowingly—then it had to be punished.

The South in 1865

In the South there was resentment. Southerners had lost the war, and they resented the implied inferiority of losers. They also thought God was on their side in the recent conflict; therefore, they concluded that might—not right—had triumphed. It was easier to admit Northern strength than Northern rightness. Southerners had no enthusiasm for submission to Northern-dictated reconstruction, but they had no choice. Therefore they turned to rebuilding their region, but they did so with resignation, frustration, and hatred. Fannie Downing summed up the Southern attitude in a widely circulated poem entitled "Dixie":

> To die for Dixie!—Oh, how blest
> Are those who early went to rest,
> Nor knew the future's awful store,
> But deemed the cause they fought for sure

As heaven itself, and so laid down
The cross of earth for glory's crown.
And nobly died for Dixie.
To live for Dixie—harder part!

Indeed it did seem that to live was harder than dying for Southerners in the immediate months following the end of hostilities. Out of a population of some six million whites, a quarter of a million were dead. Many of those who did return were wounded. Mississippi in 1866, for example, spent 20 percent of its revenue for artificial limbs. At home, those who returned found neighbors missing, property destroyed, the labor system disorganized, and people suffering from want of necessities; the land was devastated, the banks had failed, factories had been destroyed by federal raiders, and public buildings had been destroyed or confiscated by a horde of Yankee officials. There was no money and little livestock; the roads were impassable; and public transportation was almost nonexistent. Rebuilding was hampered by federal regulations. The Treasury Department was busy confiscating all property of the Confederate government, which proved but an excuse for many dishonest agents to condemn anything of value for the 25 percent commission they received. Secretary of the Treasury Hugh McCulloch commented of these agents, "I am sure I sent some honest agents south; but it sometimes seems doubtful whether any of them remained honest very long." In Savannah, Georgia, alone, the government received only $8 million of the $21 million in cotton that such agents confiscated. And, finally, Southerners had lost their capital investments, $100 million in insurance and twice that amount in bank capital; the greatest single loss was the slaves. Real estate values dropped to a tenth of their prewar worth, and many homes and farms fell before the auctioneer's hammer because the owners could not pay the taxes. Southerners had good cause for despair.

Then things grew worse. The recently freed slaves interpreted freedom to mean they no longer had to work; morals, manners, and restraints on actions were associated with slavery and abandoned with the Emancipation Proclamation. Mostly illiterate and totally unprepared for their new status, the freedmen roamed the countryside waiting to be told what to do. Thousands of them died of starvation, exposure, and disease in the spring and summer of 1865. Swindlers, mostly Northerners, reaped rich rewards from their ignorance, selling them worthless finery, skin bleaches, hair straighteners, and striped pegs to mark off the forty acres of land that false rumor held the freedmen would be given on January 1, 1866.

On March 3, 1865, Congress passed legislation establishing the Freedman's Bureau to care for the exslaves. Under the direction of General Oliver O. Howard, this organization saved thousands of lives by providing free food, shelter, and medical attention, while its schools taught thousands to read and write. Southerners countered that what the Negro needed was to return to work; to Howard and his staff, such talk seemed an intention to reestablish slavery. Thus the bureau insisted on written contracts between employers and freedmen. But the Negroes were suspicious of contracts and largely refused to sign them. As a result, Southern whites began to turn against the freedmen. Before the war it had been a sign of being "trash" to mistreat Negroes; after the arrival of the bureau, mistreatment of Negroes was regarded as a test of Southern manhood. Then came January 1, 1866, with no distribution of forty acres and a mule to the freedmen; most of them then returned to work under contract, and it seemed that the Southern economy would begin functioning again. The next step was restoring the government of the Southern states to something approaching normal.

208

Lincoln's Plan of Reconstruction

The philosophy of political reconstruction was hard-fought at the national level. As president during the war, Lincoln had held that secession was illegal; therefore no state, technically, had ever left the Union. According to Lincoln, the Southern states were temporarily out of harmony with the national government, but still part of it. His philosophy of reconstruction was based on this premise. He issued his plan of reconstruction on December 8, 1863. Called the "Ten Percent Plan," it was promulgated by presidential proclamation. Under it, all high military and civil officers of the Confederacy were excluded from participation in the new governments; all other Southerners would be restored to citizenship by taking an oath of loyalty to the Constitution and swearing to abide by "all acts of Congress passed during the existing rebellion with references to slaves . . . and faithfully support all proclamations of the President . . . having reference to slaves." Confiscated property, other than slaves, would then be returned. When 10 percent of a state's electorate of 1860 had taken this oath, that state could then write a new constitution, elect a new state government, and return to harmony with the Union. Until such time as these requirements had been met, the state would be under military government. By 1865 the Ten Percent Plan had produced governments in Tennessee, Arkansas, Louisiana, and Virginia.

Lincoln did not live to see reconstruction completed, however. On April 14, 1865, less than a week after Lee's surrender at Appomattox, the president attended a play at Ford's Theater in Washington. There he was shot by John Wilkes Booth, a mentally unbalanced actor, and died the next morning, April 15, at 7:20 A.M. Another conspirator stabbed Secretary of State Seward at his home, but Seward survived. Booth escaped, but was surrounded in a barn in Maryland and was shot on April 26. Nine persons were implicated in the assassination; four of them were hanged and four imprisoned, while one was released. Lincoln's death strengthened the radical attitude toward the South; in short, it seemed divine retribution to one who preached magnanimity. Herman Melville foresaw this change in his poem, "The Martyr," in which he said, "Beware the people weeping/When they bare the iron hand."

Johnson's Plan of Reconstruction

Lincoln's death brought Andrew Johnson to the presidency. Congress was not to meet again until December, 1865, and thus reconstruction in the next several months would be under Johnson's direction. Born in Raleigh, North Carolina, of poor parents, Johnson had become a tailor. When he married at age twenty, he was still illiterate, but his wife helped him begin the process of self-education. Later he entered politics in Tennessee as a Jacksonian Democrat and rose rapidly, serving as a congressman, governor, and senator from the state. At the outbreak of the Civil War, he refused to give up his seat in the U.S. Senate. Next he served as wartime governor of conquered Tennessee. He was known to hate the property-owning class bitterly, and his elevation to the presidency was welcomed by radical members of Congress who felt the South should be punished harshly; their only fear was that Johnson might prove too vindictive. A jubilant Benjamin Wade, senator from Ohio, president pro tem of the Senate and a Radical Republican, declared, "Johnson, we have faith in you. By the gods, there will be no trouble now in running this government."

Andrew Johnson

Yet the responsibilities of office tempered Johnson, and his plan of reconstruction, when promulgated by presidential proclamation, proved remarkably similar to Lincoln's. He recognized the Ten Percent governments of Tennessee, Arkansas, Louisiana, and Virginia, and on May 29 issued a proclamation of "Amnesty and Reconstruction," which provided for military governors for the other seven rebel states and an oath of loyalty for former Confederates that included a pledge that they would "henceforth faithfully support, protect, and defend the Constitution of the United States and the Union of the States thereunder." The new state constitutions to be written in the seven states had to ratify the Thirteenth Amendment (emancipation of the slaves), repudiate the Confederate debt, and declare secession null and void. Johnson's hatred of the rich was shown by his adding to the disfranchised list anyone in the South who had been worth $20,000 at the start of the war; anyone on the list, numbering fourteen categories, had to apply for presidential pardon before he could vote again. Finally, Johnson declared his hope that literate and property-owning Negroes might be allowed to vote, but this he left to Southerners to determine.

Johnson's program was so easily met that the seven states still outside the Union quickly effected it. Constitutional conventions were called, organic documents drafted, and officials elected; by the end of the year 1865 all states except Texas, Florida, and Mississippi had met all the conditions stipulated by Johnson. Mississippi had only to ratify the Thirteenth Amendment, which it soon did. Texas and Florida complied with Johnson's conditions in 1866, and they also returned to the fold. All seven proceeded to elect governors, legislatures, and members of Congress—most of them former Confederates. For example, Alexander Stephens of Georgia, former vice president of the Confederacy, was named to the United States Senate from his state. Even more disheartening to Northerners wondering about the fruits of their late victory were the "Black Codes" enacted by Southern states. These varied from state to state, their harshness or mildness reflecting the percentage of the state's black population; but all made plain that the freedman was a second-class citizen.

Blacks everywhere were prohibited from voting or serving on juries. They could not carry weapons. Nor could they appear in public places without a pass from an employer. The Black Codes did recognize the right of freedmen to own and inherit property, to make contracts, and to sue in court—and they made it very plain that blacks were expected to return to work, for they said that blacks had to have a steady occupation and they carried heavy penalties for violations of labor contracts. The Black Codes did not offer the Negro appreciable hope of advancement in the future. Thus to Northerners the codes seemed a legal expedient for continuing slavery in practice if not in legality. The codes seemed to prove the Radicals' point that the war had been fought in vain. Where, the Radicals asked Northern audiences, were the fruits of victory? On the alleged basis of the failure of Johnson's plan of reconstruction, the Radicals, mostly Republicans, united to write a congressional plan of reconstruction.

Radical Reconstruction

The radical temper was first manifested on July 4, 1864, as opposition to Lincoln's Ten Percent Plan. With considerable heat the Radicals rammed through Congress the Wade-Davis Bill, just an hour before the session adjourned. The work of

211

Senator Benjamin F. Wade of Ohio and Congressman Henry W. Davis of Maryland, it required a majority of the voters of 1860, not just 10 percent, to swear loyalty to the Union before an acceptable state government could be established in a seceded state; the new constitutions would have to abolish slavery, disenfranchise ex-Confederates, and repudiate state debts. Some Radical Republicans thought the Wade-Davis Bill too weak, too generous—and were extremely outraged when Lincoln killed the bill with a pocket veto. They responded with the Wade-Davis Manifesto of August 5, 1864: "A more studied outrage on the legislative authority of the people has never been perpetrated. . . . The authority of Congress is paramount and must be respected."

The Radicals were not overwhelmed with sadness at the death of Lincoln and Johnson's subsequent inauguration, for they thought Johnson would punish the rebels. The Radicals saw nothing contradictory in their arguments that secession was illegal, that no Southern state had ever left the Union during the war, and then, during reconstruction, that Southern states were out of the Union and must change before reentering. When Johnson proved conciliatory, the Radicals turned against him; they became more determined than ever to enforce a congressional reconstruction on the South. Led by Charles Sumner of Massachusetts in the Senate and Thaddeus Stevens of Pennsylvania in the House, they turned on the president in a fury and on the South with a vengeance. Stevens summed up the Radical Republican attitude when he said, "The whole fabric of Southern society *must* be changed," for Southern crimes "are sufficient to justify the exercise of the extreme rights of war—'to execute, to imprison, to confiscate.' "

When Congress reconvened in December, 1865, the Radicals found the temper of the North suited their ends. Northerners were filled with righteous indignation at the Black Codes recently enacted in the South, at the election of former high Confederates to state and national offices, at the general mild tenor of presidential reconstruction. The Radicals were emboldened to act. First they refused seats to congressmen and senators from the Southern states. Next they formed a Joint Committee on Reconstruction to represent both houses of Congress. This committee consisted of six senators and nine representatives and was charged with investigating presidential reconstruction and making recommendations. It conducted hearings that produced "evidence" that the South could not be trusted as loyal, tried to embarrass the president, and drafted the Fourteenth Amendment. This amendment declared that all persons born in the United States were citizens, thereby repudiating the *Dred Scott* decision; stated that a state could not deprive "any person of life, liberty, or property, without due process of law"; and that all persons (except Indians not taxed) would count for purposes of congressional representation, thereby repealing the three-fifths compromise of the original Constitution. In short, the amendment was designed to enfranchise Negroes but disenfranchise former Confederate leaders. Tennessee, of the former eleven Confederate states, ratified the Fourteenth Amendment when it was submitted to the states. The Radicals then restored Tennessee to the Union on July 24, but left the other ten Southern states under military rule.

The Radicals also pushed a measure through Congress to continue the Freedmen's Bureau. President Johnson vetoed it, stating that the Southern states should perform such tasks, and he likewise vetoed a civil rights bill forbidding states to discriminate among their citizens on the basis of race or color—a measure designed to strike down the Black Codes. Congress was able to override the president's vetoes on these measures but not on other critical legislation. The Radicals thereupon turned to the election of 1866 as a solution, hoping to garner enough Radicals in Congress to override all vetoes. The election of 1866 became a referendum between president and Congress to see who would direct reconstruction.

Johnson made a speaking tour between August 28 and September 15, a "swing around the circle," as he phrased it, visiting key cities to support congressional candidates favorable to his point of view. His speeches were long, rambling, and often incoherent—as were his usual speaking efforts. Radicals pictured the president as ignorant, crude, a Confederate sympathizer, and a drunk. The last charge stuck to Johnson particularly, all because of one previous offense. On inaugural day in March, 1865, Johnson was convalescing from an attack of typhoid fever (or malaria) and drank too much brandy on an empty stomach in order to nerve himself for the ceremony. His speech was much too long, trailing off into incoherence before he received the oath of office. Even afterward, he tried to launch into another speech before he compassionately was led away. The Radicals never allowed him to forget the episode—and used it to ridicule him in his "swing around the circle."

In that election campaign, the Radicals also capitalized on race riots in Memphis and New Orleans, and they received strong support from the newly formed Grand Army of the Republic (the GAR), which consisted of Union Army veterans. Finally, the Radicals appealed to businessmen for support, pointing out that Southerners traditionally stood for a low tariff, cheap money, and other policies inimical to business. The result of the election was conclusive—in both houses of Congress the Radicals had far more than the two-thirds majority necessary to override presidential vetoes. Reconstruction would be by Congress, not the president; further, reconstruction would be radical, not conciliatory.

The Radicals Triumphant

One of the Radicals' first acts, as much to test their strength as to insure continuing Republican victories, was to enfranchise Negroes in the District of Columbia, despite a plebiscite vote of 6525 to 35 against it. Next came an extension of the Negro franchise to the territories. As Congress had always governed the territories and the District of Columbia, both acts were clearly within congressional power. However, on March 2, 1867, came the Tenure of Office Act, which prohibited the president from removing government officials without senatorial consent, even those the president had appointed himself, such as his cabinet; violation was punishable by fine and imprisonment. This act, of doubtful constitutionality, was followed by one that was clearly unconstitutional. This was the Army Act, which forbade the president to issue orders to the Army except through the commanding general of the Army, nor could the president remove Ulysses S. Grant from that position or station him outside Washington without the consent of the Senate. The Army Act directly violated the president's constitutional charge to be commander-in-chief of the Army. It was intended to prevent the president from controlling the Army, for the Army would enforce reconstruction and Grant was working closely with the Radicals.

Their tactics now legislated into law over the president's veto, the Radicals turned to reconstruction itself. The First Reconstruction Act was passed on March 2, 1867; it stipulated that no legal governments existed in the ten Southern states still outside the Union. These states were divided into five military districts commanded by generals, who were charged with registering voters, including Negroes and excluding those disfranchised by the Fourteenth Amendment (that is, former Confederates), and holding elections for constitutional conventions. New state constitutions then would be drafted, to include the same voting rules as in the Fourteenth Amendment. These constitutions likewise had to ratify the Fourteenth Amendment (this would count for ratification—and was necessary to carry it— although these states were considered outside the Union). When such constitutions had been drafted, ratified by the people, and approved by Congress, then Southern representatives would be seated in Congress and federal troops would be withdrawn. Congress subsequently found it necessary to pass the Second, Third, and Fourth Reconstruction acts, mainly to implement the intent of the First.

Under terms of these acts, the military commanders proceeded in a generally honest and efficient manner. When the voting rolls were completed, 703,000 blacks and 627,000 whites had been registered, with Negro majorities in Alabama, South Carolina, Louisiana, and Florida. In the remaining six states the Radicals and blacks together held a majority. "Carpetbaggers" (Northerners who came South, many with their entire worldly possessions in a carpetbag suitcase, usually with the intention of getting rich) and "scalawags" (Southerners who cooperated and conspired with the carpetbaggers) gained control of all ten states' new governments. Seven states were hurriedly admitted in time to vote in the election of 1868, and all were back in the Union by 1870. These carpetbag-scalawag governments generally tried to introduce reforms into the South, reorganizing county government, the judiciary, and the system of taxation. They also sponsored relief of the poor along with other humanitarian measures, and they provided for universal, compulsory, and integrated public education. Such measures cost money, and taxes were raised and raised again. When direct taxation proved insufficient, state indebtedness skyrocketed. The running expenses of the governments of Alabama and Florida increased 200 percent under the carpetbag-scalawag governments, Louisiana's expenses increased 500 percent, and Arkansas an astronomical 1500 percent. Nor was the money wisely spent. Governor H. C. Warmouth of Louisiana spoke for most carpetbaggers and scalawags when he stated, "Corruption is the fashion. I do not pretend to be honest." On an annual salary of $3000, Warmouth amassed a fortune of $500,000—while Louisiana's indebtedness increased by over $48 million.

The individuals directing reconstruction, both at the state and national levels, realized that they needed the Negro vote to stay in power, and they took steps to insure the black franchise. Most Freedman's Bureau officials, along with Northern teachers and missionaries who came South, worked hard to register Negroes and to persuade them to vote a straight Republican ticket. Another agent of the Republican Party was the Union League. Originating in Ohio in 1862 on the premise that "loyalty should be organized," the Union League began moving South shortly after the close of the war, appealing principally to blacks. Part of the initiation oath was a statement that secession was illegal, an oath that Southern whites generally found unacceptable. Meeting in secret, with rituals, passwords, and an initiation ceremony that appealed to the uneducated, the Union League became a bastion of Republican supremacy in the South.

From the national level came the Fifteenth Amendment, ratified on March 30, 1870, which stated that the right to vote could not be abridged "on account of race, color, or previous condition of servitude." When the Supreme Court gave evidence of ruling some of this legislation unconstitutional, the Radicals indicated they would not tolerate interference. Earlier, in 1866, in the case *Ex Parte Milligan*, the Supreme Court had ruled martial law unconstitutional where civil courts were operating and ready to try offenders. Then on March 17, 1868, came the case *Ex Parte McCardle*, involving the jailing of a Mississippi editor under terms of a reconstruction act of 1867. Fearing that the court would declare the act unconstitutional, for it denied the writ of habeas corpus, the Radicals passed a law withdrawing appellate jurisdiction from the Supreme Court in cases involving such a writ. Johnson vetoed the measure, but it passed over his veto. Thereafter the Supreme Court did not challenge reconstruction measures. In 1869, in the case *Texas* v. *White,* for example, the court ruled that Texas had never seceded, but it refused to take a stand on the validity of reconstruction.

Johnson's Cabinet

Next the Radicals turned their attention to the chief executive, the last bastion of opposition to their complete dominance of the government. Andrew Johnson perhaps was not the strongest president the nation had seen to his day, but he by no means was as bad as he has been pictured. He had inherited Lincoln's cabinet but was unable to control it as Lincoln had done. Lincoln's cabinet had been chosen for political reasons more than for ability, and thus the men whom Johnson could not control were generally politicians of low caliber. The only noteworthy exception was Secretary of State William H. Seward. During the Johnson administration, Seward managed several pieces of diplomacy bringing credit to the nation. In March, 1867, the Russian minister in Washington, through Seward, offered the United States a chance to purchase Alaska. Negotiations produced a price of $7,200,000—of which $200,000 was used to induce congressmen to vote for "Seward's Folly" or "Seward's Icebox." Seward also ordered the occupation of the uninhabited Midway Islands in the Pacific, and negotiated an agreement with Nicaragua allowing the United States to build a canal there if it so desired. Seward, also through negotiation, enforced the Monroe Doctrine by pressuring the French régime of Napoleon III to withdraw its troops from Mexico, thereby allowing Benito Juaréz to capture and execute the would-be dictator of Mexico, Maximilian.

Finally, Seward negotiated with England on the question of the *"Alabama* Claims."* During the Civil War the Confederate ships that had been built in England had done an estimated $15 million worth of damage to American shipping. Confederate agents also had used Canada as a staging area for attacks into the United States, such as the one at St. Albans, Vermont. All such claims were lumped together under the label *Alabama* Claims because the *Alabama* was the most famous of the Confederate commerce raiders. England at first refused even to discuss the *Alabama* Claims. However, a rising militancy in Germany disposed England to peace with the United States, as did American suppression of the Fenian (Irish revolutionary) raids into Canada. The Fenians were recent Irish immigrants to the United States who hoped to stir a war between their new homeland and their traditional enemy, Great Britain, by creating border incidents. The Johnson administration suppressed these raids, thereby avoiding war. In January, 1869, Britain and the United States signed a treaty, the Johnson-Clarendon Convention, calling for arbitration of their claims against each other. However, Charles Sumner fought the measure in the Senate, declaring that the *Alabama* and other Confederate raiders had prolonged the war; thus, he said, the United States was entitled to "indirect damages"—which he estimated at approximately $2 billion. Sumner suggested that England might abandon Canada so that the United States could acquire it and thereby settle the debt for indirect damages. Sumner argued so persuasively that the Senate rejected the Johnson-Clarendon Convention by a vote of fifty-four to one. (Subsequently, in 1871, the Treaty of Washington provided for arbitration, was satisfied, and the claims arbitrated; the United States received what Seward had asked, approximately $15 million.)

Johnson's Impeachment

While Andrew Johnson could not claim credit for these good aspects of his administration, so he could not be blamed for the bad aspects of it—which generally centered around reconstruction. His opposition to the Radical program had started talk of impeachment in 1866, talk that grew the following year, and which came to a head early in 1868. The crisis came over Johnson's attempt to remove Secretary of War Edwin M. Stanton, who was loyal to the Radicals. Johnson's real desire, however, was to test the constitutionality of the Tenure of Office Act. In August, 1867, Johnson offered the post to General Grant, who first accepted, then rejected the offer at the behest of the Radicals. Then on February 21, 1868, Johnson dismissed Stanton outright and installed General Lorenzo Thomas in the office. Stanton refused to be ousted, however, and barricaded himself in the secretary of war's office. Thus there were two secretaries of war: Thomas, who held title and attended cabinet meetings, and Stanton, who physically occupied the secretary's office and had the archives.

The Radicals were overjoyed with Johnson's actions, believing they had grounds for impeachment. This, according to the rule of succession then in force, would bring Benjamin Wade, president pro tem of the Senate, to the chief executive's office. The charges of impeachment were drawn by the Joint Committee on Reconstruction, headed by Thaddeus Stevens, not by the Committee on the Judiciary in the House, as they should have been. Eleven charges were brought to the House for a vote. The first eight charges dealt with Johnson's attempts to remove Stanton. The ninth charged the president with violation of the Army Act. The tenth, drawn by Benjamin F. Butler, one of the most profane men in Congress, charged the president with making "with a loud voice certain intemperate, inflammatory and scandalous harangues" against Congress and the laws of the United States and thereby bringing "the high office of president of the United States into contempt, ridicule, and disgrace, to the great scandal of all good citizens." And the eleventh charge was a summary and partial repetition of the first eight charges. Stripped of their superfluous verbiage, these articles of impeachment accused Johnson of removing Stanton, as had always been a president's option to remove cabinet members he no longer wished; of asserting his constitutional prerogative as commander-in-chief of the Army; and of making speeches offensive to congressmen. None of these fitted the constitutional requirement for impeachment—"high crimes and misdemeanors." Nonetheless, the House on February 24, 1868, voted 126 to 47 for impeachment.

The Senate then sat as a high court of impeachment, with Chief Justice Salmon Chase presiding. Proceedings began on March 5 and dragged on to May 16. It was a theatrical trial in which the Radicals even tried to implicate Johnson in Lincoln's assassination. The vote on March 16 was thirty-six for conviction, nineteen for acquittal—one short of the required two-thirds majority. The Radicals then secured a postponement of the final vote to allow them to pressure one senator to change his vote. Senator E. A. Ross of Kansas was their main target. Reportedly, Benjamin Butler commented, "Tell the . . . scoundrel that if he wants money there is a bushel to be had." Ross remained firm, however, and on May 25 the final vote was thirty-five for conviction, nineteen against. Johnson escaped conviction, but his effectiveness was so reduced that the Radicals continued to dominate reconstruction.

The Election of 1868

The Radicals also dominated the Republican Party, and at their convention of May 20, 1868, in Chicago, they nominated Ulysses S. Grant for president and Schuyler Colfax for vice president on a platform endorsing Radical reconstruction. Grant was without a political record—in fact, he had voted for the Democratic candidate in 1856 and had supported Stephen A. Douglas in 1860. Nor were his views on national affairs widely known—if he had any views. Andrew Johnson sought the Democratic nomination in 1868, but the party knew he could not win. Tainted by their image as the party of secession, the Democrats sought an acceptable Northerner to head their ticket when they gathered at New York City on July 4. Eventually they settled on Governor Horatio Seymour, former governor of New York and former Union general, along with Francis P. Blair of Missouri, to head their ticket. Seymour was not widely known, so the Democrats desperately needed a good issue on which to campaign. The best they could do, with foreign affairs quiet, was the money issue. During the Civil War large numbers of "greenbacks"—paper money without gold or silver backing—had been issued; after the war, these were being redeemed in gold, thus reducing the amount of paper fiat money in circulation and working a hardship on farmers and the creditor class. The Democratic platform therefore appealed for payment of the war debt in more greenbacks, and it settled for a mild attack on the excesses of Radical reconstruction.

During the campaign the Republicans postured themselves as the party of "hard money," and they capitalized on their attitude during the recent war. Voters were asked to cast their ballots "the way they shot." This tactic was called "waving the bloody shirt." Democrats were pictured as the party of rebellion, the Black Codes, and financial disaster. Angus Cameron of Wisconsin typified bloody shirt politics in a speech in which he declared, "The cure for all the evils we endure—all of them spawned by rebellion—is not to be found in conciliation . . . but in sustaining the party that restored the Union of the fathers, clad now in the white robes of freedom, unsullied and irreproachable." Grant carried twenty-six states to Seymour's eight and was easily the victor in the electoral college by a vote of 214 to 80. A close examination of the totals showed that Grant had received only 310,000 more popular votes than Seymour, and his total included approximately 700,000 Negro votes. Thus the Radicals quickly pushed the Fifteenth Amendment through Congress in 1869 and pushed for its ratification by the states.

Grant and Reconstruction

Ulysses S. Grant proved a naïve president, one easily controlled by the Radicals —just as they had anticipated. They were free to continue their repressive reconstruction policies. Southerners grew more and more unhappy in this milieu. When they resisted reconstruction, they met with fines, jail sentences, and other forms of coercion. Therefore they turned to extralegal and illegal activities to prevent Negro voting; they, too, realized that continued carpetbag-scalawag government depended on black suffrage. Their weapons were the Ku Klux Klan, the Knights of the Golden Camellia, and dozens of lesser known such organizations—a Southern counterpart to the Union League. These "night-riding" organizations were formed to combat lawlessness, prevent black voting, rid communities of undesirable Freedmen's Bureau officials and other Northerners, and, in general, to bring a return of white supremacy. Their weapons were secrecy and, at times, brutality. By preying on Negro superstition and fear, they began making themselves felt by 1870. Radicals in Congress responded to the Klan's growing influence by passing the Force Acts on May 31, 1870, followed by the Ku Klux Klan Act of April 20, 1871; both were designed to suppress the Southern whites and to threaten martial law. They were passed because Democratic candidates had made serious inroads into Radical Republican supremacy in Congress in the off-year election of 1870. Despite these laws, however, the Southern demands for a return to self-government grew instead of diminished.

The Election of 1872

As the election of 1872 approached, the Radicals were noticeably nervous. Whites had regained control of four Southern states and could be expected to vote Democratic. Also, the Republican Party was split in 1872. A liberal faction with the avowed aim of unseating Grant had developed within the party. Led by Carl Schurz, a German immigrant who opposed the growing corruption of the Radicals, the Liberal Republicans met in convention in Cincinnati on May 1, 1872, to nominate Horace Greeley for president and B. Gratz Brown for vice president. Greeley was an unfortunate choice; a newspaperman for thirty years, he was an outspoken ultraliberal who favored a high tariff, believed in isolationism in international affairs, and was given to enthusiasms that colored his judgment. Fellow newspapermen bitterly denounced him to such an extent that Greeley, on one occasion, said he did not know whether he was running for the presidency or the penitentiary.

The Democratic Party realized it had little chance of victory unless it joined with the Liberal Republicans, and therefore it also nominated Greeley (although in 1866 Greeley had publicly labeled the Democrats "the traitorous section of Northern politics"). The Radical Republicans gathered on June 5 at Philadelphia to renominate Grant happily, although they dropped Schuyler Colfax in favor of Senator Henry Wilson of Massachusetts for vice president. On election day, November 5, Grant triumphed easily, carrying all except six states (all south of the Mason-Dixon line) and winning a popular majority of nearly 800,000; in the electoral college Grant received 286 votes, while Greeley got none, for he died shortly after the election and before the electoral college convened.

After Grant's sweeping victory in 1872, he became more conciliatory toward the South. Nor did the Democrats despair; although soundly defeated, they waited for the return of Southerners to control of their states. Southern whites noticed Grant's mellow mood and became more insistent in their demands to control their own affairs. The Freedmen's Bureau died in 1868, economic sanctions were applied locally to recalcitrant Negroes, and Democrats gradually resumed office. By 1876 only three states were still in the hands of carpetbag-scalawag governments: Florida, South Carolina, and Louisiana. The other eight could be expected to vote Democrat.

The Grant Scandals

Also, Democrats could look toward the election of 1876 with hope because of the scandals of the Grant administration. Grant seemed bent on destroying the Republican Party, mainly by ineptitude and naïveté. Those qualities that had made Grant a great general did not make him a great president. He regarded the presidency as a gift bestowed on him by a grateful nation. Disliking politics, he let Congress run the country. He was honest personally, but was willing to accept gifts, such as a $100,000 home and a $75,000 library. And he was independent, appointing his cabinet without consulting the Radicals. His first cabinet actually contained some men of ability, such as Hamilton Fish as secretary of state; for the most part, however, he relied on his old Army friends and businessmen for advice. A business failure himself, Grant excessively admired success in business. Unfortunately, the businessmen the president chose were not as honest as he, and they misused his trust. Theirs was an age of business expansion—as well as corruption—and having Grant's ear often aided them in their schemes.

The only scandal to become public knowledge during Grant's first administration stemmed from his gullibility when talking with the captains of industry. Railroad speculators Jay Gould and Jim Fisk convinced the president that the sale of government gold would hurt farm prices. With Grant's assurance that no government gold would be released, Gould and Fisk began buying up gold and soon cornered much of the market. Prices soared to astronomical heights as businesses sought to acquire gold to meet their foreign commitments. On September 24 the stock exchange was in such a panic that a collapse of the economic system seemed imminent. Grant at last realized on September 24, known as "Black Friday," what was afoot and ordered the Treasury Department to release $4 million in gold—and the conspiracy collapsed. Grant was guilty only of extreme innocence, but Gould and Fisk had made a fortune.

During the election of 1872 came hints of yet another scandal, one related to the construction of the transcontinental railroads. This concerned the Crédit Mobilier, a construction company which actually built the Union Pacific Railroad. Operated as a separate company, it was owned by members of the board of directors of the Union Pacific and was paid excessively high amounts for construction work of far less value. To prevent congressional inquiries into the practices of the Crédit Mobilier, its owners employed Oakes Ames, a congressman from Massachusetts, to give or to sell at a good discount shares of the stock to key members of Congress. Even Schuyler Colfax, the vice president, took stock. A congressional committee investigated in 1873 and discovered that the Crédit Mobilier had been paid $73 million to perform $50 million worth of work. The $23 million difference went to the stockholders of Crédit Mobilier stock as profits that ran as high as 100 percent annually. The construction company for the Central Pacific, known as Crocker and Company (although its real name was the Contract and Finance Company), had returned even more handsome profits. Revelation of this scandal came just as the Panic of 1873 was descending on the nation, and hard-pressed citizens were angered at huge profits for the favored few.

Grant's second administration was a dreary chronicle of scandals, some very close to the president himself. In March, 1873, Congress voted the president and itself very generous pay raises, in reality long overdue, but the move aroused strong public protest by making the raises retroactive for two years. Because of the outcry at the "Salary Grab," the increases were rescinded. Then came revelations that Secretary of the Treasury W. A. Richardson had awarded contracts to collect unpaid taxes to a friend, John D. Sanborn. Sanborn was receiving a 50 percent commission to collect $427,000, much of which he split with high Republican officials. The "District Ring" was yet another scandal. It involved the governor of the District of Columbia, Alexander Shepherd, who enriched himself and his friends through what he called "honest graft." By this he meant kickbacks for awarding public utility franchises. When Grant appointed Shepherd to the newly created commission for the district in 1874, the Senate indignantly refused to ratify the appointment.

The two scandals that came close to Grant personally were those called the Whiskey Ring and the Belknap scandal. In the first, Benjamin H. Bristow, who succeeded Richardson as secretary of the treasury, discovered a conspiracy that involved Grant's private secretary, Orville E. Babcock, and several prominent Republicans; they had defrauded the government of approximately $100,000 annually through false reports about collections of the whiskey excise tax. Grant refused to believe that Babcock was guilty, and he interfered so strongly at Babcock's trial that the secretary was saved from prison. Grant thereupon appointed him to another office. The Belknap scandal involved Secretary of War William W. Belknap's acceptance of bribes in return for appointment and retention of Indian post traders, who were raking in huge profits by swindling their Indian charges. Impeachment proceedings were instituted against Belknap, but Grant allowed him to resign "with great regret" before the impeachment charges could be voted. A lesser scandal broke that involved the Navy Department and the sale of business to contractors. Finally, there was a scandal in the New York City Customs House. Until 1874 the tariff laws allowed customs inspectors to condemn shipments for fraud; such shipments were then sold, half the proceeds going to the government and the other half divided among informants, appraisers, and lawyers. Investigation revealed that many legitimate shipments had been declared fraudulent, with the proceeds finding their way into the Republican campaign fund in New York, and GOP Senator Roscoe Conkling as the immediate beneficiary.

President Grant, in his final message to Congress, alluded to the scandals of his administration, admitted errors of judgment, but defended his intentions. He pleaded his lack of political experience prior to 1868 as a cause. What he did not allude to was an act of Congress that became law under his signature, an act that farmers and miners believed to be a national scandal. On February 12, 1873, the Coinage Act abolished the coining of silver because little silver was being brought to the treasury. The creditor class came to believe that this "Crime of '73" was part of a "gold conspiracy" on the part of the hard-money faction. They turned away from the Republican Party to agitate for easy money in the Democratic Party or in fringe political parties that started to cater to their demands. The Greenback Party was devoted entirely to this issue, and in 1876 nominated Peter Cooper, a New York philanthropist, for president.

The Election of 1876

The Republican Party gathered for its convention in Cincinnati on June 14, 1876, to find Ulysses S. Grant favorable to the idea of a third term. Certain of the Radicals, the hardcore professional politicians, were encouraging Grant in this direction. The liberals turned away from the general, however, principally because businessmen were tired of scandals and the exactions of corrupt politicians. The liberals, known as "Half-breeds," had sufficient power to prevent Grant's renomination. Their candidate was James G. Blaine, a congressman from Maine. Yet even Blaine was tainted with corruption; as Speaker of the House from 1869 to 1875, he had helped—and profited from—certain railroads. Evidence of his profiting was contained in private correspondence known as the "Mulligan Letters." Blaine might yet have had the nomination had he not, in a speech, referred to the Radicals, then called "Stalwarts," as "all desperate men, bent on loot and booty." This speech so angered the Stalwarts, especially Roscoe Conkling, that they blocked Blaine's nomination. The choice then fell on a compromise candidate, Rutherford B. Hayes, governor of Ohio, for president and William A. Wheeler of New York for vice president.

The Democrats gathered at St. Louis on June 27 in a jubilant mood. The Panic of 1873 was yet lingering, the scandals of the Grant administration were well known, and the Republicans were divided. Victory seemed assured, a sweet prospect to a party that had been out of office for sixteen long years. In fact, these years out of office and the Democrats desire to return to it brought unity to the delegates, a unity that transcended differences about the tariff, federal aid for internal improvements, and the question of cheap versus hard money. They nominated Samuel J. Tilden, governor of New York, and Thomas A. Hendricks of Indiana to head their ticket. Tilden, a millionaire corporation lawyer, had won an excellent reputation as a reform governor of New York. During his administration the notorious Boss Tweed and his gang had gone to the penitentiary, and Tammany Hall had been routed (temporarily).

Privately to friends, Hayes predicted his own defeat at the outset of the campaign. To win victory, he resorted to waving the bloody shirt. In his letter of acceptance of the nomination, written on July 8, he agreed that "peace" meant the "permanent pacification of the South." By August he was declaring, "the vast majority of the plain people think of this as the main question in the canvass—A Democratic victory will bring the Rebellion into power." By election day he could say, and almost believe, that a Democratic victory would mean "the poor colored men of the South will be in a more deplorable condition than when they were in slavery." Hayes had to wave the bloody shirt because actually there was little difference between him and Tilden. Both were honest and had gubernatorial records to prove it, both favored civil service reform, and both favored little regulation of industry and commerce.

On election day, November 7, newspapers reported a Tilden victory. He had amassed 4,284,020 popular votes to Hayes' 4,036,572—almost a quarter of a million plurality. But the electoral college returns from Louisiana, Florida, and South Carolina, as well as one electoral vote from Oregon, totaled twenty votes, and all were in dispute. Without these twenty votes, Tilden had 184 electoral votes to Hayes' 165; to win, Tilden needed only one of the twenty disputed votes, while Hayes needed them all. Republican national headquarters in New York City wired key carpetbag-scalawag leaders in each of the three Southern states to hold their votes for the party. The result was two sets of election returns from each of the three states, with Congress left to decide between them. The nation was thrown into confusion as it waited breathlessly for a victor to be announced—and the Constitution made no provision, then or now, for settling disputed electoral college returns. While Congress deliberated, Grant notified the Army in each of the three

221

Southern states to prevent molesting of the ballot boxes. Democrats were enraged that canvassing boards in the three states were under Republican control, and they in some instances resorted to violence and intimidation. Reportedly, the Democratic national headquarters offered a million dollars to the Louisiana canvassing board to cast its votes for Tilden; the offer was rejected.

In Congress, debate over procedure grew quite heated. Republicans wanted the ballots counted in the Senate, where they had a slight majority. Democrats preferred the House, which they had controlled since the election of 1874, or a joint meeting of the two houses, since they had a numerical superiority that way. Finally, in late January, 1877, Congress created an Electoral Commission to decide the election. This commission was to consist of five senators, five congressmen, and five justices of the Supreme Court. Five Republicans and five Democrats would represent Congress, while two of the justices were Democrats, two Republicans, and one an independent (and therefore supposedly unbiased). The Illinois legislature promptly elected the independent justice to the United States Senate, leaving only Republican justices from whom one could be picked for the Electoral Commission. Therefore, every vote by the Electoral Commission was eight to seven, each on straight party lines, and all twenty electoral votes went to Hayes.

Outraged Democrats threatened a filibuster in Congress to prevent Hayes' getting these votes and being installed as president. There followed, reportedly, a meeting at the Wormley Hotel in Washington at which a compromise was effected. Republicans promised the withdrawal of Army troops from the three Southern states still under reconstruction governments; this implied a return to white (and Democrat) rule in the South. Southerners also exacted a promise that at least one of Hayes' cabinet choices would be from the South and that they would control the patronage in their region of the nation. Economic concessions included the promise of general federal aid for internal improvements in the late Confederate states and federal subsidies for the Texas and Pacific Railroad. With these concessions, Southerners agreed to the election of Hayes, and on March 2 the president of the Senate announced the election of Hayes, who was inaugurated on March 5 (because March 4 fell on a Sunday).

The Compromise of 1877

The "Compromise of 1877" meant the end of Radical reconstruction in the South. All troops were withdrawn, dooming the carpetbag-scalawag governments in Louisiana, Florida, and South Carolina. By the summer of that year, Southern whites were completely in power again. They immediately began to repeal state legislation passed by the Radicals, just as Southern whites had in the other states as they regained control. In the process, they repealed integrated education—and compulsory education as well. They also rejected the Republican Party, which led to one-party rule. They reduced taxes, enforced strict economy, and wrote long, detailed state constitutions to give their elected officials as little power as possible. The restored leaders of the white South were labeled "Bourbons," after the French aristocrats who returned to power after the fall of Napoleon. However, they largely were businessmen—not planters—who depended on Negro votes to keep them in office, just as had the carpetbaggers and scalawags. The move to restrict the Negro franchise, and with it more Black Codes, came at the turn of the twentieth century when the Bourbons were being turned out of office by Populist-Democrats. The economic attitude of the Bourbons was almost identical with that of the industrialists and financiers then running the Republican Party in the North, and a gradual process of industrialization began in the South.

The South, then, was "reconstructed" between 1865 and 1877, but not as Northern Radical Republicans had intended. Nor was the end product what most Southerners thought they wanted. Politically the Union was whole again, but socially and economically it was not. The tragedy of reconstruction may have been, as liberals declared, that it did not go far enough; or the tragedy may have been, as Southern conservatives said, that it went too far. All could agree that change had occurred, but few were happy with what that change had wrought. Grave problems remained to be solved—but the Union had been preserved.

The Indian Wars

If there was a region of the country where reconstruction and Northern-Southern hatreds had little impact, it was the West. This region largely ignored the fights and the bitterness that sparked the years 1865–77 in the older regions of the country. Much as the East had turned to building after the War of 1812, so the West turned to self-improvement after the Civil War. Westerners were ready to dig precious metals, run cattle, establish farms, and strip forests, along with developing territorial and state governments in what had been largely a wilderness. But before any of these things could be done—and it would take several decades, not just twelve years—the native inhabitants had to be confronted and removed.

Originally the Great Plains region had been labeled the Great American Desert in geography books, and in 1825 Congress decreed that the Indians should be moved there. Advancing technology and changing techniques of pioneering brought white settlers to those plains just before and immediately after the Civil War, however, forcing a new look at the reservation system. This look was taken by the Department of the Interior, created in 1849 and entrusted with overseeing the Indians. The department's Bureau of Indian Affairs gradually evolved the concept of two big reservations in the West in the face of encroaching settlers. Between 1865 and 1867 a series of treaties was negotiated with the major plains tribes providing for the two reservations. The first of these was to be on the southern plains; called the Indian Territory (Oklahoma), it would be home for the Cheyenne, Comanche, Kiowa, and Kiowa Apaches, as well as the Five Civilized Tribes already there. To the north, the second reservation would be in the large area west of the Missouri River (principally in modern South Dakota); it would be home for the Sioux and the northern tribes.

Other tribes, such as the Apaches of the Southwest and the Modocs of Oregon, were to be crowded onto individual small reservations. The inducement used to secure treaties with these tribes, as well as those on the plains, was the promise of an annual distribution of presents. Overall Indian Bureau strategy at this time was to crowd the Indians onto reservations where they would be given training in farming and induced to take up "civilized" pursuits—in short, to make the Indians carbon copies of other frontier Americans.

Helping reduce the Indians to reservations was the slaughter of the buffalo. In 1865 there were an estimated 10 to 30 million of these shaggy beasts roaming the plains. They constituted an indispensable part of the Indians' way of life. Thousands of these animals were killed to feed the workers on the transcontinental railroads, but the mass destruction began when eastern tanners discovered that buffalo hides could be turned into excellent leather. Between 1868 and 1880 the herds on the plains were virtually exterminated, the hunters taking only the hides and the choicest cuts of meat and leaving the rest to rot. Later the bones were collected to be ground up and used as fertilizer. In 1873 the Santa Fe Railroad alone shipped 754,529 hides to market. With the destruction of these herds—and the buffalo was almost extinct by 1880—the Indians were forced either to raid to earn a livelihood or else turn to the government for subsidies.

Yet these Indians needed little excuse to raid. Such had been their way of life for centuries. They had hereditary chieftains, but most plains tribes followed war chieftains who gained their positions by being successful raiders. Also, the measure of a warrior's wealth was the number of horses and mules he possessed, and these usually were gained by theft. A brave therefore gained social, economic, and political position by being a successful thief and murderer—at least, that was how the American frontiersman saw it. And, after all, these tribes had warred upon each other for centuries before the arrival of American settlers.

To the advancing frontiersmen, the Indians were making unproductive use of the land. To them, the land belonged to the United States by right of conquest. The Indian was living on his land as he had lived for centuries; to him the Americans represented a real physical and psychological threat. Might made right in that era, and both races appealed to the final arbiter of the age—force. Theirs was a tragic conflict of cultures. Finally, Indian wars were good business for frontier merchants without scruples. For them there was profit both in the reservation system and in the wars. Beef and other supplies had to be delivered to the reservations, which meant profitable contracts. And during Indian wars, the troops that were sent to a region meant hay and grain contracts to feed the Army's horses and supply contracts to feed the soldiers. These merchants used their local newspapers to stir an occasional Indian scare in the interests of business.

Trying to maintain a lasting, if not completely honorable, peace in this incendiary situation was the Indian-fighting Army of the post–Civil War era. No longer were these troops a part of the Grand Army of the Republic patriotically preserving the Union, but a peacetime force with little public understanding or appreciation. An economy-minded Congress reduced the size of the Army until by 1874 it numbered only 27,000 men. That same economy-minded Congress decreed that Civil War surpluses had to be exhausted before new materials could be ordered. Thus the soldiers frequently were sent into battle in under-strength numbers and with obsolete weapons and equipment—on a private's pay of thirteen dollars a month.

In reducing the northern tribes, principally the Sioux, there were three distinct wars: that of 1862–63, that of 1865–67, and that of 1875–76. The first Sioux war occurred during the Civil War, the result of Indians being swindled out of their land. More than 700 lives were lost during the uprising. General Henry Hastings Sibley defeated the Sioux in a series of engagements; then when they surrendered, thirty-eight of their leaders were hanged at Mankato.

The second Sioux war occurred just at the end of the Civil War, the result of a miners' rush to Montana over the Bozeman Trail. This trail ran through the heart of Sioux hunting grounds. Chief Red Cloud protested treaty rights to this region, but to no avail, and the Sioux attacked all along the trail. The only major engagement of this two-year war worthy of special note was the Wagon Box Fight of August, 1867. Thirty-two soldiers with magazine rifles barricaded themselves

224

behind wagons and held off 3000 Sioux—a forecast of the inevitable defeat of the Indians through technological advance. The second Sioux war ended indecisively. In 1867 a congressional committee made a report stating that the Army was to blame for starting the war and ordered peace with the Sioux. The intent was to settle them on reservations where they would have homes, begin farming, and forget tribal ways.

The third Sioux war broke out in 1875 as the result of the Black Hills gold rush. The presence of gold was confirmed in the Black Hills in 1874, and negotiations began with the Sioux to get them to cede these lands. The Sioux refused because the Black Hills were sacred to them. When the Sioux refused, the Army troops stationed in the vicinity were removed, miners swarmed in, and the Sioux left their reservations. General Alfred Terry sent word to Chief Sitting Bull that the Sioux had to return to their reservations by February 1, 1876, or the Army would move against them. Sitting Bull replied, "You won't need any guides; you can find me easily; I won't run away."

Terry's strategy was a favorite of the Army at the time: a three-headed strike designed to enclose the renegades. General George Crook was to move north from Wyoming, Colonel John Gibbon was to come eastward from Montana, and Terry would march westward from the Dakotas. Crook's column was turned back at the Rosebud River. Terry's column managed to link with that of Gibbon at the Yellowstone River. There they found much Indian "sign," and George Armstrong Custer, a lieutenant colonel (and former Civil War brevet major general), was sent ahead with elements of the Seventh Cavalry. His orders were to exercise caution. Custer had different ideas, however. He was smarting from a presidential rebuke; he had testified in the Belknap scandal, which had angered Grant. He also wished to rise again in the Army, and thought a spectacular victory might win promotion. His scouts reported large bodies of hostiles in the region of his advance, but he disregarded their advice. On June 25, 1876, he came upon an encampment of Sioux and Cheyenne on the Little Big Horn River. He ordered an attack, splitting his force into two parts, one commanded by Major Marcus Reno and the other by himself. Custer made his famous stand, and he and 225 men were killed. Reno saw the futility of fighting such a superior force and managed to escape with his 150 soldiers and scouts. Custer's massacre had little effect on the outcome of the Sioux war. Terry pursued the Sioux and Cheyenne and forced them to surrender, although Sitting Bull fled to Canada and would not return to the reservation until 1881.

Related to the Sioux wars was the campaign against the Nez Percé. Part of their reservation in Oregon was thrown open to settlement by Grant without consulting the Indians, and in the winter of 1876–77 they fled. Under Chief Joseph, the Nez Percé departed, apparently for Canada. They were pursued a recorded 1321 miles in seventy days, with many skirmishes, before the Indians simply grew tired and quit. Chief Joseph summarized the futility of the Indians' fight in his surrender speech. "Hear me my chiefs," he said, "I am tired: my heart is sick and sad. From where the sun now stands, I will fight no more forever." This campaign alone cost almost $2 million, not including the property destroyed.

On the southern plains, the war was against the Comanche, Kiowa, and Kiowa Apache. By the end of the Civil War, these Indians in theory had been confined to reservations in the Indian Territory. Yet they continued to raid almost at will into Texas and Kansas. By 1874 this raiding had grown so extensive that the secretary of the interior turned to the Army for help. All Indians off the reservations were

Crazy Horse

BORN beside Rapid Creek, South Dakota, Crazy Horse (whose Indian name was Ta-shunca-Uitco) was a strange, quiet Sioux youth, serious and thoughtful. His skin and hair were so light that he often was mistaken by passing frontiersmen for a captive white child; by his people he was called "Light-Haired Boy" and "Curly."

Growing to manhood, he was wild and adventurous, hating the reservations and the encroaching whites. He married a Cheyenne girl and thus had close ties with that tribe; after he came to prominence as a warrior, many braves from that tribe joined with him. During the Sioux wars of 1865–68, Crazy Horse participated, but as a warrior not a leader. By 1876 and the last great Sioux war he had become a war chief. On January 1, 1876, he and his followers refused to return to the reservation as ordered by the Army following the Black Hills gold rush. On March 17 Colonel J. J. Reynolds struck his village, destroyed the 105 lodges in it and captured his horses; however, Crazy Horse rallied his braves, trailed the soldiers twenty miles, and recaptured the horses. On June 17 it was Crazy Horse and his warriors who turned back at Rosebud Creek the 1300 soldiers led by General George Crook, preventing them from making their rendezvous with General Alfred Terry.

Crazy Horse then led his band north, where he joined with Sitting Bull's followers on the Little Big Horn River. On June 25 he was in command of the warriors who massacred General George Custer and 225 troopers at that famous engagement. Then with 800 warriors he went into winter quarters in the Wold Mountains near the headwaters of the Rosebud. His village suffered a surprise winter attack on January 8, 1877, by soldiers commanded by Colonel Nelson A. Miles, and his followers were demoralized and dispersed. Crazy Horse fought on for four more months before surrendering with 1100 men, women, and children at the Red Cloud Agency in Nebraska on May 6.

An Army officer at this time described Crazy Horse as five feet eight inches tall, lithe and sinewy, and with a weathered visage; "The expression of his countenance was one of great dignity," the officer wrote, "but morose, dogged, tenacious and melancholy. . . . He was one of the great soldiers of his day and generation." On September 5, 1877, officers at a nearby Army post became convinced that Crazy Horse was plotting an outbreak and ordered him arrested. When troops came to his lodge, he drew a knife and began fighting. In the struggle he was mortally wounded in the abdomen, either by his own knife or by a soldier's bayonet. His death deprived the Oglala Sioux of one of their most able leaders.

declared renegades subject to punishment for their crimes. A five-pronged attack against these raiders was initiated, centering on the Texas Panhandle region. More than 3000 troops were engaged in the drive that saw fourteen battles fought during the winter of 1874–75. During one of these engagements, Captain (later General) Adna R. Chaffee made history when he spurred his men on with the shout, "If any man is killed, I will make him a corporal." By the summer of 1875 the Indian spirit had been broken. Their women and children had been taken captive and were on the reservations. The men soon straggled in. Seventy-five of their chiefs were arrested, tried, and sentenced to imprisonment in Florida. A few years later they were allowed to return to their people.

In the Southwest, principally in New Mexico and Arizona, were the western Apaches, subdivided into groups known as the Warm Springs, Chiricahua, San Carlos, and White Mountain Apaches. These bands gradually had been rounded up and forced onto San Carlos Reservation in Arizona—several thousand of them where once only a few hundred had lived. There they considered themselves uncomfortably crowded. There also they were shorted on their rations by unscrupulous Indian agents. Unaccustomed to farming, they could not raise enough to eat, and their food rations were so short they were near starvation. A final humiliation was that they were not allowed to make or drink their native beer, called *tiswin*. In May, 1885, a group of them determined on confrontation. They drank *tiswin*, then confronted their immediate keeper, a young lieutenant who did not know what to do with them; the lieutenant telegraphed the departmental commander, General George Crook, for instructions, but the telegram was lost. In panic when nothing had happened in two days, the Apaches fled the reservation for Mexico under command of their hereditary chief, Nachez, and their war chief, Geronimo.

Crook organized pursuit, guided by Apache scouts hired to track their brothers. Tired of running, the renegades met with Crook on March 25, 1886, and surrendered. On the return trip to San Carlos, however, a wandering whiskey peddler sold his wares to Geronimo, and that chief with thirty-eight followers (including women and children) returned to the Mexican Sierra. During the public outcry that followed Geronimo's escape, Crook was removed as commanding general of the department, to be replaced by General Nelson A. Miles. With almost 5000 troops at his command, Miles tried to force the Apaches to surrender by hard pursuit. When that failed, he sent Lieutenant Charles B. Gatewood and two friendly Apaches to negotiate a surrender. Gatewood persuaded Geronimo and the renegades to meet with Miles, which they did at Skeleton Canyon, Arizona, on September 3–4, 1886. There they were promised two years' imprisonment in Florida and then a return to Arizona, as well as reunion with their families in Florida. Four days later all were sent to Florida, but not to be united with their families; the men were at Fort Pickens and the women and children at Fort Marion. Nor were they returned to Arizona; they, and the Apache scouts who had fought alongside troops in Arizona, were kept prisoners of war until 1913 and never were allowed to return to the desert Southwest. Instead they were moved to the Indian Territory in 1894, there to remain.

On these reservations the Indians grew more and more unhappy and frustrated, and they turned to mysticism to recapture past glories. Among the Sioux on the northern reservations, there spread a mystic religion usually known as the "Ghost Dance cult." This was a blend of Christianity with native religion, which taught that the Americans were all to be killed and that Indians, both living and dead, would be reunited in an earthly paradise where there would be no disease and where the buffalo would return. The symbol of this cult was a "ghost shirt," a sack-like affair usually made of cotton and decorated with mystical symbols. The medicine men even said that the wearers of such shirts would be invulnerable to bullets. The craze probably would have died a natural death, but the Indian agents panicked and called the soldiers to suppress it.

When the troops arrived in the late fall of 1890, the Indians fled the reservations. During the flight, Sitting Bull was killed; and during the roundup of reservation-jumpers several tragedies occurred. The worst of these came during the final days of December when 500 soldiers surrounded 300 Sioux, two-thirds of them women and children, at a little Dakota creek called Wounded Knee. The Indians refused a call to disarm, whereupon the troops began firing indiscriminately into the camp; 146 Indians died in what amounted to an execution. One witness commented about the burial in a mass grave the following day, "It was a thing to melt the heart of a man, if it was a stone, to see the little children, with their bodies shot to pieces, thrown naked into the pit."

After 1890 the Indian became an administrative problem, rather than a military menace. The reservation had become a police system where the Indians were fed and where halfhearted attempts were made to teach them to farm. Gradually, however, the national conscience was being awakened to their plight. This began in 1881 with publication of Helen Hunt Jackson's *A Century of Dishonor,* which was an historical account of governmental injustice in its treatment—and cheating—of the Indians. Next came her novel, *Ramona,* a love story of injustice to California natives. The book sold 600,000 copies, and the public, now aroused, began demanding better treatment for these wards of the nation.

The problem was a philosophical one—what was to be done with the Indian? Some argued that these native Americans should be allowed to shape their own destinies through traditional tribal ways. Others insisted that the only future for the Indian was through assimilation, a nice word that meant "taking the white man's road." Rising to the fore as leader of the assimilationists was Henry Dawes, senator from Massachusetts. Born in 1816 at Cummington, Dawes completed grade school and the academy in his home town, then secured a degree at Yale College. After teaching school for a few months and writing for local newspapers, he began reading law and in 1842 was admitted to the Massachusetts bar. This soon led him into politics; he served in the lower house in his state, 1848–49 and 1852, and was elected to the state senate in 1850. Then in 1857, running as a Republican, he won a seat in Congress, a position he would hold until 1875. There his seniority brought him considerable power; this he used to write antislavery legislation, protective tariffs, especially for textiles, and other matters of benefit to his home state. Also, he introduced legislation to provide for daily weather reports (which eventually led to the establishment of the Weather Bureau).

Entering the Senate in 1875, he was a New England Yankee with high cheekbones and a gray beard—and a strong desire to help the Indians in the way he thought they should be helped. This he achieved as chairman of the Senate Committee on Indian Affairs. Included in the legislation he engineered were acts to provide funds for educational facilities on reservations and to bring the Indians under federal criminal laws.

However, he is best remembered for one act, named after him. Originating from his belief that Indians should be brought into the American political and economic

Geronimo

GERONIMO was born in Arizona's No-doyohn Canyon in June, 1829. As he grew to manhood, he apparently was indolent, for he was called Goyakla—"He Who Yawns." In 1858, however, his mother, wife, and three children were killed by Mexican scalp-bounty hunters. "I could not call back my loved ones," he later stated, "I could not bring back the dead Apaches, but I could rejoice in revenge." During the next fifteen years he rose in stature as a war leader among his tribesmen. John Clum, an agent to the Apaches who arrested Geronimo in 1877, described him as "erect as a mountain pine, while every outline of his symmetrical form indicated strength and endurance. His abundant ebony locks draped his ample shoulders, his stern features, his keen piercing eye, and his proud and graceful posture combined to create in him the model of an Apache warchief."

Forced onto the reservation at San Carlos, Arizona, Geronimo was a minor leader in the Apache outbreak of 1881. General George Crook and his soldiers pursued the Apaches to Mexico and forced them to return, but in 1885 they fled San Carlos again, angry at being cheated on their rations and unhappy with regulations that forbade many of their tribal customs. This time Geronimo was a principal war chief. Pursued by American and Mexican troops, the Apaches conducted many raids on both sides of the international boundary.

In March of 1886 they met with Crook to discuss surrender terms, but thirty-nine of them, including Geronimo, escaped into the Sierra yet again. For four months they were pursued by 5000 American soldiers and a like number of Mexican troops, plus many bounty hunters, but they never were forced into battle. Finally, in September, Geronimo agreed to surrender to General Nelson A. Miles, who had replaced Crook in Arizona; Geronimo was promised that he and the Apaches would be imprisoned for two years in Florida and then returned to Arizona. President Grover Cleveland ignored these terms, however; the Apaches were imprisoned at Fort Pickens, Florida, then transferred in 1888 to Mount Vernon Barracks, Alabama, and finally taken in 1894 to Fort Sill, Oklahoma. There they were interned as prisoners of war, although they were allowed to prosper as farmers.

Geronimo later toured with a "Wild West" show, was an "attraction" at the Omaha and Buffalo expositions, and was exhibited at the St. Louis World's Fair in 1904. He died at Fort Sill in 1909, still a prisoner of war.

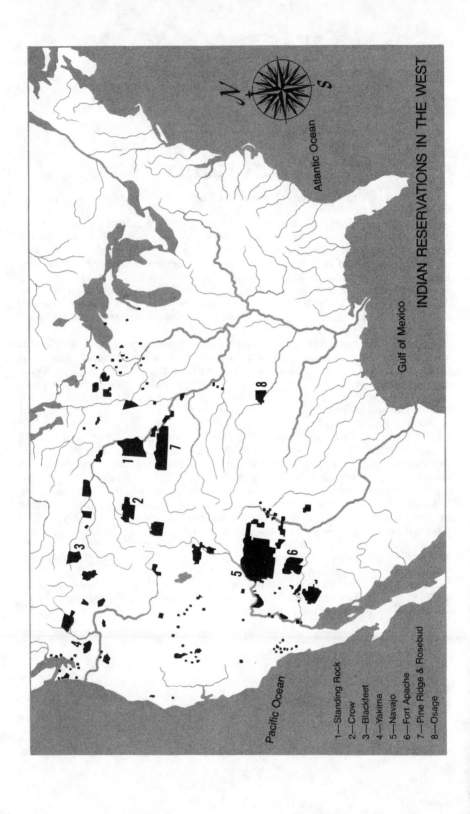

INDIAN RESERVATIONS IN THE WEST

Atlantic Ocean

Gulf of Mexico

Pacific Ocean

1—Standing Rock
2—Crow
3—Blackfeet
4—Yakima
5—Navajo
6—Fort Apache
7—Pine Ridge & Rosebud
8—Osage

system instead of clinging to their tribal ways, the Dawes Severalty Act became law in 1887; this provided for dissolving the tribes as separate legal entities and for wiping out tribal ownership of property. The land was to be granted individually, 160 acres to heads of families for farming or 320 acres for grazing, and could not be alienated for twenty-five years. The latter restriction was made to keep unscrupulous whites from cheating the Indians into signing away their property. The government also appropriated funds for additional schools for the Indians, schooling which generated severe cultural conflict. Parents of Indian children tended to discount the importance of education, making the children hard to discipline in the classroom. The only weapon the teacher had was the threat of expulsion—exactly what most Indians, parents and children, devoutly wanted. Youngsters educated in white ways found themselves socially isolated as well. Thus the government began boarding schools, taking the children away from the influence of the tribe. But when the child returned, he discovered there was no place on the reservation to use his new education; if he had learned a trade, no one was there to employ him. Most quickly reverted to tribal ways of life and forgot what they had been taught.

Further changes in Indian policy came in 1906 with passage of the Burke Act. This provided that the Indian did not get citizenship when he took his 160 acres, as under the Dawes Act, but when he got title to the land twenty-five years later. Finally, in 1924 all Indians were granted citizenship. The theory behind all this legislation was to make the Indian an individual landowner and a taxpaying, voting citizen. But such was not the case. Division of the land had not produced ability to farm, for few Indians had developed or were interested in the necessary skills. The land that was allotted soon passed out of Indian hands, and the former owners lapsed into poverty and squalor. They became recipients of government charity. In 1934, a decade after citizenship was extended the natives, came the Wheeler-Howard Act (or Indian Reorganization Act), which was expanded in 1936. Allotments of land ceased; there was to be no further alienation of Indian lands. The Indians were encouraged to revitalize their tribal organizations—in fact, to incorporate and hold the land jointly. The government had at last recognized that the Indians had an inherent right to rule themselves. In the next fifteen years, Indian-owned livestock increased from 171,000 to 361,000 head, and the value of farm produce jumped from $1,850,000 to $49 million. Even the amount of Indian-owned land jumped by 4 million acres. Yet no permanent solution had been achieved. Today the Indian is still groping for a solution to his problem; the whites are not going to disappear and leave the land to them again, nor is the technological revolution going to evaporate. Neither is the Indian going to vanish. His final destiny is yet to emerge.

Gold and Silver Rushes

Settlers of the frontier were quick to take advantage of the removal of the Indians—although they did not always give credit to the federal government for expending the funds for that removal. As the Indians were penned on reservations, and even before, these frontiersmen came to wrest wealth from the land. Their methods were extractive in nature, generally centering on mining, ranching, and farming, and, to a much lesser extent, fishing and timbering. The removal of the Indian threw open almost half the land mass of the nation. Men free from the Civil War but unable to return to tame employments sought adventure in the West. Confederate veterans with nothing to return to, newly arrived immigrants looking for a place to begin, criminals seeking a place to start over again safe from prosecution—all went west, to join those few who had gone in that direction before the Civil War.

The first and most obvious lure was quick riches: the mineral frontier—gold and silver. This movement began in the Sacramento Valley of northern California in January, 1848, on property belonging to John Augustus Sutter. An immigrant to California in 1840, Sutter had established a farm and ranch; there in early 1848 his men began constructing a mill. While they were digging the mill race they found gold. Sutter wanted to keep the news secret, for he realized that his property would be overrun in the stampede for quick riches. But such news could not be suppressed. By the spring of 1848 the rush had begun from San Francisco and was spreading to Oregon, British Columbia, Hawaii, Mexico, Peru, and Australia. Then in December, 1848, President Polk confirmed the existence of gold in California in his last annual message to Congress. Schools closed as teachers and pupils alike headed west. Lawyers abandoned clients, doctors their patients, merchants closed shop. As one newspaper commented, "Everything is neglected save the manufacture of shovels."

In California the Argonauts learned the techniques of mining, principally from Mexicans who rushed to the digs. Most of the early discoveries were in stream beds —placer gold (particles of the metal that had broken from the "mother lode" in the mountains and had washed downstream). All a man needed to go into business was a shovel, a washing pan, and a little water in which to swirl the dirt so that mud and sand were separated from the grains of gold. Where the pay dirt was rich, the Forty-Niners refined their methods by building a "cradle," a crude box rocked by the operator with one hand while dipping dirt and water in with the other. The rocking motion washed away the debris, and the gold particles settled to the bottom where they were held by cleats. The "long tom" was similar to the cradle but of greater length; it was a long box through which a stream of water was directed and into which the miner shoveled raw earth.

The California miners evolved a code to regulate life in the gold fields. The federal government made no attempt to regulate or tax the produce of the mines, although the gold and silver was taken from the public domain. Each community therefore drafted its own "miners' code" and was ruled by a miners' association that elected officers, set the rules for the size and registration of claims, and listened to disputes in open miners' court. The size of claims varied according to the district, but usually was about fifty by one hundred feet. The water essential to placer mining belonged to the man who used it first, even though he might divert it from the stream to a sluice box and leave other claimants downstream without water. And a claim had to be worked to be held. When Congress in 1866 finally made provisions for mining on the public domain, it did so by enacting, for the most part verbatim, the miners' code of the West.

These same miners' associations also dispensed justice, as there usually was no federal, state, or territorial law enforced in the mining districts. When claim jumpers became too bold or criminals resorted to violence too often, the miners tried them in open court. With no jails—and little patience—they meted out prompt and simple justice to those they found guilty. The sentences were few in number—hanging, flogging, or expulsion. Bret Harte's classic "Outcasts of Poker Flats" is a story of expulsion. But most of the miners were hard-working. They labored day

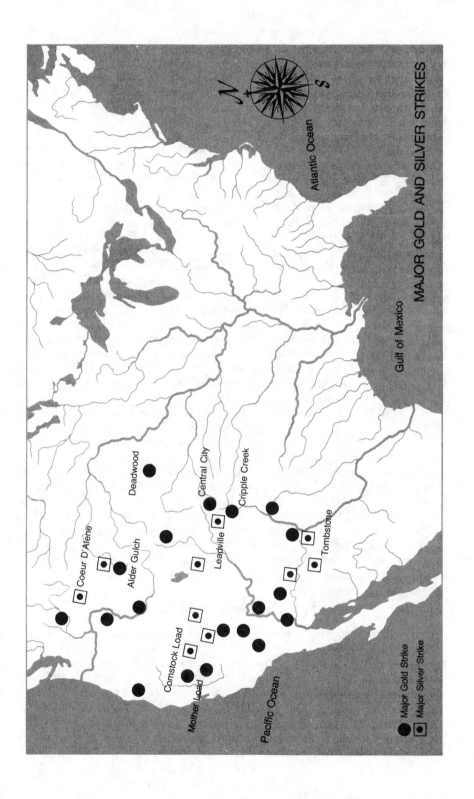

MAJOR GOLD AND SILVER STRIKES

Atlantic Ocean

Gulf of Mexico

Pacific Ocean

Deadwood

Central City

Cripple Creek

Leadville

Tombstone

Coeur D'Alene

Alder Gulch

Comstock Load

Mother Load

● Major Gold Strike
▣ Major Silver Strike

after day for "dust," standing for hours waist deep in icy streams. At night they lived in primitive shacks and ate uninviting meals of coffee, beans, and greasy pork, washed down by strong coffee. In such conditions, even in good weather, they suffered from diarrhea, dysentery, chills, fevers, and malaria. Their diversions were also few, for their towns likewise were uninviting—canvas and board shacks where the miners could drink and gamble. As one miner dolefully wrote home: "There's nothing to do but hang around the saloons, get drunk and fight, and lay out in the snow and die."

Eventually the placer gold was gone, and the miners tracked it upstream to the mother lode. There it was embedded in quartz, which meant tunneling, stamp mills, and other expensive machinery that could be financed only by corporations. Thus the Forty-Niners were faced with the prospect of going to work on a twelve-hour shift in the mines or of pushing across the Sierra in search elsewhere for placer gold. This is what many of them did—they became restless, rootless prospectors of the thousand hills of the West. In Arizona they discovered silver in 1856, in Colorado in 1858-59 in the famous "Pike's Peak or Bust" boom, in Nevada in 1859 at the Comstock Lode rush, in Montana and Idaho during the Civil War, and in the Dakotas in 1875-76 during the Black Hills rush. At each of these strikes there was a similar turbulent experience. They named their towns with such colorful appellations as Whiskey Bar, Skunk Gulch, and Hell's Delight. Then the placer gold would be gone, the corporations would enter, along with jails, churches, and schools, and the frontier would pass on. And when copper became the metal most sought during the electrical revolution, it also was mined by corporations. These corporations paid relatively low wages: $2.50 to $3.00 a day for a twelve-hour shift. The miners believed they were being exploited, and they organized unions that demanded higher wages and better working conditions. Thus the miners were ready, toward the end of the nineteenth century, to participate in the protest movement.

But in the rough, raw process of seeking gold, the prospectors, the Forty-Niners, and their descendants performed a vital service for the United States. They opened the West, hastening settlement by decades. California, Arizona, Nevada, Colorado, Montana, and the Dakotas owe territorial status and/or statehood in large measure to their mineral riches. The mining fields also provided an outlet for population from the East. And the product of the mines—gold and silver—financed much of the post–Civil War industrial boom in the United States. Finally, the miners attracted ranchers and farmers, for they had to be fed, and they paid high prices in the process. In fact, many ranchers and farmers found their occupations more profitable than did the miners.

The Cattleman's Empire

The cattlemen's empire of the era had its origins deep in south Texas in a triangle bounded by the cities of San Antonio, Corpus Christi, and Laredo. The region was a cattleman's dream: the climate was mild, the grass grew tall, and predatory animals were few. From the time of the first Spanish penetrations, cattle had escaped from the missions, had run wild, and had proliferated until they numbered in the millions. The basic animal of this industry was the longhorn, more a type than a breed. Brought to Mexico from Spain, and then from Mexico to Texas, he was of nondescript color, produced coarse and stringy meat, and had a vicious temper. Early American settlers brought cattle from the eastern United States, and they interbred with the longhorns. The result was an animal slightly different from the original beast: the horns were longer, the body heavier and rangier, and the color variations unlimited. Spaniards also contributed the horse, a wiry mustang pony descended from Arabian stock and trained to work cattle. Spaniards also provided almost all the ingredients of the open-range cattle industry except the grass and water. The saddle, lariat, chaps, boots, and the techniques of handling cattle from horseback all were adopted and adapted by Americans from Spanish antecedents.

At the conclusion of the Civil War, there were some five to seven million of these wild cattle in Texas, free to anyone who would round them up and brand them, or they were for sale at four to five dollars a head. In the cities of the North, where rapid industrialization was going forward, the workers were hungry for meat. Texans returned from the war to find their Confederate money worthless and their economy wrecked. They had beef—but no market. In the North there was money —but no beef. And a steer brought forty dollars on Northern markets. The four-dollar cow had to be brought to the forty-dollar market. The longhorns themselves provided the connection, for they could walk sixty miles without a drink of water. Texans decided to trail the cattle to the nearest railhead, Sedalia, Missouri. Thus was born the trail drive.

In the spring of 1866 a few Texas ranchers drove herds up what became known as the Shawnee Trail (or Sedalia Trail). But that first year of the "long drive" was almost the last. Not yet experienced in trail driving, the cowboys found the half-wild cattle difficult to manage. And armed mobs of angry Missouri farmers, halting the drives at county lines, shot or stampeded the cattle, for they feared these herds would infect their own animals with "Texas Fever," a disease to which longhorns were immune but which they carried with their ticks. Also, residents of Arkansas were equally impoverished by the Civil War; they stampeded herds in order to have beef available when they went hunting.

It was Joseph G. McCoy who provided a solution. This young cattle dealer had an idea—run a rail line out to the middle of the prairie, beyond the line of farmers, and there establish a railhead for shipping cattle. The Kansas Pacific Railroad liked the idea, carried it out, and thus was born Abilene, Kansas. To publicize this railhead, McCoy hired Jesse Chisholm, a half-breed Cherokee, to pioneer a trail southward and to tell cattlemen of the town. In 1867 only 35,009 head of cattle reached Abilene, but a new era had begun. Returning drovers spread the word throughout Texas, noting that few settlements, wooded areas, or angry farmers would be encountered on the "Chisholm Trail." In the next four years more than a million head of Texas cattle were loaded at Abilene and shipped to Kansas City and Chicago packing houses, or as feeders to Iowa, Nebraska, Missouri, and Illinois farms for fattening on corn.

Then the advancing farmers' frontier made it necessary to shift the long drive westward again. The next major trail to develop was the "Great Western," or, more simply, the Western. Its railhead first was Ogallala, Nebraska, served by the Union Pacific Railroad; later it ran to Dodge City to be served by the Santa Fe. By 1876 the Western had supplanted the Chisholm Trail as the major northward artery of cattle traffic. This trail extended northward to Montana and Idaho to stock ranches then developing in those territories. Texas had become the breeding ground, while the yearlings went north to be fattened for market.

237

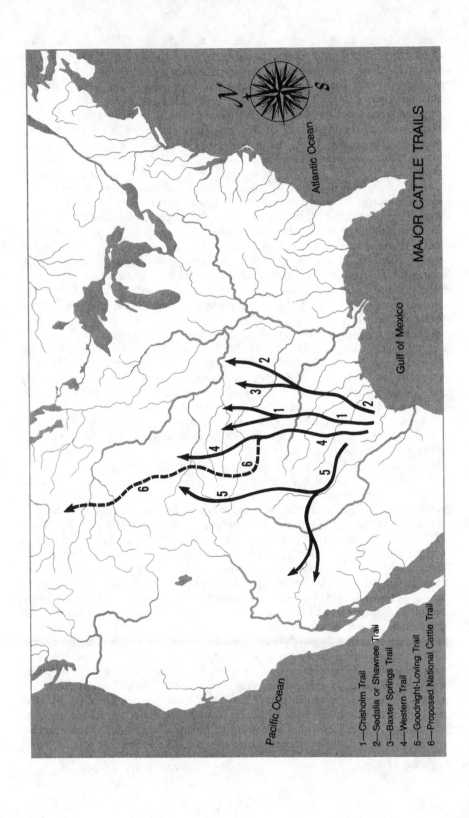

MAJOR CATTLE TRAILS

Atlantic Ocean

Gulf of Mexico

Pacific Ocean

1—Chisholm Trail
2—Sedalia or Shawnee Trail
3—Baxter Springs Trail
4—Western Trail
5—Goodnight-Loving Trail
6—Proposed National Cattle Trail

The Texas cowboys who pushed the cattle northward were filled with exuberance and confidence, although they faced heat and thirst, stampedes and Indians, rustlers and armed homesteaders. Charles N. Harger described one of these cattle drives in *Scribner's Magazine* in 1892:

A herd of a thousand beeves would string out to a length of two miles, and a larger one still longer. It made a picturesque sight. The leaders were flanked by cow-boys on wiry Texas ponies, riding at ease in great saddles with high backs and pommels. At regular distances were other riders, and the progress of the cavalcade was not unlike that of an army on the march. There was an army-like regularity about the cattle's movements, too. The leaders seemed always to be especially fitted for the place, and the same ones would be found in the front rank throughout the trip; while others retained their relative positions in the herd day after day.

At the start there was hard driving, twenty to thirty miles a day, until the animals were thoroughly wearied. After that twelve to fifteen miles was considered a good day's drive, thus extending the journey over forty to one hundred days. The daily programme was as regular as that of a regiment on the march. From morning until noon the cattle were allowed to graze in the direction of their destination, watched by the cow-boys in relays. The cattle by this time were uneasy and were turned into the trail and walked steadily forward eight or ten miles, when, at early twilight, they were halted for another graze. As darkness came on they were gathered closer and closer into a compact mass by the cow-boys riding steadily in constantly lessening circles around them, until at last the brutes lay down, chewing their cuds and resting from the day's trip. . . .

When skies were clear and the air bracing, the task of cattle-driving was a pleasant and healthful one. But there came rainy days, when the cattle were restless, and when it was anything but enjoyable riding through the steady downpour.

He noted that the singing of cowboys to a herd at night produced some oddities: "It was not uncommon to hear some profane and heartless bully doling out camp-meeting hymns to sooth the ruffled spirits of a herd of Texas steers, a use which might have astonished the fathers and mothers of the churches 'back in God's country,' could they have known of it." Such was the life of the men who took the range-cattle industry from Texas out onto the Great Plains and the Rocky Mountain states.

The business entered a real boom period about 1880, and more young Texans went up the trail than ever before. The boom began when a British parliamentary committee discovered that American cattle could be raised in the United States, shipped live to England, and still sell for less than British cattle. The reason was that American cattle largely were fattened on grass on the public domain, not on costly, privately owned land. This parliamentary committee announced its findings, triggering a rush to invest in the business—for the profits in it amounted to a staggering 33 percent annually. Gouty squires began competing with New England businessmen to own stock in ranching corporations. This produced overstocking of the range by 1886. The summer that year was hot and dry, and cattle entered the winter in poor condition. The winter of 1886–87 was one prolonged blizzard, and resulting losses were staggering. Some cattlemen in the spring of 1887 saw as high as 80 percent of their herds dead. After this disaster, ranching changed drastically; the range was fenced, windmills provided water, and blooded stock replaced the longhorn. The open-range cattle era died with the winter of 1886–87. But ranching had produced territorial status and/or statehood for Wyoming and to a lesser extent for New Mexico, Colorado, Montana, Idaho, and parts of the Dakotas and Nebraska, along with Texas.

The Farmers Empire

Less romantic than mining or ranching, but equally valid, was farming. The rancher and the miner did not worry excessively about title to their land, but the farmer did. Basically the farmers' frontier was made possible by several land laws: the Homestead Act of 1862, which provided 160 acres free to heads of families; the Timber Culture Act of 1873, which offered an additional quarter-section if part was planted in trees; the Desert Land Act of 1877, which provided 640 acres at minimal cost if the land was irrigated; and the Timber and Stone Act of 1878, which provided up to a quarter-section of timber or mineral land for $2.50 per acre. Also providing incentive for settlement of the West by farmers was the widespread sale of land by the railroads from their generous grants. They, along with steamship companies, advertised in Europe for immigrants. Through the government's generosity, the amount of land in private ownership devoted to agriculture rose from 407 million acres in 1860 to 871 million acres in 1900.

The bonanza rush to cultivate the Great Plains was encouraged not only by the railroads and steamship companies, but also by local residents themselves; their goal, of course, was to drive up property values. Many prices were inflated beyond the true value of the land in terms of what it would produce, but still the price was much lower than that of comparable land in Europe and in the eastern United States. Thus it did have a lure—which was enhanced by such tracts as the one issued by Dakota Territory in 1870 (written by George A. Batchelder):

> Think of it young man, you who are "rubbing" along from year to year, with no great hopes for the future, can you accept for a little while the solitude of nature and bear a few hard knocks for a year or two? Lay aside your paper gloves and kid gloves. Work a little. Possess your soul with patience and hold on your way with a firm purpose. Do this, and there is a beautiful home for you out here. Prosperity, freedom, independence, manhood in its highest sense, peace of mind and all the comforts and luxuries of life are awaiting you. The fountain of perennial youth is in the country, never in the city. Its healing, beautifying and restoring waters do not run through aqueducts. You must lie down on the mossy bank beneath trees, and drink from gurgling brooks and crystal streams. . . .
>
> Young men predominate in the West, while maidens are scarce; therefore I say to you, get yourself a wife and bring her with you. You will be happier and more contented, and, I have no doubt, make money faster.
>
> To young women I would say just a word. Out here
> "There is no goose so gray,
> but, soon or late,
> Will find some honest gander
> for a mate."
> Therefore, attach yourself to some family emigrating, and if you are over 21 years, your 160 acres of land, to which you are entitled, and your other attractions, will soon find you a nest and a mate.

Such advertisements had the desired effect. The pilgrims came in increasing

240

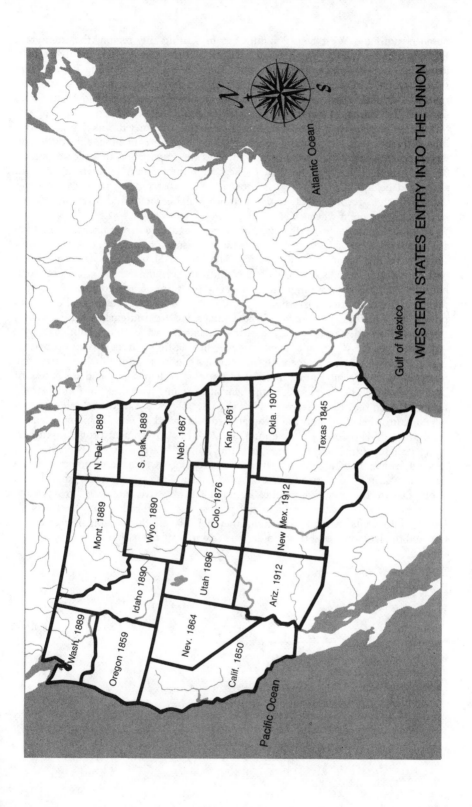

N. Dak. 1889
S. Dak. 1889
Neb. 1867
Kan. 1861
Okla. 1907
Texas 1845
Mont. 1889
Wyo. 1890
Colo. 1876
New Mex. 1912
Wash. 1889
Idaho 1890
Utah 1896
Ariz. 1912
Oregon 1859
Nev. 1864
Calif. 1850

Atlantic Ocean

Gulf of Mexico

Pacific Ocean

WESTERN STATES ENTRY INTO THE UNION

numbers until the West began to fill. Yet in settling this region, the immigrant farmer had to evolve new pioneering techniques. A log cabin could hardly be built in an area so devoid of trees, and thus the sod hut was devised. Barbed wire replaced split-rail fences for the same reason. Dry-land farming evolved to conserve moisture. Technological improvements, such as John Deere's steel plow and James Oliver's less expensive chilled-iron plow, also helped settle the West. Other innovations included multiple plowshares mounted on a mechanized sulky, grain drills, harvesting methods which were improved by use of the cord binder in 1880, and the mechanical reaper. Another innovation was the importation of different strains of seed, such as "Turkey Red" winter wheat from the Crimea. This wheat was hard and could be introduced only as improved methods of milling were developed—methods such as revolving rollers that permitted higher yields and more bread from higher-gluten content wheat.

These farmers were bedeviled by grasshopper plagues, recurrent drought, and blizzards, by falling prices and rising costs, and by isolation and loneliness. But they stuck it out and became too productive. The United States had a vast surplus of wheat by the mid-1880s, along with a surplus of corn and other agricultural commodities. The farmer was caught in a squeeze—the price of his produce was falling, the cost of transporting his crops to market was rising, and generally hard times prevailed. Therefore the farmer, like the miner and the cattleman, had grievances that made him ready to join the protest movement of the late nineteenth century.

The American West—the frontier—also had lasting effects on the American character. It was an area where the dominant traits were individualism, freedom, inquisitiveness, ingeniousness, materialism, strength, democracy, and a laxness of business morals. The people were impatient of restraint, yet willing to follow strong leadership. On the frontier most individuals were on the same economic level, leading to a firm belief in political programs for the good of the "common man"—implying programs for social amelioration as well as government programs encouraging individualism, freedom of opportunity, and the acquisition of wealth. They favored lenient land legislation, internal improvements at government expense, a protective tariff, and a strong central government—yet paradoxically they had a strong distaste for authority, a belief in individual initiative, and gave lip service to the free enterprise concept. And in the process of transforming the West from a frontier into a vital part of the nation, they helped heal the wounds of reconstruction and the late war—and they molded the character of the nation.

Chapter Ten

The Expansive Age

Politics: An Overview

IN the two decades following reconstruction, politics and economics were bedfellows to an extent never before or since approached in American history. The age was one where social preeminence was gained through great wealth. To a nation conquering the West and industrializing, politics was somehow "dirty." Thus politicians from the Grant administration to the end of the nineteenth century were nearly all mediocre, even incompetent—and too often dishonest. A few captains of industry, meanwhile, were using politicians to compile astounding fortunes. "We are the rich," wrote one such industrial aristocrat of that era, Frederick Townsend Martin; "we own America; we got it, God knows how; but we intend to keep it if we can. . . ." Of the issues of the day, he said, "When we are discussing pro and con the relative merits of candidates or the relative importance of political policies, the discussion almost invariably comes down to a question of business efficiency. We care absolutely nothing about statehood bills, pension agitation, waterway appropriations, 'pork barrels,' state rights, or any other political question, save inasmuch as it threatens or fortifies existing conditions."

The moral and intellectual tone of politics during this age was the lowest in American history—but the voters got what they deserved, for they failed to hold party or politician responsible. There were few political issues of burning national interest. Those debated were the tariff, the currency, and civil-service reform—issues not exactly at the "gut level" to ordinary citizens. The result was that politics was left to politicians, and their masters, and the two major parties grew increasingly unresponsive to the wishes of the public. Few politicians were concerned with the public interest, and in state and city governments there was a growth of bossism and political machines. The two major parties were evenly balanced in popular support, although the Republicans won national elections more often than did the Democrats. In theory the Republicans favored a strong national government and economic expansion, while the Democrats favored states' rights and limited federal government; in practice, however, these distinctions became blurred, with the Republicans representing big business and western farmers and the Democrats becoming the party of white supremacy in the South and of the urban poor in the North—with both under conservative national leadership.

243

Rutherford B. Hayes

The Hayes Administration

Rutherford B. Hayes, elected by a minority popular vote in 1876, was not outstanding in ability or particularly colorful, but he was honest and hard-working. Honoring the Compromise of 1877, he withdrew federal troops from the South, and he appointed a Tennessee Democrat, David M. Key, as postmaster general, a position with great patronage power. Yet the Democrats never allowed him to forget the method of his election. In their speeches they referred to him as "His Fraudulency" and "Old Rutherfraud," and in the House, which they controlled, they introduced bills calling for an investigation of the recent election.

Hayes' major fight was to end the spoils system and to establish some type of civil service system. To accomplish this, he appointed the Liberal Republican, Carl Schurz, as secretary of the interior with orders to hire on merit. Also, he issued an executive order designed to prevent federal employees from engaging in political action: "No assessments for political purposes of officers or subordinates should be allowed," he stipulated. This ended a practice dating from the days of Andrew Jackson, under which office holders were expected to contribute 10 percent or more of their salaries to the party coffers. "No officer," Hayes declared, "should be required or permitted to take part in the management of political organizations, caucuses, conventions or election campaigns." This order brought Hayes into conflict with the Stalwart Republicans led by Roscoe Conkling, especially when Hayes fired Chester A. Arthur and others from their posts in the New York Customs House for violating his executive order.

The other major issue of Hayes' term related to the currency. The Crime of '73 rankled western miners producing silver and farmers who wanted inflation. Congress in 1878 responded to their demands by passing the Bland-Allison Act, which ordered the Treasury Department to purchase $2 million to $4 million in silver each month and coin it into silver dollars at a ratio of sixteen to one with gold. Hayes vetoed the bill, but it passed over his veto. Thereafter the Treasury bought the minimum amount monthly—not enough to inflate the currency but too much for hard-money advocates. In the end Hayes lost favor with both sides. Even his attempt to reform the civil service had the same effect: too much for some, too little for others, and the Stalwarts worked to thwart his renomination. This they did so well that he did not seek a second term.

The Election of 1880

Again in 1880 the Republicans were so divided between Stalwarts and Half-breeds that they found it difficult to select a candidate when they gathered in convention. The Stalwarts wanted Grant to run again—and he was willing—but the Half-breeds prevented it. Finally the nomination went to James A. Garfield of Ohio, with the vice-presidential nomination going to Conkling's henchman in the New York Customs House, Chester A. Arthur. The Democrats responded by nominating a little-known former Union general from Pennsylvania, Winfield Scott Hancock, a hero of the Battle of Gettysburg, and William H. English. A meaningless campaign followed, one of the dullest in American history, with Garfield on election day winning a plurality of only 9464 votes out of nearly 9 million cast. In the electoral college the vote was 214 to 155 in favor of Garfield.

During the campaign Garfield apparently had come to an understanding with

James A. Garfield

the Stalwarts, but on taking office he disputed with them over appointments to the civil service. He broke with Roscoe Conkling by naming James G. Blaine as secretary of state, angering Conkling. And he named Liberal Republicans to the customs house in New York City, whereupon Conkling resigned his Senate seat. Conkling thought he would be reelected to the Senate by the New York legislature, humiliating the president; but that body surprised him by naming someone else. Stalwart fortunes turned downward thereafter. Even more fatal to Stalwart fortunes was the crazed act of Charles Guiteau, a disappointed office-seeker who, on July 2, 1881, shot Garfield. Guiteau stood over the body and shouted, "I am a Stalwart; Arthur is now President of the United States." Garfield did not die until September 19, during which time there actually was no president. Garfield was incapacitated, and Arthur could not exercise power. Fortunately no great emergencies occurred.

The Arthur Administration

Chester A. Arthur had been a spoilsman all his life, and his ascendancy to the presidency seemed a calamity to the nation. But Arthur rose to the occasion and proved the best president since Lincoln. He broke with the Stalwarts, steering a neutral course between the two factions of the party. He vetoed a rivers and harbors bill as pork-barrel legislation, he reorganized the cabinet, and he vigorously prosecuted the Star Route frauds in the post office. In the West, the mail was often carried by wagons and horses under contract. Investigation in 1881 showed that a senator from Arkansas and the second assistant postmaster general of the United States had conspired with Star Route bidders to award contracts paying excessive amounts, then splitting the excess with the contractors. The trials of these individuals in 1882–83 revealed fraud on ninety-three routes and a $4 million loss to the government. However, high Republican officials actively helped those indicted, and no convictions resulted. Arthur also tried for a tariff reduction; a tariff commission he appointed in 1882 recommended reducing the tariff on many items, but when the bill came before Congress, lobbyists were able to keep the tariff as high as ever in the "mongrel tariff" of 1883.

Arthur rose above his image as a spoilsman best, however, in pushing for reform of the civil service. For twenty years reformers had denounced the spoils system and demanded reform, but nothing had been done. Federal jobs continued to be allotted to members of the winning national party—with resulting incompetence, extravagance, and corruption. The murder of Garfield spurred Congress to action, and Arthur actively supported the effort. The result was the Pendleton Act of 1883. This provided for a Civil Service Commission, headed by three members who were to administer "open competitive examinations" so that federal employees would be selected on a merit basis. Federal service was classified into grades. And the act forbade assessing federal employees for political purposes. Only about 12 percent of all federal nonmilitary positions were put under civil service at that time, but the president was authorized to expand the list at his discretion. Subsequent presidents have done so, and today about 80 percent of all federal positions are covered by the civil service. Unfortunately these reforms have not eliminated incompetence, extravagance, and corruption. Mediocre persons fill the bureaucracy—and mediocrity is a cancer that votes to sustain itself. Mediocre functionaries designed tests to select employees on the basis of mediocrity rather than merit, and like a runaway cancer,

Chester A. Arthur

this has never been cured. Equally unfortunate was another effect of this "reform": politicians thereafter had to turn to business, unions, and other special interests for campaign funds, thus becoming tools of the highest bidders.

The Election of 1884

Arthur compiled a creditable record during his years in office, but in the process he pleased neither the reformers nor the party regulars. As a result, he was not renominated. The Republicans in 1884 turned instead to James G. Blaine of Maine, who had been trying for the nomination for eight years. Called the "Plumed Knight" by his admirers, Blaine was magnetic, a spellbinding orator, but he was tainted by the railroad stock scandals; letters implicating him survived, the "Mulligan Letters," across the bottom of one of which he had written "Burn this letter." The Democrats nominated Grover Cleveland—blunt, honest, and sound on the money question, a reform governor of New York. The Republicans hurriedly checked into Cleveland's background for political scandal, but to their surprise could find none. However, they did discover that as a young man Cleveland had been named in a paternity suit. He had never denied the charge, true or untrue, and had supported the child. Nor did he deny the charge during the months of the campaign.

The race of 1884 was dirty, based more on personalities than issues. Both platforms were alike except on the issue of the tariff; the Democrats straddled the issue, while the Republicans favored an increase. Liberal Republicans, called "Mugwumps," swung to support Cleveland. Their manifesto stated, "We should elect Mr. Cleveland to the public office he is so admirably qualified to fill and remand Mr. Blaine to the private life which he is so eminently fitted to adorn." Democrats gathered at Republican rallies to chant, "Burn that letter, burn that letter," while Republicans gathered at Democratic rallies to chant, "Ma, Ma, where's my Pa?" The Democrats were so certain of victory that they began replying, "Gone to the White House, Ha, Ha, Ha." New York proved the decisive state in a close election, and Cleveland won. Nationally Cleveland had a plurality of just 23,000 in the popular voting but a majority of twenty-three votes in the electoral college.

The Cleveland Administration

Cleveland generally is regarded as the ablest president between Lincoln and Theodore Roosevelt, even though he was not a man of great insight. His economic views were as conservative as those of any Stalwart Republican, and he lived up to the adage that "A public office is a public trust"; honest himself, he favored legislation for no particular class. He summed up his beliefs when he vetoed a ten-thousand-dollar appropriation for drought-stricken farmers with the comment, "The lesson must never be forgotten that though the people support the government, the government should not support the people." During his term, he put an additional twelve thousand federal jobs under civil service, angering both the reformers, who wanted more, and Democratic Party faithful, who wanted jobs after being out of office for twenty-four years. He also vetoed rivers and harbors bills as pork-barrel legislation.

He made the most enemies, however, by vetoing hundreds of pension bills,

249

Grover Cleveland

angering the Grand Army of the Republic, the Union veterans organization. He believed that a majority of these pension bills stemmed from fraudulent claims. Congress, responding to GAR pressures, passed a general pension bill giving benefits to all Union veterans suffering from disabilities, no matter how incurred; Cleveland likewise killed this with a veto, leading to further charges that the Democrats were the party of treason and rebellion. In reality, Cleveland was sympathetic to genuine veterans' needs, and the total appropriation for pensions increased during his administration. He also instructed the secretary of the interior to inspect past grants of public lands to the railroads, lumbering, and cattle interests and to recover that land granted under fraudulent pretenses. Subsequently the secretary of the interior recovered 81 million acres. And during Cleveland's first term the Interstate Commerce Act was passed, providing for federal regulation of the railroads. Finally, he tried to lower the tariff, which angered businessmen and manufacturers. Cleveland argued that the government should not protect the businessman, just as it did not protect the consumer. In 1888 came the Mills Bill, a genuine effort to lower the tariff. The bill was blocked in the Senate, however, and the issue went into the election of 1888.

The Democratic Party easily renominated Cleveland at its St. Louis convention on June 5, 1888, although his vice president, Thomas A. Hendricks, was replaced by Allen G. Thurman of Ohio. The Republicans gathered on June 19 in Chicago. First they turned to Blaine, but he had become a hypochondriac and, on the grounds of poor health, refused to run. He suggested as an alternative a little-known Indiana lawyer, Benjamin Harrison, grandson of William Henry Harrison, a man whose record was almost unknown. The convention agreed, naming Harrison and Levi P. Morton of New York to head the ticket.

During the campaign some big businessmen contributed to both Democrats and Republicans, hoping thereby to be friends with whichever won. Other businessmen chose sides openly; for example, J. P. Morgan and Andrew Carnegie donated large sums to the Republicans, while August Belmont and James J. Hill bankrolled the Democrats. The Republicans collected $4 million in campaign funds, some of which went for outright bribes, as to the head of Tammany Hall in New York City; that Democratic organization then did nothing for Cleveland and he lost the state as a result. Also, a Republican wrote a letter to the British ambassador to the United States asking which of the two candidates England most wanted to win; that individual was indiscreet enough to answer that England most wanted Cleveland to win. The letter was published, and the British-hating Irish of New York City voted for Harrison. On election day Cleveland secured 5,537,857 popular votes to Harrison's 5,447,129 votes; yet in the electoral college Harrison won by a vote of 233 to 168.

Matthew Quay, the Republican Party boss who engineered the election of Harrison, began advising the president on appointments. When someone he recommended failed to be appointed, Quay was asked by a friend, "Doesn't Harrison know you made him President?" Quay responded, "No, Benny says God did it." Harrison soon learned the facts of political life, however; he later said, "When I came into power, I found that the party managers had taken it all to themselves. I could not name my own Cabinet. They had sold out every place to pay the election expenses." This was not quite true. Harrison did get to name Blaine his secretary of state.

Benjamin Harrison

The Harrison Administration

The Republicans early in 1889 had control of both houses of Congress and the presidency—and they had a surplus in the treasury. To end the surplus, Congress reduced taxes and raised expenditures. First, they proved extremely generous with pensions. Corporal Tanner, a robust partisan, was named commissioner of pensions, and he approached his task with the joyous shout, "God help the surplus." He granted all new requests for pensions, even opening the files of those applications already refused to approve them; he even gave retroactive raises. His extravagance became so flagrant that he finally was forced to resign, but Congress on June 27, 1890, passed the Dependent Pensions Act providing for all veterans of the Union Army. Any person who had served ninety days or more in the federal Army during the Civil War was to receive a pension of six to twelve dollars per month if incapacitated from any source. Appropriations for pensions rose from $81 million annually when the Republicans came into office to $135 million annually by 1892.

Another raid on the surplus, this one of more help to the nation, came when Congress voted money to build steel ships for the Navy—enough ships to raise the American Navy from twelfth to fifth in the world. Republicans decided, however, that the best end to the surplus was to raise import duties to such a height that little revenue would be raised from them; the result was the McKinley Tariff, passed October 1, 1890. This raised import taxes to unprecedented heights and substantially increased the number of protected items; duties averaged about 50 percent on all incoming items. And, as a sop to western states, Congress passed the Sherman Silver Purchase Act on July 14, 1890. This raised the amount of silver to be purchased by the Treasury Department each month to 4.5 million ounces, to be used to issue treasury certificates redeemable in gold. In the next three years this action put an additional $156 million into circulation, but was not enough to satisfy free-silver advocates. That Congress of 1890, which became known as the "Billion Dollar Congress" because the budget that year was the first ever to exceed a billion dollars, also passed the Sherman Antitrust Act to regulate big business. But it was their action on the tariff that most angered the nation, and in the off-year election of 1890, eighty-eight House seats changed from Republican to Democrat hands.

The Election of 1892

In the election of 1892 the Republican Party leaders sensed defeat. Without enthusiasm they renominated Harrison, with Whitelaw Reid of New York for vice president, when they met at Minneapolis on June 7. Business was bad and businessmen refused to back the Republicans, abandoning Harrison. The Democratic convention met at Chicago on June 21 to nominate Grover Cleveland for a third try for the presidency; his running mate was Adlai Stevenson of Illinois. During his four years out of office, Cleveland had been practicing law with a Wall Street firm that did most of the legal work for J. P. Morgan's bank. The Democrats had an ample campaign fund, thanks to business contributions. And the Mugwumps supported Cleveland. Yet the campaign was not enthusiastic; as one critic declared, "Each side would have been glad to defeat the other if it could do so without electing its own candidate." What excitement there was that year was provided by the Populists (officially entitled the People's Party); this was an agrarian party with support from various farmers' organizations. It had nominated James B. Weaver of Iowa for president and James G. Field of Virginia for vice president on a free-silver platform (free and unlimited coinage of silver at a ratio of sixteen to one with gold). The Democrats made deals with the Populists in several Midwestern states, agreeing to withdraw their local candidates in favor of the Populists in the belief that if Cleveland did not win outright, the Populist vote would throw the election into the House of Representatives, where the Democrats had a majority. But Cleveland easily carried the election, getting a plurality of 381,000 votes over Harrison and an electoral college majority of 277 to 145. The great surprise of the race was Weaver, the Populist, who received more than a million popular votes and twenty-two electoral votes. Clearly, the Populist Party had made a creditable showing in its first national race.

Cleveland's second term proved even more conservative than had his first. On the money question he stood for gold with the fervor of a Republican, so much so that some liberal Democrats talked of joining the Populists. Also during his second term, the Panic of 1893, which would last four long years, began, putting approximately 4 million out of work. Cleveland took no relief measures; instead he worked to maintain federal solvency. He could not get Congress to reduce the tariff, and he was forced to call out troops to suppress the Pullman Strike of 1894. He did get Congress to enact an income tax law, but in 1895 the Supreme Court declared it unconstitutional. Still more voters talked of joining Populist ranks as a result. The approach of the election of 1896, therefore, seemed a time when the Populists might supplant one of the two older parties.

The Election of 1896

The Republicans in 1896 were confident of victory as they approached their convention. The party boss that year was Mark Hanna, a wealthy Ohio businessman who aspired to be kingmaker. Like Alexander Hamilton, Hanna believed that there should be a close relationship between government and business. And he had a candidate ready when the convention met, a candidate whom he had been grooming for several years—William McKinley of Ohio, author of the McKinley Tariff of 1890. When the convention met, Hanna had sufficient votes secured to win the nomination, and he presented his candidate as "Bill McKinley, advance agent of prosperity." The Republican platform endorsed a protective tariff and ignored everything else except the currency issue. On the latter the platform stated party opposition to the free coinage of silver unless other commercial nations agreed to it likewise, a highly unlikely event.

The Democrats met in turmoil at their convention. Southern and western delegates came determined to seize control from eastern delegates because of alarm at Populist advances. The platform committee could not agree on a report demanding tariff reduction, an income tax, and free coinage of silver; a minority report called for the gold standard except by international agreement. To resolve the differences, six debaters were chosen, three for each side. Seemingly the gold standard debaters were winning until the final argument by William Jennings Bryan, a thirty-six-year-old congressman from Nebraska, who declared:

> There are two ideas of government. There are those who believe that if you just legislate to make the well-to-do prosperous, their prosperity will leak through on those below. The Democratic idea has been that if you legislate to make the masses prosperous, their prosperity will find its way up and through every class that rests upon it. . . . Having behind us the producing masses of this nation, and the world, supported by the commercial interests, the laboring

interests, and the toilers everywhere, we will answer their demand for a gold standard by saying to them: You shall not press down upon the brow of labor this crown of thorns, you shall not crucify mankind upon a cross of gold.

This "Cross of Gold" speech not only carried the convention to vote for the free-silver plank, but also secured Bryan the nomination for president. The People's Party thus lost its reason for existence, and when it met in convention later, it also nominated Bryan for president.

The election of 1896, for the first time since 1860, saw a clear difference between the two parties; the question of free silver had become symbolic of the differences between capitalism and agrarianism. Handsome, magnetic, a spellbinding orator, Bryan was naive and provincial with few ideas and little experience, but he brought hope to the farmer and the laborer fighting the business oligarchy. The election was a David-and-Goliath contest. The Republicans were well-financed with ample funds secured from businessmen. Hanna conducted a "front porch" campaign, keeping McKinley on his front porch in Canton, Ohio, to which reporters faithfully trekked to have lemonade and hear McKinley's pronouncements, written by Hanna. Bryan stumped the country systematically, journeying 18,000 miles by railroad and speaking personally to an estimated five million people. The Democratic campaign fund amounted only to about $700,000, just slightly larger than Standard Oil's contribution to the Republican Party.

As the campaign neared its end in November, fear gripped the East that Bryan would win. Employers told their workers that in the event of a Bryan victory, they need not come to work the day after election as jobs would be ended. Bryan, who was deeply religious, was pictured as the "apostle of atheism, repudiation, and anarchy." Banks let it be known that farmers who voted for Bryan would have their mortgages called in—and the secret ballot was as yet largely unknown. And satire was employed. Senator Joseph Foraker, a leading Republican, was asked if Bryan's title, "Boy Orator of the Platte," seemed appropriate; it did, replied Foraker, for as he recalled the Platte was six miles wide at the mouth but only six inches deep. In the closing days of the campaign, prices for farm produce rose because of crop failures in Europe. The price of wheat almost doubled. Farmers in the Midwest, suddenly happy, returned to their Republican allegiance, and McKinley received over 600,000 votes more than Bryan and carried the electoral college 271 to 176. McKinley was inaugurated in March, 1897, leaving big business to dominate the economic and political scene for another four years. The election had one other result—the Populist Party was dead.

The Growth of Business

While 1877–97 were not politically inspiring years, they were years of tremendous growth in manufacturing, transportation, communication, and commerce. In fact, the age from the end of the Civil War to the turn of the twentieth century is best characterized as an era of industrial growth and rapid economic expansion. Capital invested in manufacturing rose from one billion dollars to ten billion; this rapid growth, combined with amazing agricultural productivity, moved America from a third-rate power to potentially the strongest nation on earth. One of the major factors making possible this rapid growth was rich soil and vast mineral resources. Other factors included accumulated capital for investment, stemming from a half century of trade and manufacturing; an easily secured source of labor, which resulted partly from natural population increase and partly from the steady flow of immigrants from Europe; political unity over a large area, providing a large market in which there were no local trade restrictions, no customs barriers, and no threatening neighbors; peace, which meant that little of the nation's resources went for an army; government support that extended protection and assistance through tariff barriers; a banking system and fiscal policy that benefited creditors; direct grants and easy sale of public resources; low taxes; easy communication, which stemmed from Samuel F. B. Morse's invention, the telegraph; judicial protection, with the courts using the Fourteenth Amendment to declare strikes to be unlawful deprivation of corporations of their property without due process of law; a philosophical basis that applied Darwin's theory of evolution to society at large, to say that the most successful businessmen were those that nature intended to survive; and a national system of transportation, the railroad, to bring raw products to the factories and distribute manufactured goods from them.

Southerners had been able to block federal legislation authorizing a subsidy for a transcontinental railroad before the Civil War. When the war began, however, Southerners walked out of Congress and action swiftly followed. On July 1, 1862, Congress chartered the Union Pacific Railroad Company to begin building westward from Missouri and the Central Pacific Company to begin building eastward along the thirty-eighth and thirty-ninth parallel route. These companies were given generous inducements: free right of way, free use of minerals and timber, ten sections of public land free for each mile of track laid, and a loan of $16,000 per mile of track across the plains, $32,000 per mile of track in the foothills, and $48,000 per mile of track in the mountains. When these inducements proved insufficient to stimulate fast construction, Congress in 1864 doubled the amount of free land to twenty sections of public land for each mile of track laid, and it stipulated that the government loans constituted a second mortgage. With these subsidies from the public purse, the building of a railroad became profitable.

Little work began in earnest until after the Civil War ended. Then ample labor became available, and financing could be arranged. Finally, Oakes Ames of Massachusetts and his brother devised a scheme to make fortunes for the directors of the Union Pacific. They set up a construction company called the Crédit Mobilier of America. Its principal stockholders were members of the board of directors of the Union Pacific. The board of directors voted contracts—at exorbitant rates—to their construction company to build the railroad. The excess became profits for division among the "boys." When congressmen became too inquisitive about the high cost of building the transcontinental, they were allowed to buy—even were given—shares of stock in the Crédit Mobilier. The Central Pacific's board of directors imitated their eastern competitors, and both began driving their men to lay track and still more track. Each mile meant profits.

One writer described the process of laying track as it was perfected:

A light car, drawn by a single horse, gallops up to the front with its load of rails. Two men seize the end of a rail and start forward, the rest of the gang taking hold by twos until it is clear of the car. They come forward at a run. At the word of command, the rail is dropped in its place, right side up, with care, while the same process goes on at the other side of the car. Less than thirty seconds to a rail for each gang, and four rails go down to the minute!

Colonel Grenville M. Dodge, chief engineer for the Union Pacific, was an experienced military man, as were many of the workers, and he easily trained them to drop shovels at a moment's notice and grab rifles to fight Indians. Buffalo Bill Cody was hired to slaughter meat for the workers, and soon gained the fame that would make him a "Wild West Show" attraction for many years.

As the rails crept westward, a succession of end-of-track towns sprang up. Tent and frame shacks blossomed overnight, featuring dance halls, saloons, and gambling dens designed to separate the workers from their pay. When end-of-track got too far ahead of the town to give easy access, the houses were disjointed and canvas, sheet iron, and lumber were loaded on the cars to be moved forward. "What had been Julesburg in the morning became Cheyenne at night," one worker later declared. On the Central Pacific, however, such towns were comparatively quiet, for the Chinese workers imported to build that line were not such easy prey for the gamblers, the bartenders, and the dance-hall girls.

Both lines raced forward as they entered Utah. Both wanted to be first to reach the Mormon settlements and win their business, but the great spur was President Lincoln's earlier ruling that the Great Basin region was mountainous, although it in fact was flat desert. Because of this ruling, the companies building across it received $48,000 per mile subsidy for easy work. Incredible amounts of track were laid, as much as ten miles per day, during this race. And both companies began projecting their track beyond the point where they would meet; they contemplated laying parallel tracks across the nation. But Congress intervened and decreed that the rails should meet at Promontory Point (near Ogden), Utah. Prominent company officials and honored guests gathered there on May 10, 1869, as a polished laurel tie, bound with silver, was put into place. The final rails were then laid, to be held in place by spikes of gold and silver from various western states. To President Grant went a telegram stating, "The last rail is laid, the last spike driven. The Pacific Railroad is completed." The continent had been spanned.

Four other transcontinentals would be completed in the following three decades, most of them using the same methods of finance and construction pioneered by the Union and Central Pacific railroads. The Atchison, Topeka, and Santa Fe (usually called the Santa Fe) began in 1859 when Cyrus K. Holliday secured a charter from the Kansas legislature to build from Atchison on the Missouri to the state capital of Topeka. That done, he dreamed of extending his track southwestward along the old Santa Fe Trail, and by 1876 he was at Pueblo, Colorado. Then he built south through Raton Pass and reached Albuquerque in 1880. Transcontinental ambitions followed, realized through his acquisition of the Atlantic and Pacific charter, given in 1866 as a thirty-fifth-parallel road with the usual subsidies. Northern Arizona proved difficult to cross, but on November 14, 1885, the Santa Fe reached the Pacific in Southern California.

The Texas and Pacific was chartered in 1871—with the customary subsidies—as a thirty-second-parallel route, to build from Marshall in East Texas to San Diego. By 1876, however, track had reached only to Fort Worth. At that time it was acquired by Jay Gould, well-known railroad promoter and participant in the Black Friday affair. Gould hired Grenville Dodge to oversee construction, and work began across West Texas. Meanwhile, the Southern Pacific was building eastward along the same parallel. The Southern Pacific was the brainchild of the "Big Four" of California railroading, the men who had built the Central Pacific—Collis P. Huntington, Charles Crocker, Mark Hopkins, and Leland Stanford. They determined to build the Southern Pacific to block competition and thereby hold a monopoly on rail transportation into California. By 1877 they were at Yuma Crossing, reached Tucson in 1880, and were racing for El Paso. Gould and the Big Four concluded an

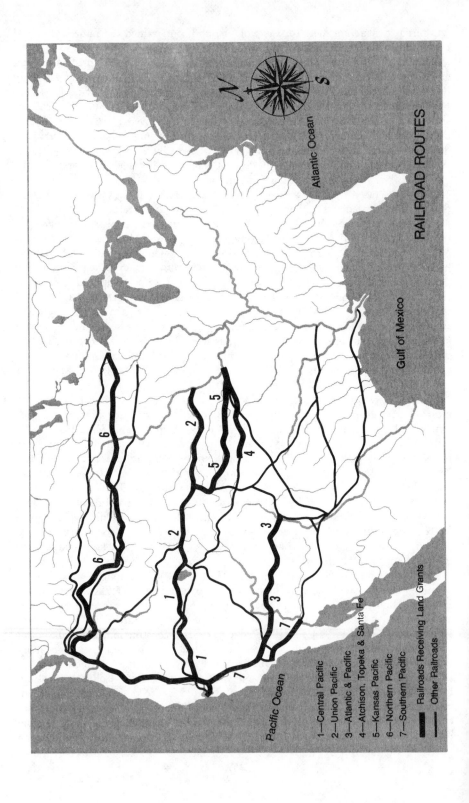

Atlantic Ocean

Gulf of Mexico

Pacific Ocean

1—Central Pacific
2—Union Pacific
3—Atlantic & Pacific
4—Atchison, Topeka & Santa Fe
5—Kansas Pacific
6—Northern Pacific
7—Southern Pacific

━━━ Railroads Receiving Land Grants
——— Other Railroads

RAILROAD ROUTES

agreement that the Texas and Pacific would join the Southern Pacific at El Paso and that the Texas and Pacific's subsidies west of El Paso would be transferred to the Big Four. Congress refused to endorse this transfer, however, whereupon the Big Four determined to make their way to the Mississippi. Buying up various short lines and connecting them, Southern Pacific officials saw their track reach New Orleans by way of Houston in 1882.

The Northern Pacific was as speculative as the other roads. Chartered on July 1, 1864, it was to run from Lake Superior to Puget Sound, and was to receive not twenty but forty sections of land in the western territories; but no loan was extended. Jay Cooke and Company, widely known for its sales of government bonds during the Civil War, represented the firm, and construction began in 1870. By the Panic of 1873, it was at Bismarck, North Dakota—and there stopped when Cooke's bank failed. Construction proceeded slowly until Henry Villard, a German immigrant and journalist, began buying its stock as the representative of German banks; in 1881 he secured control, pushed construction, bought the Oregon Railroad and the Oregon Steam Navigation Company, and reached Portland in September, 1883, with track; steamboats then moved the freight to Seattle until 1887 when track reached that city.

The last major transcontinental was the Great Northern, the brainchild of James J. Hill. A Canadian immigrant, he acquired title to the St. Paul and Pacific Railroad, a 200-mile line, in the Panic of 1873. By 1893, building conservatively and correctly, he reached Seattle with track. His road was not overcapitalized—nor was it publicly subsidized—and it cost less to maintain, for it could carry long, heavily laden trains with few repairs. His was the only transcontinental to survive the Panic of 1893 without bankruptcy. A final attempt was made to construct a transcontinental in 1905, when the Chicago, Milwaukee, and St. Paul Railroad began building toward Puget Sound; in 1925 this venture collapsed in what was the biggest receivership in American history to that point—nearly half a billion dollars.

Eastern railroaders were not slow to learn from the financial mispractices of western railroaders. They too wanted to milk the public for as much as possible. Cornelius Vanderbilt's New York Central constituted a near-monopoly on traffic between Chicago and New York City, while the Baltimore and Ohio Railroad was milked by the Garrett family until it went into receivership in 1896. These tycoons cooperated with other big businessmen to charge the highest possible rates for the worst possible service. The sloppy construction methods resulted in numerous wrecks; excessive shipping costs caused land values along the right-of-way to decline; and the manipulations of railroad securities ruined many innocent investors, for promoters offered high dividends to attract investors, then allowed the companies to go into receivership. When questioned about such practices, Commodore Vanderbilt snapped, "The public be damned. What does the public care for the railroads except to get as much out of them for as small a consideration as possible? I don't take any stock in this silly nonsense about working for anybody's good but our own. . . ."

Regulating the Railroads

The greatest evil of the railroads was the excessive rates they charged on the short haul. Between major cities, where there was competition, rates were kept low; but between small towns the railroad had a natural monopoly and charged extremely high rates, even higher on occasion over short distances than over longer ones where there was competition. The "short haul evil" led to a rising chorus for "reform," starting at the state level. The first railroad regulation came in Massachusetts in 1869; the commission created there had no punitive power, only the right to investigate and make public the abuses it found. By 1880, fourteen states had copied the Massachusetts law. But these did not work as intended; such commissions had no way to enforce their findings and thus correct evils, so they had become a convenient dodge for the railroaders. Anyone complaining was told to see the regulatory agency—as if the agency was to blame for not correcting any evils, not the railroads. Also, if a state became too overbearing, railroad executives threatened to end service to that state. Reformers thus found the problem to be national in scope, not local, and reformers turned in growing numbers to protest at the national level.

The strictest state law had been passed in Illinois in 1870. This empowered a commission to prevent unjust discrimination in freight rates and to regulate them. The railroads fought this act all the way to the Supreme Court, but in the case of *Munn* v. *Illinois* (1877) the Supreme Court ruled that railroads were clothed with a public interest and therefore were subject to public regulation; this was done by a court turned liberal by appointments during the reconstruction era. Later, however, the Court reversed itself in the case *Wabash, St. Louis and Pacific Railroad* v. *Illinois* (1886), usually called the *Wabash* case. This decision, which struck down the state regulatory laws on grounds that the states had exceeded their authority by enacting legislation restricting interstate commerce, reflected the appointment of more conservative and property-minded justices. During the mid–1880s, in a series of decisions beginning with *Santa Clara County* v. *Southern Pacific Railway Company* (1886), the high court reinterpreted the Fourteenth Amendment. That amendment stated that no state could "deprive any person of life, liberty or property without due process of law"; the Court decided that a corporation was a "person" just as was an individual citizen, and that the states attempting to regulate railroad corporations were depriving them of their property. Moreover, the Court widened the application of the "due process" clause, which originally had been designed to prohibit the confiscation of property or other arbitrary violations of individual rights, to void any regulation that prohibited a corporation from making a "reasonable profit" on its investment and said that the courts, not the states, should decide how much profit was reasonable. By striking down state regulation of the railroads, the Court thereby made inevitable a federal regulatory act for the railroads, which came in February of 1887.

The Interstate Commerce Act forbade discriminatory rates, thereby outlawing the so-called short haul evil. It also struck down pooling arrangements whereby competing companies pooled their holdings to avoid competition. Railroads were required to post copies of their rates "in every depot or station . . . in such places and in such form that they can be conveniently inspected." Rates were to be "reasonable and just," and could not be changed without ten days' notice. The act also established the Interstate Commerce Commission, the first independent federal regulatory agency, to consist of five men, no more than three from the same political party, each to serve a six-year term. The ICC had the authority to require the attendance and testimony of witnesses, the submission of documentary evidence, and receipt of annual reports from the companies. Also, railroads had to institute a uniform system of accounting. Fines could be levied by the ICC for violations not to exceed $5000 for each day of an offense; corporations and their agents were subject to such fines, and infractions were made a criminal offense.

The Interstate Commerce Act seemed to answer the reformers' demands, but in truth there was no ready solution to the conflict between railroaders and their critics. During the era when the railroads had been constructed, investments had totalled in the hundreds of millions of dollars; afterward, in the 1870s, 1880s, and 1890s, each corporation was striving to make a profit on the huge investment that had been required. During this era of protest about high railroad profits and arbitrary practices, the rate of return on investments for the railroads—their profits —actually totaled less than one percent per year. Yet the reformers could see no connection between prices charged and return on investment, and they demanded yet more change. In the process they added momentum to the so-called progressive movement of the late nineteenth century.

Despite the protests of the reformers, the railroads had performed a vital function for the nation—goods could be transported easily over a vast area. The railroad reached almost every town of any size (events subsequently would show that the railroads had overbuilt extensively). Through easy transportation and the many other aids and inducements that industry received in the post–Civil War years, fortunes were made with incredible rapidity as America industrialized at a dizzy pace. Immense wealth was the reward of entrepreneurs. Before the sectional conflict, $100,000 was considered a fortune; only twenty-five New Yorkers and nine Philadelphians possessed a million dollars each to that time. By 1890, however, standards had changed drastically. The Vanderbilts had $300 million, the Astors $250 million, and Andrew Carnegie, Marshall Field, and Jay Gould each had well above $100 million. There were more than 3000 "ordinary" millionaires, a hundred of whom had untaxed annual incomes of more than a million dollars.

Steel Production

In this expanding industrial age, steel was king. Steel had been a scarce commodity until the Civil War; prior to that conflict, steel was expensive and used largely for cutlery. Even after the war, the iron horse literally rode on iron rails. Widespread use of steel came only after the process of its manufacture was simplified and the new method widely applied. An American, William Kelly, a Kentucky manufacturer of iron kettles, actually invented the new process very early, but no one paid any attention, calling his product "Kelly's fool steel." Then came the Bessemer Process in the 1850s; Henry Bessemer, an Englishman, stumbled on the same process and popularized it. This new method consisted of blowing cold air on red-hot iron, causing the metal to become white-hot by igniting the carbon and thereby burning away the impurities. The Bessemer Process was welcomed in the United States, one of the few nations that had abundant coal for fuel, rich iron ore, and other essentials for making steel, all within close proximity to each other.

Unfortunately for the United States, however, the steel industry was chaotic and disorganized—until Andrew Carnegie organized it. A poor immigrant lad from Scotland, he saved his money, invested it wisely, and making good business connections, he emerged as a leader in the infant steel business. During the Panic of 1873, he and his associates expanded by erecting a new steel plant at Pittsburgh. There, as elsewhere in his expanding empire, Carnegie concentrated on producing quality products and the lowest possible price, a free-enterprise concept that moved his company forward rapidly. By 1877 he was producing one-seventh of the Bessemer steel in the United States. Next he invested in coking coal, necessary in the steel-making process. Eventually he controlled all aspects of steel production, including

Andrew Carnegie

AN undersize lad whose parents came to America in 1848 when he was only thirteen, Andrew Carnegie through his rise from "rags to riches" symbolized the opportunity of America in the late nineteenth century. The son of a handloom weaver of radical inclinations, Carnegie inherited a hatred for privilege based solely on birth. In Allegheny, Pennsylvania (now part of Pittsburgh), young Carnegie took employment as a bobbin boy in a spinning mill at $1.20 per week. Soon he had risen to a position as clerk in the office of the cotton factory employing him, and at night he studied double-entry bookkeeping. Next he became a messenger boy in the telegraph office in Pittsburgh, simultaneously studying telegraphy at night. This led to a promotion in 1852 to a job as telegraph operator—while at night he studied debating and familiarized himself with Shakespeare's plays and other forms of culture.

In 1853 Carnegie was hired as personal clerk and telegraph operator to Thomas A. Scott, the Pennsylvania Railroad's division superintendent at Pittsburgh. Six years later, through the same hard work that had marked his career, Carnegie was division superintendent at Pittsburgh. During the Civil War he helped organize the military telegraph system in the East.

As he rose in the business world, he gradually made wise investments that brought handsome returns—in Adams Express stock, in a sleeping car company, in the Pittsburgh Locomotive Works, in the Pennsylvania oil fields, and in the Keystone Bridge Company, a firm building iron railroad bridges. In 1865 he resigned his position with the Pennsylvania Railroad to concentrate on his growing involvement in iron—and then steel—production. Gradually he came to dominate a partnership, formed with Thomas A. Scott and J. Edgar Thompson (president of the Pennsylvania Railroad), that owned several steel-making furnaces. Everywhere in the enterprise he insisted on quick adoption of innovations to improve his product and cut costs.

In 1873 his firm erected the J. Edgar Thompson Steel Works at Pittsburgh and secured lucrative contracts for steel rails from the Pennsylvania Railroad, insuring success for the company. A good organizer and administrator, Carnegie surrounded himself with able associates, such as Henry C. Frick and Charles Schwab, men equally hard-driving and energetic. These individuals actually ran his growing plants while he lived in New York City, meeting men of letters, traveling, and formulating policy. By the 1880s Carnegie was concentrating on vertical integration of his firm so that it owned (or leased) its own ore beds, coal fields, limestone deposits, ore ships, and railroads. By 1899, when the Carnegie Steel Company was organized as a New Jersey corporation, it was capitalized at $320 million, and returning an annual profit of $40 million. The "Napoleon of the Smokestacks," as Carnegie was called, was receiving personally some $25 million of this.

In 1901, following sale of his company to J. P. Morgan's new United States Steel Corporation, Carnegie spent the remainder of his life giving away most of his fortune, for he felt he would die "disgraced" with so large a sum of money. Principal among his philanthropies were the donation of 7500 church organs, the funding of a pension plan for retired professors, and the establishment of free libraries in more than 2800 towns and cities in the United States. By the time of his death in 1919, he had disposed of $350 million, while endowments he established have continued to benefit the nation. A firm believer in the free-enterprise system, Carnegie contributed greatly to the industrialization of America.

ownership or leasing of iron ore beds, coal fields, limestone deposits, ore ships, and railroads, along with steel works.

Eventually Carnegie's expansion brought him into conflict with J. Pierpont Morgan. "Jupiter" Morgan, as the banker was known, had made a legendary reputation for himself as a Wall Street financier. He had reorganized railroads, insurance companies, and banks. An impressive man, he had massive shoulders, shaggy brows, piercing eyes, and a bulbous red nose—along with a strong record of integrity. By 1900 Morgan's bank had invested heavily in the production of steel-pipe tubing. Carnegie let it be known he was thinking of entering the same field; his real intent was to force Morgan to buy out the Carnegie Steel Company, for the canny Scot was tired of the game. Carnegie's agents haggled with Morgan for eight straight hours before emerging with $440 million in cash for Carnegie alone. Later, to his disgust, Carnegie learned that Morgan had stood ready to pay twice that sum to obtain control of the steel company.

Morgan took the Carnegie holdings, consolidated them with his own companies, and established the United States Steel Corporation, capitalized at one billion dollars—America's first billion-dollar corporation. This one corporation alone represented more investment than the total estimated wealth of the United States in 1800. And Morgan, within a few years, made the corporation actually as valuable —and profitable—as its capitalized value.

The Petroleum Boom

If the age was that of steel, its fuel was oil. Prior to the Civil War, petroleum was little known. What oil there was had been found in stream beds and seeps and was used as patent medicine and back-rub ointment. Then in 1859 came E. L. Drake's discovery in western Pennsylvania at a depth of 69.5 feet. Called Drake's Folly at first, the product soon became known as "Black Gold." Drake's well produced only twenty barrels a day, but that sold for twenty dollars a barrel. The chief use found for oil was as an illuminant—kerosene lamps. Many operators entered the field because it was so profitable, but the competition was fierce and the price of oil fell disastrously and made long-range corporate planning impossible. Into this arena stepped John D. Rockefeller.

At the end of the Civil War, Rockefeller had $50,000 that he had earned in the grain and hay business. Surveying the petroleum industry, which was chaotic and fragmented, he decided it was useless to attempt to control all sources of supply, for oil was being discovered in many small fields; rather Rockefeller determined to control the output at one stage—refining. Thereby he could dictate terms to the whole industry, could stabilize production and prices, and could make a good profit on his investment. With his $50,000 he acquired control of a refinery. Next he turned his attention to efficient means of production, forming alliances and business connections with the ablest men in the industry to establish a monopoly of brains. Eliminating competitors by underselling them in selected markets, he made up the losses with profits earned where competition was less. He showed no pity in dealing with his competitors; mercilessly he drove those out of business who refused to join with him, and carefully he saved his profits for reinvestment rather than spend them on high living.

Next he worked on transporting his product, developing the rebate system. Seemingly he was paying the same price to the railroad for transportation as everyone else, but he was shipping so much oil that he could demand—and get—a return of part of his fees. Thereby he could ship at a lower price than his competitors, could sell for less, and could drive them out of business. Later, when his company grew still larger, he instituted the drawback, which meant that the railroads paid Rockefeller's company part of the fees they charged for transporting his competitors' oil. Such practices were not against the laws of that day, and his competitors were trying to do the same thing; Samuel Downer, one competitor, summed up the industry attitude when he declared, "I am opposed to the whole scheme of rebates and drawbacks—without I'm in on it." As many were "in on it" as could force the railroads to pay.

In 1870 Rockefeller and associates formed Standard Oil Company of Ohio with capital assets of a million dollars. By 1872 the company had eliminated most competition in the Midwest and controlled a fifth of the national refining capacity. Still expanding, he moved rapidly ahead. In 1882 came the Standard Oil Trust, whereby he and his competitors formed a holding company in which they placed the stock in their companies; Standard Oil Trust, with Rockefeller at its head, then operated all these firms as a single unit to provide yet more profits to all. When Ohio ordered this trust dissolved as a conspiracy in restraint of trade, it was incorporated under the easier laws of New Jersey in 1889. Then years later the whole conglomerate was legally combined into Standard Oil Company of New Jersey. Through this trust company, Rockefeller controlled 95 percent of the national refining capacity. Always, however, he stressed economy of operation. He hired chemists and production experts to devise cheaper methods; he created his own sales force to eliminate the middleman's profits; he even acquired companies to build his own barrels, supply acids, and other needed items. And in everything he hired the best possible men.

Technological Development

In the field of electricity, there were rapid developments during this period. Thomas Alva Edison, a self-educated man with little basic scientific knowledge, devised a satisfactory filament to produce light from electricity in 1879, and three years later the Edison Electric Company opened a power plant in New York City. A rival concern, headed by George Westinghouse, perfected alternating current generators, so that power could be transmitted long distances. A Yugoslav immigrant, Nikola Tesla, devised an alternating-current motor, and Westinghouse's company patented the invention. In 1895 Westinghouse managed to harness the power from Niagara Falls, and, in 1892, Edison's company changed its name to General Electric.

In communications, Western Electric, established in 1878 as a holding company, came to control 80 percent of the nation's telegraph lines. Postal Telegraph was its nearest competitor. The telephone, invented in 1876 by Alexander Graham Bell, a Scotch immigrant studying deafness, came into rapid use. A number of the companies licensed to use the Bell patent were then tied together into a holding company. Finally, Western Union and the Bell companies, along with Postal Telegraph, agreed to end their competition by forming a single vast holding company, American Telephone and Telegraph, eventually to become the largest corporation in America.

Other captains of industry were quick to realize the value of the holding com-

John D. Rockefeller

WHEN his personal fortune passed $100 million, John D. Rockefeller was giving his children an allowance of only ten cents per week. This thrift reflected both his business philosophy and his own hard origins. Born in Richmond, New York, in 1839, he knew poverty as a lad. When he was fourteen, his family moved to Cleveland, where, after attending high school for two years, he went to work as a clerk and bookkeeper in a commission house. There his ability brought him advancement and, at age nineteen, a junior partnership in Clark, Gardner and Company. Eventually this became Rockefeller and Andrews Company.

During the Civil War Rockefeller hired a substitute to fight for him (a common practice at the time) and amassed a modest fortune in the grain and hay business, supplying these items to the Union Army. After the war his company involved itself in the petroleum industry at the refining level. Hard driving and hard working, Rockefeller expanded rapidly, by 1879 controlling more than 90 percent of the refining capacity of the nation. This was consolidated first as the Standard Oil Trust of Ohio, then later as Standard Oil Company of New Jersey. By this time the firm had investments not only in oil but also in railroads, iron, steel, banking, and other interests. After 1895, by which time Rockefeller's fortune was so great as to be indeterminate —but estimated at one billion dollars—he gradually turned direction of Standard Oil over to associates, retiring officially in 1911.

A devout Baptist all his life, as well as a diligent worker and a thrifty person, Rockefeller devoted himself more and more to philanthropy after he retired. Since 1855, when he took his first job, he had donated regularly to his church and to other charities, but in his old age he gave away an estimated $600 million. Most of this went to the Rockefeller Foundation, the General Education Board, and the Rockefeller Institute for Medical Research, in addition to the University of Chicago (which he had helped found in 1890). He spent the last thirty years of his life in search of longevity, dying in 1937 just short of the 100-year mark. By this time he had outlived most of his associates, as well as most of his enemies. However, the children of some of the men he bested in business never forgave him, and through their writings his business practices and ethics constantly were called into such question that his reputation suffered.

pany and the trust as a means of avoiding competition. The trend toward consolidation continued at a rapid pace in the last years of the nineteenth century. By 1890 the value of all property in the United States was estimated at $65 billion, of which $25 billion represented the assets of the large corporations. Cynics began saying that U.S.A. stood for United Syndicates of America. By that time there were over 300 trusts, including many controlling items of common use such as salt, nails, leather, and tobacco.

The Display of Wealth

As men moved to multi-millionaire status, a few of them began acquiring symbols of their new status, giving all a bad name. In New York a list was made of those eligible to be on guest lists of the finest homes; this list consisted of *the* 400 families of New York. Other cities saw similar lists compiled. These would-be aristocrats filled their garish mansions and imitation palaces with paintings, books, tapestries, and bric-a-brac from the Old World. Culture became a badge of position. J. P. Morgan never bothered to inspect a $100,000 Vermeer he acquired; the picture itself was incidental. A swarm of dealers in rarities descended on the cities to supply the desired objects, complete with warranties of excellence. Another way to display wealth was through parties, usually given with the help of an etiquette book —generally not read sufficiently to prevent over-display. For example, at one party, given at the Waldorf-Astoria Hotel in New York City in 1899, the guests ate from golden plates; the party cost $10,000 for forty people, or $250 apiece, at a time when that constituted six-months' wages for the average worker. A Mrs. Martin Bradley spent $250,000 on one party, creating such a furor that she and her husband left for Europe. Such antics were reported in the popular press and gave the rich a bad image.

Yet when criticism arose—or when the Socialists, Communists, and anarchists protested—there were those who defended the wealthy, rightly insisting that laissez-faire capitalism was a positive good for all. In 1889 Andrew Carnegie published an article entitled "Wealth" in the *North American Review* in which he said:

> The Socialist or Anarchist who seeks to overturn present conditions is to be regarded as attacking the foundation upon which civilization itself rests, for civilization took its start from the day that the capable, industrious workman said to his incompetent and lazy fellow, "If thou dost not sow, thou shalt not reap," and thus ended primitive Communism by separating the drones from the bees. One who studies this subject will soon be brought to the conclusion that upon the sacredness of property civilization itself depends—the right of the laborer to his hundred dollars in the savings bank, and equally the legal right of the millionaire to his millions. To those who propose to substitute Communism for this intense Individualism the answer, therefore, is: The race has tried that. All progress from that barbarous day to the present time has resulted from its displacement. Not evil, but good, has come to the race from the accumulation of wealth by those who have the ability and energy that produce it.

There were many who failed to agree with Carnegie, however. They were not of necessity Communists or anarchists or Socialists but rather people who wanted changes in the system of free enterprise in America to favor the less productive. When these people at long last did begin to turn their attention to breaking up the trusts, they tried first at the state level. Just as in the realm of railroad regulation, however, the reformers quickly learned that the "problem" was national in scope. Thus they focused their energies at the federal level—only to discover grave constitutional problems. The federal government, under the Constitution, had the power to regulate only interstate commerce—and most manufacturing took place within a single state. Reformers also had to overcome the conviction that the government should not interfere with business in any way, that the hands-off policy of the federal government to that time was what had brought America to industrial greatness, that antitrust legislation, if any, should be left to the states. But state regulation had failed, as in the *Wabash* case of 1887 when the Supreme Court had ruled that a state could not regulate industry, for thereby it deprived the corporate person of its property without due process of law.

Reformers continued to work, however, and in 1890 came "An Act to Protect Trade and Commerce Against Unlawful Restraints and Monopolies," better known as the Sherman Antitrust Act. Passed on July 2, 1890, this act was based on the power of Congress to regulate interstate commerce. It made combinations and contracts "in restraint of trade among the several States or with foreign nations" illegal. The attorney general was empowered to prosecute violators, who could receive heavy fines and jail sentences; also, victims of combinations in restraint of trade could receive triple damages. But the act was vague, its terms ill-defined. Prosecution was left to the federal government, not the wronged individual, and Harrison, Cleveland, and McKinley were not inclined to prosecute. Examples of the vagueness of the law became evident soon after passage, as in 1895 when Attorney General Richard Olney, after proving that the Sugar Trust controlled 98 percent of the sugar refined in the United States, lost his case in the Supreme Court because, said the court, he had failed to prove the trust sought "to put a restraint upon trade and commerce" thereby. However, at the same time, the act was used to prosecute four labor unions as combinations in restraint of trade. And the industrialists were protected by this law; to complainants they could answer, sue under the antitrust act.

The Farmers' Protest

The rising chorus of protests against the railroads, the monopolies, and the trusts was led by farmers, who suffered from falling prices for their produce along with rising prices for what they bought. As one said, "The farmer sells wholesale and buys retail, but he pays the freight both ways." The first attempt to organize the farmers for meaningful action came in 1867 when Oliver Hudson Kelley, a clerk in the Department of Agriculture, started an organization called the Patrons of Husbandry, popularly known as the Grange. Kelley saw the Grange as a way to spread information about scientific farming, but it quickly became a vehicle for farmers' protests, especially against the railroad. By 1874 the Grange had almost three-quarters of a million members, most of them in the Midwest. Receiving no satisfaction from their grievances about the so-called short haul evil and the high rates of banks and insurance companies, the Grangers determined upon political action. In the mid-1870s they began offering candidates for public office and, to their surprise, winning control of several state legislatures. Promptly they enacted legislation to control the railroads, as in Illinois. However, these laws often proved poorly drafted and unenforceable, despite the Supreme Court approval extended in the case *Munn* v. *Illinois*. The Grangers also attempted to establish cooperatively owned factories, stores, and sales agencies, but these largely failed through inexperience and ignorance; additionally, the farmers did not support their cooperatives when the trusts undersold Grange stores.

The Grange movement subsided late in the 1870s because of such reverses, to be replaced by the Greenback Party, whose demand was inflation. From 1865 to 1900 there was a period of deflation. The Greenback Party, organized in 1870, demanded that Congress print millions of dollars of paper money not backed up by gold or silver. In the election of 1878 the Greenback Party polled a million votes and elected fifteen congressmen, but was unable to persuade the conservative national government to enact its proposals. Thereafter the party declined rapidly. In 1880 its presidential candidate, James B. Weaver, received only 300,000 votes. As the party declined, however, its demands were taken up by other groups dedicated to the free and unlimited coinage of silver.

Then, during the 1880s, farm prices rose slightly, reducing farmers' discontent. However in 1887 prices fell again. The result was a wave of foreclosures that raised farmers' ire and led to still another attempt at political agitation. The Southern Farmers' Alliance, started in Texas in the late 1860s as a social organization, and the Northern Farmers' Alliance, established in 1880 and centered in the Midwest, made attempts in the mid-1880s to ally into a large national organization. The Southern Alliance preferred to work within the Democratic Party, however, while the Northern Alliance, joined by former Greenback Party members, decided to form the People's Party (Populists).

Leaders of the People's Party were colorful: James Baird Weaver of Iowa, "Sockless Jerry" Simpson, and Mary Elizabeth Lease of Kansas (who urged farmers in most unladylike tones to "raise less corn and more hell"). In 1890 the Populists elected nine congressmen and carried several Midwestern state legislatures. The next year they organized still more formally, and they met in Omaha in national convention in 1892 to nominate James B. Weaver for president. Their platform called for direct election of United States senators, for the initiative and the referendum on legislation, for government ownership of railroads, telephones, and telegraph, for a graduated income tax, for a shorter workday for labor, and for currency inflation. They also wanted government warehouses in which to store farm produce. Their candidate, Weaver, received 1,042,000 popular votes and twenty-two electoral votes, sufficient to encourage the party greatly. They began looking forward to the election of 1896 with much anticipation.

Labor Unrest

Just as farmers were angry, so also were factory workers. Appalling laboring conditions in the factories aroused concern—even hatred—at the same time that a few rich people were throwing parties at which cigarettes were lighted with one-hundred-dollar bills. Laborers between 1865 and 1900 had to be content with a basic wage that changed little: $1.50 per ten-hour day. Children as young as ten were working the same hours. In Southern cotton mills, children working at the looms on the night shift were kept awake by having cold water thrown in their faces, while little girls cutting fruit and vegetables in the canneries worked sixteen-hour days during the harvest season. Industrial accidents were common in the United States; in fact, the American accident record was the highest of any industrialized nation at the time, for there were few laws requiring safety devices. Unrestricted immigration provided a source of cheap labor and helped kill strikes. Periodic layoffs were common during cyclic readjustments in the economy. When recessions came, the trusts simply shut down factories without notice. Yet another evil was the company town where conditions were miserable; tyrannical bosses ran these towns and high, even exorbitant, rates prevailed.

Prior to the Civil War there had been attempts to start labor unions, but these were killed by economic panics in 1837 and 1857. The first post-Civil War attempt to organize workers was done by the National Labor Union, started in Baltimore in 1866. By 1868 it claimed 600,000 members, but it oriented itself toward political action, even running a candidate for president in 1872 on a labor reform ticket. It failed to survive the Panic of 1873; founded on idealism, it was not realistic enough to survive.

Equally impractical was the Noble and Holy Order of the Knights of Labor, organized in 1869 at Philadelphia by Uriah S. Stephens. The Knights of Labor admitted all workers to membership, save lawyers, bankers, stockbrokers, liquor dealers, and professional gamblers. Its aims were "to secure to the toilers a proper share of the wealth they create." They also aimed to organize cooperatives to produce and distribute goods. The Knights made little headway until Terence V. Powderly became Grand Master in 1879. Powderly was a Pennsylvania machinist who organized more than thirty cooperatives. He opposed the strike as a weapon, but his union received its biggest boost when it supported a strike against Jay Gould's Missouri Pacific Railroad in 1885—and won, even forcing Gould to rehire hundreds of union men whom he had fired. This success brought so many recruits to its banner that union membership jumped to over 700,000, and the union planned a May Day rally in Chicago in 1886 to demonstrate for the eight-hour day. The choice of cities proved unfortunate, for in Chicago a bitter strike against the McCormick Harvester Company was in progress. At the rally at Haymarket Square on May 3 a bomb was thrown at the police; one officer was killed and several were injured. A riot followed, during which an additional seven policemen and four civilians were killed and hundreds were injured. The bomb-thrower was never found, but eight anarchists were arrested and placed on trial, more for being anarchists than for any bomb-throwing. All were found guilty, and seven were sentenced to hang; five actually went to the gallows. Later, liberal Governor John P. Altgeld of Illinois freed the surviving three, charging the judge with "malicious ferocity."

Tainted by the Haymarket violence, the Knights of Labor died quickly as public opinion turned against them. They were supplanted by a different type of union, the "business union" or "craft union." The American Federation of Labor was organized in 1886 by Samuel Gompers, a New York cigar maker who urged his followers to give a day's work for a day's pay and who reminded them that a profit for the employer was of benefit to the worker. Gompers aimed to win members not from all laborers but from skilled workers within certain crafts. Each craft was organized as a local union, with the local unions affiliated under the national banner of the AF of L. Gompers insisted on regular payment of dues to provide each union and the national organization with a strike fund; he insisted on full-salaried organizers to enlarge and discipline the membership. And he had no political aspirations; rather he aimed to force business to bargain collectively with union members (not with all workers). Gompers believed an essential goal was the "closed shop," meaning a factory that employed only union members. By 1892 the AF of L had 250,000 members and was making satisfactory progress in its efforts to bargain collectively. Then came two violent and losing strikes.

In 1892, with Andrew Carnegie in Europe, Henry Clay Frick as president of the

Samuel Gompers

THE great organizer of American skilled labor was thirteen when he immigrated to the United States from his native London, England, in 1863. His father, a cigar maker, had sent young Gompers to a Jewish free school for four years, then had apprenticed him to a shoemaker at age ten. A few months later, however, he was apprenticed to his own father to learn the cigar making trade, which he followed in New York City after the family moved there. There in 1864 he joined the Cigarmakers Union. In his spare time he attended lectures and participated in debates at Cooper Union, and he joined the Odd Fellows and the Foresters.

At the shop where he worked, pay was given by the piece and talking was allowed. His fellow workers often rolled his quota of cigars while he read to them, often from labor and economics tracts, even the writings of Marx and other socialist and Communist thinkers. Gradually he formed his own philosophy, which was prounion and pro-workingman but not antibusiness. Gradually he rose through the ranks of the Cigarmakers Union, which was reorganized following the Panic of 1873, becoming president of the local union and then a founder and first president of the American Federation of Labor in 1886. He would hold this office, except for one year, until his death in 1924.

His was the decision that kept the AF of L from trying to create cooperative stores and from accepting leadership from "theorizers" and intellectuals. Rather, he worked for a union wherein members would get higher wages, more leisure time, and better working conditions.

Today some of his theories doubtless would get him kicked out of many unions. For example, he did not want the workers to try to run the business; leave that to management, he said; nor did he want his union to enter politics directly. During World War I he urged laborers to support the war effort, and he argued that the strike should be labor's weapon of last resort. A practical man, his attitude toward new doctrines or theories was "study your union card, . . . and if the idea doesn't square with that, it ain't true."

Carnegie Steel Company announced a cut in wages because of a profit squeeze. The AF of L refused to accept this. Frick responded on July 1, 1892, with a lockout; he closed the Homestead Plant in Pennsylvania and hired 300 Pinkerton detectives to protect company property. The Pinkerton operatives came to the plant on barges; the strikers, knowing the schedule, met the detectives at the docks with guns and dynamite, and a pitched battle was fought on July 6. After several hours of fighting that left three guards and ten workers dead, the Pinkertons surrendered and were escorted roughly out of town. Frick then asked for and received protection from the state militia; 8000 guardsmen were supplied by the state governor. Public opinion, at first sympathetic to the workers, turned against them when an anarchist tried to kill Frick. Slowly the workers drifted back to their jobs, their cause lost.

The following year saw the beginnings of the Panic of 1893, a severe depression that lasted some four years. Wages were cut, millions were thrown out of work, and labor disputes grew in intensity. The major battle came in Illinois at the Pullman Palace Car Company works near Chicago. Even before the panic, railroad companies and their workers had a long history of strife. American railroads had an appallingly high accident record because of the sloppy construction methods used to lay track; as late as 1907 an average of twelve workers a week were being killed on American railroads. Railroad workers could not get insurance, so they organized "brotherhoods" to offer mutual protection to widows and orphans. When steel rails were laid, longer trains and longer hauls became common, meaning more work.

In contrast with the railroad brotherhoods was the American Railway Union, organized by Eugene V. Debs, himself a fiery railroad worker. In 1894 at the Pullman plant, one-third of the workers were summarily laid off and the other two-thirds had their wages cut by 40 percent. However, company officials refused to lower the rent on housing in the company town of Pullman; the rent there already was 25 percent higher than similar housing elsewhere. A delegation of workers protested peacefully—and all were fired, whereupon the rest of the employees went on strike. They appealed to Debs' American Railway Union for aid, which he gave in the form of money and by having his 150,000 union members refuse to handle Pullman cars. Railroad officials responded by firing all workers who refused to handle Pullmans; the American Railway Union thereupon called a general strike, and all rail service west of Chicago was brought to a halt.

Railroad officials found little sympathy from Governor John P. Altgeld of Illinois, so they appealed to federal officials for help, asking that Army troops be sent in. The Constitution stipulates that federal troops can be sent into a state only by request of local authorities—and Governor Altgeld would not request them—but that was no deterrent to President Cleveland and his attorney general, Richard Olney. Olney, a former railroad lawyer, decided that the troops could be employed to keep the mail moving. On July 2, 1894, Olney secured an injunction under the Sherman Antitrust Act to prevent the union from interfering; two days later, Cleveland ordered 2000 soldiers to Chicago to safeguard the mail. The injunction against the union was so broad in scope that it practically forbade Debs and his union to continue the strike; when they ignored it, they were arrested, tried for contempt (without jury trial), and sentenced to six months in jail. With union leaders in jail, the strike collapsed by July 20. Debs emerged from prison a martyr, a convert to socialism, and a dedicated enemy of capitalism.

The Homestead and Pullman strikes illustrated the widening differences between capital and labor. Also, they showed how federal troops and federal courts were being used as strikebreakers. In short, the Interstate Commerce Act, intended to curb the trusts, had become an aid to big business. Yet in spite of the evils suffered by labor during this era, the workers did not turn to the unions in large numbers. By 1898 there were an estimated 17 million factory workers in America, but only half a million union members. In frustration at the failure of workers to turn to them, as well as because of federal aid to businessmen, some extremists tried to subvert the union movement to more violent measures to force concessions from the captains of industry.

Conditions in the anthracite coal mines of Pennsylvania were so wretched that some miners turned to acts of terrorism. Murders and beatings were performed by a group known as the "Molly Maguires," a radical offshoot of a fraternal group known as the Ancient Order of Hibernians, incorporated in Pennsylvania in 1871 for charitable purposes. In 1875 the anthracite coal miners of eastern Pennsylvania went on strike between January and June; hunger forced them back to work and to accept a 20 percent cut in pay. The Philadelphia & Reading Railroad employed Pinkerton detectives, notably James McParlan, who secured evidence that saw twenty-four miners arrested, held, and tried early in 1876; all were found guilty and ten were hanged, reducing the appeal of extremist union tactics.

The last major effort at extremist union tactics came in 1905, when William "Big Bill" Haywood organized the International Workers of the World, known both as the IWW and the Wobblies. The IWW believed in direct action to accomplish its goals of anarchistic syndicalism. Members of this union wanted to abolish the government and replace it with a national syndicate of workers, who would own the factories and run them. Most of the members of this union came from the West and were largely unskilled—men working in lumbering, mining, dock labor, fruit-growing, and similar rough occupations. In the Northeast, the IWW concentrated on the textile mills, and in 1912 it won a bloody strike at Lowell, Massachusetts. But it opposed American entry into World War I and thereby died quickly, overwhelmed by patriotism.

Labor did make tangible gains in the period 1865–1900: the contract labor law that allowed businessmen to hire workers overseas and bring them under contract to work in the United States for a specified period of time in return for their passage money was abolished. In 1868 Congress established the eight-hour day on public works, and in 1892 it extended the eight-hour day to government employees. Finally, labor managed to get a host of state and local laws enacted on safety standards—more often ignored than enforced. Labor also had found its tools of organization. But despite its failures, laborers in the United States did not turn to violent socialist political action as workers did in Europe; they worked, waited, and lobbied for federal regulation and became ready recruits for the so-called progressive movement that would sweep America at the turn of the twentieth century.

Urban Conditions

Rapid industrialization had produced another class eager to join the progressive movement, the city dweller. In 1840 only one in twelve Americans lived in urban areas. By 1860 the ratio had increased to one in six, and by 1900 to one in three. Many of these city dwellers were factory workers who crowded in as industry grew. During the period there was no urban planning—just growth. Immigrants swelled city populations, along with farm lads moving to town. City development was mainly in the hands of real-estate operators who cut the land into squares, built houses, and laid out streets with little thought to beauty, health, or recreational needs. City fathers felt they had performed their function when they supplied water, fire and police protection, and garbage collection. There were few, if any, restrictions about crowded living quarters, just as there was little worry about how rooms were ventilated or about plumbing. American cities rapidly were becoming slums with growing crime and vice problems.

Because few people paid attention to local government, the results were disastrous. In 1890 James Bryce wrote, "With few exceptions the city governments of the United States are the worst in Christendom—the most expensive, the most inefficient, and the most corrupt." He was right to a disheartening extent. The career of Boss William M. Tweed of New York City well illustrated his point. Tweed, as president of the board of supervisors of New York City , placed his cronies at critical points and swindled the city for an estimated $45 million to $100 million before he was exposed. Contractors were expected to pad their estimates for work, then split the excess with the Tweed Ring. Tweed had judges, policemen, and even newspaper reporters on his payroll. Thomas Nast, a cartoonist, was Tweed's downfall; his cartoons showing Tweed and his cronies were exceedingly effective, for, as Tweed said wrathfully, the people could not read but they could "look at the damn pictures." Tweed was brought to trial and convicted for his crimes.

Yet even though corrupt bosses such as Tweed were exposed, the city slums continued to grow. The extremely poor lived in the cities in conditions barely endurable. Tenements spread as the middle class moved to the suburbs, tenements that were tiny apartments, overcrowded, often lacking sanitary facilities. Dozens crowded into rooms too small for a single family, while rising land prices caused landlords to build on the land to the extent that nothing was left for trees, grass, or recreational areas. Those who protested were evicted. Yet these poor could vote— and with other alienated Americans they were ready to legislate change. Their day arrived approximately with the turn of the twentieth century.

Chapter Eleven

A Restless Republic

The Progressive Revolution

THE last years of the nineteenth century and the early years of the twentieth century seem, in nostalgic retrospect, to have been a time of Fourth-of-July speeches, quiet strolls in the sylvan countryside, and ice-cream socials on spacious lawns. Yet these were momentous years, during which a revolution was occurring—a quiet revolution, a peaceful revolution, an unnoticed revolution, but a revolution nonetheless. It was fought not with bullets but with ballots, not with flashing swords but with slashing words, not with armies conquering territory but with a philosophy that conquered minds and hearts. Almost four decades would pass before this revolution was completed and the national government subverted from the intent of the Founding Fathers. Yet the substantive fact of this revolution occurred between 1897 and 1917—and the country was left irrevocably changed.

This progressive revolution in brief was a shift in philosophic position when eighteenth- and nineteenth-century liberals suddenly became twentieth-century conservatives and when eighteenth- and nineteenth-century conservatives became twentieth-century liberals, at least in their attitudes toward the central government. The Federalists, who were the conservatives of their day, favored a strong federal government; their position was often called "Hamiltonian." And the Jeffersonians, the liberals of their day, had favored a weak central government. During the progressive revolution, however, the labels were reversed; the "liberals" suddenly were those speaking in favor of a strong central government, while the "conservatives" shifted to a position favoring states' rights. This dramatic change reversed national attitudes of more than a century's standing, again with the "liberals" winning out. The central government was immeasurably enlarged and strengthened by the progressive revolution.

Roots of Conservatism

No revolution springs forth the product of a day or a single event. The roots of the progressive revolution were buried deep in American and world history. The progressive revolution was in part a reaction to a philosophy that sprang from Charles Darwin's *The Origin of Species*. Published in 1859, this work argued the process of natural selection of the species most fitted to survive. Darwin's philosophy outraged religious fundamentalists, but it was espoused by some scientists. Then a British philosopher, Herbert Spencer, applied Darwin's theory of survival of the fittest (a catch-phase coined by Spencer) to society and declared that evolution was synonymous with progress. Spencer's books enjoyed a wide sale in the United States, and they helped convert some churchmen such as Henry Ward Beecher. But it was William Graham Sumner who completed the conversion of Darwinism to a social philosophy. The most fit societies survived, while the less fit perished, said Sumner, a Yale professor; likewise, the most fit individuals not only survived but prospered, while the less fit became ordinary workers—or perished. Businessmen welcomed the doctrine of "Social Darwinism," for it loaned a patina of respectability to their business practices. Social Darwinism held that reform—that is, government interference in the marketplace—was interference with the process of natural selection and thus contra-survival. Sumner was consistent; he held that government should not aid the businessman, just as it should not aid the common man. He believed there should be no tariff, no give-away of the public domain, nor any of the other practices of the day that helped the captains of industry make great fortunes. For this consistency of belief, businessmen turned against Sumner.

Opponents of Capitalism

Precursors of the progressive revolution were the men who early opposed the doctrine of Social Darwinism. In 1883 sociologist Lester F. Ward published a denunciation of the doctrine in his *Dynamic Sociology*, a book received so coldly that it sold only 500 copies. He argued that man had used science to benefit himself in numerous ways; if man used natural law in science to his benefit, why also should he not use the social sciences for the betterment of man? Thus he welcomed social intervention by the government—which meant he favored federal programs of social amelioration. Other disciplines than sociology were involved in the attack on Social Darwinism. Richard T. Ely, John R. Commons, and Edward Bemis—young economists—declared their belief that the government should be used for social betterment; these young economists banded together to found the American Economic Association, which early declared its belief in the "positive assistance" of the state. Then came economist Thorstein Veblen, whose *Theory of the Leisure Class* (1899) and many other volumes attacked the pretensions of the rich; in them he used data drawn from sociology, biology, and anthropology to support his thesis that the government should be used for social betterment.

Attacks on Social Darwinism also came from philosophers such as Henry George, who authored *Progress and Poverty* (1879). In this book George argued against what he believed Social Darwinism had produced: "monstrous wealth and debasing want." His answer was a "single tax" that would appropriate all increases in the value of land for the benefit of society as a whole. In 1888 Edward Bellamy published a novel entitled *Looking Backward, 2000–1887*, in which he argued for the nationalization of all industry and equal wages for all. His novel had wide influence.

Support also came from novelists such as Stephen Crane and William Dean Howells, whose naturalistic writings sensationalized the hardships of the poor. Educationists such as Charles W. Eliot of Harvard challenged the role of education as a supplier of technicians for industry, while theologians such as Dwight L. Moody and Mary Baker Eddy preached social action. Washington Gladden organized a movement known as the "Social Gospel," through which he promoted the social responsibilities of the church for aiding the poor and remaking society to the benefit of the ordinary citizen. Finally, philosophers such as John Dewey and William James revolted against impersonal determinism and developed the philosophy of pragmatism, which, among other things, claimed that man's intelligence could be harnessed by government for social betterment. Lawyers such as Oliver Wendell Holmes and Louis Brandeis carried the new philosophy into the courts to urge the weight of social factors in achieving "justice."

The intellectual protesters of Social Darwinism provided a philosophy of social betterment, but they could not transmute cold philosophy into hard votes on election day. This service was provided by the "Muckrakers," a band of sensational journalists whose stories stirred the conscience of the nation and focused attention on alleged abuses. Muckraking got its name from a 1906 speech by Theodore Roosevelt, in which he likened the sensationalist journalists to the man in *Pilgrim's Progress* who was offered a heavenly crown for his "muck-rake." The sensationalists accepted Roosevelt's appellation and wore it with pride.

Muckrakers included such men as Lincoln Steffens, who wrote of political scandals at the municipal level; David G. Phillips, who showed how some senators were representatives not of the people but of certain special interests; Thomas Lawson, who exposed the stock manipulations of Wall Street financiers; Samuel Hopkins Adams, who detailed the patent medicine fraud; and Ida Tarbell, who dramatized the methods used by John D. Rockefeller in building Standard Oil. Other Muckrakers attacked the trusts, the meat packing industry, slum conditions in the cities, bribery, corruption, and many other evils. Muckraking novels were written by Upton Sinclair, Jack London, David Graham Phillips, Booth Tarkington, and William Allen White.

And there were more serious attacks by reputable authors. John Spargo penned *The Bitter Cry of the Children* to expose the hard realities of child labor and child exploitation by factory owners. Ray Stannard Baker in *Following the Color Line* described the pitiful condition of the Negro, while George K. Turner in *Daughters of the Poor* purported to show how poor girls were trapped into white slavery. Gustavus Myers wrote a "Bible" of facts for the muckrakers in his *The Great American Fortunes;* in this book he detailed how some millionaires had made their fortunes through the connivance of a corrupt government that aided them in acquiring title to public land, public-utility franchises, and rich mineral deposits. Myers' book gave the muckrakers and the progressive movement facts and figures to cite. And Burton J. Hendricks in *The Story of Life Insurance* so exposed that industry that the state of New York was moved to regulate its insurance companies. These men did much to dispel the myth of American innocence.

Progressive Strength

The muckrakers, scholars, and philosophers stirred the conscience of the nation and galvanized a broad segment of the population into political action. What was called the progressive movement drew its support from diverse groups; the farmers angry at practices of the railroads joined, as did workers indignant at their lot and intellectuals who considered reform fashionable. Other progressives included the newly emerging middle-class professional men such as lawyers not profiting from

William Graham Sumner

THE Summer home at Patterson, New Jersey, in which William was born in 1840, was poor in wealth but rich in intellectualism. His father was unskilled and moved several times before settling at Hartford, Connecticut; there he worked in the repair shop for the Hartford and New Haven Railroad. However, with his family he discussed what he had read and thought, and William grew to manhood in an intellectual environment. After attending the local public schools, he entered Yale University, studied hard, and was ordained an Episcopal priest. There, also, he became friends with young men who later would be leaders in business and industry.

Gradually his thoughts turned from religious matters to questions of economic and social impact, and in 1872 he returned to Yale as a professor of political and social science. There, with a head "magnificently bald," he taught hundreds of students and gave public lectures on his evolving beliefs about society and economics. These involved a sound monetary system backed by gold, the right of business to grow big and bigger, no government interference with business, reform of the civil service, and opposition to socialistic schemes to remake the world. One of his favorite topics was the "Forgotten Man," by which he meant the middle-class, hard-working taxpayer who had to bear the cost of supporting a bungling and inept government's "social quackery."

His only published book during his life was *Folkways,* which appeared in 1907, three years prior to his death in 1910. However, he published numerous essays in popular and scholarly magazines, making himself both the father of modern American sociology and a leading defender of the free-enterprise system. Businessmen and leaders in industry loved to quote him—except when he called protective tariffs economic quackery and detrimental to business.

A stern, moral man, Graham hated sham, poor logic, and bad thinking. Also, he remained consistent and unbending in his total dedication to a totally free capitalistic system. For this reason he had a host of enemies and detractors, few of whom matched his intellectual stature.

the corporations, ministers and religious leaders who sensed their influence slipping into the hands of businessmen, educators tired of training technicians, small businessmen who were being squeezed out by the trusts, and women who wanted the vote and prohibition. The progressive movement thus was broadly based and spread over the country.

Their aims were diverse—almost too diverse. Some wanted to reform the cities; the cities were not meeting fire, sanitation, police, school, and recreational needs, and their governments were notoriously corrupt. Other progressives were angry at the political machines at the state and local level, machines built on immigrant votes. For others the motivation was the lack of a "social conscience" on the part of the captains of industry. There were progressive demands for regulation of the trusts, for the ballot for women, for national prohibition, for industrial safety legislation. Sometimes one segment of the progressive movement would collapse, and sometimes parts of the movement were working in opposition to yet other parts, while occasionally all segments would unite to fight for a common cause. "White Collar" workers constituted the voting strength of the progressive movement, and their only method of economic protest was the ballot; they did not have labor unions or trade associations. Leadership came from this same urban middle class, usually college-educated and frequently self-employed, native-born Protestants.

Local Reform

The progressive movement, like the Grangers, attempted reforms first at the local level. Demands for municipal reform had begun in the 1870s, but the first notable successes came in the 1890s. Tom Johnson was elected mayor of Cleveland in 1901 and held office until 1910. He had read Henry George's *Progress and Poverty,* but had rejected the "single tax" theory; however, he had begun to think, and he decided as mayor to break the grip of corporations on the city. First he had a tax study made, producing a great map showing every lot in the city and how much it was taxed; then the city reevaluated its tax base on a more equitable basis, raising the taxes of the corporations and reducing those of individuals. After a lengthy court battle, Johnson and the progressives won. Another Ohioan, Samuel "Golden Rule" Jones of Toledo, likewise managed to prove that municipal government did not have to be corrupt. The movement for municipal reform peaked with the creation of the city commission form of government; this originated in Galveston following the disastrous flood there in 1900. By 1914 some 400 other cities had copied the idea of independent administrative commissions.

Municipal reform was a long, difficult task, however, and the progressives turned to the state level to achieve their goals. The leader at the state level was Robert M. LaFollette of Wisconsin. His state was firmly in the hands of the railroading and lumbering interests. In 1900 La Follette won the governorship—despite opposition from old-line Republicans—by fighting the campaign chiefly on the issues of a direct primary and tax equalization. He also advocated direct election of United States senators, the initiative, referendum, and recall, legislation to regulate business, and an informed public. In subsequent elections, La Follette secured a progressive majority in the legislature, and with it he enacted what became known as the "Wisconsin Way." This included: a railroad commission with power to fix rates based on the investment of the railroad; a state income tax law; an antipass law that forbade the giving of free passes to politicians to ride the railroads; an antilobby law; a corrupt-practices law limiting the amount that politicians could spend to win election; the initiative, referendum, and recall; conservation, particularly of forests; and cooperation of the University of Wisconsin in improving the state, especially through extension work. La Follette, his work done at the state level, sought and was elected to the United States Senate, where he continued to push for progressive legislation; for example, in 1915 he secured the La Follette Seamen's Law that radically altered working conditions on ocean-going, river, and lake vessels, regulated seamen's wages, and controlled conditions of employment on such vessels. Another successful progressive state governor was Hiram Johnson, who battled to push the Southern Pacific out of California state politics, then moved up to the national Senate.

Yet, as at the local level, progressives found that the center of power in the United States was not at the state level but in Washington. Thus they transferred their attention there, only to find their way blocked by President William McKinley. The last Union veteran to occupy the presidency, McKinley was friendly, kindly, and lovable. However, he was inclined to follow the advice of party leaders such as Mark Hanna. Fortunately for McKinley, prosperity returned to the nation, ending the Panic of 1893, just about the time he entered office. Poor foreign wheat crops spurred sales of American grain, bringing more money to the farmers. Also, gold was discovered in the Klondike and fresh strikes were made in Colorado; these new sources of specie appreciably increased the amount of currency in circulation and appeased the debtor class. Thus the Republicans could claim to be the party of prosperity.

The Republicans could offer one other picture of itself to the public—that of capitalist-progressive. Progressives had been talking of grass-roots politics, of returning power to the people by overthrowing the corrupt political machines to elect honest congressmen. Several senators elected in 1896 were themselves business millionaires; rather than pay corrupt politicians to secure their wishes, businessmen were turning to politics personally to secure what they wanted. Mark Hanna entered the Senate in 1897, to be welcomed by Rhode Island's Senator Nelson W. Aldrich, a wealthy businessman whose daughter had married the son of John D. Rockefeller. These businessmen-turned-politicians were not corrupt party hacks, but they certainly were not democrats; they believed in government by the meritorious. An example of their style of statecraft was the Dingley Tariff of July 7, 1897, which raised duties to an all-time average high of 57 percent.

The Election of 1900

McKinley's first administration was more concerned with foreign affairs than domestic crises, however. In that realm he bumbled through, more by weakness of American opposition than from any personal or administration brilliance. Thus as the election of 1900 approached, McKinley was riding a crest of popularity. In that election year there were fringe parties trying to exploit discontent, but they proved more comedy relief than real opposition. The Social Democratic Party met on March 6 to nominate Eugene V. Debs for president, while the Populists split, part to support Bryan and part to follow the standard of Wharton Barker of Pennsylvania. The Republicans met in jubilant mood in Philadelphia on June 19 to renominate McKinley, and to select the hero of the late Spanish-American War and governor of New York, Theodore Roosevelt, for vice president. Their platform endorsed Repub-

William McKinley

lican foreign policy and the gold standard (which had become law on May 14—the Currency Act, which firmly committed the United States to the gold standard). The Democrats gathered at Kansas City on July 4 to renominate William Jennings Bryan and to select Adlai E. Stevenson for vice president on a platform opposing "imperialism" and the gold standard. Imperialism proved the main issue in an otherwise lackluster campaign, at the end of which McKinley was swept back into office. McKinley's slogan, "the full dinner pail," proved attractive to 7,218,491 voters, while Bryan pulled 6,356,734 popular votes; in the electoral college the vote was 292 to 155 in McKinley's favor.

McKinley had hardly begun his second term when he decided in September to attend the International Exposition at Buffalo, New York. There on September 6 he was shot by an anarchist, Leon Czolgosz. McKinley lingered until September 14 before dying and leaving Roosevelt president by accident. Roosevelt had been placed on the ticket at the insistence of Thomas Platt, Republican boss in New York, who wanted to get TR out of state politics—and an assassin's bullet had put Roosevelt in the chief executive's chair. This whim of fate did not please leaders in the business community or in the party; Mark Hanna commented in anger, "Now look, that damned cowboy is President of the United States."

Roosevelt's First Term

Roosevelt later admitted that when he assumed office he had no "deliberately planned and far-reaching scheme of social betterment." His sole aim was to be elected president in his own right. Even if he had wanted to make sudden and sweeping changes, he could not have done so because Congress was solidly in the hands of the old-line Republican leadership. Nelson W. Aldrich of Rhode Island was Republican leader in the Senate, and Joseph G. "Uncle Joe" Cannon was Speaker of the House. Thus Roosevelt moved cautiously. He retained McKinley's cabinet, and he consulted Aldrich and Cannon extensively on such matters as his speeches to Congress and his proposals to it. Very quietly, however, he began using the president's patronage power to appoint men loyal to himself and to break Mark Hanna's hold on the party. Quietly he reorganized the Republican Party to make it answerable to him—yet at the same time his appointments were of men markedly more able than those appointed by McKinley. By 1904 Roosevelt's maneuverings had been completed; the GOP had not become progressive, but it did answer to Roosevelt. Hanna's death early in 1904 completed the shift.

When the Republicans convened in convention on June 21, 1904, they quickly nominated Roosevelt for president, along with Senator Charles W. Fairbanks of Indiana for vice president. A month later, meeting in St. Louis, the Democrats selected Alton B. Parker, Grover Cleveland's law partner in New York, and Henry G. Davis of West Virginia to head their ticket. The electorate was not interested, and business failed to contribute to the party that twice had nominated Bryan. Roosevelt's campaign manager solicited funds from the trusts, and they contributed despite the president's progressive stance—or perhaps because of it. Well financed, the Republicans swept to victory. Roosevelt won by an unprecedented margin of 2.5 million popular votes, receiving 7,628,461 to Parker's 5,084,223 and, in the electoral college, 336 to 140. At last he was president in his own right. However, Eugene V. Debs, the Socialist candidate, received some 400,000 popular votes (four times as many as he had received in 1900), making Roosevelt think that more "reform" might be useful.

Bureau of Printing and Engraving

Theodore Roosevelt

BORN in 1858 and Harvard-educated, Roosevelt studied law and was admitted to the New York bar. He served one term in the New York legislature before going west to ranch in the Dakotas. In 1889 he was appointed to the United States Civil Service Commission. In 1895 he became head of the New York City police force for two years, followed by an appointment as assistant secretary of the navy in the McKinley administration until the outbreak of the Spanish-American War. During that conflict he gained considerable fame with the Rough Riders in Cuba, returning to win election as governor of New York despite Republican Party opposition.

Roosevelt was flamboyant and aggressive, colorful and domineering. Born to wealth and privilege, he simultaneously was sympathetic to the demands of the progressive movement, although during Republican quarrels on progressive issues he had remained loyal to the party rather than breaking with it as others had done.

Roosevelt was a believer in capitalism, but with strong modifications. For example, in 1906 and again in 1907, despite opposition from many commercial interests and small businessmen, he urged Congress to do what leaders of the great industrial combinations wanted: amendment of the Sherman Antitrust Act to permit federal licensing of corporations and provide a federal supervisory power over the big concerns engaged in interstate commerce. He argued that national regulation was necessary because combinations of laborers and farmers were inadequate to police the industrial giants, and because state regulation was likely to be erratic, inefficient, or radical; moreover, he argued, national regulation of big business would not only prove beneficial to big business, it would protect investors and the general public. Finally, he wanted to introduce a higher moral tone into business. And he was the first Republican president since Lincoln to exert strong executive leadership.

The Square Deal

Roosevelt called his stance toward the role of the federal government "The Square Deal," implying reform. He believed that public discontent over the practices of big business had to be met, but in a way that would preserve capitalism. In March, 1902, he instructed his attorney general to bring suit against the Northern Securities Company, a trust organized by railroad barons James J. Hill and Edward H. Harriman to control freight rates to the West Coast. The case lasted from March 10, 1902, to March 14, 1904. In this case the Supreme Court ruled, by a five-to-four decision, that the company was a conspiracy in restraint of trade (as defined by the Sherman Antitrust Act) and ordered it dissolved. Roosevelt proceeded to institute a total of forty-four suits against the big corporations, including the "beef trust," the American Tobacco Company of James Duke, and even Standard Oil; thereby the president won a reputation as a trust-buster and became a hero to the progressives. In truth, big business was not checked, but it did become aware that the federal government was alert to illegal combinations. Roosevelt knew this. "We draw the line against misconduct," he said, "not against wealth."

Just as he tried to enforce the Sherman Antitrust Act, so also Roosevelt worked to strengthen the Interstate Commerce Commission. On February 19, 1903, Congress passed the Elkins Act to forbid rebates and to require the railroads to adhere to their published rates; the act was passed mainly at the behest of the railroads as a tool to fight Standard Oil and the other trusts that were forcing them to give rebates and drawbacks. Then on June 29, 1906, came the Hepburn Act, actively pushed by Roosevelt. The president's proposal would have extended quite broad powers to the ICC, but he had to compromise. The Hepburn Act gave the ICC the power to set maximum "reasonable" rates, and it provided for quick appeal to circuit courts and the Supreme Court; moreover the burden of proof for reversing ICC decisions on rates was placed on the railroads, although they were given the right to secure injunctions suspending ICC decisions until the courts could rule on such cases. The Hepburn Act also authorized the ICC to impose a uniform system of bookkeeping on the railroads. Finally, the Hepburn Act extended the powers of the ICC to include regulation of storage, refrigeration, and terminal facilities, as well as sleeping and express cars and pipeline companies. In 1910 the same power was granted the ICC to govern rates of telephone and telegraph companies.

Both the Hepburn and the Elkins acts were early examples of federal meddling in business for noble reasons, but which proved disastrous in the long run. Between 1897 and 1906—the years between the Panic of 1893 and that of 1907—the railroads had expanded considerably. However, the Hepburn Act deprived railroad management of control over maximum rates (while the Mann-Elkins Act of 1910 would remove their control over minimum rates). Thereafter, as prices and wages rose, the railroads repeatedly sought general rate increases, but most of the time the ICC, responding to public pressures, granted them little or nothing. Progressives such as Louis D. Brandeis and Senator Albert Cummins proved legalistic economic illiterates in their opposition to the railroads; their "righteous indignation" overshadowed or covered in the public mind their ignorance of the industry under attack and of the economic issues. Denied the right to price their services, the railroads were forced to cut back on maintenance and upgrading of their stock and roadbeds. (Ironically, when the federal government nationalized the railroads during World War I and federal bureaucrats began looking into the situation, the first thing accomplished was the rate increases that the ICC had denied railroad management since 1910!)

Moving in another direction, Roosevelt in May, 1902, tried to force arbitration in the public interest in a United Mine Workers' strike against anthracite coal mines. On March 22, 1903, this arbitration commission awarded the union a 10 percent wage hike, but it did not force union recognition as a bargaining agent as the strikers had demanded. Previous presidents had intervened in strikes to aid employers; Roosevelt had demonstrated a willingness to use the presidential power to force a negotiated settlement in the public interest—thereby greatly angering mine owners such as George F. Baer and the House of Morgan. Roosevelt further demonstrated his attitude when, on February 14, 1903, Congress established a Department of Commerce *and Labor,* thereby implying that the government would favor neither side but would safeguard the "public interest."

Other progressive legislation in the Roosevelt years included conservation, a subject close to the president's heart. In 1902 he helped secure passage of the Newlands Act, which provided that funds from the sale of public land would be used for reclamation projects (that included building giant dams in the West for irrigation purposes). And with the assistance of Gifford Pinchot, director of the Forest Service, Roosevelt increased national forest lands by 130 million acres, and he withdrew from the public domain almost 90 million acres that contained mineral deposits and water-power sites. Legislation also was passed during Roosevelt's administration that made common carriers in interstate commerce responsible for workers' injuries—and liable for them. Finally, on June 30, 1906, came the Pure Food and Drug Act and the Meat Inspection Act. (Much of the impetus for this legislation came from Socialist Upton Sinclair's hard-hitting attack on the meat packing industry in his novel *The Jungle.*) These acts provided for federal inspection of the packing houses, and they prohibited the sale of harmful foods and drugs, while all had to be labeled to show contents.

Republican fortunes turned downward somewhat because of the Panic of 1907, a severe but short-lived depression that forced several railroads into bankruptcy and led to bank closings and unemployment. As a result of this panic, Congress authorized commissions to study ways to strengthen the national financial structure; eventually from such work would come, in 1913, the Federal Reserve Act to establish the Federal Reserve System that would regulate the supply of money and the credit supply. Roosevelt was sufficiently frightened by the panic to approve the merger of United States Steel and the Tennessee Coal and Iron Company, a merger that liberal critics said would lessen competition, but which brought increased efficiency.

The Republican convention met in Chicago on June 16, 1908, and nominated Roosevelt's hand-picked successor, Secretary of War William Howard Taft of Ohio, for president and James S. Sherman for vice president. The Democrats gathered on July 7 at Denver and, for a third time, chose the seemingly charismatic William Jennings Bryan, no longer a "boy orator," for president and John W. Kern of Indiana for vice president on a platform pledging revision of the tariff. The campaign was quite dull. Roosevelt's progressive measures had left Bryan without an angry constituency to which to appeal, while Taft told the voters he would follow faithfully in Roosevelt's footsteps. On election day, November 3, the voters gave Taft 7,675,320 popular votes and 321 electoral votes to the "Great Commoner's" 6,412,294 popular votes and 162 electoral votes.

The Taft Administration

If the voters thought they had endorsed progressivism by electing Taft, they were to be disappointed, however. Taft in practice seemed more like McKinley than Roosevelt. Jubilant at their victory, Republicans had shouted, "Roosevelt has cut enough hay; Taft is the man to put it into the barn." However, Taft proved slow moving and slow thinking—and he definitely did not put progressive hay in the barn. A large (350-pound) man of good humor, he first displayed his ineptitude in the tariff squabble. Taft during the campaign had promised a tariff reduction and he called a special session of Congress soon after his inauguration to work on such a measure. When Congress met on March 15, 1909, however, it was dominated by Republicans such as Senator Aldrich and Speaker of the House Cannon. Progressives such as La Follette in the Senate and George W. Norris of Nebraska in the House sought Taft's aid, but they found him unwilling to fight Aldrich and Cannon. What emerged on August 5, the Payne-Aldrich Tariff, was a measure that lowered the import duties only on goods where there was little foreign competition but raised duties substantially on wool, sugar, and other items where American trusts were making huge profits. Taft signed the bill, calling it "on the whole . . . the best tariff bill that the Republican Party has ever passed." The one bright spot in the bill for the progressives was a provision for a tariff commission to make a study of import rates.

Despite this setback to progressive hopes, Taft did accomplish several goals they sought—although he did not receive proper credit for such efforts. For example, his administration was responsible for dissolving some ninety trusts (as opposed to only forty-four such dissolutions during Roosevelt's administration). And on June 18, 1910, the Mann-Elkins Act gave more power to the Interstate Commerce Commission. Congress also passed the Sixteenth Amendment providing for a graduated income tax and sent it to the states for ratification; and a Postal Savings Bank System was inaugurated.

Taft's administration was postured before the public as dominated by the trusts, however, especially on the issues of the tariff and conservation. The Payne-Aldrich Tariff was followed by the issue of Canadian reciprocity. In 1911 Taft submitted to the Senate proposals to exempt Canadian goods from import duties provided Canada allowed American goods free entry into that country. Midwesterners were angered by this measure because the only Canadian goods entering the United States were foodstuffs and raw products; as La Follette declared, "It singles out the farmer and forces free trade upon him, but it confers even greater benefits upon a few of the great combinations sheltered behind the high rates found in the Payne-Aldrich tariff." A bill embodying Taft's recommendations passed Congress, but Canadian nationalists refused to go along, fearing such a move was but a first step toward American annexation. The residual effect of this attempt was growing agrarian discontent with the Republican Party.

On the issue of conservation, Taft, on September 15, 1909, backed his secretary of the interior, Richard A. Ballinger, in a move to sell certain water-power sites to private industry, sites that Roosevelt had withdrawn from possible sale. Ballinger represented the viewpoint of businessmen who wanted public resources sold—inexpensively—for private development. Gifford Pinchot, a Roosevelt appointee in charge of the Forest Service and a strong conservationist, protested loudly. Then he publicly denounced Ballinger for selling coal lands in Alaska to a Morgan-Guggenheim syndicate, coal lands that had been reserved for public use. Ballinger denied this assertion, Taft believed his secretary of the interior, and Pinchot was fired. The president privately believed in conservation and had actually extended conservation practices by executive orders, but a rift had been effected between Taft and the conservationists.

Finally Taft angered progressives with his handling of "Uncle Joe" Cannon, Speaker of the House. Taft disliked Cannon, but was afraid to challenge him. When he was approached by young progressives in the House, who wished to deprive the Speaker of much of his power, Taft gave them encouragement. But when the issue approached a vote, the president deserted the progressives to support the Speaker. Nonetheless, the Republican progressives, led by Congressman George W. Norris of Nebraska, pushed through the House a change in the rules that deprived the Speaker of the power to appoint the Rules Committee and to serve on it. Cannon had used his appointive power to this powerful committee to control legislation, and the change sharply reduced his virtual veto over legislation he did not like. The *Wall Street Journal* declared, "The clock has struck for Uncle Joe." It also had struck for Taft, for the progressives believed he had acted deviously. He completed this alienation when in August, 1911, he vetoed efforts to reduce the Payne-Aldrich Tariff.

The Election of 1912

As early as 1909 some progressive Republicans began looking toward the jungles of Africa for their next presidential candidate—for Theodore Roosevelt had gone hunting there when he left the White House. When Roosevelt returned in 1910, he concluded that Taft had "completely twisted around the policies I advocated and acted upon." Thus when he returned his first hello was for Gifford Pinchot, not for Taft. And he declined Taft's invitation to visit at the White House. Yet he held his peace, doing nothing that would publicize his split with the president. Roosevelt finally broke this silence when he became alarmed at Taft's use of the executive patronage to build conservative strength in the Midwest, where progressives had been strongest. In August, 1910, Roosevelt began a speaking tour of the West, where he delineated his doctrine, of "The New Nationalism." At Osawatomie, Kansas, on August 31, 1910, he espoused a number of progressive schemes, arguing that social justice could be attained only through strengthening the power of the federal government so that the chief executive would be the "steward of public welfare." He said that those concerned with property and profits "must now give way to the advocate of human welfare, who rightly maintains that every man holds his property subject to the general right of the community to regulate its use to whatever degree the public welfare may require it." His speech, which shocked conservatives everywhere, outlined what would come to be known as "The Square Deal," a program that included a graduated income tax and an inheritance tax, workmen's compensation for industrial accidents, regulation of the labor of women and children, tariff revision, and firm regulation of corporations through a powerful bureau of corporations. The result of the Osawatomie speech was that Roosevelt clearly became the leader of the progressives. Conservatives reacted with shock; Senator Henry Cabot Lodge declared that Roosevelt had become "little short of a revolutionist."

On January 21, 1911, progressive Republicans met to form the National Progres-

Bureau of Printing and Engraving

William Howard Taft

sive Republican League, with the purpose of wresting the presidential nomination away from Taft in 1912. The driving force in this faction was Senator Robert M. La Follette, who wanted the nomination for himself, however. But many progressive Republicans hesitated to support La Follette, preferring Roosevelt. The former president believed that 1912 would be a Democrat year and preferred to wait until 1916 to seek reelection; thus he was not averse to allowing La Follette to run in 1912—and go down to defeat. Then on February 2, 1912, La Follette, exhausted and worried, delivered a rambling and repetitive speech—little short of a complete mental breakdown. Many of La Follette's followers deserted him in favor of Roosevelt, and on February 24, 1912, the ex-president announced, "My hat is in the ring." Thereby he acquired the undying hatred of La Follette and his Midwestern supporters.

In the Republican primaries in the spring of 1912, Roosevelt easily won, showing he had strong support at the grassroots level. When the Republican convention gathered at Chicago on June 18, however, more than a third of the delegates' seats were contested. The Republican National Committee, composed mainly of Taft supporters, proceeded to give 235 of 254 contested seats to Taft's people, thus preventing Roosevelt's nomination. Taft was nominated on the first ballot, along with James S. Sherman for vice president. Roosevelt told his delegates, "We stand at Armageddon, and we battle for the Lord." He and his followers bolted the Republican Party and met in Chicago on August 5 to hold a Progressive Party convention; with financial support from Frank Munsey, a newspaper magnate, and George W. Perkins of U.S. Steel, the party nominated Roosevelt for president and Hiram Johnson of California for vice president on a platform calling for progressive social reforms. Roosevelt, when questioned about his health, said he felt fit as a bull moose, thereby giving his party a symbol and a nickname.

This split in the Republican Party presaged victory for the Democrats, who gathered jubilantly in convention on June 25 at Baltimore to nominate the reform governor of New Jersey, and former college professor and president, Woodrow Wilson, on the forty-sixth ballot. His running mate was Thomas R. Marshall of Indiana. Their platform called for the abolition of monopolies, a tariff only for revenue, banking reform, and a curb on the use of injunctions in labor disputes. In the campaign that year, Wilson managed to win the former followers of William Jennings Bryan—the rural and small-town voters—through the same religious appeal; Wilson, a staunch Presbyterian, was of the same fundamentalist mold as Bryan. Wilson also proved extraordinarily popular with the progressive voters, pulling them away from Roosevelt to some extent. President Taft made several sad speeches, so conservative they sounded as if they had been written by Senator Aldrich, before he finally collapsed into silence. Roosevelt, meanwhile, had managed to win the hearts of only the Progressive Republicans; in his campaign he sought and received support from big businessmen, to whom he said he wanted only to regulate them, not to abolish their monopolies. Wilson, calling his platform the "New Freedom," replied that Roosevelt's policies would only mean federal licensing of big business to crush competition. An anarchist shot Roosevelt in the arm at Milwaukee, but he finished his speech before consenting to collapse, thereby showing his stamina. However, the voters were not overly impressed, and on election day they gave Wilson 6,296,547 popular votes and 435 electoral votes, and Roosevelt 4,118,571 popular votes and 88 electoral votes. Taft ran an embarrassing third, with 3,486,720 popular votes and eight electoral votes.

Wilson had polled fewer votes than Bryan had received in any of his three campaigns, but had won. He was a minority president, with only 41.9 percent of the popular vote. However, his votes, when combined with those of Roosevelt, totaled an impressive 69.3 percent—and Eugene V. Debs, the Socialist candidate, had received almost a million votes in addition to these, bringing the total vote for change to 75 percent. Once in office, Wilson tried to unify the Democratic Party. He named Bryan secretary of state; a New York businessman from Georgia, William Gibbs McAdoo, secretary of the treasury; and William B. Wilson, former secretary-treasurer of the United Mine Workers, as his secretary of labor. His major personal adviser was a Texan, "Colonel" Edward M. House, about whom one contemporary remarked, "He can walk on dead leaves and make no more noise than a tiger."

Wilson's First Term

Wilson worked extraordinarily hard as president to transform his campaign promises into law. On the day he took office he called a special session of Congress to lower the tariff. And he appeared before Congress in person to read his message, the first time since Jefferson's day that a president had gone before the legislative body. The result was the Underwood-Simmons Tariff of 1913, providing substantial tariff cuts, the first since the Civil War, and introducing some element of European competition in the American market. To replace the lost revenue, Representative Cordell Hull introduced an amendment to the Underwood Tariff calling for the Sixteenth Amendment to the Constitution—allowing for an income tax. The amendment set rates which, at the time, seemed ridiculously high—one percent on income above $4000 a year, rising another one percent on income over $20,000 a year to a total of 6 percent on income above $500,000 a year.

Rather than lose the momentum of reform working in his favor, Wilson held Congress in session through the hot summer months. On May 31 came the Seventeenth Amendment to the Constitution, providing for the direct election of senators, which then was sent to the states for ratification. Then came the first major revision in the nation's banking and currency system since the 1840s. Following the Panic of 1907, Congress had provided for a National Monetary Commission to study the nation's currency and banking system. Senator Nelson W. Aldrich, head of that commission, proposed a privately controlled central bank similar to the Second Bank of the United States. Conservative Democrats such as Congressman Carter Glass preferred regional banks supervised by a federal board, while rural Democrats such as William Jennings Bryan wanted a national system under the complete control of the central government. Wilson's call for reform was aided by the report of Democrat Congressman Arsène Pujo, published early in 1913, which used fake statistics to prove that the money trust was the greatest monopoly in the country. Although Pujo's attacks were unjustified either on legal or economic grounds, Louis Brandeis popularized his arguments in his book, *Other People's Money and How the Bankers Use It*. The result was the Glass-Owen Act, which was signed into law on December 23, 1913. This created twelve Federal Reserve Banks, to be "owned" by the private banks in each of the twelve districts; these Federal Reserve Banks could rediscount notes, issue a new type of inflationary paper currency (Federal Reserve notes), and fulfill other banking functions. National banks (chartered by the federal government) were required to be members, while other banks were encouraged to join. The federal government retained control of the system through the Federal Reserve Board of seven members, each appointed to staggered fourteen-year terms by the president. These banks would serve as the federal depositories. At first there was great opposition to the Federal Reserve System from bankers, but within a year nearly half of all banks in the nation were members of the system. By the late 1920s the number of members had grown to some four-fifths of all banks.

By 1914, when Wilson began moving on more regulatory legislation, many big businessmen were in total agreement with him. Teddy Roosevelt had held that there were good and bad trusts that should be regulated; Woodrow Wilson held that all trusts were evil and should be destroyed so that competition would result. Roosevelt favored regulated monopoly, while Wilson favored regulated competition (an admittedly fine distinction)—a stance with which most businessmen agreed. Moreover, many big businessmen, especially those in public service enterprises, wanted to bring their industries under governmental regulation by expert, nonpolitical commissions. The electric utility industry, for example, sought to have itself regulated by state commissions because these could legalize its monopolistic status and stave off municipal ownership, as well as continued control and harassment by corrupt or inept local politicians. Executives of Prudential Life Insurance Company, U.S. Steel, and the "Beef Trust" were avid supporters of federal regulations of their respective industries.

Thus in September, 1914, when Wilson proposed the Federal Trade Commission Act, he did so with the blessing of most of big business. This act provided for a Federal Trade Commission to replace the Bureau of Corporations, and it had the power to investigate corporations, receive reports, and issue cease and desist orders to prevent "unfair methods of competition." On October 15 that same year Congress passed the Clayton Antitrust Act, which declared several business practices to be illegal; however, Wilson lost interest in this bill when it was so loaded with amendments that, as some progressives said, it had so few teeth it could not chew milk-toast. Interestingly, the act specifically declared that labor and agricultural organizations were not conspiracies in restraint of trade, and it forbade the use of injunctions in labor disputes unless property was in danger of irreparable injury.

Other bits and pieces of interventionist legislation in Wilson's first term included the Smith-Lever Act of May 8, 1914. This provided for agricultural extension work through the land-grant colleges under the Department of Agriculture. And on March 4, 1915, came the La Follette Seamen's Act, which aimed at improving the conditions under which sailors in the merchant marine worked. Wilson by this time, however, was turning away from progressive legislation; only with reluctance did he sign the La Follette Seamen's Act. He turned aside pleas from women's suffrage organizations, answering them with a states' rights argument. He backed Southern cabinet members in their introduction of Jim Crowism in his administration. And he gave no aid to a child labor bill because he thought it unconstitutional. His last progressive move before his thoughts turned to reelection was to appoint Louis Brandeis to the Supreme Court on January 28, 1916.

The Election of 1916

The Republicans met in their convention on June 7 at Chicago to nominate Charles Evans Hughes, an associate justice of the New York Supreme Court, for the presidency and Charles W. Fairbanks of Indiana for vice president. The Progressive Party met the same day in Chicago and named Theodore Roosevelt their candidate,

Woodrow Wilson

but he refused to run, saying he would support Hughes; whereupon the Progressives endorsed Hughes—and disintegrated. The Democrats met a week later, June 14, at St. Louis to renominate its ticket of 1912, Wilson and Marshall. To appeal to the voters, who were yet in a progressive mood, Democratic congressmen pushed through a host of progressive legislation that summer and early fall. On July 11 came the Federal Highway Act, providing for federal funds for road construction. On July 17 Congress passed the Farm Loan Act that set up twelve Farm Loan Banks to provide credit to farmers and which aided farmers' cooperatives. On August 11 Wilson signed the Warehouse Act, which allowed farmers to deposit certain commodities at licensed warehouses and receive receipts that they could use as collateral for loans. The Keating-Owen Child Labor Act was passed on September 1; it banned from interstate commerce all goods manufactured with child labor. (The bill was declared unconstitutional by the Supreme Court in the case *Hammer* v. *Dagenhart* in 1918, whereupon Congress passed a heavy tax on goods produced with child labor—an act that would later be declared unconstitutional.) The Adamson Act of September 3 dictated the eight-hour day on interstate railroads, while the Workmen's Compensation Act placed some half million federal employees under workmen's compensation. Finally Wilson signed the Emergency Revenue Act of September 8, doubling the rate of taxation under the income tax.

With these measures enacted into law, Wilson could posture himself before the progressives, farmers, and laborers as their champion—without saying that, simultaneously, he had greatly enlarged the interventionist function of the federal government, seriously weakening states' rights and dramatically changing the role of the federal government.

In the campaign of 1916 the Republicans had intended to use war preparedness as a major issue, but Wilson preempted them with the slogan, "He kept us out of war." In 1914 Europe had been plunged into the abyss of war; Wilson had prevented American entry, however, and could pose as a statesman. The Republicans' worst enemy proved to be Hughes himself, who was a poor campaigner. He talked vaguely of a firmer stand for the rights of Americans and of neutral nations during the European war. Roosevelt campaigned strenuously for Hughes—which probably hurt the Republicans. Finally Hughes tried to pose as a progressive, which proved disastrous; this posture disenchanted conservatives, while the progressives already supported Wilson and refused to change. Early returns on election night, November 7, indicated a victory for Hughes, and he went to bed thinking he had been elected. The vote from the far West defeated him, however; during the campaign he had snubbed Hiram Johnson of California, and that state went for Wilson by 4000 votes—giving national victory to Wilson. The incumbent received 9,127,695 popular votes and 277 electoral votes to Hughes' 8,533,507 popular votes and 254 electoral votes. The Socialist and Prohibition candidates had garnered 4.4 percent of the popular votes, while Hughes received 46.2 percent, and Wilson was reelected with 49.4 percent of the vote—making him twice a minority president.

Before inauguration day the following March, Congress passed two measures popular with the progressives and labor. On February 5, 1917, came a bill providing for a literacy test for immigrants; it passed over Wilson's veto after having failed to pass vetoes in 1897, 1913, and 1915. And on February 23 the Smith-Hughes Act provided for vocational education in secondary schools across the nation. Yet the progressive movement had lost its internal direction, for as with all progressive movements it had engaged America in a war for however idealistic motives. Wilson's second term was occupied with foreign, not domestic affairs. The progressive movement had come into focus during the McKinley administration, gathered strength from the war with Spain, and moved the United States from its isolated and insulated position in world affairs to involvement in the greatest war the world had ever known.

The Annexation of Hawaii

Foreign affairs first came into sharp focus at the end of the Harrison administration early in 1893. In Hawaii a group of American planters led a revolt against the native dynasty of Queen Liliuokalani. This revolt curiously was tied to the McKinley Tariff of 1890. Previously, by a treaty of 1875, Hawaiian sugar had entered the United States duty free, but the McKinley Tariff gave a bounty of two cents a pound to American sugar growers, thus making annexation seem enticing to Hawaiian growers. Led by Sanford B. Dole, the planters rose in rebellion in January. American Marines came ashore at the orders of the American consul, John L. Stevens, and, at a critical point, brought victory to the rebels. On February 1 the American flag was raised, and on February 14 a treaty of annexation was signed. Grover Cleveland, who came to office in March, 1893, withdrew the treaty, however, and sent a confidential agent, James H. Blount, to investigate. Blount reported that the revolution had been engineered by American elements and Consul Stevens, not by native Hawaiians. Cleveland tried to restore Queen Liliuokalani, but Dole refused to concede; the president then reluctantly recognized the Republic of Hawaii on August 7, 1894. Thus it remained until 1898, when, at the height of the Spanish-American War and expansionist fever, it was annexed to the United States by a joint resolution of Congress, becoming an American territory.

The Spanish-American War

American expansionism won its greatest triumph in the Spanish-American War. The crisis originated in Cuba in 1895 when an insurrection against Spanish rule began, caused by the Panic of 1893 and falling prices that hurt Cuban sugar growers, many of whom were American (or operating with American capital). The rebels deliberately attacked American property, hoping thereby to cause American intervention—but Grover Cleveland refused, although the government and the public kept a close watch on developments. Spanish officials, hoping to end the insurrection quickly, sent General Valeriano Weyler to Cuba, and he instituted such repressive measures, including the use of concentration camps, that he was nicknamed "Butcher." American humanitarianism was roused by Weyler's repression— and that humanitarianism and concern was further stirred up by newspaper owners who hoped to sell papers thereby. In New York City the *Journal* of William Randolph Hearst and the *World* of Joseph Pulitzer vied with one another to report the most lurid atrocity stories of Spanish brutality—without worrying about accuracy. Both sent batteries of reporters and artists to Cuba with orders to provide lavish accounts of cruelty and suffering. Hearst reportedly told one artist, "You furnish the pictures, and I'll furnish the war." These correspondents complied with stories of Cubans massacred and tortured, of noncombatants starved in concentration camps, and of young women subjected to indignities. Some of the stories were true, many were exaggerated, and some were manufactured—but all were effective in stirring public opinion.

Grover Cleveland was not moved by the public outcry, however. He believed that both sides in Cuba were to blame and that there was no justification for American intervention. He issued a proclamation of neutrality; when Congress passed a resolution favoring recognition of Cuban belligerency, he ignored it. He did offer America's good offices to mediate the conflict, but Spain refused. There the matter rested when McKinley came to office in March, 1897. At first McKinley was disposed to move cautiously. He renewed the offer to mediate, which was again rejected, and he protested to Spain officially about the "uncivilized and inhuman" conduct of the war in Cuba. Spain, fearing the protest foreboded intervention, recalled Weyler, modified its policy of concentration camps, and took steps to grant the island qualified autonomy. By the end of 1897 it seemed that the threat of war had diminished. Also, prosperity was returning to the country by 1897 as the Panic of 1893 lost its force, and businessmen began opposing war as a threat to their new-found prosperity.

Early in 1898, however, the situation changed rapidly. On February 8, Hearst's *Journal* published a letter written by Dupuy de Lôme, the Spanish minister in Washington and stolen from the mails in Havana; the letter described McKinley as a weak man and a "bidder for the admiration of the crowd." Many Americans were saying worse of the president—Theodore Roosevelt had said that McKinley had "no more backbone than a chocolate eclair"—but the public was outraged by a foreigner characterizing the president in such a manner. De Lóme resigned quickly, but his letter had brought war closer. Then on February 15 came even more startling news; the American battleship *Maine* was blown up in Havana harbor, killing 260 American sailors. The vessel had gone there in January on a "friendly" visit— its real purpose to protect American lives and property by its presence. Most Americans believed that the Spaniards were responsible; Roosevelt called it "an act of dirty treachery." Actually, the Spanish government was doing everything possible to avoid incidents. A U.S. naval court of inquiry subsequently found that the sinking was done by a submarine mine, but the perpetrators were never named.

Only a strong chief executive could have kept the country out of war following the sinking of the *Maine,* and McKinley was not that. Congress voted $50 million for preparedness, while "Remember the *Maine*" became a national chant. On March 27 McKinley proposed that Spain grant an immediate armistice with negotiations for permanent peace to follow, and that there be an immediate end of concentration camps. On April 9 Spain accepted these terms, but nonetheless McKinley on April 11 went before Congress to ask for power to use armed force to end hostilities in Cuba—in short, a declaration of war. "In the name of humanity," he said, "in the name of civilization, in behalf of endangered American interests," Congress should agree; nowhere in his message did he say that Spain had accepted his earlier demands. Congress probably would not have cared, for its members were not about to be cheated out of a war. On April 19 by a joint resolution Congress recognized the independence of Cuba, authorized the president to use force to throw the Spaniards out, and, through the Teller Amendment to the resolution, disclaimed any American intention of annexing Cuba. President McKinley signed this resolution on April 20; four days later Spain declared war on the United States, whereupon Congress needlessly declared war on Spain on April 25.

The regular Army of the United States at the outbreak of war numbered only 28,000, but Congress authorized an increase to 68,000 and a call for 125,000 volunteers. Spain had an army of 130,000 men, 80,000 of them already in Cuba. (However, Spanish officers were paralyzed by fear of certain defeat.) Nor did the Ameri-

William Randolph Hearst

THE son of a California miner who struck it rich and subsequently became a U.S. senator, Hearst was born in San Francisco in 1863. During his youth he was characterized as brilliant and spoiled, able and headstrong. Expelled from Harvard for his conduct, he returned to San Francisco to take control of the *Examiner,* a newspaper owned by his father—and to fulfill the promise seen in him earlier.

Through sensationalism, then in style among journalists, and capable management, he made the *Examiner* one of the most successful newspapers on the West Coast. In 1895, he purchased the New York *Journal* to engage in a battle with Joseph Pulitzer for journalistic supremacy in that city. The result was called "yellow journalism," as both papers exaggerated and sensationalized the news, in the process helping the cause of political reform—and perhaps causing the Spanish-American War.

Next came Hearst's entry into politics. After supporting William Jennings Bryan in 1896 and 1900, Hearst ran for Congress in New York and served two terms (1902–06), and he made a strong bid for the Democratic nomination for president for himself in 1904, only to lose to Alton B. Parker. Afterward Hearst remained a power in the party, thanks largely to his growing chain of newspapers.

He bought papers in some cities and started them in others, fashioning the largest chain of newspapers in America. Next he added magazines, including *Cosmopolitan, Harper's Bazaar,* and *Good Housekeeping.* In the process he made millions, but he prized his own beliefs over money; for example, his opposition to American entry into World War I, evident in his publications, cost him advertising dollars. His opponents labeled him an isolationist, a super-patriot, and stubborn—and he was.

A man who loved art and castles, he acquired both with zest and appetite. During the depression he turned away from the New Deal to become far more conservative. He died in 1951, still very much the lord of his domain.

cans have an overall plan for conducting the war. Only in the Navy was there strength; in 1898 the American Navy was fifth in the world, far superior to the Spanish Navy in ships, gunnery, and personnel. Thus it was little surprise that the U.S. Navy performed brilliantly. On April 27, Commodore George Dewey led his Asiatic Squadron from Hong Kong, acting under orders from Assistant Secretary of the Navy Theodore Roosevelt (sent on February 25 without authorization), which called for an attack on the Spanish Philippines in case of a war with Spain. Dewey sailed into Manila Bay on May 1, calmly calling his famous slogan, "You may fire when ready, Gridley." When the firing ceased, the Spanish fleet had been destroyed with no damage to the American ships. The Spaniards still held Manila, but an expeditionary force arrived that summer and Manila fell on August 13. The Spaniards surrendered to General Wesley Merritt and a rebel force commanded by Emilio Aguinaldo. Dewey was promoted to admiral and became the first hero of the war—but in the heat of victory few Americans noted that a war begun to free Cuba had been subverted to an imperialistic venture.

Meanwhile, a fleet departed Spain late in April, eluded an American blockade, and slipped into Santiago harbor in Cuba. For a time it was feared this fleet was headed for the United States, causing some panic along the Eastern seaboard. Actually the fleet was antique, had not a single battleship, and most of the ships were constructed of wood; it was sent more as a gesture to Spanish honor than a threat to the United States. Once the fleet was found at Santiago, Admiral William T. Sampson led an American naval force to the scene and bottled up the Spaniards.

In the United States, the War Department was hopelessly confused as it tried to mobilize, train, organize, and equip an army. General Nelson A. Miles, commanding general of the Army, proved inadequate to the task of leadership; thus it was the volunteers who led in the fighting.

On June 14 an army of 17,000 men, including the famed Rough Riders (commanded by political figures Colonel Leonard Wood and Lieutenant Colonel Theodore Roosevelt), sailed from Tampa, Florida, under overall command of General William R. Shafter. For lack of transport, the Rough Riders had to leave their horses behind. The force landed near Santiago de Cuba amidst scenes of fantastic incompetence. It took five days for the troops to get ashore. Fortunately there was no enemy resistance. Once landed, Shafter moved toward Santiago. On the way, two small battles were fought, El Canay and San Juan Hill. In both engagements the Rough Riders led in the fighting, and Theodore Roosevelt emerged as another hero of the war. Marching on toward Santiago, Shafter's troops were riddled by sickness to the extent that Shafter was ready to abandon the campaign.

Fortunately, the Spanish commander at Santiago decided he had lost and ordered the fleet under Admiral Pascual Cervera out of the harbor. As it attempted to escape, the American fleet destroyed it. Admiral Sampson quieted his sailors with the comment, "Don't cheer, boys. The poor devils are dying." The Spanish fleet destroyed, the commander at Santiago decided to surrender, and General Shafter granted him liberal terms. His surrender ended effective Spanish resistance in Cuba. Shortly thereafter, General Miles finally led regular troops ashore at Puerto Rico, but a quick Spanish surrender there spoiled Miles' ambitions of a great victory and political gain for himself.

Through the French ambassador in Washington, Spain sued for peace, and an armistice was signed on August 12. The peace conference opened in Paris on October 1, and the Treaty of Paris was signed on December 10. In this agreement, Spain recognized the independence of Cuba, and it ceded to the United States the territories of Puerto Rico, Guam, and the Philippines. For the Philippines the United States agreed to pay $20 million. This treaty had been bought at the price of 5462 American deaths—only 379 of them in battle, the rest from disease and food poisoning.

The chief debate on this treaty in the Senate centered on annexation of the Philippines. This feature was denounced by intellectuals, traditionalists, the Anti-Imperialist League, Democrats, a few Republicans, and economic interests such as sugar growers. Favoring it were the expansionists, the navy lobby, most Republicans, and the Protestant clergy (who saw in the Philippines a field for fruitful missionary work). Unexpectedly, William Jennings Bryan, who opposed expansionism, spoke in favor of annexation (anticipating his renomination for the presidency in 1900), and some Democrats voted for the treaty. It passed on February 6, 1899, by a vote of fifty-seven to twenty-seven.

Two days previous to this vote, Emilio Aguinaldo began the Filipino Insurrection. He and his followers had fought alongside the Americans to overthrow the Spaniards, believing that the United States wanted independence for them just as it did for Cuba. When they learned differently, they rose in a war that continued until 1902; during this conflict the Americans employed methods unpleasantly reminiscent of Butcher Weyler's tactics, including concentration camps, and at a cost of $170 million and 4300 American lives. Not until 1946 would the Philippines be granted independence. Cuba was more fortunate, however. It was granted its independence on May 20, 1902, after American occupation forces had built good roads and hospitals and had trained Cubans for independence. The status of residents in Hawaii, Guam, and Alaska was settled over the years by congressional and court action. The residents of these possessions were granted American citizenship and, eventually, territorial status: Hawaii by an act of 1900 and Alaska in 1912; Guam became a protectorate with a military (usually Navy) man as governor. Puerto Rico saw an end to military government in 1900 by terms of the Foraker Act; the governor and upper chamber of the legislature were appointed in Washington and the lower house locally elected. Puerto Ricans were granted citizenship in 1917, and in 1951 were given commonwealth status.

Next to become a problem in foreign policy was China. The ancient Chinese government was feeble, and the country was being carved into "spheres of influence" by powerful Western nations. With American trade in China thus threatened, Secretary of State John Hay attempted a solution on September 6, 1899, when he proposed what became known as the "Open Door" policy—all nations would have the same rights and privileges with no discrimination in matters of tariff duties, port fees, or railroad rates. Other nations with influence in China were not enthusiastic, but Hay announced that since no one had disagreed, the United States would regard the Open Door policy as binding. Nationalistic Chinese, led by a secret society known as the Boxers, were ashamed at the weakness of their country and determined to rid it of all foreigners; this climaxed on June 20 when all diplomatic personnel in China were besieged in the British embassy in Peking. An international expeditionary force marched into Peking and lifted the siege on August 14. An indemnity was demanded of the Chinese government, and it was forced to acquiesce. The American share of $25 million was used mainly to educate Chinese students in the United States.

Attitudes Toward Latin America

The inauguration of Theodore Roosevelt as president saw a shift in the emphasis of American foreign policy to Latin America. There thoughts were turning to the construction of a canal through Central America. In 1901 the United States and England had agreed to the construction of such a canal under American auspices through the Hay-Pauncefote Treaty, which gave the United States the right to build the canal, fortify it, and control it; in return the United States agreed to open it to all vessels without discrimination. Then on January 4, 1902, the New Panama Canal Company, a French concern, offered to sell its rights to build an isthmian canal to the United States for $40 million; however, this transfer had to be approved by Colombia (or New Granada as it then was known) since that nation owned what now is Panama. On January 22, 1903, the Hay-Harran Treaty was signed to grant the United States a ninety-nine year lease, for which the United States agreed to pay Colombia $10 million and an annual rental fee of $250,000.

The Hay-Harran Treaty was rejected by the Colombian senate, however; the New Panama Canal Company lease was about to expire (in October, 1904), and the Colombian senators preferred to wait until then so they could secure the $40 million that the United States was willing to pay for the concession. Roosevelt proved unwilling to wait, and with support from the French and the Panamanians a revolt began on November 3, 1903. Led by Philippe Bunau-Varilla, an agent of the New Panama Canal Company, the Panamanians declared their independence. At a critical moment in the revolution, American gunboats prevented Colombian troops from reaching Panama in order—said the commander—to protect the American right of transit across the isthmus under terms of a treaty of 1846. With almost indecent haste, the Roosevelt administration recognized the new republic (November 13) and on November 18 signed a treaty with the new government giving the United States sovereign rights in perpetuity to a strip of land ten miles wide for $10 million and a $250,000 annual payment. Work on the canal began quickly, was well organized, and proceeded smoothly. It opened in 1914 with much American pride. Roosevelt was criticized at the time and later for his actions during the Panamanian revolution; in 1911 he replied to his critics, "I took the Canal Zone and let Congress debate; and while the debate goes on the Canal does also." In 1914 the Democrats attempted to pay Colombia $25 million for the loss of Panama, but Republicans blocked the attempt; the sum was finally paid in 1921.

Roosevelt had one other major addition to Latin American policy, his corollary to the Monroe Doctrine. When Germany, England, and Italy used force to collect debts from Venezuela, Roosevelt answered them on December 6, 1904, by stating that the United States alone would police Latin American nations guilty of "chronic wrong doing." This right was exercised in the Dominican Republic in 1905, in Cuba in 1906, and later, during Taft's administration, in Honduras, Haiti, and Nicaragua. Finally, in foreign affairs, Roosevelt mediated the Russo-Japanese War of 1904–05. Representatives of the two powers met at Portsmouth, New Hampshire (the Portsmouth Conference), and managed to terminate the conflict. However, Roosevelt did not get the indemnity that Japan wanted, thereby earning some hatred for America. Nevertheless, Roosevelt negotiated a "Gentleman's Agreement" concerning Japanese immigration to the United States. There was rising fear in America, particularly in California, of what was regarded as a "Yellow Peril"—that the country would be inundated with Orientals who would work cheaply. In October, 1906, the San Francisco Board of Education ordered ninety-three Japanese children segregated in a separate school. Roosevelt through pressure managed to get this ruling, which stung Japanese pride, reversed. To prevent such occurrences in the future, he negotiated an agreement in which Japan agreed to issue no more pass-ports to its citizens to emigrate to the United States; this agreement was unofficial, hence the name Gentleman's Agreement. Fearful that Japan might think the United States weak, however, Roosevelt ordered the "Great White Fleet" of American war-ships around the world—to stop in Japan—in order to impress Japan and other world powers. Perhaps this move had an influence, for in November, 1908, came the Root-Takahira Agreement, an executive agreement, not a treaty; in this docu-ment the United States and Japan agreed to maintain the status quo in the Pacific, to uphold the Open Door policy in China, to respect each other's possessions, and to support the "independence and integrity" of China.

Taft as president carried forward Roosevelt's policies—but without Roosevelt's flair. Construction of the Panama Canal prompted intervention in Latin America several times—to protect the American investment; intervention also was prompted to protect other American business investments. For these reasons, Taft's use of troops to insure stability in Latin America became known as "Dollar Diplomacy." On May 19, 1910, Taft sent Marines into Nicaragua, he said, to protect American lives; the result was that New York bankers gained control of the National Bank of Nicaragua, and the Marines were sent again in 1912, to remain until 1933, to pro-tect this investment. American funds also flowed into Haiti and the Dominican Republic at Taft's urging. The president also urged American investment in a Chinese purchase of Manchurian railroads; Russia and Japan, both with interests in these railroads, were angered at Taft's proposal, bringing hatred and suspicion of Americans even though American businessmen did not invest in this venture. Simi-larly, Latin Americans hated and resented American investment and intervention in Latin America. Dollar Diplomacy clearly did not win friends.

Woodrow Wilson, when he came to office in 1913, changed the tone of Ameri-can involvement—but not the net result. Wilson was primarily an idealist, never uncertain of his moral position. He, Secretary of State William Jennings Bryan, and Secretary of the Navy Josephus Daniels were all devoutly religious, war-hating men. But the opportunity to use force for moralistic purposes—to uplift benighted broth-ers to the south—was too powerful for them to resist. Wilson spelled out his atti-tude on foreign policy in a speech given at Mobile, Alabama: "The United States will never again seek one additional foot of territory by conquest," he said, but instead would seek "the development of constitutional liberty in the world." This speech changed the historic thrust of American foreign policy. In the past the nation had extended its system of government, economics, and social structure through conquest; thereafter the thrust would be idealistic imperialism. Every war —and almost all foreign entanglement—would be moralistically justified, to use Woodrow Wilson's war phrase, as making the world safe for democracy. Wilson's call echoed some thread in the American spirit and set the tone for the next half century of American foreign policy. Forgotten was the "balance of power" concept that had sustained America for a century and a half (and Europe for much longer) as the United States rushed to sustain Wilson's puritanical ideas.

The Mexican Adventure

In his speech in Mobile, Wilson was addressing himself specifically to the case of Mexico. There a revolution had occurred that caused a lingering American involvement. American business interests had approximately a billion-dollar investment in Mexico, which had been ruled since in 1877 by Porfirio Díaz. Then, in a revolution that began in 1910 and culminated in May, 1911, Díaz was overthrown by Francisco I. Madero, a liberal idealist who had little government experience. Madero was, in turn, overthrown in February, 1913, and then murdered by Victoriano Huerta, who was encouraged and abetted by Henry Lane Wilson, American ambassador to Mexico. Businessmen in the United States urged President Wilson to extend quick recognition to the new regime, but Wilson stubbornly refused to recognize what he called a "government of butchers." Wilson hoped his withholding of recognition would bring a quick collapse of Huerta's administration and a return to constitutional government. This action reversed a trend set in Jefferson's day of extending American recognition to de facto governments, and it forced the United States into a policy of extending recognition on the basis of moral purity rather than political necessity.

Wilson's refusal to extend recognition to Huerta's regime brought a counterrevolution in Mexico, an uprising led by two men in the north, Venustiano Carranza and Francisco ("Pancho") Villa, and one man in the south, Emiliano Zapata. Wilson in June, 1913, offered American offices in mediating between Huerta and the Carranza forces, but both sides refused. The United States then assumed a policy of watchful waiting and persuaded England to stop purchasing oil from Mexico. Wilson offered American aid to Carranza, but was rebuffed again (Carranza would have lost popular support by dealing with the hated Yankees). Next, on February 3, 1914, Wilson revoked the embargo on arms sales in Mexico, thereby allowing guns to be sold to Carranza's forces. Still Carranza did not win, leaving Wilson searching for a way to bring constitutional government to Mexico as he had promised the world he would.

Wilson's opportunity for intervention came in April, 1914. American warships had been patrolling the Gulf of Mexico to prevent the landing of arms for Huerta, even seizing the customs house at Vera Cruz to forestall the landing of German weapons. Then on April 9 one of Huerta's officers arrested several American sailors who had gone ashore at Tampico; a superior officer realized the mistake and ordered the sailors released immediately, and he issued an apology for the incident. But the American admiral in charge of the fleet demanded that the Huerta government fire a 21-gun salute to the American flag by way of apology. This the Huerta government could not do, for it would cause revolution among the Yankee-hating populace. Fighting took place on April 21–22 between Americans and Mexicans, during which 126 Mexicans were killed and 195 wounded; American casualties were 19 killed and 71 wounded. By April 30 some 6700 American troops were engaged at Vera Cruz—yet had accomplished nothing to topple Huerta. Even Carranza's followers were threatening to join Huerta in opposing the Americans.

Argentina, Brazil, and Chile—the so-called ABC powers—offered to mediate the dispute between the United States and Mexico on April 30, and Wilson gladly accepted. Delegates met at Niagara Falls, Canada, from May to July, 1914, seeking a mutually satisfactory end to Mexican-American difficulties. Before a solution could be achieved, word came that on July 15 Huerta had abdicated before advancing Carranzistas. Carranza occupied Mexico City on August 20, and American forces withdrew entirely from Mexico. The whole Mexican problem seemed to be at an end, especially when Wilson extended recognition to the Carranza government.

Yet all was not peaceful in Mexico. There Pancho Villa was angry that he had not been given a proper place in the government, and he led a revolution against Carranza. Intent on showing he was no tool of Yankee imperialists—thereby gaining popular support for his revolution—Villa, on January 11, 1916, stopped a train in northern Mexico, took sixteen Americans off, and shot them summarily. Then on March 9 Villa raided Columbus, New Mexico, killing nineteen more Americans. Wilson ordered 6000 American troops across the border under command of General John J. ("Blackjack") Pershing to capture Villa. These troops moved as much as 300 miles into Mexico, but never captured the wily Villa. However, they did force Villa to run, to hide, to retreat until his revolutionary thrust was dissipated and his force hurt by defections. In January, 1917, realizing the approach of World War I, Wilson ordered Pershing to withdraw from Mexico. The sum total of Wilson's moralistic intervention south of the Rio Grande was lasting Mexican hatred of the "Colossus of the North," while Villa remained at large. However, the troops under Pershing had received valuable combat experience that would serve them well in the world conflict then emerging.

In the two decades 1897–1917, the progressive spirit swept much of America. Progressives were elected first at the local level, then at the state level, and finally were swept into office nationally. They enacted much legislation intended to ennoble mankind and change human nature. Some of the reforms were needed. Some were beneficial. But none had the desired effect. People remained people. Corruption continued. Sloth and laziness were not eliminated. Yet in the process of liberalizing the country, a revolution had occurred. Thereafter every quack peddling economic or social nostrums set up his stand in Washington, hopeful of securing federal enactment of some law to change mankind. And the federal bureaucracy began to expand with geometric progression.

Chapter Twelve

Wide Open All the Way

Background to War

AMERICANS have been a people given to hyperbole—how else could they have believed that their involvement in the European conflict of 1914–18 was to fight a "war to end all wars." But they did believe Woodrow Wilson's phrase and sang jauntily as they marched aboard ships to participate in that distant conflict. They believed it because to them it seemed plausible, because to them it seemed that a defeat for tyranny at that time would end forever any attempts to subvert democracy. Such did not prove to be the case; the right of men to govern themselves has had to be defended in almost every generation, not just once. Then, now, and always the words of Patrick Henry will hold true. Security has never proven worth its price of chains and slavery. New catch-phrases have been invented periodically —have had to be invented periodically—to inspire men to fight. Wilson's phrase served that purpose in 1917–18.

The origins of the conflict in Europe were deep and involved; they stemmed from industrialization, imperialism, nationalism, and militarism. Fighting began in August, 1914, between Germany, Austria-Hungary, and Turkey on one side and England, France, and Russia on the other. At first Americans congratulated themselves that they were not involved; as late as 1916 Wilson referred to the war as "a drunken brawl in a public house." The president accurately reflected public sentiment when, on August 4, 1914, he issued a proclamation of American neutrality and urged the people to be neutral in both thought and deed. But Americans could not be neutral. They had strong educational, social, cultural, economic, and sentimental ties with England and France; moreover, they were shocked by the German invasion of Belgium in specific violation of a treaty signed in 1839.

Economic Impact of the War

The immediate effect of the war in the United States was economic, as European combatant nations liquidated their holdings. Soon, however, war orders began to pour into American factories, and the economy boomed. Then, despite an embargo on war loans to combatant nations, the State Department on October 15, 1915, quietly allowed such loans. By 1917, when the United States entered the war, American bankers had loaned the allied nations approximately $2.3 billion—but Germany only $27 million. Moreover, most American trade was with England and France, for England controlled the seas. On November 3, 1914, England declared the North Sea a war zone and mined it, seizing American ships trying to reach Germany—all in direct violation of the rights of neutral nations. Americans tended to accept the British blockade quietly because of inherent American sympathy for the Allies and because a retaliatory embargo on England would have hurt American farmers. Thus the United States had a growing economic interest in an Allied victory.

Yet another reason why the United States came to favor the Allied cause was because of skillful manipulation of American public opinion by England. The undersea telegraph cables that ran to the United States passed through Great Britain last as they left Europe; British censors used their control of the cables to fill American newspapers with their point of view and with stories of German atrocities. The Germans were pictured as molesters of women and killers of children. The British also had heavy investments in American newspapers, so editorial policies were often pro-British. Thus in the war of propaganda, the British proved much more skillful and better masters of American psychology than did the Germans.

At first the German High Command hoped to win the war in Europe before American influence could become a factor, but they were stopped short of Paris in the Battle of the Marne in September, 1914. Then the Germans turned to the use of the submarine as a means of preventing shipping from reaching England and France. On February 4, 1915, Germany proclaimed a war zone around the British Isles and warned that neutral ships inside that area would be attacked by submarines. Because a surfaced submarine was vulnerable to attack, the captains of these craft could not follow previous rules of warfare, such as stopping and searching enemy merchantmen and sinking them only after making provisions for the safety of crew and passengers. The sinking of merchant vessels without warning seemed horrible to Americans. Yet the German announcement of unlimited submarine warfare inside the war zone around England was premature. At the time Germany had only twenty-one operative submarines and could not enforce its proclamation effectively. On February 10 Washington vigorously protested the German announcement, warning that it would hold Berlin accountable for unlawful sinkings of American ships.

The first encounter between the United States and Germany over submarine warfare came when Americans traveling on foreign vessels were torpedoed. On March 28 one American died when the British ship *Falaba* sank in the Irish Sea. Then on May 1 three more Americans died when the American tanker *Gulflight* was sunk. The serious crisis over submarine warfare came over the sinking of the British liner *Lusitania,* which was torpedoed on May 7 and sank within eighteen minutes, carrying 1198 people to their deaths, including 128 Americans. Few Americans knew that the ship had been carrying munitions and that the Germans had publicly warned passengers not to sail on it. Coupled with the German use of poison gas at Ypres on April 22, the sinking of the *Lusitania* seemed particularly horrible to the American public. Then on May 13 a lengthy story appeared in American newspapers about German atrocities in Belgium, supposedly written by the former British ambassador to the United States, Lord Bryce. The story was filled with fabrications, but the American public believed it—and was ready for war. Yet in Philadelphia on May 10 Woodrow Wilson said that a nation did not have to use force to prove it was right: "There is such a thing as a man being too proud to fight." A series of stiff diplomatic notes were exchanged by the United States and Germany between May 13 and July 21. Wilson's second note was so stiff that Secretary of State William Jennings Bryan resigned rather than deliver it, for he felt it meant war. Secretly the German High Command ordered submarine commanders not to sink passenger liners, and on February 16, 1916, agreed to pay an indemnity for the American lives lost on the *Lusitania*.

New trouble arose early in 1916 on the same score. On February 8 the Germans declared that enemy merchant ships would be sunk without warning after March 1. Wilson reiterated his doctrine of strict accountability, yet he sent his unofficial advisor, "Colonel" House, to Europe on what proved a fruitless search for peace. Then on March 24 a German submarine torpedoed an unarmed channel steamer, the French ship *Sussex,* injuring several passengers. Wilson responded by threatening on April 18 to sever diplomatic relations with Germany if that nation did not abandon unrestricted submarine warfare. This threat was sufficient to bring a pledge on May 4 from the Germans that they would not torpedo any merchant vessel without warning. Wilson seemingly had won a great victory—and could go into the election of 1916 with the claim that he had kept the nation out of war. At the same time that the election was being held, Wilson, without fanfare, was gradually preparing for war. On June 3 the National Defense Act expanded the Army to over 200,000 men. On August 29 the Council of National Defense was created, consisting of six cabinet members, with advisory representatives from business, labor, transportation, and industry. On September 7 a Shipping Board was established to be responsible for defense planning.

The president made one last attempt to secure peace. In December, 1916, he sent notes to each warring power asking what its terms for peace would be. Germany did not bother to reply, while England and France made exorbitant demands. Finally, on January 22, 1917, Wilson in a speech to the Senate expressed the hope that a just and lasting peace could be achieved in Europe, a "peace without victory," and outlined his ideas for a league of nations to protect the peace. Germany shattered Wilson's hopes for peace on January 31 by announcing that it was resuming unrestricted submarine warfare. The German High Command realized this announcement made war with the United States inevitable, but hoped to crush England and France before the United States could contribute sufficient men to influence the course of the war.

The Zimmermann Note

Americans still hoping to avoid war were further shocked when on March 1 the State Department released the Zimmermann Note. Written by German Foreign Secretary Alfred F. M. Zimmermann, this note, addressed to Mexican officials, proposed that if war between the United States and Germany should come, the Mexicans should invade the United States and reconquer its former holdings. The note had been intercepted by British naval intelligence and passed to the State Department on February 25. Then, in March, 1917, came word of the Russian Revolution, in which the czar was forced to abdicate and a republic was established. Wilson, at last, could go to war in the belief that it was the "democracies" against Prussian autocracy.

On March 12 Wilson ordered that American merchant vessels going to the war zones should be armed. That same day German submarines sank an American ship. On April 2 Wilson went before a special session of Congress to ask for a declaration of war; in it he enumerated German transgressions against our shipping and our neutral status, saying that "the right is more precious than peace" and calling for a crusade to make the world "safe for democracy." On April 4 the Senate voted for the declaration 82 to 6; two days later the House concurred by a vote of 373 to 50.

America's Fighting Force

America's foremost problem at the outbreak of war was to expand its armed forces rapidly. To do this, on May 18 Congress passed the Selective Service Act calling for the registration of all men between twenty-one and thirty years of age (the act was amended on August 31, 1918, to include men between eighteen and forty-five). Ultimately some 24 million men would register, of whom nearly three million were called to active duty, all of them unmarried and without dependents; conscientious objectors were exempted from the draft (or assigned to noncombatant duties). In addition, the National Guard was activated immediately, while some 1,250,000 men volunteered, bringing the total number of men who served to 4,791,172. The allied nations of Europe were extremely anxious that American troops be rushed to Europe to participate in the fighting as soon as possible for reasons of morale. Therefore an American Expeditionary Force was readied and arrived in France on June 26, 1917, under the command of General John J. Pershing. One of Pershing's aides, recalling the French aid to Americans during the Revolutionary War, announced the American arrival with the statement, "Lafayette, we are here!" British and French tacticians wanted to distribute the American troops among seasoned combat units already in the field, but Pershing insisted that the AEF be maintained as a separate unit. President Wilson backed him in this demand, and in October his troops were assigned the Toul sector east of Verdun and came under fire on October 21.

Pershing's troops took part in thirteen major operations during the next year, and they acquitted themselves with distinction. The first distinctly American operation did not come until September, 1918, however, when these troops fought at Saint Mihiel. It was in this operation that Brigadier General William Mitchell directed an aerial assault involving about 1500 Allied airplanes, demonstrating the devastating effectiveness of air power. Americans served with equal distinction with British and French units, as at the Battle of the Marne, at Chateau-Thierry, and at Belleau Wood. By July, 1918, the tide of battle was turning, as the American contribution swung the advantage to the Allied side. On July 15 the Germans started a final drive at Rheims, but 85,000 American troops, fighting alongside the British and French, stopped them. Then on September 26 the Americans committed 1.2 million troops to a major drive at the Meuse River–Argonne Forest sector and drove the Germans back. Meanwhile, the American Navy, under Admiral William S. Sims, had made a major contribution to the Allied effort. Admiral Sims established the convoy system for conveying war supplies from the United States to Europe, while American warships helped the Allied fleets fight German submarines. By the fall of 1918 German troops were retreating on almost every front, and by the second week in November the retreat had become a rout. The German High Command had no recourse but to ask for an armistice, which was signed on November 11, 1918. The United States had suffered 325,018 casualties, including 116,516 killed, 204,002 wounded, and 4500 missing in action.

The Home Front

Yet the true impact of World War I was felt by most Americans at home, not on the front. At no time in history had the nation been so regimented—or freedom so restricted. To coordinate the economic activities of the country, six major committees were established by the federal government. The most important of these was the War Industries Board, created in July, 1917, to coordinate government purchases and eliminate waste. The chairman of the committee was Bernard Baruch, a Wall Street financier, and under his direction it exercised strong control over manufacturing, price-fixing, and the purchase of supplies. This was done mainly under terms of the Overman Act of 1918, which gave the president the powers necessary to direct industrial production.

Financing the war was another major area of effort by the government. The Emergency Loan Act of April 24, 1917, authorized a bond issue of $5 billion. This was supplemented by other legislation that authorized yet more "Liberty Bond" drives and that by 1919 raised $21 billion, or about three-fifths of the cost of the war. Additional revenues were raised by increasing the income tax to an unprecedented height and by a great variety of new excise taxes. Secretary of the Treasury William Gibbs McAdoo believed in paying as much as possible of the cost of the war through current taxes, and he raised about one-third of the $35 billion spent by this method.

"Food Will Win the War" proclaimed posters all across the country in 1917, and food was almost as important as money in the campaign against the enemy. Woodrow Wilson established a Food Administration on his own initiative, which was authorized by Congress on August 10, 1917, by terms of the Lever Act. The Food Administration, along with the Fuel Administration, was charged with controlling production, cutting waste, and setting prices. Taking charge of these two agencies was Herbert Hoover, a mining engineer turned humanitarian who had earned a great reputation between 1914 and 1916 as supervisor of the attempt to feed hungry Belgians. He provided farmers with an assured market at a fixed price by establishing a Government Grain Corporation; farmers responded by increasing wheat acreage from 45 million acres to 75 million acres in two years and by increasing total food production by 24 percent. Hoover opposed retail price-fixing, which he believed would lead to black markets, and thus there was some increase in prices. The Fuel Administration raised production 50 percent, but a fuel shortage plagued the country. Hoover had to declare a series of "coal holidays" early in 1918.

Organized labor fared well during the war. Samuel Gompers and other labor leaders pledged no strikes. In return they were promised government support for the eight-hour day and recognition of collective bargaining, along with wage increases to keep pace with inflation. A National War Labor Board served as a quasi–supreme court for labor disputes. Labor and industry each named five representatives to the board, with two chairmen representing the public. Thus there were no strikes or lockouts except among such radical unions as the International Workers of the World. Such cooperation by organized labor meant giant gains for it, and membership jumped from 2,716,900 in 1914 to 4,169,000 in 1919.

Moving food, fuel, and men to the war zone severely taxed America's transportation system, while the production of ships and aircraft was equally important. When the railroads proved unable to move goods to the ports, the government stepped in. In December, 1917, Wilson nationalized all railroads under a Railroad Administration, headed by Secretary of the Treasury McAdoo. Utilizing experienced railroad men, he ran all the lines as one unified system—and moved goods and men. In return for their "cooperation," the railroads received rents equivalent to their average profits in the years 1914–17. Movements of goods and men at sea was dictated by the Shipping Board, while the Emergency Fleet Corporation was established to oversee the construction of more ships. Finally, an Aircraft Production Board was established, promising to deliver 22,000 planes. Failure to deliver this absurd number of aircraft led to harsh public criticism, but the board did deliver 1185 DeHaviland bombers and 5460 Liberty motors.

The area of greatest change in the United States during the war was in the field of civil liberties. Democratic countries are at a distinct disadvantage during total war, for freedom has to be curtailed in order to achieve victory—yet they state they are fighting for those very freedoms curtailed. Wilson recognized this early in the war when he said, "to fight you must be brutal and ruthless, and the very spirit of ruthless brutality will enter into the very fibre of our national life." Contributing much to the spirit of public brutality was the Committee on Public Information, created on April 14, 1917, and administered by George Creel. Its task was to publicize the war effort, which it did by printing an estimated 75 million pieces of literature and employing some 150,000 writers. This literature was pure propaganda; it accused the Germans of starting the war and pictured them as barbarians capable of every type of atrocity. American hatred of things German reached fantastic heights. German-language newspapers were banned; departments of German were abolished at most universities; even the lowly frankfurter was renamed the "liberty pup" to avoid the appearance of a German name.

On June 15, 1917, came the Espionage Act, providing fines of $10,000 and twenty years in prison for those aiding the enemy, obstructing recruiting, or promoting disloyalty in the armed forces. Further, it empowered the postmaster general to ban from the mails any matter that in his opinion was seditious. In 1919 the Supreme Court upheld this act in the case *Schenck* v. *United States;* Justice Oliver Wendell Holmes wrote that Schenck's pamphlets had encouraged resistance to the draft and were therefore a "clear and present danger."

Other legislation followed the Espionage Act, designed clearly to enforce total public support of the war. On October 6, 1917, came the Trading With the Enemy Act, which allowed the president to censor messages going to foreign powers. On November 16 the president, by executive order, required enemy aliens to register. In the spring of 1918, on May 16, Congress passed the Sedition Act as an amendment to the Espionage Act. This amendment went much farther in stifling dissent. It provided for punishment of anyone obstructing the sale of Liberty Bonds, interfering with the war effort, or using "disloyal, profane, scurrilous . . . language about the form of government of the United States." This act was so worded that federal judges could impose long sentences on anyone who opposed the war in any public way, even jailing anyone who said the war was contrary to the teachings of Christ or that it made some manufacturers rich. And officials used these dictatorial powers, for approximately 1500 persons were arrested for seditious statements. The Supreme Court upheld this legislation; in 1919, in *Abrams* v. *the United States,* the court ruled that distributing pamphlets criticizing the government for sending troops into Russia (the expeditionary force fighting against the Communist regime) was a violation of the act. The most famous case involving the Sedition Act was the conviction of Eugene V. Debs on September 14, 1918. For interfering with recruiting, Debs was sentenced to ten years in jail and his citizenship was revoked. The Supreme Court upheld his conviction in 1919, and in 1920 Wilson refused to commute his sentence. (On December 24, 1921, President Warren Harding released him from prison, but without restoring his citizenship.) As late as February 20, 1919 (after the war had ended), Socialist Victor L. Berger was sentenced to twenty years in prison for violation of the Sedition Act.

Even after the armistice, peace did not return on the home front, for new enemies of freedom had surfaced. The rise of Russian communism, coupled with the founding of a Communist movement in the United States, led to what the radicals labeled a "Red Scare" in the country. With good reason, the Department of Labor deported 249 Russians in December 1919, while Attorney General A. Mitchell Palmer, in January, 1920, authorized raids on suspected Communist cells that resulted in over 4000 arrests and 556 deportations. Then, on May 5, 1920, came the arrest of Nicolà Sacco and Bartolomeo Vanzetti on a charge of murder. Sacco and Vanzetti were convicted in 1921 on the basis of hard evidence, but radicals pictured the two as innocent martyrs and stirred popular protests. Six years later, on August 23, 1927, they were executed after prolonged public debate about their guilt or innocence.

Finally as a result of the war, there were two constitutional amendments. During the war, prohibitionists urged an amendment to "dry up" the country, saying it would save badly needed grain for the war effort. The Eighteenth Amendment was passed by Congress and went into effect on January 16, 1920. The Volstead Act of October 28, 1919, defined as intoxicating any beverage with more than one-half of one percent alcohol content, made the Internal Revenue Bureau responsible for enforcing the measure, and prohibited the manufacture, sale, or transport of such beverages in interstate commerce. The Nineteenth Amendment was passed by Congress and became effective on August 26, 1920; this women's suffrage amendment was passed on the argument that women would not be gullible enough to vote for rascally politicians and thus would bring about better government.

Making the Peace

Woodrow Wilson emerged from the war more than an American hero. He had the sincere admiration of much of the Western world. His "Fourteen Points" calling for a just peace had struck a responsive chord, even in Germany, for the world was indeed weary of fighting. The Germans, realizing the war was lost, had asked for an armistice—granted on November 11, 1918—under the terms of the Fourteen Points. On November 18 Wilson announced he would attend the peace conference personally, but the announcement triggered sharp partisan political fighting. Henry White, a diplomat, was the sole Republican on the commission Wilson was taking to Europe—and the Republicans had captured both houses of Congress in the November general elections. To be politically acceptable, Wilson's commission should have included prominent Republicans such as Henry Cabot Lodge, some other senators, and possibly Theodore Roosevelt.

Wilson arrived in France on December 13, 1918, to make a triumphant tour of

France, England, and Italy. He was cheered everywhere—until later when he fought against the nationalistic interests and exorbitant claims of some of these countries; then the adulation faded. The peace conference began at Versailles on January 12 in an atmosphere tinged with national aggrandizement and idealism. Wilson fought to prevent a division of the spoils, fought for the mandate system of trusteeship of former German colonies, and urged creation of the League of Nations. Some points he won; others he lost. He was forced to concede ownership of former German colonies in the Pacific to Japan, but on February 14, 1919, the conference provisionally accepted a covenant for a League of Nations. Wilson sailed for the United States in mid-February determined to win acceptance of the League covenant. "Colonel" House warned him to be prepared for some compromise, but the president retorted, "I have found you get nothing in this world that is worth-while without fighting for it."

On February 26 the president met with members of the Senate and House to discuss the League of Nations and foreign affairs—but the politicians were unhappy. Two days later Senator Lodge of Massachusetts delivered a stinging speech against it, and on March 2 thirty-seven Republican senators signed a letter rejecting the League and calling for modifications; these included provisions that a nation need not accept a mandate of the League against its will, that members could withdraw on two years' notice, that the League could not regulate immigration, and that American participation would not infringe on the Monroe Doctrine.

Early in March the president returned to Versailles, where final decisions were made on reparations and territorial possessions. Amidst bitter debate, the Allied leaders forced Wilson to concede several points. Germany was made to pay a heavy amount of reparations, was forced to admit it was guilty of starting the war, and was stripped of territory (such as Alsace-Lorraine). Wilson returned to the United States confident that he could get senatorial confirmation of the treaty despite his inflexibility. He submitted it formally on July 10, after which it was bottled up in the Senate Foreign Relations Committee for two months. In an attempt to force the issue, the president started a speaking tour in September that led him to the American West. After thirty-seven speeches, he had a paralytic stroke on September 26 while crossing Kansas; this left him very ill during his remaining months in office —and left the League without a public champion. In November the Foreign Relations Committee of the U.S. Senate recommended passage of the treaty—with fourteen amendments. Wilson would accept no compromise and urged Democrats to vote against the changes. The altered treaty failed on November 19 by a vote of thirty-nine for to fifty-five against. The final vote on March 19, 1920, was forty-nine for the treaty to thirty-five against. To end the war formally, the government made separate treaties with Germany, Austria, and Hungary; these were ratified on October 18, 1920.

The Election of 1920

The election of 1920 was really an extension of the fight over the League of Nations treaty. The Republican convention, meeting June 8 in Chicago, nominated Senator Warren G. Harding of Ohio for president and Governor Calvin Coolidge of Massachusetts for vice president. (Coolidge had made an instant national reputation in 1919 when he called out the National Guard to end a police strike in Boston.) The Republican platform rejected the League of Nations, but promised

Henry Cabot Lodge

DERISIVE poems have been written to express the sense of class among Bostonians of the nineteenth century, and by almost everyone's definition both the Cabot and Lodge families ranked at the top of lists of distinguished families in that city. John E. Lodge, owner of clipper ships and a merchant, married Anna Cabot, and to them in 1850 was born Henry Cabot Lodge, who twenty-one years later graduated from Harvard, married a cousin, and went to Europe for a year. Afterward he went to Harvard Law School.

After editing the *North American Review* for three years, Lodge returned to Harvard to complete the first doctor of philosophy (Ph.D.) awarded there in the field of political science. During the next several years he wrote many works of history, biography, and political science, gave public speeches, penned essays, and taught history at Harvard.

The family's sense of public service soon led him into the arena of politics. As a conservative Republican, he was first elected to the Massachusetts House of Representatives; this success was followed in 1886 by election to Congress, where he served three terms. He entered the Senate in 1893 and served until his death. He also attended every Republican National Convention from 1884 to 1924.

A hard worker, a clear thinker, an excellent writer, and a forceful orator, he soon became a major force on the national stage. He stood for sound money, a high tariff, a strong navy, and American expansion in Panama and the Philippines; he was against women's suffrage, the Eighteenth Amendment, and foreign meddling in American affairs. During Theodore Roosevelt's years in office, Lodge was a close advisor on foreign affairs, on which he was the acknowledged master in the Senate. When Woodrow Wilson tried to secure American entry into the League of Nations, Lodge led the fight against it, sure that his own view was that of the majority of Americans. The presidential election of 1920, which the Republicans won, seemed to vindicate his viewpoint. In 1924 he died in Cambridge, Massachusetts.

support for an "association of nations." The Democratic convention met on June 28 in San Francisco and nominated Governor James M. Cox of Ohio for president and Assistant Secretary of the Navy Franklin D. Roosevelt for vice president. The platform called for strict adherence to the League treaty. Harding managed to appeal both to opponents and supporters of the League, while masterfully calling for a "return to normalcy." He waged a front-porch campaign that promised a return to the old-time virtues, a repeal of war taxes and controls, and a healing of public divisions. The public responded warmly, giving Harding 16,143,407 popular votes and 404 electoral votes; Cox trailed with 9,130,328 popular votes and 127 electoral votes. Interestingly, Eugene V. Debs, although in prison, received 919,799 popular votes as the Socialist candidate.

Warren Gamaliel Harding was as unlike Woodrow Wilson as possible—perhaps this is why the Republicans nominated him for the presidency. Born on a farm in Ohio in 1865, he had taught school, studied law, and sold insurance before buying the *Marion Star* and editing it. With the help of powerful Senator Joseph B. Foraker, Harding entered Ohio politics, and in 1914 he was elected to the United States Senate. There he was noted for his geniality and for his strict adherence to conservative Republican policies.

As president, Harding realized his inability to lead Congress and thus relied on his cabinet—which was surprisingly strong: Charles E. Hughes as secretary of state, Herbert Hoover as secretary of commerce, Harry M. Daugherty (an Ohio crony) as attorney general, Andrew W. Mellon as secretary of the treasury, and Albert B. Fall as secretary of the interior. In his inaugural address Harding rambled to an astonishing extent, filling time with platitudes, verbiage and bad grammar (an English writer called it the most illiterate statement ever made by the head of a civilized government). Following Harding to Washington and the presidency was a group of Ohio friends and hangers-on, who played poker with the president and who became known as the "Ohio Gang." Yet Harding, despite his critics, accomplished much.

The first major problem of the Harding administration was the depression that descended on the country in May, 1920, and lingered for some two years. It was triggered by Wilson's sudden balancing of the budget after the war and by the return of some four million servicemen to peacetime employment. Harding called Congress into special session on April 11, 1921, to ask for economy, a national budgetary system, reform of internal taxes, tariff legislation, protection for agriculture, and a reduction in railroad costs. Congress responded by establishing the Bureau of the Budget, regulation of the grain futures commodity market, and passage of a Revenue Act eliminating the wartime excess profits tax. In fact, Secretary of the Treasury Mellon proposed so many tax reductions in the next few years that political cartoonists regularly depicted another slicing of the "tax mellon," thereby gaining for Mellon a reputation as the greatest secretary of the treasury since Alexander Hamilton. Then on September 19, 1922, came the Fordney-McCumber Tariff, which raised the duty on manufactured goods to a level 25 percent above the rate of the high Paine-Aldrich Tariff of 1909. Harding described the result as the greatest work in tariff history.

Harding made his mark on the federal government in other ways. His appointments at almost every level were from the conservative ranks—most of them very praiseworthy. Charles G. Dawes became the first director of the budget and performed very well. Ex-President Taft became chief justice of the Supreme Court to the satisfaction of much of the country. Harding also made three other appoint-

Warren G. Harding

ments to the court in his short tenure: George Sutherland, Pierce Butler, and Edward T. Sanford, all of them conservative.

The major feat of the Harding administration came in the field of foreign affairs under the strong leadership of Secretary Hughes. At Hughes' suggestion, Harding called a Washington conference on disarmament and Pacific affairs. This conference met on November 12, 1921, and the delegates were astounded to hear Hughes suggest that first day that the attending powers scrap much of their tonnage of warships. On December 13 the United States, England, France, and Japan signed the Four-Power Pact, in which they agreed to respect each others' insular possessions in the Pacific. Then on February 6, 1922, came the Nine-Power Pact (signed by the Big Four plus Italy, China, Belgium, Portugal, and the Netherlands), in which all guaranteed China's territorial integrity and the Open Door policy. And that same day of February 6 came the Five-Power Treaty (the Big Four plus Italy), in which all agreed to tonnage quotas for battleships; this set a ratio of 5:5:3:1.75:1.75 for England, the United States, Japan, Italy, and France respectively. Some students of foreign affairs claim that these treaties delayed war in the Orient for ten years and in the West for fifteen years.

By the off-year election of 1922 the postwar depression largely had ended, yet the Republicans saw their majorities reduced in both houses. General discontent with the Harding administration was evident in the land, along with the circulation of ugly rumors about scandals in high places. Most of these scandals were not proved until after Harding's death, but they were common knowledge in Washington by the summer of 1923. Harding learned of the public distrust of his administration, worried about it, and set about touring the country to restore confidence in himself. In June, 1923, with a party of sixty-five, he began a 7500-mile tour that included Alaska. On his return to San Francisco from Alaska, Harding suddenly became very ill and died on August 2. His widow assiduously collected—and destroyed—his personal correspondence that might have proved his innocence (or guilt) in the scandals subsequently uncovered.

The Coolidge Years

Calvin Coolidge, the nation's thirtieth president, immediately caught the fancy of an industrializing nation that longed for simpler days by his first act. The son of a Vermont country storekeeper, he was visiting his father when awakened on the morning of August 3 to be told of Harding's death. He dressed, prayed, then descended to the family dining room, where by the light of two kerosene lamps his father administered to him the oath of office. His father, of course, was not empowered to administer the oath and it had to be repeated in Washington later in order to be legal, but the newspapers gave wide coverage to so romantic a beginning.

Coolidge was a dour, colorless, cold New England Yankee who seemed almost the exact opposite of Harding. Educated at Amherst, he had been admitted to the Massachusetts bar in 1897, had entered public life the following year, and had risen to become governor of the Bay State in 1918. A solid conservative, he believed in governmental economy and in aid to business without restrictions. Then in 1919, when the Boston police went on strike, he called out the National Guard with the statement, "There is no right to strike against the public safety by anybody, anywhere, at any time," a statement that helped to win him the nomination as vice president in 1920 as a compromise choice. Taciturn, suspicious, moody, he was a colorless president. Yet Coolidge was a stronger chief executive than historians generally have pictured him. When he entered office, the Republican Party was in disarray. It had lost much of its majority in Congress in the elections of 1922, the Harding scandals were just being revealed, and farmers in the Midwest were greatly discontented. Just a year after taking office, Coolidge won election easily in his own right, and when he left office in 1928 the party was stronger yet.

A Puritan by nature, Coolidge had no sympathy with those guilty of misconduct in government. Thus he worked to clean house and to prosecute the malefactors. The first case involved Charles R. Forbes who, as director of the Veterans' Bureau, allegedly resold supplies for personal profit and who made special arrangements with contractors. Indicted for defrauding the government, Forbes was convicted and sentenced to federal prison. The Ohio Gang was found to have been selling protection to bootleggers, as well as profiting from the sale of permits to draw liquor from government warehouses. Thomas W. Miller, the alien property custodian, went to prison for taking bribes, while Attorney General Harry Daugherty was brought to trial for receiving bribes from persons violating prohibition and from monies received through the alien property custodian; Daugherty was not convicted on these charges, but Coolidge did force his resignation.

The most sensational scandal involved the naval oil reserves (proven oil deposits on public lands that had been set aside for use by the Navy). Secretary of the Interior Albert B. Fall had persuaded President Harding to transfer the naval oil reserves from the Department of the Navy to his own department, then had leased the reserves at Teapot Dome, Wyoming, and Elk Hills, California, to oil men Harry F. Sinclair and Edward L. Doheny. Fall in return had received "loans" totaling $350,000. A senatorial committee headed by Thomas J. Walsh of Montana secured proof of this corruption, and charges were brought. Fall was convicted of accepting bribes, fined $100,000, and sentenced to a year in jail; yet Sinclair and Doheny were found innocent of bribery, although Sinclair was convicted of contempt of court.

The Election of 1924

Coolidge—and through him, the Republican Party—was not tainted by this corruption, for he was meticulously honest. Moreover, as the election of 1924 approached, the Coolidge administration backed measures of wide public popularity. On May 26, 1924, came the Immigration Quota Act, which restricted annual immigration to 2 percent of the number of each nationality resident in the United States according to the census of 1890; this measure was popular with Americans who wanted to restrict immigration. Congress also was considering the McNary-Haugen Bill, which called for the federal government to buy surplus commodities such as corn and wheat at high prices and to resell them at a loss on the world market. Coolidge in 1927 would veto the measure, just as in 1924 he vetoed the Soldiers' Bonus Act, yet these policies did not hurt the Republicans in 1924.

The ruling party held its convention first, meeting on June 10 in Cleveland. Coolidge was easily nominated to head the ticket, with Charles G. Dawes of Illinois as his running mate. The Democratic convention convened two weeks later in New York City—and seemed hopelessly deadlocked. The conservative Southern branch of the party backed William Gibbs McAdoo, former secretary of the treasury, while the liberal Northeastern wing of the party wanted New York's Alfred E. Smith. On

Calvin Coolidge

the one hundred and third ballot the delegates compromised on John W. Davis, a West Virginian by birth and a lawyer for J. P. Morgan and Company. His running mate was another compromise choice, Charles W. Bryan of Nebraska, brother of William Jennings Bryan. A major issue at the Democratic convention was the Ku Klux Klan, which had been revived in the South about 1915; the Klan of this era bore no resemblance to its predecessor of reconstruction days, but it was strongly anti-Catholic, anti-Negro, and anti-Jewish. A resolution to include in the Democratic platform a plank condemning the Klan failed by one vote.

As both Coolidge and Davis were conservative, the liberals that year of 1924 decided to launch a third party. On July 4 the Conference for Progressive Political Action met in Cleveland. Usually labeled the Progressive Party, it had no connection with the "Bull Moose" party of 1912. The choice of this gathering was Senator Robert M. La Follette of Wisconsin, then sixty-nine years of age but still vocally liberal, along with Burton K. Wheeler, a Democratic senator from Montana. The platform condemned monopoly and called for nationalization of railroads and electric power companies, demanded a lower tariff and recognition of collective bargaining as a weapon of labor unions, and quixotically asked an abolition of war. But there was never any real doubt that Coolidge would win the election—which he did handily with 15,718,211 popular votes and 382 electoral votes to Davis' 8,385,283 popular and 136 electoral votes. La Follette polled 4,831,289 popular votes and carried the thirteen electoral votes of his native state of Wisconsin. La Follette's defeat caused the Progressive Party to dissolve almost immediately.

The four years during which Coolidge served as president in his own right were unspectacular. A frugal man himself, he cut government expenditures severely, reduced taxation, and reduced the national debt rapidly. Andrew Mellon continued as secretary of the treasury with the same policies as he had under Harding, to the great pleasure of the country. Curiously, Coolidge during his years in office, despite his dour nature, was extremely popular with the public—which apparently wanted a quiet, dour man in office during an era of rapid social and economic change. He appointed Dwight W. Morrow as ambassador to Mexico, thereby restoring good relations with that nation, relations that had deteriorated badly since the days of Woodrow Wilson and intervention. Also, the Kellogg-Briand Pact, which was an attempt to outlaw war as an instrument of national policy, was ratified by the United States and France (and eventually by sixty-two nations). Finally, under Coolidge's direction, the United States sent observers to the League of Nations and American jurists sat on the World Court of the League of Nations, although the United States never joined that organization. In the summer of 1927 Coolidge made the cryptic remark, "I do not choose to run for President in 1928," which he followed up by not seeking the nomination of his party. He retired from public office on March 4, 1929, without playing any role in the choosing of his successor. He returned to Northampton, Massachusetts, where he completed his autobiography.

The Election of 1928

In 1928 the Republicans gathered at Kansas City, Missouri, where they selected Secretary of Commerce Herbert C. Hoover for president and Senator Charles Curtis of Kansas for vice president. The platform stressed that the Coolidge policies would continue to be followed. Among the Democrats, there was only one candidate who seemed to have a national following—Al Smith of New York. Smith was a moderate progressive who twice had been governor of New York, but who called for reforms that would aid the farmer and labor unionists. His running mate, selected by the convention that met in Houston on June 26, was Senator Joseph T. Robinson of Arkansas.

The campaign that year was one of the most colorful—and bitter—in years. The Democratic platform promised enforcement of Prohibition, but Smith said he would work for repeal of the Eighteenth Amendment. Further, Smith was a Roman Catholic (the first to be nominated for president), an Irishman, and had a strong New York accent. Some Republicans stirred racial and religious prejudices in behalf of Hoover, a Protestant of old American stock. Finally, Hoover called Prohibition "a great social and economic experiment, nobel in nature and far-reaching in purpose," which appealed to Southern conservatives, as did his speeches about rugged individualism. Hoover won with 21,391,993 popular and 444 electoral votes to Smith's 15,016,169 popular and 87 electoral votes. Significantly, Hoover carried five former Confederate states, while Smith won majorities in the twelve largest cities in the nation. Later Franklin D. Roosevelt would lay the foundations of the new Democratic Party along the urban lines where Smith had scored. In the election of 1928, Americans showed again that they preferred a conservative president, one in keeping with the actuality of the age but who was able to cope with foreseeable change. And the eleven years following the end of World War I saw more changes in society than during any such span of time before. The era has been described as the "Age of the Flapper," the "Dry Decade," the "Era of Wonderful Nonsense," and the "Jazz Age." It was all of these, for in the decade following the end of World War I Americans were restless, with a craze for entertainment, a passion for frivolity, and an insatiable appetite for sensational journalism. There were stunts and escapades, records were set and broken, and sexuality dawned on the "puritanical" Republic. There was the alleged kidnapping of Sister Aimee McPherson in 1926 and the discovery of the bodies of the Reverend Edward Wheeler Hall and Mrs. James Mills (the choir leader of his church) found shot to death on an abandoned farm near New Brunswick, New Jersey, to titillate the country.

The Twenties

F. Scott Fitzgerald caught the spirit of the Roaring Twenties in such novels as *This Side of Paradise* and *The Great Gatsby*. He called those years "the gaudiest spree in history"—with much truth. Marathon dances (continuous dancing by couples night and day as long as the contestants could keep awake) became an overnight craze; the first such marathon was held in New York City on March 31, 1923, with a record of twenty-seven hours set, followed less than three weeks later in Cleveland with a record of ninety hours nineteen minutes. Another craze was flagpole sitting; the American record was twenty-three days seven hours, set by Alvin "Shipwreck" Kelly in Baltimore and reported nationally by newspapers.

Women's fashions reflected the sudden change in national attitudes. The "flapper" became the rage—bobbed hair, rouge and "kissproof" lipstick, tight felt hat, two strings of beads, bangles around the wrists, flesh-colored stockings, and skirts up to, or even above, the knees. Flapper dresses concealed women's breasts and hips, while the wearers smoked cigarettes openly, drank from flasks, and, in general, tried to hold their own with men.

The "Noble Experiment" proved a dismal failure. To enforce the Volstead Act, the federal government employed some 1500 agents, yet in 1924 the United States Chamber of Commerce estimated that the value of liquor smuggled into the country was in excess of $40 million. Illicit distilling provided far more gallons for drinking than did smuggling—and between 1919 and 1929 U.S. production of corn sugar (which could be used to make corn whiskey) increased 600 percent. The "drys" discovered to their dismay that social behavior was difficult to legislate. Defying Prohibition became a national pastime and the subject of national humor. Two Prohibition agents became famous—Izzy Einstein and Moe Smith. They worked in New York City as a team for two years, using a wide variety of disguises, and provided colorful copy for reporters.

Not so colorful or humorous was the growth of organized crime that Prohibition bred. Entrepreneurs such as Al Capone built a monopoly in large cities such as Chicago by supplying illegal spirits, and enriched themselves by hundreds of millions of dollars. More than 500 murders occurred in Chicago in the decade of the 1920s, as gangsters fought each other for this lucrative monopoly with profits estimated at an annual $60 million. Capone was convicted of tax evasion in 1931, but the syndicate he built survived—and expanded into legitimate businesses with the huge profits made from bootlegging.

The hallmark of the 1920s was the new music that swept the country. Called jazz, the music originated among southern blacks and was a blending of the spiritual-march played at funerals; the attitude of New Orleans' "hell-hole," which said, "Live it hard while you can"; and the music of the "blues," which was a combination of vocal music with the horn and implied that the only thing man could do was cry. Jazz began in New Orleans, moved to St. Louis, Kansas City, and Chicago during the war, and in the 1920s swept the nation. White musicians imitated the blacks and called their product Dixieland, while the youth of the day evolved new dances to accompany it. The black bottom emphasized sinuous hip movements, while the Charleston was more strenuous. The older generation had to be content with the fox trot. Religious fundamentalists saw the new music and the new dances, known popularly as "syncopated embracing," as a breakdown of moral standards. Despite their condemnations, both jazz and dancing spread.

On college campuses, the revolt of youth was even more pronounced. In the previous generation, kissing generally led to marriage. Suddenly "necking" became popular, although it did not necessarily lead to marriage. College coeds adopted the flapper dress, showing not only their ankles but also their knees, while their male companions donned raccoon coats and straw hats, carried flasks, and tried to drive new sports cars. Simultaneously, girls abandoned old fashions in swim wear for one-piece swim suits that were close-fitting.

The response to these new modes of dress and behavior by women—and men— varied with the attitude of the observer. To the young it seemed a glorious revolution; to the religious fundamentalists it seemed a challenge to orthodox Christianity. One minister warned that "low-cut gowns, the rolled hose and short skirts are born of the Devil and his angels and are carrying the present and future generations to chaos and destruction." In Philadelphia a committee on dress reform questioned ministers for opinions, then designed a "moral gown." It featured loose-fitting sleeves reaching below the elbow and a hem that came to within seven and one-half inches of the floor. In the Ohio legislature a bill was introduced prohibiting females over the age of fourteen from wearing a "skirt which does not reach to that part of the foot known as the instep." Ladies were arrested for indecent exposure, ministers thundered from pulpits, and moralists predicted damnation, but women's fashions were irrevocably changed.

This demise of familiar patterns of conduct and dress caused many Americans to focus their attention on the achievements of individuals. Indeed, in no period of American history had there been such hero worship: of aviators, explorers, adventurers, and sports figures. Bobby Jones (golf), Bill Tilden (tennis), Babe Ruth (baseball), Jack Dempsey (prize fighting), Red Grange (football), and Gertrude Ederle (the first woman to swim the English channel) became household words—while Charles A. Lindbergh captured the imagination of the world by flying solo from New York City to Paris in June, 1927.

Hero worship was but one response to the collapse of familiar patterns of conduct. Intolerance and bigotry were another. The war had bequeathed to the next decade a legacy of fear of foreigners and a hatred of change. It was this environment that produced a resurgence of the Ku Klux Klan—and of an antievolution crusade to prevent the teaching of Darwinistic theories in the public schools. Science, according to the fundamentalists, was the culprit causing change in America; science was the work of the Devil to tempt God-fearing Christians. Fundamentalists organized into Bible Crusaders and the Anti-Evolution League to lobby for a ban on the teaching of evolution (as well as passage of "blue laws" to govern conduct). North Carolina, Oklahoma, Mississippi, Alabama, Tennessee, and Texas responded to this pressure and passed laws against the teaching of evolution. In Dayton, Tennessee, young John Scopes agreed to teach evolution in his classes to promote a court test of these laws. His trial in July, 1924, attracted thousands to the small town of Dayton and pitted Clarence Darrow, for the defense, against William Jennings Bryan, who was there to aid the prosecution. Scopes was found guilty and fined (later the state supreme court upheld the conviction and the law but rescinded the fine).

Rapid Changes

Perhaps abetting such changes and such laws was the growing urbanization of the country. The census of 1920 revealed that for the first time in American history more than half the nation's population was living in urban areas. Farm population was declining as young people moved to the cities seeking new opportunities. Leading this movement was the southern Negro who, beginning during World War I, migrated northward and settled in cities such as New York, Philadelphia, Washington, Chicago, and St. Louis (and westward to Los Angeles). By 1930 the black population of New York City was 300,000—and climbing—turning Harlem into a black slum and creating a problem that neither time nor money has solved. Facilitating this movement to the cities was the automobile, which became increasingly available to the average citizen. Annual auto production rose from 1,518,061 in 1921 to 4,794,839 in 1929, while the price declined proportionately. Automobiles brought a demand for good roads, and together these ended the isolation of rural America, gave birth to suburbs, stimulated the petroleum industry, and accelerated pollution of the air.

Yet another force in the remaking of American society was the entertainment industry. Movies and radio were forms of mass entertainment that became big business. By 1922 some 40 million movie tickets were sold weekly, while three million homes had radios. By 1929 the sale of movie tickets had doubled, while radio ownership had jumped to ten million. The National Broadcasting Company (NBC) was formed in 1926 and the Columbia Broadcasting System (CBS) the following year to provide programs for the proliferating number of radio stations. And both the radio industry and movie companies promoted a mass production–mass consumption culture. To attract large audiences, the motion picture industry made pictures that appealed to as many people as possible, while advertisers sponsoring radio shows wanted—demanded—that their messages reach the maximum number of people possible. The radio networks developed a telephone "polling" system to determine what share of the national audience was listening to a particular program; those that did not pull a high rating were dropped. Such trends in the broadcasting and motion picture industries reflected the increasing portion of major industries that were tied to the desires, fads, fancies, and purchasing power of the masses of Americans. The day of the giant corporation, mass production, and mass consumption was at hand.

And the 1920s were years of mass production. In fact, the government under both Harding and Coolidge seemed dedicated to the credo that government should be small while business should be free to grow. And this policy produced an unparalleled prosperity. Spectacular advances were made in the production of electric power, in durable consumer goods, in the construction of suburban homes and urban skyscrapers, and in leisure items. The post–Civil War period had seen the erection of the basic industrial capacity and of a nationwide transportation system; the post–World War I period saw that capacity turned to the production of consumer goods. By 1929 one American in five had an automobile, while radios, home appliances, and prepared foods were in common use. Mass advertising and installment buying created both the desire for these goods and the means of acquiring them, and together they wrought a drastic change in American Society. Those who did not like the changes in American society could retreat into religious fundamentalism, join the literary intellectuals who fled to Paris, or content themselves with sweeping damnations of the country.

In business itself, there was a movement toward consolidation of industries unequaled since the post–Civil War period. Secretary of Commerce Herbert Hoover encouraged this movement in the name of industrial efficiency by gathering statistics, seeking out foreign markets, and allowing competing firms in an industry to form trade associations to share information, standardize tools, and set prices— thereby increasing productivity. The Supreme Court in 1925 endorsed this activity in the *Cement Manufacturers' Protective Association* case. Iron, steel, mining, banking, manufacturing, distributing, electronics, automobiles—all fell into the hands of giant conglomerates. The public was delighted with this process, while both Harding and Coolidge appointed to the Federal Trade Commission men hostile to enforcement of the antitrust laws.

Hurt by this change were the labor union and the farm. For thirteen consecutive years membership in trade unions declined from a peak of over four million at the end of the war, while the farmer was the victim of overproduction. By 1929 government warehouses bulged with surplus corn and wheat, while farmers' real income dipped ever lower. Low wages, monopolistic conglomerates, and retail price-setting did produce increasing profits for the manufacturers, however, and this stimulated an orgy of speculation on the stock market. Fortunes were made overnight as buyers purchased shares of stock on margin, waited for a rise in prices, then sold and took their profits. The "Great Bull Market" began in March, 1928, and continued without interruption for nineteen months, with stocks quadrupling in price and the daily turnover rising from about one million to eight million shares.

The Great Crash

Herbert Hoover thus came into office during a wave of prosperity and optimism. His first seven months in office were a "honeymoon," during which editorial writers lamented the death of the Democratic Party. Then, with chilling suddenness, the nation spiraled downward into economic depression. Credit was overexpanded in the stock market and in the area of installment buying; industry was overexpanded; agriculture was overexpanded and underpaid; technology was unable to absorb the expanding work force; and the world suddenly had embarked on tariff wars that slowed the exporting of American goods. On October 24, 1929, the crash came. Brokers fought to unload their holdings, and sales on the stock market rose to unbelievable volume on Monday and Tuesday, October 28 and 29. By mid-November, 40 percent of the paper value of common stocks had been cancelled. Tall, plump, moon-faced Herbert Hoover—shy, stiff, and in high collar—the man who had fed the Belgians and who had come to office celebrated as humanitarian, the "Great Engineer," faced the hair shirt of depression.

Chapter Thirteen

Paying the Piper

The Depression

THE event that most shaped the American national psychology in the twentieth century did not arrive with martial music nor with bullet and bomb nor yet with nuclear reaction. Its birth was announced by pandemonium in corporate offices, and by stunned workers receiving the infamous "pink slip" that notified them of termination of employment. Its adolescence was marked by the marching of veterans demanding payment of a bonus for having served in the Great War, by perhaps the most cynical political maneuvering in American history, and by the election to the presidency of a man promising to kill the monster with nostrums. In its maturity, men stood in soup lines, families migrated in search of work, shanty-towns dotted the countryside, and the voters endorsed legislation that redefined and even defied the Constitution. Yet its death came not from demands, nostrums, or legislation, but from the most terrible war of recorded history. This event was the Great Depression of 1929, which ended with the coming of World War II.

Hoover's Reaction

The agony of the American public during this economic trauma became the personal agony of the president. Herbert Hoover believed in individualism, initiative, liberty, and moral equality; "you cannot extend the mastery of government over the daily working life of a people," he responded to cries for governmental intervention, "without at the same time making it the master of people's souls and thoughts." His first reaction to the stock-market crash was to voice optimism. On October 25 he stated that the economy was "on a sound and prosperous basis." In the hope that he could prevent a vicious downward spiral in the economy (that is, a slump followed by a discharge of workers, followed by a decreasing ability to make purchases, leading to yet a bigger slump, huge unemployment, farm foreclosures, and business failures), he held a series of conferences at the White House at which he urged businessmen not to cut wages or fire workers, to build new plants and buy new equipment, and to avoid price cuts. Simultaneously, he urged labor leaders not to seek higher wages, Congress to vote funds for federal public works, and governors to expand state construction projects. But, of course, the nation continued to slide toward a deeper depression.

The depression was worldwide, and most nations responded by enacting protectionist legislation. Tariffs everywhere rose to dizzy heights, even in the United States. Congressman Willis C. Hawley of Oregon introduced a tariff bill in the House in May, 1929, which was revised upward in the Senate by Reed Smoot of Utah and emerged to receive Hoover's signature as the Hawley-Smoot Tariff; this made 890 revisions—upward—of the Fordney-McCumber law and raised duties to the highest level in American history.

Herbert Hoover tried to end the Depression within a constitutional framework. He believed that the federal government should not enter the field of direct relief: "Prosperity," he declared, "cannot be restored by raids on the public Treasury." He did, however, advance expenditures for public works such as roads, federal buildings, and conservation facilities such as Hoover Dam on the Colorado River. By 1932 the national government was spending approximately $500 million annually on public works.

Hoover would not supply funds for direct relief, however. When private agencies and local resources proved inadequate, he appointed Colonel Arthur Woods to head an Emergency Committee for Employment. Woods' task was to work with state and local officials and with private organizations to coordinate the various relief agencies. Hoover also attempted an expansion of the nation's credit. In late 1929, under Hoover's prodding, the Federal Reserve Bank reduced its rediscount rate from 5 to 4.5 percent, and in October, 1931, he pressured businessmen to form the National Credit Corporation to loan money to banks and corporations. When the latter proved inadequate, Hoover reluctantly agreed to more drastic legislation. With his token backing, Congress, in January, 1932, established the Reconstruction Finance Corporation (RFC). This corporation could loan up to $2 billion to banks, railroads, insurance companies, and other businesses facing bankruptcy.

When the Depression worsened and hunger stalked the land, Hoover agreed in March, 1932, to the distribution of the 40 million bushels of wheat and five million bales of cotton held by the federal government as surplus commodities. (He insisted that the food and cloth be distributed by the Red Cross rather than the federal government.) Then in June, 1932, he agreed to allowing the RFC to loan up to $300 million for direct relief and $1.5 billion to the states for self-liquidating public works. And in July, 1932, came approval of the Home Loan Bank System to aid householders about to lose their homes.

The Depression grew worse by 1932, with almost 10 million unemployed. Despondent men began talking of revolution, but they were a small minority. Yet there were many panaceas suggested, and even some radical action. For example, in the summer of 1932 came the Veterans Bonus March. Congress in 1924 had voted a bonus to veterans of World War I, payable in 1945. In February, 1931, Congress, over Hoover's veto, passed an act allowing veterans to borrow up to 50 percent of their bonus funds. In May and June, 1932, hundreds of veterans marched to Washington to support the Patman Bill, which would have authorized immediate payment of full bonuses to all veterans. When Congress adjourned in July without passing this measure, thousands of veterans were in Washington—and in an ugly mood. When trouble threatened, Hoover ordered out federal troops. Commanded by General Douglas MacArthur, the Army dispersed the veterans. Few knew that the president personally provided funds to transport many of the veterans home. And in the Midwest, militant farmers instituted a strike to force prices up. Under Milo Reno, the National Farmers' Holiday Association led strikes at Sioux City, Council Bluffs, and Des Moines, Iowa, that saw highways blockaded.

Herbert Hoover

Politics and the Depression

Herbert Hoover became the great villain of the Depression. Those who ate rabbits called them "Hoover Hogs"; most shanty-towns were labeled "Hooverville"; and those sleeping under newspapers named them "Hoover Blankets." In truth, the president proposed several pieces of legislation that would greatly have mitigated the rigors of the Depression, legislation that embodied the heart of Roosevelt's New Deal. Hoover's program was not enacted into law by Congress because of rabid partisan politics. The Democrats smelled victory in 1932 because of the national suffering. They saw little reason to throw away that expected victory by passing legislation that would satisfy the population to the benefit of the Republicans. The Democrats had gained control of the lower house of Congress in the off-year election of 1930 and used their majority there to bottleneck Hoover's programs. John J. Raskob, national chairman of the Democratic Party, sent squads of propagandists around the country to pin a depression label on the Republican Party; called "mud-gunners," these squads did their work with great efficiency, while Democratic congressmen (along with Republicans seeking to disassociate themselves from the administration) voted against Hoover's proposals.

The Election of 1932

The Republican convention in Chicago in June, 1932, was dreary and dejected. Sensing defeat, the delegates renominated Hoover and Curtis without enthusiasm and issued a platform calling for emergency loans to the states for relief, tariff protection, banking reform, and cooperatives for farmers. They tried to avoid the issue of Prohibition. The Democratic convention of June 27, also meeting in Chicago, was in marked contrast to the Republican gathering. The leading candidates for the nomination were John Nance "Cactus Jack" Garner, Speaker of the House of Representatives from Texas, and Franklin Delano Roosevelt, the governor of New York. Roosevelt's backers persuaded Garner to accept the vice-presidential nomination and thereby secured for their aristocratic candidate the nomination for president on the fourth ballot. In his acceptance speech, Roosevelt gave his era a name: "I pledge you, I pledge myself, to a new deal for the American people." However, his explanation of the New Deal was vague and general.

In the campaign that followed, Roosevelt—a New York aristocrat, Harvard graduate, and former assistant secretary of the navy who had overcome poliomyelitis—campaigned fearlessly on some issues: he was foursquare for relief both by federal dole and by "make work"; he promised recovery for the economy without burdening the budget; and he talked vaguely of reforming the national government. There was never any doubt that Roosevelt would win. Even Hoover knew it, as he pointed out with bitter realism that Roosevelt's promises of work for all were cruel because they were impossible of fulfillment. Roosevelt tried to insure his victory through use of a group of men he gathered to write his speeches, his "brain trust": Raymond Moley, professor of public law at Columbia University; Hugh S. ("Ironpants") Johnson, army general, lawyer, and businessman; and James A. Farley, who served as campaign manager. As election day neared, Hoover gradually lapsed into silence. Colonel Sam Robertson of Texas summed up the mood of that election in a telegram to Ross Sterling, the governor of the Lone Star State, advising him that it was a bad year for incumbents: "You are an in. You cannot win in such a time as this.

Thomas Jefferson, George Washington, or Abe Lincoln, if in office today, could not be reelected. The voters of 1932 are as rational as the mob who crucified Christ." On November 8, Roosevelt received 22,809,638 popular and 472 electoral votes, while Hoover received a surprising 15,758,901 popular votes and 59 electoral votes. Roosevelt had received his mandate to attempt a "new deal."

The Hundred Days

Roosevelt swept into office on a wave of optimism. To a nation wallowing in gloom, he seemed a "laughing revolution." In his inaugural address he declared, "The only thing we have to fear is fear itself," and he said he would use the executive authority to deal with the emergency then facing the nation. His cabinet members were a diverse lot: Cordell Hull of Tennessee as secretary of state; James A. Farley of New York as postmaster general; Harold Ickes as secretary of the interior; Henry A. Wallace as secretary of agriculture; and Francis Perkins as secretary of labor. Some of these appointees were former progressive Republicans, some were Southerners, and most were not from within the Democratic Party's hierarchy.

One of the president's first acts was to convene Congress in special session to deal with the crisis of the Depression. Because Roosevelt had refused to announce before his inauguration any of his policies, the country had come to a virtual economic standstill. Banks had shut to avoid financial collapse, and cities were using scrip instead of currency. In the Midwest, farmers were in revolt; milk trucks were being overturned and mortgage sales forcibly halted. During the next three months —the famous "hundred days"—Roosevelt secured from Congress almost everything he asked. Well he might, for he had overwhelming majorities in both houses of Congress, many of the members acutely aware that they had ridden into office on the president's coattails. On taking office, Roosevelt had declared a bank holiday, stopping all transactions in gold and silver. Congress, which met on March 9, passed that same day the Emergency Banking Act, which approved the bank holiday and gave the president broad powers over money and banking. On April 19 the president officially took the nation off the gold standard by forbidding gold exports.

Legislation followed in such rapid succession that it was difficult to keep abreast of the changes. Federal salaries were reduced, and two constitutional amendments were added—the Twentieth, which ended the "lame duck" session of Congress and established January 20 as the day for inaugurating presidents; and the Twenty-first, which repealed Prohibition. As a relief measure, the administration secured legislation creating a Civilian Conservation Corps, which hired young men to work on reforestation and other conservation projects. Hoover's idea of loaning money to the states for public works was reemployed, while home and farm owners were extended government credit to refinance their mortgages. To promote recovery from the Depression, the administration secured passage of several acts: the Trade Agreements Act, which empowered the president to negotiate lower tariff arrangements to promote foreign trade; the Beer and Wine Revenue Act, which legalized certain alcoholic beverages and which brought needed revenue to the treasury; the National Industrial Recovery Act, which established the National Recovery Administration (NRA) and empowered it to draw up "fair competition codes" supposedly to stimulate competition and get people back to work; the Gold Reserve Act, which devalued the dollar to 59.06 cents; and the Agricultural Adjustment Act, which sought to raise farm prices and reduce production.

Bureau of Printing and Engraving

Franklin D. Roosevelt

Federal public works to provide jobs included such diverse elements as the Tennessee Valley Authority Act, which created the Tennessee Valley Authority (TVA) with power to construct dams and power plants; and the Civil Works Administration, which evolved into the infamous Works Progress Administration (WPA) that hired 2.5 million men by 1935 to lay sidewalks, rake leaves, and even paint murals on post office walls. There were also such measures as the Securities Exchange Act, which provided a regulatory agency for the stock market; the Federal Communications Commission (FCC), to regulate interstate and foreign communication; and the Federal Housing Administration (FHA), to insure homes and build new ones.

The Second New Deal

The public at large responded to Roosevelt's "first" New Deal by increasing the Democratic majority in Congress in the off-year election of 1934. But average businessmen and property-owners had become increasingly hostile. And by 1935 it was clear that Roosevelt's measures had not ended the Depression—or even seriously reduced unemployment. Thus he came before Congress in 1935 asking for a "Second New Deal" that supposedly would help the underprivileged. Congress rubber-stamped his proposals, which included a National Labor Relations Act (requiring management to bargain collectively, allowing the closed shop, and creating the National Labor Relations Board to judge claims of unfair labor practices); a Social Security Act, to provide old-age benefits and unemployment compensation (with the aim of getting old people off the labor market); and a Wage and Hours Act, which set minimum wages and maximum hours in the nation's chief industries. These, along with dozens of other bills and acts creating myriad agencies and commissions, vastly extended the influence of the national government into fields it never before had entered. At the same time the president was concentrating power in his own hands to a degree, a dangerous degree, never before reached in American history.

The Supreme Court and the New Deal

The Supreme Court noted some of the radical innovations of the New Deal—and courageously ruled against them. The NRA was ruled unconstitutional in the case *Schechter Poultry Corporation* v. *United States* (May 27, 1935), and the AAA likewise in *United States* v. *Butler* (January 6, 1936). Four of the nine members of the court were conservative in the Jeffersonian sense of strictly interpreting the Constitution; three were liberal in the Hamiltonian sense of loosely interpreting the Constitution; while the other two were moderates, one moderately liberal and the other moderately conservative. Both the NRA and the AAA were ruled unconstitutional by five-to-four decisions. Roosevelt determined to change the complexion of the court, but with characteristic deviousness he decided to wait until after the election of 1936.

The Republicans met on June 9 in Cleveland to nominate Governor Alfred M. Landon of Kansas as their party's standard bearer, with Colonel Frank Knox of Illinois for vice president. The platform was a promise to repeal the New Deal and return power to the states. The Democrats met on June 23 in Philadelphia to renominate Roosevelt and Garner on a platform defending the New Deal. In the campaign that followed, Landon proved a colorless, even inept campaigner. Most newspapers vigorously supported the Republican candidate, but this proved insufficient to bring victory. Roosevelt used the radio effectively, as he had for the past three years in his famous "fireside chats," and he had welded divergent, even opposing, factions into an effective party that included Southerners and blacks, farmers and urban dwellers, and reformers and cynically corrupt city machines. On November 3 the electorate gave Roosevelt the mandate he sought. The president received 27,752,869 popular and 523 electoral votes (along with more than a three to one majority in both houses of Congress) to Landon's 16,674,665 popular and 8 electoral votes (he carried only Maine and Vermont).

The election over, Roosevelt moved to neutralize the Supreme Court. As six of the justices were more than seventy years old, he proposed that "where there are incumbent judges of retirement age who do not choose to resign," the president could appoint an additional justice to the court for each justice over seventy who did not retire, up to a number of six additional judges. The "Court Packing Bill" was introduced on February 5, 1937, but to Roosevelt's astonishment, Congress—even members of his own party—fought it bitterly. And the public supported the court. The bill died in Senate committee. However, the president got what he wanted. One judge retired voluntarily on May 18, allowing the president to appoint Hugo L. Black, a former Ku Klux Klansman turned liberal. Three more resignations by 1939 allowed Roosevelt to realign the court to his satisfaction, and thereafter it ruled New Deal actions constitutional, including minimum wage laws, upholding the National Labor Relations Board, and the right of the federal government to use the taxing power to provide pensions.

Roosevelt's Second Term

Also in his second term, Roosevelt moved still farther to the left. Labor unions, encouraged by the Wagner-Connery Act, went on strike to fight for union recognition and the closed shop, while the National Labor Relations Board quickly gained its prolabor reputation. The loss of 28,400,000 man-days of work due to strikes in 1937 in part accounted for the ensuing economic tailspin. National productivity had not yet returned to the level of 1929 when this began; the Roosevelt administration tion labeled the downward slant of the economy a "recession," but names mattered little to the four million additional people who became unemployed as a result. Roosevelt reacted by blaming businessmen, accusing them of price-fixing, and launching trust-busting activities better suited to finding a whipping-boy than providing true remedies. Simultaneously, he moved still farther left in asking for appropriations for relief and public works, thereby increasing the national debt.

The Roosevelt administration during its first years in office did try to raise revenues by revising the tax system. The Revenue Act of 1935 had raised rates on individual incomes above $50,000, on inheritances, corporate earnings, gifts, and "excess" profits; in 1936 came a drastic raise on corporate profits (reduced somewhat in 1938). Yet taxation did not provide sufficient financing for the grandiose schemes of the New Deal; the result was deficit financing. The public debt of the nation at the end of fiscal 1933 was $22.5 billion; six years of Roosevelt's policies had almost doubled it to $40 billion—with ensuing suffering for those on fixed incomes. By 1938 the nation was becoming disenchanted with FDR. The New Deal, for all its rhetoric, its legislation, and its invasion of private and property rights, had not ended the Depression or even done much to reduce unemployment. In short, it was a failure, although its adherents refused then (and now) to admit as much. The voters in 1938 sensed the failure, however, for the Republicans scored substantial gains; they, with the aid of conservative Democrats, thereafter had sufficient strength to halt expansion of the New Deal. Moreover, war in Europe —and possibly the Pacific—seemed about to erupt, and Roosevelt became more and more enmeshed in foreign affairs, to the benign neglect of domestic affairs.

Social Changes

Because the 1920s had been prosperous, comfortable, optimistic, the 1930s were traumatic for most Americans. Suddenly everything was turned upside down. Even the outward appearance of the cities changed, with former stockbrokers on the sidewalks selling pencils or apples, with unemployed men welcoming arrest because it meant warmth and food in jail, with shanty-towns appearing in and around the industrial cities, with desperation, hard times, discomfort, and pessimism the hallmarks of the age. For the farmer the Depression had begun after World War I, but it became more intense during the 1930s. Owners, renters, and sharecroppers alike suffered, and prices for commodities skidded still lower; few could sell their produce for enough to pay costs—at a time when much of the population was hungry, and despite the farmer working as hard as ever. However, the farmer could usually raise sufficient food to have a full table—which meant he was better appreciated by his city kin, many of whom moved back to the land they had abandoned for high-paying industrial jobs. For the city dweller out of work—and without farm relatives —there was the shame of the soup line. Children suffered from malnutrition, with rickets increasing; in New York City, for example, the city health department found 20.5 percent of the school children suffering from malnutrition.

Other Americans took to the road in the hope that opportunity lay in distance. The nation had long been one of wanderers, but the Depression set off a wave of nomadism unparalleled in previous years. Teen-aged tramps became adept at "riding the rails," while refugees from the dust-bowl of the Midwest (erroneously called Okies, implying that all were from Oklahoma) piled their few possessions onto aging automobiles and headed west. California, which became a Mecca for many wanderers, took steps to turn away as many of them as possible at its borders.

The Depression was equally traumatic for the middle class. Unemployment among college graduates did not match the unemployment among those with less education, but the threat of losing a job—and the lowering of income—was difficult indeed for the educated to bear. Professional men not on salaries saw their incomes dwindle seriously, while those living on income from capital investment saw both income and capital shrink. This hardship caused some social and political writers to speculate on the death of the middle class and the resultant influence on America. Perhaps the hardest hit of the middle class were teachers. Retrenchment was in order in the public schools in order to save tax dollars; the result was inadequate education for a generation. Colleges and universities, both public and private, suffered budgetary cuts, but it was their students who suffered most. The student of the 1930s frequently had to make severe sacrifices to remain in college; life there was grim and earnest—education was a privilege, and the students knew it.

Yet for all the hardships, socialists were surprised to discover that hard times did not mean an end to the family as a social institution. Instead, family ties grew stronger as members of each unit drew together for survival. Divorce rates plum-

337

meted, leading those who studied this phenomenon to suggest with bitter humor that poverty either was good for marriages or else few could afford divorce.

Intellectuals and the Depression

The Depression had a similar influence on American intellectuals for the most part. Many artists and writers had been appalled at the materialism of the 1920s and had fled the country, either literally or figuratively. Perhaps it was the pessimism of the 1930s (or the prospect of power and influence) that appealed to the so-called intellectuals, for those who had fled began returning, while those who had stayed at home began reentering the mainstream of American life. John Steinbeck addressed himself to the impact of the Depression—and captured some of its frustrations—in his *Grapes of Wrath,* while playwright Clifford Odets concentrated on political themes (*Waiting for Lefty*). Other writers flourishing in this period included William Faulkner, Thomas Wolfe, and Ernest Hemingway, and the federal government subsidized unemployed artists, writers, and composers, just as it did laborers and farmers.

Most of these "intellectuals" turned optimistic and tried to promote "cultural nationalism," with emphasis on American forms of art, literature, and music. Actors found the Depression a golden age, for radio and motion pictures proved profitable forms of escapism and provided employment—and riches—for them. A few intellectuals gave way to despair, however, and turned to extremist answers, among them communism. For a time intellectuals considered it fashionable to carry a membership card in the Communist Party, or at least to voice openly a sympathy for the aims of that organization; many of these intellectuals later would be embarrassed by their espousal of communism during the 1930s, but at the time it seemed somehow "significant" to meet in conspiratorial groups and whisper the word "revolution." And some 100,000 Americans actually applied for visas to go to Russia; the majority of them quickly returned to report that the "workers' paradise" was more hell than heaven.

By 1940 the number of unemployed still numbered 7.5 million, roughly 14 percent of the civilian labor force. Perhaps it was America's concentration on economic affairs that had caused it to be so ignorant of events transpiring across the Atlantic. Because the democratic process had been preserved in the United States despite the Depression, it was difficult for most Americans to realize that democracy had been killed in some European nations by economic dislocations. Yet Americans during the 1930s were isolationist to a high degree. Even Roosevelt in the early years of his tenure as chief executive had largely ignored foreign considerations. The only innovation in foreign policy early in the New Deal was to recognize the Communist régime in Soviet Russia in the vain hope that it would stimulate foreign trade and also restrain Japan somewhat. Similarly, Secretary of State Cordell Hull wanted trade barriers reduced, and in 1934 Congress passed the Trade Agreements Act, which allowed the executive branch of government to negotiate treaties providing for a reciprocal lowering of tariffs; by 1939 twenty-one such treaties had been negotiated. Contrary to Hull's hopes, these treaties did not stimulate foreign trade, the level of which remained far below what it had been in the 1920s.

Only in Latin America did Roosevelt's policies redound to American benefit. There he instituted what became known as the "Good Neighbor Policy." This meant a repudiation of interventionism and Dollar Diplomacy; it meant a respect for the sovereign independence of other American nations; and it meant frequent consultation, as at Montevideo in 1933, at Buenos Aires in 1936, and at Lima in 1938. Later the Organization of American States (OAS) would grow from these conferences.

Isolationism

As international relations deteriorated in Europe and Asia in the mid-1930s, as dictators invaded Ethiopia and China, Americans responded with their typical isolationism. Only at rare times in the nation's history had its citizens really been concerned with global needs or with balance-of-power politics on the international scene. The rise of Adolf Hitler to power in Germany, with the resultant persecution of the Jews; the emergence of Benito Mussolini and fascism in Italy; and the emergence of war lords as masters of Japan, with the subsequent invasion of China and Manchuria—these hardly seemed threats to America. Scholars promoted this sense of isolationism by publishing studies that allegedly proved World War I had resulted from a conspiracy of Wall Street bankers, munitions makers, and British propagandists. Motion pictures and novels emphasized the horrors of World War I —and its futility. Students in colleges and universities affirmed their hatred of war by taking the "Oxford Oath," a pledge never to fight. Congress responded to this public attitude by passing a neutrality act in 1935, which prohibited the sale of arms and munitions to all belligerents and forbade American citizens from traveling on belligerent vessels. In 1936 came yet another neutrality act, this one embargoing loans to belligerent nations. When the Spanish Civil War began in July, 1936, many American liberals immediately forgot their oaths against war and went to Spain to join combat against Franco. Yet another neutrality act was passed in 1937 forbidding individual Americans to export arms to belligerent nations or to loan them money, but specifically authorizing the export of articles other than arms and munitions if the buyer paid cash and carried the goods away in his own ships.

The net effect of this American attitude and these laws was to encourage the very aggression they were intended to halt. Hitler believed that in the event he made war on England and France, the United States would take no part and would insist on cash payment for goods. The Japanese came to believe that Americans were soft and would not resist their takeover of the Pacific world. By October, 1937, when Roosevelt finally came to realize the world drift toward holocaust, the damage had been done. World war again loomed on the horizon.

Chapter Fourteen

Confronting the World

Conditions in 1940

RARELY in human history has a nation so underestimated its power as did the United States in the 1930s. Under the influence of pacifist propaganda, many Americans came to believe that wars were engineered by industrialists, stockbrokers, and profiteers, while, simultaneously, they were led to believe that the German war machine was invincible. Charles A. Lindbergh, famous as an aviator, used his position to push his ideas about the power of the Nazis' air force. Many Americans read —and believed—such statements, and interpreted them as meaning that France and England would be destroyed in the event of war and therefore the United States should not help them. Then, after the Roosevelt administration allowed the Japanese to attack Pearl Harbor in a "surprise" bombing, the United States flexed its muscles, built a war machine, and vigorously prosecuted the conflict its policies had encouraged into happening.

Yet never before in human history had a nation so idealistically fought—not for territorial gain, not for economic gain, nor yet for gratitude. America poured forth its treasure and its industrial output and its young men for the right of nations to determine their own political destinies, for human decency, for justice, and for the survival of freedom. Five years after the war ended, the United States again had to send its youth, it supplies, and its money to far-off Korea on a similar mission. Idealism was expensive, both in treasure and in lives, but it was thought preferable to spend these than to lose sight of American ideals and to endanger national security through cowardice. The United States had become the world's greatest power—and sadly learned the high cost of this burden between 1940 and 1953.

Causes of World War II

The causes of World War II were essentially the same as those that had brought World War I—nationalism, greed, racism, and the search for power. Adolf Hitler, coming to office as chancellor of Germany in 1933, chose to blame his country's losses in World War I on the Jews, to break the Treaty of Versailles, to rearm Germany, and to expand in the name of uniting all German-speaking people. In 1935 he began building his army and air force; in 1936 he remilitarized the Rhineland;

340

that same year he joined Japan to form the Berlin-Tokyo Axis (joined by Italy in 1937); in 1938 he seized Austria and part of Czechoslovakia; and in 1939 he occupied Prague and the remainder of that nation. England and France had done nothing to oppose these moves except seek to appease Hitler. With the seizure of Prague in the spring of 1939, the English prime minister, Neville Chamberlain, was forced by public indignation to promise Poland aid in case of German aggression. Hitler chose to fight, but only after a treaty with Russia on August 23 that promised no war between his country and the Communists. On September 1 the German army invaded Poland from the west and the Red Army attacked from the east; within two days France and England declared war on Germany.

Meanwhile, in the Pacific, Japanese war lords had gained control of their government and were pushing for their sun to rise over Asia. In 1931 they ordered the occupation of Manchuria, where they established a puppet government. The United States protested only mildly, so in July, 1937, the Japanese army invaded China. Again the United States protested, this time by denouncing Japan as an aggressor and a treaty-breaker. The Japanese reply came in 1938, when Tokyo announced the end of the Open Door policy in trade and industry. The American reaction was to give six-months' notice of termination of the reciprocal trade agreement of 1911; yet Japan continued to purchase scrap iron, gasoline, and other war materials in the United States. The United States loaned some $70 million to the Chinese government to purchase war supplies.

By the spring of 1940 Roosevelt, certain that German victory was imminent, was determined to involve the United States in the European war. Between April 9 and June 22 the German army occupied Norway, Denmark, Belgium, the Netherlands, and France. Japan responded by conquering most of the former Dutch colonies in the Pacific. Roosevelt named a National Defense Advisory Commission to coordinate the economic aspects of war preparations, and the first peacetime draft system was established through the Burke-Wadsworth Act, which called for all men between twenty-one and thirty-five to register. Also during that summer of 1940, through indirect sales, the United States began providing arms and ammunition to England; most of this equipment was surplus from World War I. Then on September 2 the United States transferred fifty overage destroyers to Great Britain in exchange for ninety-nine-year leases on eight naval and air bases in Newfoundland, Bermuda, the Bahamas, British Guiana, and other Western Hemispheric British possessions. This "Destroyer Deal" marked the end of American neutrality, a point that was not missed in the presidential elections that fall.

The Election of 1940

The Republicans gathered in Philadelphia on June 28, 1940, to find their party divided. Eastern delegates had an internationalist point of view and favored intervention, while Midwestern and Western delegates remained isolationist. After a spirited battle, Wendell Willkie was nominated on the sixth ballot for president, with Senator Charles L. McNary of Oregon for vice president. Willkie was a corporation lawyer from New York and president of Commonwealth and Southern who had fought valiantly against the TVA and who had made a national reputation as a champion of the free-enterprise system and critic of the New Deal, while McNary was known as a friend of the farmer. The Democrats gathered at Chicago on July 15 to shatter precedent and nominate Roosevelt for a third term; "Cactus Jack"

Garner broke with the president on the third-term issue and was dropped from the ticket in favor of Henry A. Wallace of Iowa. Both party platforms promised to keep America out of war (in terms reminiscent of Woodrow Wilson's pledge of 1916), to aid England in every way short of a declaration of war, and to ready the country's defenses. In short, both platforms were similar on foreign policy. On domestic issues, the Democratic platform stressed the positive results of the New Deal, while the Republicans attacked it as dictatorial, wasteful, bureaucratic, and undemocratic. Even the third-term issue was not enough for Willkie, however. Roosevelt was swept into a third term, although with a smaller majority than he had received in 1936, netting 27,307,819 popular votes (55 percent) and 449 electoral votes to Willkie's 22,321,018 and 82. To the surprise of everyone, even the Democrats, they increased their majorities in both houses of Congress. The voters apparently wanted experience in the White House during a time of crisis; Roosevelt chose to interpret his victory to mean endorsement of all-out support for England.

The Coming of War

During 1941 the United States moved steadily toward war. In his annual message to Congress on January 6, 1941, Roosevelt recommended a lend-lease bill to aid the Allies; goods, rather than money, would be loaned to England, to be paid for after the war. Congress enacted the measure on March 11 after spirited debate, and the movement of these goods began (lend-lease aid would total $51 billion before the end of World War II). The German High Command, naturally, wanted to prevent these goods from reaching England, and it ordered its submarines to sink American merchant ships; Roosevelt responded on September 11 by ordering American naval vessels to shoot on sight at German submarines in American defense waters, and on November 17 Congress passed legislation allowing the arming of American merchant ships. Also that year, by agreement with Denmark, the United States occupied Greenland for defensive purposes and on July 7 occupied Iceland to prevent a German occupation. (Iceland had declared its independence from Denmark and invited the Americans in.) And on August 14 came the Atlantic Charter after a secret meeting between Roosevelt and British Prime Minister Winston Churchill. This agreement called for no territorial aggrandizement by either nation after the war, for the right of self-determination for all nations, for freedom of the seas, for freedom from want and fear, and for postwar arms reductions that would make the seas peaceful highways of commerce for all nations.

War with Japan became inevitable when, on September 27, 1940, that nation signed a three-power pact with Germany and Italy calling for mutual assistance in case any of the three was attacked. Russia was specifically exempted, meaning the treaty was aimed solely at the United States. This agreement in hand, the Japanese moved into French Indo-China, knowing it meant eventual war with the United States and England. The American response was to order a halt of sales of gasoline to Japan and a presidential order freezing all Japanese assets in the United States on July 26 (a step also taken against German and Italian assets). Then, as the Japanese prepared for a surprise attack on the United States, they sent Saburo Kurusu as a special envoy to join with ambassador Kichisaburo Nomura in Washington for negotiations; they promised Secretary of State Cordell Hull that Japan would evacuate Indo-China if in return the United States would restore trade with Japan. Hull responded on November 26 with an ultimatum that the Japanese leave China and

Indo-China and respect the Open Door policy. Japan rejected the Hull demands on December 1.

American military intelligence experts had broken Japanese codes and were aware that a surprise attack was imminent. Admiral Husband E. Kimmel and General Walter C. Short, who commanded the naval and army units at Pearl Harbor, were warned to be prepared, but only in general terms. Then on December 6, when hard knowledge of the impending attack was in hand, George C. Marshall, commanding general of the Army, sent a telegram to General Short warning him; the telegram was delivered after the attack began. At 7:55 A.M., Sunday, December 7, waves of Japanese aircraft struck the naval base at Pearl Harbor and other military facilities in Hawaii, sinking five of the eight battleships there and damaging the others; in all, nineteen ships were sunk or disabled, and 2343 soldiers and sailors were killed. The degree of Roosevelt's guilt in failing properly to warn Short and Kimmel has never been properly assessed, but there is no doubt that the attack had the effect Roosevelt wanted—isolationism ended with dramatic suddenness, and "Remember Pearl Harbor" became a battle cry for winning the war. Congress declared war on Japan on December 8, and three days later Germany and Italy responded by declaring war on the United States. The conflict had begun.

The Home Front

World War II demanded even greater mobilization than had the war of 1917–18. The selective service processed nearly thirty-seven million men, of whom ten million were finally drafted. They, along with volunteers, swelled the armed forces to more than twelve million men and women (who were allowed to enlist in the Army, Navy, Air Corps, Marines, and Coast Guard). Women also replaced men in the factories, while farmers, white and black, migrated to the cities to become "war workers" punching a time clock. In 1940 there were fifty million people gainfully employed in the United States; this figure rose to sixty-four million by 1945 —ending the unemployment of the Depression, as the New Deal failed to do.

Within a remarkably short time the American industrial and economic system was converted to the needs of wartime. The War Production Board, under the direction of Donald Nelson, mobilized all resources of war, while the National War Labor Board mediated labor disputes (although strikes continued to plague the government, forcing Roosevelt to seize the railroads on December 27, 1943, to avert a walkout). Peacetime goods disappeared from store shelves as factories concentrated on the materials of war. Aircraft production, for example, totaled only 21,000 in 1939 but jumped to 96,356 in 1944, while the output of tanks, guns, ammunition, and ships kept pace. To feed not only the American military establishment but also to contribute to the needs of England, China, and Russia, farmers expanded their acres under cultivation despite shortages of labor and of parts for farm machines, while a system of rationing was instituted for civilians, who were encouraged to grow "victory gardens" at home. Because of high wages prevailing in industry simultaneous with a decrease in consumer goods, the government created the Office of Price Administration (OPA) to prevent great inflation. The OPA had the authority to set ceilings on wages and prices and did its job so effectively that the cost of living rose only 31 percent between 1939 and 1945. At the time no one seriously challenged the constitutionality of this intrusion into the realm of private property by the national government, and more freedom was lost.

343

Another method of controlling inflation was to raise taxes. About two-fifths of the war cost of $320 million came from taxes. The remainder came from the sale of war bonds and from loans, and the national debt rose by 600 percent to $247 billion. But taxes and rationing and limits on prices did not depress the economy; rather, government spending stimulated the gross national product, which jumped from an annual total of $72 billion in 1939 to $198 billion in 1945. In short, the war did what the New Deal had failed so miserably to accomplish; it ended the Depression.

Finally the war brought some curtailment of civil liberties on the home front. Suffering most were the Japanese-Americans; by presidential order, the secretary of war ordered the removal of 110,000 Japanese-Americans and Japanese citizens from the West Coast to internment camps in the interior. The Supreme Court upheld this order in 1943 in the case *Hirabayashi* v. *United States* and in 1944 in *Korematsu* v. *United States*. There was an Office of War Information (similar to George Creel's committee of World War I), but it stirred little hysteria and did little to curtail civil liberties. Actually there was little need for such an office, because Hollywood film makers and radio programmers, along with newspapermen, voluntarily had been presenting, in almost hysterical tones, the anti-German, pro-British line. Critics of the government were allowed to speak, if in muted tones, and the election of 1944 proceeded as scheduled. The Republicans met in Chicago on June 26 to nominate Governor Thomas E. Dewey of New York for president and Governor John W. Bricker of Ohio for vice president. The Democrats also met in Chicago, but in July, knowing that Roosevelt wanted a fourth term; this they gave him on the first ballot. Yet Southern dislike for Wallace was sufficient to prevent his nomination for the second spot; this went to Senator Harry S Truman of Missouri, who was not too closely identified with the New Deal and was from a border state. Campaign oratory centered more on personalities than on issues, and Roosevelt won easily. He received 25,606,585 popular and 432 electoral votes to Dewey's 22,014,745 and 99. The voters apparently did not want to change leadership during the course of the war, especially since by 1944 the allied cause was approaching victory despite early losses.

The War Fronts

In Europe, the United States moved in concert with its allies, England, the Free French under Charles DeGaulle, and the Russians, who had been attacked by Germany in June, 1941. In February, 1942, British and American military authorities formed the Combined Chiefs of Staff; General George C. Marshall came to dominate this body, while General Dwight D. Eisenhower as commander of American forces in the European Theater would come to dominate military movements in his area. Eisenhower's first thrust was to dislodge the Germans from Tunis, Morocco, and Algeria, which was completed on May 13, 1943. Next came landings in Sicily in July, 1943, followed by the invasion of the mainland in September of the same year. In a long and costly drive up the Italian peninsula, the Allies liberated Rome in June, 1944. Italian soldiers never were enthusiastic for this war, and thus the Allies mainly were fighting Germans in Italy.

Meanwhile, the Allies had been softening Germany by sending waves of bombers to pound the Third Reich. By 1943 this bombing had reached epic proportions, the German air force had been reduced to token opposition, and factories had been

344

blown to rubble. Supplies from America were easily reaching England because the German submarine offensive had been ended by radar, sonar, antisubmarine missiles, and convoy tactics. On June 6, 1944, under General Eisenhower's overall direction, landings were made at Normandy. Victories rapidly followed, with Paris liberated in August; Brussels, Antwerp, and Luxembourg by September 11; and the Allies raced toward the Rhine. Russian offensives in the east divided German attention and tied up dozens of divisions on that front. Then in December, 1944, the Germans mounted their last great offensive at Bastogne. Known as the Battle of the Bulge, the Germans were finally stopped—after 77,000 American casualties. American troops crossed the Rhine on March 7 and were at the Elbe by April 11; there, for political reasons, they halted to allow the Russians to take Berlin. The two armies came together at Torgau on the Elbe on April 25. Five days later Hitler committed suicide in Berlin; other high Nazi officials did likewise or fled into hiding. The German General Staff, which took command at Hitler's death, accepted terms of unconditional surrender on May 7 at Reims, France—and the war in Europe was over.

In the Pacific the war began with serious defeats for the United States: Pearl Harbor bombed; the Philippines, Wake Island, Guam, and Midway bombed the same day; a Japanese invasion of the Philippines on December 10 and final conquest on April 9. General Douglas MacArthur evacuated to Australia, where he became Allied commander for the Southwest Pacific theater. The Japanese army easily conquered Malaya on January 31, Singapore on February 15, and most of the Dutch East Indies by early in March; in Indochina they conquered Burma, and by September, 1942, they were within thirty miles of Port Moresby, New Guinea, from which they could easily mount an invasion of Australia. Moreover, they had bombed Dutch Harbor, Alaska, and had occupied Attu, Agattu, and Kiska in the Aleutian Islands. For the first several months of the war, therefore, it seemed the Japanese were invincible as they occupied a million square miles of territory. Thereafter, however, the war turned against them, but three long, bloody years were required to reconquer what they had taken and force their surrender.

The Japanese advance in the Pacific actually was halted in two decisive naval battles: one in the Coral Sea and the other at Midway. The first occurred May 4-8, 1942, with three Japanese carriers sunk or damaged; the second came on June 3-6, when a Japanese naval force proceeding toward Midway Island was routed and four of their aircraft carriers sunk. The Allied counteroffensive began on August 7, 1942, when American Marines landed on Guadalcanal and Tulagi islands in the Solomons; the Navy under Admirals Chester W. Nimitz and William F. Halsey prevented Japanese reinforcements and gave the Marines time to secure these islands. There followed a series of "island-hopping" campaigns in which the United States Marines won incredible victories over an entrenched foe and made many names familiar to Americans—Tarawa, Makin, Saipan, Guam, Iwo Jima, Okinawa. Meanwhile, the Army was securing New Guinea and then, between June 19, 1944, and February 24, 1945, reconquering the Philippines.

The islands that the Marines secured were used as air bases from which to launch air strikes against Japan, while Lord Louis Mountbattan and General Joseph W. Stilwell were recapturing Burma and driving the Japanese from China. Then in July, 1945, air attacks on Japan increased; bombs were being used to soften the island empire for invasion. Military experts believed that the Japanese would fight to the death and that the United States would suffer a million casualties in the

Douglas MacArthur

IT was natural for Douglas MacArthur to follow a military career, for his father was a distinguished soldier. Born in 1880 at an army post in Arkansas, he moved from post to post as a youngster, never doubting that fame one day would be his. Appointed to the Military Academy in 1898, he finished at the head of his class and accepted a commission.

In the next decade and a half, he served at several posts, rising to the rank of major by 1917. During World War I he displayed his genius as organizer of the 42nd Infantry Division and commander of the 84th Infantry Brigade. Twice wounded, he was colorful, enthusiastic, and courageous, emerging from the war a brigadier general.

After the war, as commandant of the Military Academy, he updated the curriculum and modernized it. Then for eight years he served at home and in the Philippines, winning promotion to major general in 1925. Five years later, in 1930, he was appointed chief of staff of the Army by President Herbert Hoover. Serving during the Depression, he had the task of breaking the Veterans Bonus Army and sending it home, just as he constantly pleaded with Congress for funds with which to update and modernize the Army.

Dwight D. Eisenhower, who served as MacArthur's aide during these years, later commented that he had learned much about dramatics from MacArthur. The general did have a sense of the dramatic about him: he wore few ribbons, no weapons, and, often, no insignia of rank, yet he obviously enjoyed command.

Retiring from the Army in 1937, he went to the Philippines as military advisor with the rank of field marshal. There in the summer of 1941 he was recalled to active duty to command the Army's forces in the Far East. He then led his troops to victory over Japan, displaying a mastery of modern warfare. After the war he stayed in Japan to administer the military occupation, bringing many changes there.

In 1950, when the Communist North Koreans invaded South Korea, he became the commander of the United Nations' troops fighting there. Harry S Truman removed him from this office after MacArthur declared, "There is no substitute for victory." MacArthur returned to a hero's welcome, a speech before a joint session of Congress, mention as a Republican candidate for president in 1952, and the board chairmanship of Remington Rand. He died in 1964, still exemplifying the motto of West Point: "Duty, Honor, Country."

battle. The invasion became unnecessary, however, owing to the invention of the atomic bomb. A cooperative effort of British and American scientists, working under the Manhattan Project, readied and tested this nuclear device, which was used twice against Japan in August, 1945. Franklin Delano Roosevelt did not make this decision, however, for just as the war was coming to a successful close he died suddenly on April 12, 1945. The presidency devolved on a political accident named Harry S Truman.

". . . I felt like the moon, the stars, and all the planets had fallen on me," commented Truman later when recalling his reaction to being told he was president. Born in Jackson County, Missouri, he was a veteran of World War I, a failure in the haberdashery business, and a political product of the Tom Pendergast machine, which brought him from county judge to the United States Senate by 1934. A man of mediocre intelligence and few talents, Truman soon was wishing he was back in the Senate, but he could not avoid the responsibilities of the presidency. He even placed a sign on his desk in the White House stating, "The Buck Stops Here." And it was he who made the decision to use the atomic bomb on Japan in an effort to save American lives by forcing a surrender. On August 6, 1945, the first bomb exploded over Hiroshima, and three days later a second was dropped on Nagasaki. The next day, August 10, Japan agreed to an unconditional surrender, and on August 14 the war officially ended. The formal terms of surrender were signed aboard the battleship *Missouri* on September 2.

Truman and War Diplomacy

Truman's next problem was diplomatic. During the war years, many agreements had been signed between the United States and its allies concerning the goals of the war. Most of the struggle had been between England and Russia, with the United States vacillating between the two powers—but most often siding with Russia. Advisors in the Roosevelt administration, as well as the president himself, could not see—refused to see—that Joseph Stalin, dictator of Russia, intended that Europe should be left in chaos and misery in order that it could easily be brought under Communist domination. Winston Churchill realized what was happening and spoke against it, but Roosevelt refused to listen. The Russians gave many clues to their intentions; they refused to share military information, did not acknowledge the $11 billion worth of lend-lease aid furnished by the United States, and dealt only with Communist groups in European nations instead of with the legitimate governments. Yet Roosevelt insisted on cooperating with the Soviets, even to allowing them almost everything they demanded, however unreasonable.

The first major planning for the "peace" that would follow the war began in January, 1943, when Roosevelt and Churchill met at Casablanca. There Churchill announced that the goal of the war was "unconditional surrender" of the Axis powers. Then in August that year, at Quebec, Secretary of State Cordell Hull met with British Foreign Minister Anthony Eden and Russian Foreign Minister V. M. Molotov; there the three agreed to a European Advisory Commission to formulate postwar policy for Germany, and there the Soviets agreed to declare war on Japan when Germany surrendered. Then another meeting was held in November, 1943; from this Cairo Conference came a statement signed by Roosevelt, Churchill, and Generalissimo Chiang Kai-shek that the Allies would wage war on Japan until it surrendered unconditionally, that all possessions taken from China by Japan would be returned, that Japan would be stripped of its Pacific possessions, and that Korea would become an independent nation. Immediately afterward, Roosevelt and Churchill met Stalin at Teheran, Iran, where the Russians agreed to coordinate their attacks on Germany from the east with the invasion from the west.

During 1944 most of the planning centered on establishing an international organization to keep the peace. This would evolve into the United Nations, which formally was established at San Francisco with representatives of forty-eight nations in April–June, 1945. Then in February, 1945, came the final conference of the "Big Three"—Roosevelt, Churchill, and Stalin. Meeting at Yalta, they agreed that Germany would be divided into four zones to be occupied by the Americans, French, English, and Russians; that Germany would pay reparations for damages it had inflicted on other nations; and that other nations would have democratic caretaker governments until free elections could be held to determine their future. Also, Russia again agreed to enter the war against Japan, in return for which it would receive Manchuria and all possessions it had lost to Japan in 1905. Truman participated at the last of these wartime conferences, the one at Potsdam in July and August, 1945. Handicapped by inexperience and poor advisers, Truman agreed to yet more concessions favorable to Russia, including bits of territory and control over the Balkan nations. Thus the war ended on Russia's terms and to Russia's postwar advantage.

Demobilization

Under the inexperienced leadership of Truman, the United States began dismantling its military apparatus as quickly as possible after the Japanese surrender. Most of the old New Dealers left the administration, to be replaced by machine politicians, Truman cronies, and businessmen with little national experience. Price controls were removed with great haste, taxes were reduced with no effort to pay off the war debt, money was made plentiful, and government war plants and surplus materials were sold at ridiculous prices. By 1947 the armed forces were down to 2 million men, the cost of living jumped some 30 percent, the economy was marked by endless strikes, and consumer goods were in such short supply and great demand that bribes and under-the-table deals were necessary to secure new automobiles, nylons, furniture, and appliances. The housing shortage was monumental, and workmanship on almost everything was deteriorating, as labor leaders made preposterous demands for inflationary raises for their followers.

Simultaneously, it became apparent in 1946 that the Russians were not living up to their agreements to allow free elections in the Balkan nations. Even the United Nations, which had been approved by Congress and which had established its headquarters in New York City, could do nothing—except show itself as a place where delegates argued endlessly. And from the war-crimes trials in Europe and Japan came incredible tales of inhumanity during the recent conflict, tales of millions killed or mutilated, of individual and national brutality on a scale never before known in human history. Simultaneously, millions were starving in Europe and Asia. All the while Harry Truman kept vacillating and issuing sunny statements and recommending international largesse with taxpayers' money. Little wonder that newspapers began calling 1946 "The Year of Frustration."

The voters reacted to Truman's mediocrity in November by electing a Republican majority in both houses of Congress (for the first time since 1930); the Republican

Bureau of Printing and Engraving

Harry S Truman

slogan, "Had Enough?" appealed to the public. The result was a decided turn toward the right in politics. On March 21, 1947, came congressional approval of the Twenty-second Amendment to the Constitution, prohibiting a president from serving more than two full terms and half of another (it was ratified on February 26, 1951). Then in June came the Taft-Hartley (Labor-Management Relations) Act, which passed Congress over Truman's veto. This act empowered the president to secure an eighty-day injunction to halt a strike endangering "national health or safety"; it required unions to give sixty-days' notice before beginning a strike; it outlawed secondary boycotts, jurisdictional strikes, and the closed shop; it declared that a union could not refuse to bargain collectively, that a union had to issue financial statements, and that union officials had to sign anti-Communist oaths. Then in July, 1947, came the National Security Act, which brought the Army, Navy, and Air Force (which was made a separate service by the act) under a Department of Defense, thereby relegating the secretaries of army and navy to noncabinet status, to be replaced by the secretary of defense.

Truman belatedly got tough with labor union leaders, although he was trying to maintain the Rooseveltean coalition of minority groups, city dwellers, farmers, and labor to ensure a Democratic victory in 1948. On May 21, 1946, he ordered a government seizure of the soft coal mines when John L. Lewis led his United Mine Workers on a bitter and prolonged strike. Also that spring Truman seized the railroads and called on Congress for authority to draft all striking workers; Congress did not grant this, but Truman's threat caused the unions to bargain seriously and to return to work. When John L. Lewis again ordered the coal miners on strike in November, 1946, Truman had his attorney general obtain an injunction against the walkout. Lewis ignored the order, for which he and his union were fined.

The Cold War

And, finally, Truman began to get tough with the Russians. Gradually he was forced to conclude that the Russians were not keeping their agreements in the Balkan nations and that they were stripping East Germany in the name of reparations. Winston Churchill, on a tour of the United States, gave a name to what the Russians were doing. At Fulton, Missouri, on March 5, 1946, the former British prime minister stated that the Soviets were erecting an "iron curtain" between Eastern and Western Europe. Yet Henry Wallace, now secretary of commerce in Truman's cabinet, decided that a stiffening of American policy toward Russia was warmongering; at a speech in New York City, he delivered a strong pro-Russian address in which he stated, "I realize that the danger of war is much less from communism than it is from imperialism." Secretary of State James F. Byrnes, then negotiating with the Soviets in Paris, threatened to resign unless Truman repudiated what Wallace had said. This Truman did—claiming innocence when in fact he had seen and approved the speech in advance—and he fired Wallace from the cabinet. Wallace thus became a focal point for pro-Russian groups, and they rallied in an attempt to secure him the Democratic nomination for president in 1948.

On March 12, 1947, the president announced the "Truman Doctrine." This doctrine called for containment of Soviet expansion and aid to Greece and Turkey, which were in danger of falling to armed Communist minorities from within. The doctrine also offered aid to other nations threatened by a Communist coup, while in June came the Marshall Plan calling for aid to stimulate the recovery of European economies ravaged by the war. And early in 1948 came the appropriation of $5 billion for the European Recovery Program. Then, without Soviet cooperation, a federal government was established in West Germany, which was admitted to the European Recovery Program. The Russians protested by blockading Berlin, a four-power city enclosed by East Germany; Truman responded with the Berlin Airlift, which saw an average of 4500 tons of supplies a day flown to the former German capital to prevent its surrender to the Communists. The Russians relented on May 12, 1949, and lifted the blockade. Finally, Truman began negotiating an alliance with England, France, Iceland, Norway, Belgium, the Netherlands, Luxembourg, Portugal, Italy, and Canada. Known as the North Atlantic Treaty Organization (NATO), this agreement pledged mutual military aid to any country in the event of an attack—and was the first American military alliance in peacetime.

The Election of 1948

As the election of 1948 approached, political pundits gave Truman little chance of reelection. The Republicans jubilantly nominated Thomas E. Dewey for president, his second try, with Governor Earl Warren of California as his running mate. Dewey read the polls and assumed he would win if he made no damaging blunders. Thus he confined his speeches to generalities and did little campaigning. The Democrats, meeting in Philadelphia on July 12, nominated Truman, along with Senator Alben W. Barkley of Kentucky, despite pressures from both right and left. Southerners became so alarmed at a strong civil rights platform plank, calling for federal legislation to protect the rights of Negroes, that they bolted the party to meet in Birmingham, Alabama. There they formed the "Dixiecrat" party and nominated Governor J. Strom Thurmond of South Carolina for president and Governor Fielding L. Wright of Mississippi for vice president, on a platform calling for racial segregation. And on July 22 the Progressive Party met in Philadelphia to nominate Henry A. Wallace for president and Senator Glen H. Taylor of Idaho for vice president. Their platform urged a soft line toward Russia as a means of achieving peace.

Truman campaigned strenuously for his programs, which he called the Fair Deal. He criss-crossed the nation by train, making speeches at every whistle stop and using the new medium of television at every opportunity. And he called Congress into special session on July 26 in a vain attempt to repeal the Taft-Hartley Act and to enact housing, civil rights, and health legislation, to raise Social Security payments, and to fight inflation with various expedients. Truman's fight, in which he pictured himself as the underdog and as a common "give 'em hell" man, brought him an unexpected victory. Despite what the pollsters predicted, he received 24,105,812 popular and 303 electoral votes to Dewey's 21,970,065 popular and 189 electoral votes. Thurmond, the Dixiecrat candidate, carried four Southern states, receiving 1,169,063 popular and 39 electoral votes, while Henry Wallace received 1,157,172 popular and no electoral votes. Truman had scored a remarkable personal victory—but the Eighty-first Congress, although controlled by Democrats, was little different in temperament from the Eightieth Congress.

Little domestic legislation passed Congress in Truman's second term. He asked for the same things: repeal of the Taft-Hartley Act (which he already had used to halt strikes) and enactment of a plethora of social legislation. All he could do was end racial segregation in the armed forces by executive order. The Fair Deal fizzled badly on the domestic front, for a recession settled on the country in 1949, one which would last until war began anew in 1950. The postwar boom had ended after driving the gross national product to $225 billion, with sixty million people employed. But the pent-up demand for goods had been satisfied by 1949, and the economy slipped downward.

On the foreign front, the administration of Harry Truman suffered even more decisive defeats. In the Far East, Truman had tried to persuade the nationalist government of Chiang Kai-shek to work with the Communists in one government; the result was that the Communists, led by Mao Tse-tung, drove the nationalists from the mainland by October 1, 1949. Chiang retreated to the island of Formosa where he established Nationalist China, which the United States continued to recognize as the legitimate government of China. This was a major American defeat, one which need not have occurred.

The Korean "Police Action"

Truman's foreign policy was founded on nuclear superiority, which meant a small army. That policy was rendered meaningless when the Russians, through espionage, secured plans for and built their own atomic bomb. Forced to spread a small army across vast stretches of the world, the United States was in a poor position to fight even a limited conventional war. Dean Acheson, the secretary of state, admitted as much when, in a speech on January 12, 1950, he stated that the American defense perimeter did not include Korea and Formosa. The direct result of this speech was a Communist North Korean invasion of South Korea on June 24, 1950. (Korea had been divided along the Thirty-eighth Parallel at the end of World War II, with the Russians controlling the northern half and the Americans controlling the southern half. The Russians had refused to allow free elections in their zone and had installed a puppet Communist regime.) Truman responded to the invasion by ordering American troops into South Korea, by sending the Seventh Fleet to the Formosa Straits, and by appealing to the United Nations. The United Nations responded by endorsing a military campaign against the North Koreans (this passed the Security Council because the Russians had withdrawn temporarily), and thus the war officially was fought by the United Nations, not the United States. Congress never voted a declaration of war, but gave tacit approval to the sending of a "police force" by voting appropriations for the action.

General Douglas MacArthur, the American military commander in Japan, assumed direction of the United Nations force. Well he might, for most countries sent only token forces; American troops bore the brunt of the fighting. At first the fighting went against the UN force and the South Koreans. But on September 15 MacArthur reversed the tide of battle by a brilliant tactic; he sent American Marines to land behind enemy lines at Inchon. The North Korean army collapsed, and by October 1, the UN troops had crossed the Thirty-eighth Parallel into North Korea. Soon MacArthur was predicting that the war would end shortly and that the troops would be home by Christmas. Two days after this pronouncement, the Communist Chinese army crossed the Yalu River into North Korea and, using human waves of troops to overrun UN positions, was driving the allies southward. MacArthur was able to evacuate his troops and regroup them near the Thirty-eighth Parallel. By January, 1951, the war had stalemated into a struggle of mutual attrition. In order to achieve victory, MacArthur wanted to bomb Chinese supply bases north of the Yalu River, a proposal Truman vetoed for fear it would bring the Russians into the

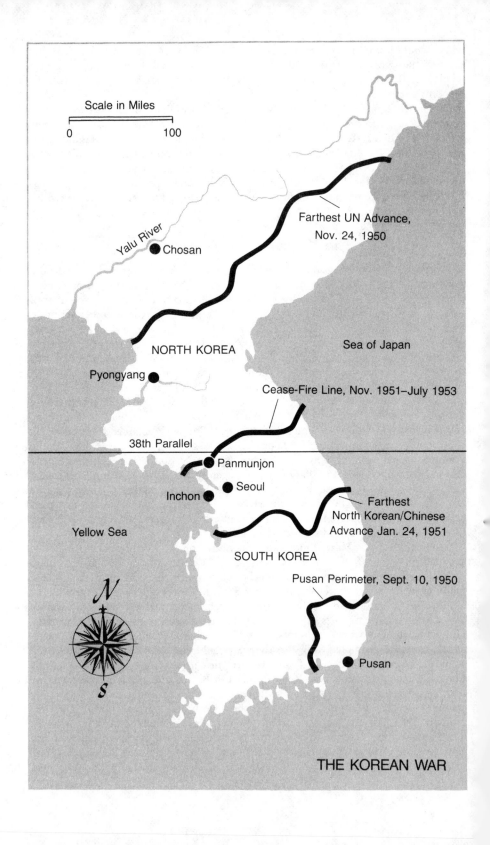

Scale in Miles

0   100

Yalu River

● Chosan

Farthest UN Advance,
Nov. 24, 1950

NORTH KOREA

Sea of Japan

Pyongyang ●

Cease-Fire Line, Nov. 1951–July 1953

38th Parallel

● Panmunjon

● Seoul

Inchon ●

Farthest
North Korean/Chinese
Advance Jan. 24, 1951

Yellow Sea

SOUTH KOREA

Pusan Perimeter, Sept. 10, 1950

N

S

● Pusan

THE KOREAN WAR

war. When MacArthur publicly disagreed with the commander-in-chief—even criticized the government—Truman, on April 11, 1951, recalled the general. MacArthur returned to thunderous approval of his stand at home. As the man responsible for rebuilding Japan and administering it following the war and as the hero of the Korean War, he was asked to address Congress and even was mentioned prominently for the presidency in 1952. Truman had blundered badly. UN negotiators began talks about an armistice with the Communists on July 10, 1951, but these talks dragged on interminably with no end in sight.

The Truman Problems

During the Korean War, galloping inflation engulfed the United States. Once again Congress found it necessary to raise taxes, vote huge expenditures for war, and adopt price-control legislation. Young men were conscripted for military service (under the Selective Service Act of 1948), and the military establishment swelled. The country seemed in little better shape than it had been ten years earlier—and then came news of scandal in Washington. Harry Vaughn, a Truman sidekick from World War I and military aide to the president, along with Assistant Attorney General T. Lamar Caudle, were tainted with stories of irregularities in income-tax collections and of accepting a deep-freeze and other gifts. Caudle was fired, along with Attorney General J. Howard McGrath.

Finally, there was the taint of Communist infiltration in the Truman administration. In March, 1947, a Loyalty Review Board had been established to screen federal employees and to discharge those about whom there were "reasonable grounds for belief in [their] disloyalty." Then, in October, 1947, the House Committee on Un-American Activities (HCUA) began investigating the extent of Communist penetration of the motion picture industry. The investigatory body discovered considerable infiltration, which led to a widespread cleanup of that industry, along with radio and television, with Communists and fellow-travelers (and a few innocent persons) being driven out. Eugene Dennis, the general secretary of the Communist Party in the United States, next was summoned to testify before HCUA, but he refused, whereupon he was indicted for contempt of Congress. He, along with ten other high-ranking Communists, was then tried under terms of the Smith Act of 1940 (which made it illegal to advocate overthrowing the government by force). On October 14 the eleven were convicted, sentenced to long terms, and heavily fined.

But the most celebrated case of this type involved Alger Hiss, long a government employee. On August 3, 1948, Whittaker Chambers, an admitted former Soviet agent, testified to HCUA that he and Hiss had been part of a Communist espionage group that had infiltrated the government in the 1930s. Hiss, who in 1948 was president of the Carnegie Endowment for International Peace, testified on August 5 with a vehement denial. President Truman, when asked about these hearings, labeled them a Republican "red herring" to discredit the Democrats, but Congressman Richard M. Nixon of California accused the president of withholding information. Hiss was indicted for perjury and, after a first trial ended in a hung jury, was convicted on January 21, 1950; he served nearly four years in jail, to become a martyr for liberal intellectuals. Next came revelations of espionage that resulted in Russia obtaining the secret of the atomic bomb; Judith Coplon, an employee of the Justice Department, and Valentin Gubichev, a Soviet consular official, were arrested on March 5, 1949, and convicted of espionage.

Robert A. Taft

MANY young men born to famous fathers feel overshadowed by the accomplishments of their parents and achieve little. Robert A. Taft was not such a case. Born in 1889 in Cincinnati, Ohio, he was nineteen when his father, William Howard Taft, was elected president of the United States. After graduating from Yale and then Harvard Law School (1913), he opened a law practice in Cincinnati. A reserved, even shy, young man, he nevertheless had driving ambition.

During World War I he served as an assistant counsel in the U.S. Food Administration, headed by Herbert Hoover, and afterward in the American relief effort in Europe. From this experience he derived a dislike for federal regulatory activities that turned him on a conservative course.

During the twenty years between 1919 and 1939 he practiced law in Cincinnati and was active in Republican circles, serving terms in the Ohio House of Representatives and Senate. In 1938 he was chosen a senator from Ohio, a position to which he was reelected in 1944 and 1950. In Washington he opposed American entry into World War II until after the Japanese attack on Pearl Harbor. After the war he approved foreign aid only grudgingly.

A staunch believer in balanced budgets, he disliked the New Deal and its philosophy, working against extensions of the federal government—but for equal opportunity for all citizens. His dislike of the excesses of labor unions led to his cosponsoring the Taft-Hartley Act of 1947, just as he fought legislation curbing business incentives and individual liberties. For these reasons he was labelled an ultra-conservative; in fact, Democrats often spoke of him derisively as "Mr. Republican," implying that all Republicans were as conservative as Taft.

Taft served from 1946 to 1952 on the Senate Republican Policy Committee, and, after the election of Dwight D. Eisenhower in 1952, he became Senate majority leader until his death. His name was prominently mentioned for the presidency in the Republican nominating conventions of 1940 and 1948, and he seemed an easy winner of the nomination in 1952 until Eisenhower placed his own hat in the ring. That year Taft lost the nomination on a close roll-call vote of the delegates. His defeat caused despair among conservatives everywhere, who then were greatly shocked by Taft's death from cancer in the summer of 1953. In the years that followed, his leadership was sorely missed.

These revelations, coupled with the Communist conquest of China, caused public opinion to swing to the right—and gave a national forum to Senator Joseph R. McCarthy. A Republican from Wisconsin, McCarthy in a speech at Wheeling, West Virginia, on February 9, 1950, electrified the nation by charging there were known Communists working in the State Department. Senator Millard E. Tydings of Maryland, Democratic chairman of a subcommittee of the Senate Foreign Relations Committee, held hearings on McCarthy's charges and called them utterly false. McCarthy thereupon used his influence to defeat Tydings for reelection in Maryland, charging that Tydings was friendly to Communist leaders.

McCarthy was aided in his campaign by the uncovering of a genuine Soviet espionage network in the United States in 1950. That summer, using information supplied by the British, agents of the FBI arrested Ethel and Julius Rosenberg and their friend Morton Sobell; they were convicted of passing nuclear secrets to Russia, and the Rosenbergs were sentenced to death and Sobell to thirty years in prison (the Rosenbergs were executed on July 19, 1953). "McCarthyism," as the liberals called the zealous search for traitors, grew and spread—with the senator gaining wide publicity. Congress responded to this new "red scare" by passing the Internal Security Act, sponsored by Senator Pat McCarran of Nevada, making it illegal to conspire to establish a totalitarian dictatorship in the United States and requiring the Communist Party and its affiliates to register with the attorney general. Truman vetoed the McCarran Act, but Congress overrode him. Then Congress passed the McCarran-Walter Immigration Act, also over Truman's veto, to keep refugees from Communist countries out of the United States.

The Election of 1952

Truman's vetoes allowed the Republicans to go into the campaign of 1952 charging the Democrats with being soft on communism. This charge had proven good political ammunition in 1950, when the Republicans gained twenty-eight seats in the House and five in the Senate, and it promised to gain the presidency in 1952. Thus the fight for the Republican nomination that year was bitter, as delegates of the party gathered at Chicago on July 7. The major contestants were Senator Robert A. Taft of Ohio, "Mr. Republican," and General Dwight D. Eisenhower. Taft was a conservative with a strong following in the party, but the delegates bolted for the Army hero who had won the war in Europe. Ike—as Eisenhower was popularly known—was nominated on the first ballot, yet Taft's supporters were appeased by the nomination for vice president of Senator Richard Nixon, widely known for his part in sending Hiss to prison. The GOP platform stressed that the Democrats were guilty of "appeasement of communism," called for an end to the dragging Korean War, blamed inflation on the Democrats, and promised a cleanup of the federal government.

In deep gloom the Democrats approached their convention, also in Chicago, on July 21. The scandals of the Truman administration, coupled with inflation, the war, and the threat of Communist subversion, spelled almost certain defeat. Truman had announced in March that he would not be a candidate for reelection, although he was eligible constitutionally (he was the last president who could serve more than two and one-half terms). The leading candidate for the nomination was Senator Estes Kefauver of Tennessee, who had presided at a special Senate committee to expose graft and the influence of organized crime in the United States. When

Kefauver failed to get the necessary votes on the first ballot, Truman's personal choice, Governor Adlai E. Stevenson of Illinois, was nominated, along with Senator John J. Sparkman of Alabama as his running mate. Stevenson proceeded to campaign with airy speeches that pleased self-styled intellectuals, but which showed little grasp of the threat of Soviet communism. Stevenson also displayed wit, charm, and even eloquence, along with a high liberal tone, but the voters were tired of both New Deal and Fair Deal. Eisenhower was swept into office with 33,936,252 popular and 442 electoral votes to Stevenson's 27,314,992 popular and 89 electoral votes.

Twenty years of Democratic control thus came to an end. The majority of Americans clearly wanted a change, one that would bring security at home, an end to the Korean War, and containment of the international Communist conspiracy. They also wanted an end to graft and corruption in Washington, along with a return of dignity at the executive level. Too many did not want an end to the social programs of the New Deal, however; once accustomed to handouts from Washington, they lacked the discipline to break the habit of depending on the federal bureaucracy for many services. Clearly, however, they did expect the general who had won the war to restore the nation to peace, serenity, and prosperity. There was no massive mandate for change, just a longing for consolidation.

Chapter Fifteen

To the Ends
of Imagination

A Nation in Transition

THE search for stability that led the voters to elect Dwight D. Eisenhower to the presidency in 1952 would be in vain. The country was about to experience the cyclic period of upheaval and change that has followed most wars. This upheaval had been postponed by the postwar boom and by the Korean War, but it would be a growing trend during Eisenhower's administration. The iceberg of tranquility that was Eisenhower was floating in a sea of disturbance, for prosperity was bringing more and yet more Americans into the upper middle class and causing them to advance idealistic—and unrealistic—demands. During the 1950s this growing band of self-styled intellectuals and self-proclaimed messiahs was moving the country dramatically to the left, promoting hedonism, immorality, racial unrest, and worship of the young. Commercial television was coming of age, intensifying the unrest of the unproductive by making them aware of goods and services they had never before realized were to be had. The colleges and universities, in mad pursuit of growth for the sake of bigness, would almost double in a decade, with liberal professors preaching an elitist philosophy to unsophisticated, naive, idealistic students who believed them. While on the surface the 1950s were placid, underneath there was seething unrest that would explode into violence and drastic change in the 1960s. Fortunately, the nation was yet a democratic republic, and the strong common sense of the public would gradually come to identify the vaporous vacuity of the liberal promise.

Ike's First Term

Perhaps it was the innate stability of Eisenhower that caused the leftist intellectuals to begin active, blatant promotion of their ideas. Most college and university professors believed themselves possessors of ultimate truth—but no one was asking them for their "answers" to all the nation's real and imagined ills. They vented their frustrations in the only way open to them—by preaching to their captive students. And the Eisenhower administration began in a way that seemed to promise a swing away from the New Deal. What the intellectuals failed to realize was that, despite his military career, Eisenhower was essentially a man of peace. Born in Denison, Texas, and growing to manhood in Kansas, Ike went to West Point and then pursued a military career that saw him commanding all allied armies in Europe and then serving as chief of staff in 1945. Retiring in 1948, he became president of Columbia University, only to be recalled to active duty in 1950 and sent to command allied forces in Europe. As president, Ike wanted domestic and foreign tranquility, and he surrounded himself with middle-of-the-roaders. Also, Ike understood that businessmen have a better grasp of political realities than do ivory-tower intellectuals, and he drew many of his cabinet members and his close advisors from the ranks of business—Charles E. Wilson of General Motors as secretary of defense and George M. Humphrey of the Mark Hanna Corporation as secretary of the treasury. Most important, he installed John Foster Dulles as secretary of state.

Even before his inauguration, Ike flew to Korea to inspect the area personally. After his inauguration, he removed the Seventh Fleet from the Formosa Straits to allow Chiang Kai-shek to invade the mainland (at least, this was the public posture Ike assumed for the move in order to cause the Communist Chinese to disengage in Korea). There even were hints that unless the Communists came to terms for an armistice in Korea nuclear weapons would be employed. These measures had the desired effect, and on July 27, 1953, an armistice was concluded providing for a demilitarized zone near the Thirty-eighth Parallel—and providing for a political conference that never was held. Finally, it called for an exchange of prisoners of war who wished to go home. Truman's policy of "no victory" had been replaced with a bolder posture. The Communists knew they either had to stop fighting or else see all of Korea fall to the allies, with no sanctuaries—and they quit.

Elsewhere in the Far East the Eisenhower administration sought to halt Communist aggression. In September, 1954, the Southeast Asia Treaty Organization (SEATO) came into being, a mutual defense pact between the United States, England, France, Australia, New Zealand, the Philippines, Thailand, and Pakistan. And a mutual defense pact with Nationalist China was signed in December of that year. Yet the militantly Communist Chinese refused to stop their aggression; halted militarily, they turned to a policy of infiltration and the promotion of local revolutions by exploiting discontent in underdeveloped nations in Southeast Asia and in Africa. Because of this Chinese militancy, the Eisenhower administration repeatedly blocked the admission of Communist China into the United Nations—to the bitter anguish of many American intellectuals who believed that the Chinese Communists were wayward children who would respond to kindness. John Foster Dulles laughed at such nonsense, preferring to deal with the Communists bluntly. Several times he prevented war by threatening massive nuclear retaliation should shooting start.

The Chinese accomplished their ends in Indochina. There Communist forces succeeded in defeating the French colonial forces, but Dulles managed an international meeting at Geneva that decreed two Vietnams, north and south, with free elections to be held by 1956 in both parts. Ho Chi Minh, who ruthlessly exterminated all opposition in North Vietnam and instituted a Communist reign of terror, refused to allow free elections in his half; thus the United States began helping the South Vietnamese with military advisors and supplies, while the North Vietnamese began a slow war of infiltration, terror, and guerrilla activities.

Foreign Affairs

In Europe the major event following Ike's inauguration was the death of Stalin on March 5, 1953. Nikita S. Khrushchev eventually won the power struggle that ensued, and he emerged as the new ruler, but on a wave of denunciation of Stalin

Dwight D. Eisenhower

and a promise of reform. No liberalism was permitted in the Soviet satellite nations, however; an uprising in East Germany in the summer of 1953 and another in Hungary in October, 1956, brought only bloody and total repression—in which the United States did not intervene except to admit refugees by special act of Congress. Ike did attempt the reunification of Germany by personal diplomacy, going to Geneva in July, 1955, for a summit conference between himself, British Prime Minister Anthony Eden, and Russian Premier Nikolai A. Bulganin. No agreement could be reached, despite public statements of better relations in the future.

Finally, the Middle East was a growing hotbed of difficulty. The region was strategically important because of known oil reserves there and because of the Suez Canal. Also a Jewish nation called Israel had been established in 1948 to the great discontent of the Arab people, who were becoming fanatically nationalistic. Egypt became the focal point of Arab nationalism under the leadership of Gamal Abdel Nasser, who in July, 1956, seized the British- and French-owned Suez Canal. Israel, denied the use of the canal, invaded Egypt in October, and were joined by British and French troops who claimed to be "protecting" the canal. The United States refused to back the British, which led to a condemnation by the United Nations of the invasion, a withdrawal of English, French, and Israeli troops, and growing Soviet influence among the Arab nationalists.

Internal Affairs

At home the Eisenhower administration had more success. Almost immediately the price controls imposed by Truman during the Korean War were removed. Cuts in government spending were effected, taxes were cut, and the budget was balanced. Also, the government began divesting itself of publicly owned utilities and natural resources, causing liberals to scream about a "give-away program." Other Republican innovations included the St. Lawrence Seaway Act of May, 1954, which opened the Great Lakes to ocean-going ships; the Housing Act of 1954, calling for urban renewal with federal matching-aid funds; the Atomic Energy Act, also of 1954, which allowed private companies to produce electricity with atomic energy; and the Agricultural Adjustment Act of August 28, 1954, providing for flexible price controls for farm produce rather than the rigid price structure of the Roosevelt-Truman years. Despite these gains, the Democrats gained control of Congress in the off-year election of 1954, allowing Lyndon B. Johnson to become majority leader in the Senate and Sam Rayburn to be named Speaker of the House; these two Texans would dominate Congress for the remainder of that decade. Possibly the reason the Democrats did so well was because of a public reaction against "McCarthyism."

McCarthy's Fight

Senator Joseph R. McCarthy of Wisconsin continued to fight the Communists in high places in the government. With the Republican victory of 1952, he was elevated to the chairmanship of the Senate Committee on Government Operations, a position he used to focus public attention on the issue. First came hearings into subversive activities in the State and Defense departments. With the aid of young helpers, such as Robert F. Kennedy of Massachusetts, McCarthy called witnesses, most of whom failed to cooperate fully. Two of his aides, Roy Cohn and David Schine, toured Europe to remove books with a Communist taint from libraries maintained by the United States Information Agency. In June, 1953, Ike responded with an attack on "the book burners," an indirect method of indicating presidential disapproval.

Then in December, 1953, the Atomic Energy Commission withdrew its clearance of J. Robert Oppenheimer, the chairman of the advisory committee to that commission. Oppenheimer was charged with associating with Communists, even of hiring them. After a hearing in the spring of 1954, the AEC concluded that Oppenheimer was loyal, but still refused to renew his clearance (in 1963, under liberal leadership again, the AEC awarded him the Fermi Award for his contributions in the field of nuclear physics, in effect reversing the 1954 ruling).

McCarthy next accused various Army officers of being "soft" on communism. The Army responded by charging that Roy M. Cohn, McCarthy's aide, had tried to exert pressure to gain special treatment for David Schine, another McCarthy aide who had been drafted. In April and May a special Senate committee investigated these charges and countercharges, during which the liberal press and intellectuals everywhere tried to whip the public into believing McCarthy was Satan incarnate, attacking him on a wide front. Before television cameras, the Army's attorney, Joseph N. Welch, portrayed McCarthy as a power-mad politician. Liberals chortled with glee—as did Communists everywhere—claiming that McCarthyism had been destroyed and the great spy-hunt was ended. Then in December the Senate condemned (but did not censure) McCarthy for abuse of that body; this action was taken for two reasons: he had spoken harshly of General Ralph Zwicker, accusing him of "shielding Communist conspirators," and he had failed to appear before a congressional committee investigating his finances.

With McCarthy "condemned" and removed from his committee chairmanship, his effectiveness in government was diminished. Nationally the press postured him as a disgraced man despite the fact that after Senator John McClellan succeeded McCarthy as chairman, the Government Operations Committee reinvestigated the Army and issued a highly critical report substantiating some of McCarthy's charges. Moreover, in 1955 the Internal Revenue Service ended up owing McCarthy money. Senator McCarthy had shown one of the great American dilemmas: how to maintain national security, yet protect civil liberties. Ironically, it was McCarthy's own liberty and civil rights that were reduced. However, by 1955 the Republicans could state that 3614 persons had been discharged from the government as security risks, but liberal critics fought back, saying that not one of those persons had been proven to be a Communist.

The Election of 1956

As the election year of 1956 approached, the country was prosperous. There had been a brief recession in 1953–54, but the economy had fully recovered. Even the farmers were sharing more fully in the prosperity, owing to a rise in farm prices. The minimum wage had been raised to a dollar an hour, more people were at work than ever before, and the gross national product had reached a record level. The Democrats thus came to their convention on August 20 without great hope of winning the presidency and demonstrated that pessimism by renominating Adlai E. Stevenson, along with Estes Kefauver of Tennessee as his running mate. The Republicans met a week later to renominate—joyfully—the team of Eisenhower and Nixon.

Again Stevenson filled the air with platitudes and high-flown rhetoric—and again he went down to defeat by 437 to 73 electoral votes and a margin of almost ten million popular votes. However, the Democrats did retain control of both houses of Congress.

Ike's Second Term

Shortly after Ike's second inauguration, the economy turned downward in a serious recession that, by April, 1958, saw five million (7.5 percent of the labor force) unemployed and industrial production dropping 13 percent. Ike increased government spending without raising taxes—with the largest peacetime deficit in history the result. Democrats smelled victory, and thus there was little domestic legislation until after the presidential election of 1960. On June 16, 1960, Congress passed the Twenty-third Amendment, which gave the District of Columbia the right to vote in presidential elections (and was ratified on March 29, 1961). Because of the recession, the Democrats picked up forty-seven House seats and thirteen Senate seats in the congressional elections of 1958.

Foreign affairs also proved more tempestuous for Ike during his second term. First came Sputnik I, a Soviet artificial satellite placed in orbit around the earth on October 4, 1957. The beeping of this tiny sphere of metal disturbed Americans greatly, for it signaled Russian possession of sophisticated rockets (which also could deliver intercontinental ballistic missiles). The American response was a crash program of massive federal aid to the public schools and the universities to train scientists and engineers, as well as to develop rockets of equal capacity. Then came the Berlin crisis of November, 1958, in which Khrushchev warned the allied powers to vacate the old capital city within six months, thereby allowing East Germany to take control of it. The NATO powers rejected this ultimatum, and war became a strong possibility. Khrushchev allowed the deadline to pass, however, for he wanted another summit meeting. Ike invited the Soviet leader to tour the United States, which he did with great exuberance in September, 1959. Khrushchev saw the cities, and he toured the farms before meeting Eisenhower at the presidential retreat, Camp David, Maryland; there they planned a summit conference for the following year.

That conference never took place. On May 1, 1960, an American U-2 photo-reconnaissance plane was shot down deep inside Russian territory. At first spokesmen for the government of the United States said the aircraft was a weather plane, but the Soviets responded by producing the pilot, Francis Gary Powers, who admitted that he had been engaged in photographic spying. On May 11, Ike admitted that he knew of the flight, that he had authorized it, and that such flights had been taking place for four years. Khrushchev vilified the president, broke off the summit meeting that was to take place, and announced that he would await the election of a new president to settle the Berlin crisis.

Likewise, the Eisenhower administration had difficulties in the Far East. In 1958 the Chinese renewed their shelling of islands (Quemoy and Matsu) held by the Nationalist government of Chiang Kai-shek. Ike responded that the United States would defend these islands against attack, but that Chiang would not be allowed to invade the mainland. Then in 1959 the Chinese invaded Tibet, claiming it belonged to China. The Dalai Lama escaped to India, but Tibet was annexed to Communist China. Finally, in 1960 students in Japanese universities rioted at the prospect of the United States arming the Japanese defense forces with nuclear weapons. These riots grew to such proportions that the Japanese government was forced to withdraw an invitation to Eisenhower to visit that nation. And in Latin America leftist demonstrations against the United States spread. In April and May, 1958, Vice President Nixon was dispatched to those nations in an effort to stop the growth of anti-Americanism. Yet the visit was unproductive, with Nixon being stoned in Peru and Venezuela by Communist-inspired mobs. In Cuba, on January 1, 1959, Fidel Castro established an openly Communist government after a five-year revolution against the dictatorship of Fulgencio Batista—and used the island republic as a staging ground for Communist revolutions in other Latin American nations.

Finally, there was seeming corruption in the Eisenhower administration. Sherman Adams, a presidential advisor, had been forced to resign in disgrace. The Democrats thus had another potent factor working for them in the election of 1960. The Democratic convention at Los Angeles, which met on July 11, saw Lyndon B. Johnson fighting hard for the nomination, but he was bested by a fellow senator, John F. Kennedy of Massachusetts. Kennedy had invested millions of dollars of his family's fortune in securing delegate votes, and in the primaries he had demonstrated a superficial wit and boyish charm that attracted many voters. He also had a brain-trust of professors from his alma mater, Harvard, to provide him with intellectual appeal, while computers simultaneously were used in a cynical search for vote-getting appeals to the public. Lyndon Johnson, a proud politician who worshiped the New Deal, was humiliated into taking the vice-presidential nomination to hold the Protestant South for the Catholic Kennedy.

The Republicans met on July 25 in Chicago to nominate Richard M. Nixon for president and Henry Cabot Lodge of Massachusetts for vice president. Ike remained aloof from the political struggle (in part for personal reasons and in part because of poor health). The Democratic and Republican platforms were similar, promising dynamic leadership at home and in foreign policy, and thus the voters had to choose on the basis of personalities. Nixon agreed to debate Kennedy on a national television broadcast, a tactical error that cost him the election; many ladies chose to vote for Kennedy because he was "handsome," others because he had "polish." Few listened to the actual content of his words, for Nixon greatly outdebated him on the issues. The election was incredibly close: Kennedy received 34,221,485 popular votes, just 112,000 more than Nixon's 34,108,684, yet he received 303 electoral votes to Nixon's 219. There were widespread and well-founded charges of Democratic vote-stealing in Texas, Illinois, and Pennsylvania, but Nixon chose to accept the result. The Democrats that year also swept to victory in both houses of Congress; the time seemed ripe for yet more New Deal legislation, however discredited such methods were.

The Age of "Camelot"

John Fitzgerald Kennedy seemed the embodiment of the liberals' dreams. He was young, handsome, rich; he had an attractive wife and lovely children; he liked music, drama, and the other arts; and he brought a brain-trust of Ivy League professors to Washington and gave them positions of responsibility. During his administration, the social life of Washington resounded to classical music, New York plays, and the laughter of the "beautiful" people. In fact, journalists named it, more aptly than they knew, "The Age of Camelot," for it seemed a fairy tale come true. At his inauguration Kennedy gave voice to the aspirations of the liberals by calling for a "New Frontier" for the American people. Moreover, Kennedy did these things with "style"—his rhetoric was flawless. He told his listeners that day not to ask what their country could do for them, but to ask what they could do for their country. To the liberals this seemed a clear invitation for them to descend on Washington to deliver the answers they had to all the ills of mankind—and a horde of academics moved toward the nation's capital. The only jarring note for old-line liberals at Kennedy's inauguration was the presence of Robert Frost, there at Kennedy's request to read a poem written for the occasion. During the 1930s and 1940s this hardy New England poet had been widely hated by liberals for some of his pungent comments; for example, he once stated that Eleanor Roosevelt and the New Deal wanted to homogenize society so the cream could never rise to the top.

Yet the Kennedy years, for all the charisma exhibited, were extraordinarily barren of results. Kennedy promised much, but delivered little. He promised a raise in the standard of living, improved education, free medical care for the aged, higher Social Security payments, and improved civil rights for minority groups. Yet in his administration the only major piece of legislation was that creating the Peace Corps (to send volunteers to developing nations to offer technical knowledge for very little pay while living under local conditions). His greatest political victory was a rules change in the House of Representatives, which liberals did not recognize as a victory, rather as a bit of dabbling in the dirt of politics.

For his cabinet, Kennedy chose Dean Rusk as secretary of state, Robert S. McNamara of the Ford Motor Company as secretary of defense, and his brother and heir apparent Robert as attorney general. Bobby Kennedy had broader powers than any previous attorney general—and he used them to stifle dissent against the Kennedy administration. For example, when retired Army General Edwin A. Walker raised embarrassing questions, Bobby had him committed to an insane asylum without trial; only loud protests by conservatives caused Walker's release. Conversely, however, Bobby did turn on certain criminal aspects of organized labor, and succeeded in convicting James Hoffa of the Teamsters' Union and getting him sentenced to prison.

President Kennedy believed in heavy government spending without corresponding increases in taxes, and the federal deficit jumped $24 billion in just three years. This massive infusion of federal money into the economy brought boom and prosperity; unemployment dropped to 5.2 percent of the work force, and the annual gross national product grew to $629 billion. Money became available for massive giveaway programs: in urban renewal, to build housing developments (which became instant slums), and for civil rights organizations. Yet businessmen, caught in the squeeze of demands for pay raises by workers without a corresponding raise in productivity, were pressured not to raise prices. For example, in April, 1962, when U.S. Steel announced a price increase, Kennedy denounced it, threatened an antitrust suit, and forced the company to rescind its price increase. As a result of such tactics, the stock market dropped. And, petulantly, Kennedy blamed the multiple defeats of his domestic proposals in Congress on businessmen, the National Association of Manufacturers, even the American Medical Association, rather than face the fact that congressmen—Democrat and Republican—were unwilling to spend the nation into bankruptcy.

Yet Kennedy, despite these defeats, maintained a remarkable hold on the media's imagination. One of his most visionary proposals was to land a man on the

John F. Kennedy

moon during the 1960s. He wanted to involve the United States in a race with Russia to be first to the moon; Congress responded by appropriating $5 billion annually for this—while Kennedy continued to pay lip service to projects to aid the poor, the cities, and the environment. The National Aeronautics and Space Administration (NASA) began work with headquarters at Houston, and moved rapidly forward, new discoveries spilling over into civilian technology and moving the economy forward.

In Latin America, Kennedy's policies saw both tragic defeat and seeming victory. On January 3, 1961, the United States broke diplomatic relations with Cuba, and six days later, with Kennedy's connivance, anti-Castro forces began training to invade their former home. That invasion came on April 17 at the Bay of Pigs; brave refugees swarmed ashore to die or be captured because Kennedy feared sending in the air support that he had promised them. Afterward he was humiliated into ransoming the captives with medical supplies badly needed in Cuba. To prevent the spread of communism in Latin America, however, he called for an "Alliance for Progress" of Western Hemispheric nations; this alliance consisted of an American contribution of money, with Latin Americans spending it. Then in 1962 came confrontation with the Soviet Union in Latin America. Russia secretly was installing in Cuba missiles capable of attacking the United States. At first the Russians denied their missiles were in Cuba, but photographs taken from spy planes proved the Russians to be liars; Kennedy rose to the occasion, ordering a blockade of Cuba and threatening nuclear war. The Russians withdrew their missiles, but Kennedy was forced to promise no further invasions of Cuba. The Cuban missile crisis brought wide acclaim for Kennedy's toughness, but it was more compromise than victory.

In Europe the Kennedy administration fared little better. In June, 1961, the president journeyed to France to meet with Charles DeGaulle, leader of that nation since 1958. Two days later Kennedy was in Vienna to meet Khrushchev, who responded to the president's appeals by erecting the Berlin wall to divide the city and to keep East Germans from their embarrassing flights to freedom and by resuming nuclear testing. Kennedy did secure a nuclear test ban treaty on August 5, 1963, with Russia and England, but only because the Soviets had completed all the tests they needed. Finally, a "hot line" providing instant communications was opened between Washington and Moscow on April 30, 1963, in an effort to reduce the risk of accidental war.

Meanwhile, DeGaulle was moving France steadily out of NATO and its American alliance. He recognized Communist China, vetoed the admission of England into the European Common Market, and pushed France's nuclear capacity by exploding an atomic bomb and by refusing to sign the Nuclear Test Ban Treaty. Also, DeGaulle steadily withdrew his support from NATO, trying to develop France as a great power—a "third force"—around which other nonaligned nations might rally.

And in Indochina the Kennedy policies moved the United States closer to another limited war in an effort to contain militant communism. In Vietnam, Ho Chi Minh was continuing his infiltration of South Vietnam and his campaign of terror. Kennedy increased the number of American troops there to 4000 in February, 1962, then added another 12,000 in January, 1963.

The Kennedy reign lasted approximately one thousand days, to be tragically cut short by an assassin's bullet in Dallas, Texas, on November 22, 1963. Lee Harvey Oswald, an admitted Communist who had just returned from Russia by way of

Cuba, was publicly charged with committing the crime single-handedly, but strong doubts remain, especially since Oswald was then killed by Jack Ruby, a Dallas night-club operator (who conveniently died soon thereafter of "heart" trouble). Lyndon Baines Johnson, who may have been dropped from the Democratic ticket in 1964, suddenly and accidentally became president of the United States. It was he who would set the tone for most of the rest of the decade.

Johnson's Policy

Johnson came to office with a reputation as the master legislator, tainted in liberal eyes by the tragic circumstances of Kennedy's assassination and his accidental emergence as president. The tall Texan was, in truth, a manipulator more at home in the proverbial smoke-filled room than in the glare of national attention. Moreover, he was at heart a Southern courthouse politician, not a man with national appeal. Yet he used his persuasive abilities to secure passage of the legislation so lavishly promised—but not delivered—by John Kennedy. In July, 1964, came the Civil Rights Act, barring discrimination in public accommodations, authorizing the attorney general to institute suits to desegregate schools, creating an Equal Employment Opportunity Commission, and expediting law suits over voting rights. Then in August came the Economic Opportunity Act, establishing the Job Corps to provide vocational training and the Volunteers in Service to America (VISTA) to combat poverty. Yet Johnson was not satisfied and promised still further gains for what he was calling the "Great Society," should he be elected in his own right.

The Election of 1964

As the election of 1964 approached, the Republicans had little hope of victory, barring some miracle. John Kennedy basically had been an unpopular president despite media worship. Barry M. Goldwater of Arizona, an articulate, polished spokesman of the conservative philosophy, had outdistanced Kennedy in polls taken prior to November, 1963, leading to a conservative takeover of the GOP prior to the convention in San Francisco on July 13. However, liberal hysteria and vengeance after Kennedy's assassination doomed the Republican's chances that election year. Nevertheless, Goldwater and his running mate, Congressman William E. Miller of New York, conducted a fighting campaign in which they called for frugality in government at home and for victory over communism. Meeting in Atlantic City, the Democrats responded by nominating Lyndon Johnson in a convention that he had carefully orchestrated, and by naming Senator Hubert H. Humphrey of Minnesota as the vice-presidential candidate. Johnson's platform included a strong civil rights plank and promised peace in Vietnam. The Democratic Party's image-makers skillfully—and inaccurately—pictured Goldwater as wishing to repeal all of the New Deal, including Social Security, and with being a warmonger unaware of the destructive potential of atomic warfare. Rarely has a candidate been so misunderstood as was the Republican nominee in 1964, and the vote went heavily against him. Lyndon Johnson was elected by the widest margin in modern history, receiving 61.1 percent of the popular vote and 486 electoral votes to Goldwater's 38.5 percent and 52 electoral votes.

The Great Society had been returned to office—and the voters reaped the "rewards." Johnson promised to eliminate poverty; Congress responded by voting

370

the Appalachian program, with $1 billion to aid the poor in eleven states. Next came the Elementary and Secondary School Education Act, giving aid to school districts, even to parochial schools. Then in July came Medicare, an adjunct to Social Security to pay the medical costs of the aged. And Congress established a Department of Housing and Urban Development, with cabinet rank, to oversee the growing crisis of the cities; Johnson appointed Robert C. Weaver the first secretary for this department, making Weaver the first Negro to hold cabinet rank.

Much to Johnson's surprise—and chagrin—these measures did not endear him to the liberals. The academic jackals who had come to Washington with Kennedy had gradually left to denounce Johnson. When he secured passage of their programs and these proved unworkable, they castigated Johnson, not their own failures—and then proposed even more unworkable schemes calling for the expenditure of more tens of billions of dollars. Any hesitancy on the president's part in espousing their utopian schemes they interpreted as oppressive authority. Johnson had given them the fruits of liberalism without the attendant cant of liberalism and without the Boston accent —and they turned on him viciously. Johnson spoke with the accent of the common man, which made him unacceptable. The great irony of Lyndon Johnson was that he cultivated the liberals and sought their benediction. Yet the more he did, the greater the denunciation, bitterness, invective—for the academic jackals considered the source more important than the achievements. The handiest club to the liberals was the war in Vietnam, and they used it to destroy the man who have given them what they said they wanted.

The War in Vietnam

The commitment of American forces in Vietnam had begun in Eisenhower's administration and had deepened under Kennedy. In 1965, however, the North Vietnamese increased their attacks with the intent of speedy victory. Johnson responded by increasing the number of American troops in Vietnam, first to 150,000, then higher and higher, until by 1968 more than half a million Americans were committed to combat; by bombing North Vietnam to halt infiltration; and by increasing diplomatic pressures on North Vietnamese leaders to negotiate a settlement. Johnson took these steps without a congressional declaration of war under the authority of the Gulf of Tonkin Resolution (on August 11, 1964, Congress had pledged American support of peace and security in Southeast Asia) and under the implied support of Congress every time it voted funds for the fighting. Of course, every escalation of the war increased American casualties, for wars are not fought without wounds and deaths.

The liberals began using the war as justification for their hatred of Johnson, thereby polarizing the country into "hawks" and "doves." Many politicians thought to use the issue to kick Johnson out of politics and boost themselves into the presidency. Senator J. William Fulbright of Arkansas, chairman of the Senate Foreign Relations Committee, held public hearings that, in essence, gave aid and comfort to the enemy, while other doves such as Senators Mark Hatfield of Oregon and George McGovern of South Dakota spoke openly at antiwar rallies. Even the most patently false charges were widely believed. Even after South Vietnam had written a constitution and had democratically elected a government, the antiwar crowd charged that the South Vietnamese government did not represent the people of that nation. And the most patently true facts about the war were not believed. When North Vietnam-

Lyndon B. Johnson

ese troops committed atrocities (such as at the city of Hué in 1968, where more than 2000 men, women, and children were butchered), the liberals raised no voice of protest.

Because of the president's slow escalation of the war, the North Vietnamese were able, with Russian and Chinese help, to meet each increase with a retaliatory increase—and the fighting dragged on. Soon the president was doing everything Goldwater had advocated, but too late to do any real good. Also, the protracted length of the war led to increasing anti-Americanism in Europe. DeGaulle, who possibly did not want an American victory because the French had been defeated in the same region of the world in 1954, demanded that all NATO forces leave French soil by 1967—and they left. Mobs stormed American embassies in most major nations of Europe, and American information libraries were burned with impunity there and in Latin America.

Johnson's Domestic Policies

Johnson's only course was to spend more and yet more money—the same answer he had for all domestic ills. Nor would he increase taxes to provide, as he said, both "guns and butter." Deficits soared in his administration, so that by the end of the eight Democratic years of the 1960s, the national debt had grown by more than $80 billion. These years were a time of prosperity, and a time when economists were led to repeat the bromides of the 1920s: that the economic cycle had been tamed. Nothing seemed impossible in this euphoric time. The poor would be no more—all would be rich. By 1968, however, this deficit financing had led to inflation soaring to a rate of 6 percent a year, hurting those on fixed salaries, the poor, and the retired—the very people Johnson had sworn he would help most. The price of the Great Society and the New Frontier would prove high indeed.

Johnson also sought to aid minority groups, probably not so much from a sense of conviction as from a desire to gain a reputation in history books for presidential greatness. Therefore he continued the policies that had begun under Harry Truman and Dwight D. Eisenhower. In 1948 Truman had sought passage of antilynching, anti-poll-tax, antisegregation, and fair employment legislation; Congress refused, but by executive decree Truman had desegregated the armed forces. Then, in Eisenhower's first term, came a Supreme Court ruling on segregated schooling; in the case *Brown* v. *Board of Education of Topeka,* the high court ruled that segregated school facilities violated the Fourteenth Amendment, thereby overturning the "separate but equal" ruling of *Plessy* v. *Ferguson* of 1896. By this judicial fiat, segregated schooling became illegal, and in 1955 the Supreme Court ruled that desegregation must proceed "with all deliberate speed." On November 25 that year the Interstate Commerce Commission banned segregation of passengers on buses, trains, and airplanes in interstate commerce. In 1957, when Governor Orval Faubus of Arkansas called out his state's National Guard to prevent the enrollment of Negroes in Little Rock's high school, Eisenhower first tried to use the courts, then sent paratroopers to force integration.

Under Kennedy, the civil rights movement grew rapidly. His rhetoric promised instant fulfillment of black dreams, even of placing "the bottom rail on top," as was the phrase during reconstruction. Martin Luther King, black leader of the Southern Christian Leadership Conference, found Justice Department automobiles and funds available to him on orders from Attorney General Bobby Kennedy, and gained a national and international reputation that brought him the Nobel Prize. More troops were used, as in Mississippi, to secure the admission of James H. Meredith at the University of Mississippi, and in Alabama, where Governor George Wallace made a show of barring registration of Negroes at the University of Alabama.

With Johnson in office the civil rights movement gained momentum, with two civil rights acts passing Congress (1964 and 1965). Civil rights marches in the South were designed to secure Northern liberals' support and to garner national sympathy more than to win gains for blacks. Outside agitators flocked to the South to incite confrontations, succeeding frequently. However, human nature could not be legislated, and feelings did not change. Moreover, the same Northerners who charged de jure segregation in the South practiced de facto segregation at home. The result of such unfulfilled promises, both by national politicians and by liberal do-gooders, led to frustration—and then violence.

The first riot came in Harlem, New York, in July, 1964; others quickly followed in the next five weeks at Rochester, New York, Jersey City, and Philadelphia. Numerous organizations tried to capitalize on the strivings of blacks, with internal bickerings for leadership that led to killings (as, for example, the death of Malcolm X of the Black Muslims, on February 21, 1965). Then in August, 1965, came the biggest race riot to date in the Watts section of Los Angeles, where thirty-four persons were killed, more than a thousand injured, and more than 600 buildings damaged or destroyed. Riot begat riot, and within the next two years almost every major city in the country experienced senseless looting, fire bombings, and shootings (especially noteworthy were the riots at Detroit and Newark). The Johnson administration's response was to reward the rioters with massive infusions of federal funds and to excuse the rioters as the victims of a "sick society"—and permissiveness only encouraged more riots.

The Supreme Court not only helped create a climate conducive to violence, but actively encouraged it with rulings that made little legal or constitutional sense, but which suited a majority of the justices' sense of "moral right." In 1953 President Eisenhower appointed California Governor Earl Warren chief justice of the high court. He and the liberal appointees of the Roosevelt-Truman years promptly turned the Supreme Court into an instrument of social activism, supplanting the legislative and executive branches of the government as chief instigators of change. The Johnson appointees (Abe Fortas and Thurgood Marshall) joined with this group to produce some startling interpretations of the law that went much farther than the desegregation cases of 1954–55. In 1962, in *Baker* v. *Carr*, the court ruled that both houses of every state legislature had to be reapportioned on the basis of equal representation (thereby making state apportionment a matter for judicial review); that same year, the court ruled that prayer in the public schools was unconstitutional. Then in 1963 and 1964 came rulings that greatly increased the "rights" of suspects in criminal cases; in *Gideon* v. *Wainwright,* the court ruled that the states must provide "free" defense counsel for indigent defendants, while in *Escobedo* v. *Illinois* it stipulated that suspects could have lawyers while being interrogated by the police. Then in 1966 came *Miranda* v. *Arizona,* in which the court declared that statements made by a prisoner under interrogation could not be used as evidence unless defendants clearly knew their rights. In short, the court was busy overturning convictions on the flimsiest of excuses, returning criminals to society to commit yet more crimes while hamstringing the efforts of the police to halt such activities. Because of these rulings by the court, convictions (on a percentage basis) declined, crime increased, the public grew increasingly afraid of the streets of major cities, and law and order became a major issue in politics.

Finally, during the Johnson administration, a "generation gap" was discovered by journalists, academicians, and sociologists. A growing number of America's young became disenchanted with their elders and with the structure of American society. Most of this alienation was the direct product of the teaching and writing of leftist "intellectuals" both inside the nation's universities and outside. From the comfort of inherited fortunes or the insularity of tenured academic positions, they preached against materialism, against free enterprise, against America's past, present, and future. Too many of the young believed such nonsense, mouthing slogans about a "sick society." Becoming doomsayers about the United States, they frothed in frustration when the nation did not disintegrate as they had predicted. Some of the young, following blindly where they had been led, sheep without reason, tried to escape reality by turning to drugs, which became fashionable to a degree until then unknown in American history; marijuana, barbiturates, amphetamines, LSD, and other varieties of mind-distorting chemicals and plants were smoked or sniffed or injected—with frequent tragic results. Organizations arose to preach violent overthrow of the American structure among campus elitists. Students for a Democratic Society (SDS), the Weathermen, and such groups even turned to active violence, beginning at the Berkeley campus of the University of California, to be imitated at Columbia and in the Ivy League, even on theretofore staid Midwestern campuses. The liberal reaction to the growing violence was to say Americans should listen to these "brilliant" students, who were the most intelligent in history; in truth, these young people may have had more facts at their disposal, but they suffered the same problems of body chemistry as every other generation in history—and they blindly refused to listen to the facts at their disposal to a degree never before equaled, while shouting down their opposition with obscenities.

By early 1968, therefore, a growing majority of Americans were disenchanted with what the Great Society and the New Frontier had produced: a seemingly endless war, deficit spending that had produced galloping inflation, racial disturbances predicated on collective guilt—and need for reparations—by whites to blacks, lawlessness in the streets, violent and alienated young people living on checks from home or else stealing from society, self-styled intellectuals predicting an American disintegration and declaring the collective guilt of Americans for everything wrong in the world, and a permissive court system that saw criminals freed and policemen chastised for arresting them. Lyndon Johnson recognized the change in the public mood, and much as he wanted another term he knew he would never get it. Therefore in March, 1968, he announced that he would not be a candidate for reelection, thereby triggering a strong fight for the Democratic nomination.

Entering the race in November, 1967, was Senator Eugene J. McCarthy, a "peace candidate" from Minnesota who conducted a low-key, under-financed campaign that, nevertheless, saw him show well in the Democratic primary in New Hampshire even before Johnson withdrew. McCarthy was aided by college students to the extent that his campaign was labeled a "Youth Crusade." After McCarthy demonstrated in New Hampshire that Johnson might be beaten, Bobby Kennedy, now a carpetbag senator from New York, tossed his hat in the ring. With family money, a thirst for power, and a horde of academic followers, he pursued the nomination despite the opposition of party regulars. His quest was ended in the California primary, however; there a crazed Arab nationalist, Sirhan Bishara Sirhan, assassinated

Kennedy. Many Americans deluded themselves that Kennedy would have won the nomination—and the presidency—except for the assassin's bullet. One senator who believed this was George McGovern of South Dakota, and he belatedly offered himself as the peace candidate; other Kennedy followers transferred their allegiance to the remaining Kennedy brother, Edward (Ted), a senator from Massachusetts, but he refused to enter the race when he saw that he had no opportunity of winning.

Vice President Hubert Horatio Humphrey was the administration candidate and hand-picked heir of Lyndon Johnson, and as such had the nomination clearly won long before the delegates convened in Chicago. Yet at the convention there was a bitter fight on the platform plank on the Vietnam War, while outside, in the streets of Chicago, a motley gang of protestors, peaceniks, flower children, and anarchists tried to prevent the convention from taking place. Only swift, decisive action by Mayor Richard Daley and the Chicago police saved the situation from degenerating into total bloodshed. Humphrey emerged with the nomination, along with Senator Edmund Muskie of Maine as his running mate, but both had been smeared by the black-shirt tactics of their youthful opponents in the streets of Chicago—which biased newspaper and television coverage had made to seem a "police riot."

Richard Nixon, by way of contrast, had easily won the Republican nomination at a Miami convention in July. He did have opposition—Governors Nelson Rockefeller of New York and Ronald Reagan of California—but the party unified under Nixon's strong leadership. His choice of a running mate, Governor Spiro T. Agnew of Maryland, was duly nominated, and the two conducted a lackluster campaign that avoided confrontation with Humphrey.

In 1968 there was a third party candidate, George Wallace of the American Independent Party. And Wallace succeeded in getting his ticket on the ballot in every state, a remarkable achievement. He made a fighting campaign under a populist banner that succeeded in attracting white ethnic voters. Meanwhile, Humphrey and Muskie were aided by Lyndon Johnson, who dramatically halted the bombing of North Vietnam late in October, ostensibly to further peace negotiations in Paris but in reality to aid Humphrey. By election day the pollsters had declared the race too close to call—and they were right. Nixon received 43.3 percent of the popular vote to Humphrey's 43.2 percent and Wallace's 13.5 percent. Wallace was defeated in his hope of throwing the election into the House of Representatives, where he would have had great bargaining power. Nixon received 302 electoral votes to Humphrey's 191 and Wallace's 45. Yet the Democrats did carry both houses of Congress. Nixon was a minority president without control of either house (the first president so elected since Zachary Taylor). Liberals sneered at Nixon's thin margin of victory, calling him a minority president; however, they conveniently overlooked the fact that he and Wallace together received 56.8 percent of the total vote—and Nixon almost certainly would have received most of these votes had Wallace not been in the race. The mood of the country definitely was shifting to the right.

Nixon's Policies

Nixon as president wanted to "de-escalate" the war in Vietnam, which he did during the next four years. "Peace with honor" was the phrase the president used to describe his intent; by this he meant that he would withdraw all American military forces while simultaneously maintaining a non-Communist government in Vietnam. Gradually he began withdrawing American troops at a steady rate, the fighting to be undertaken by increasing numbers of trained South Vietnamese soldiers. However, this required heavy infusions of American money into South Vietnam. All the while the peace conference in Paris, to which the North Vietnamese had belatedly agreed, repeatedly showed the Communist intransigence; they apparently wanted nothing short of total victory—what they could not win on the battlefield they hoped to get at the peace table through American impatience. Peace groups in the United States, who numbered in their ranks leading ministers, movie stars, and even some well-meaning senators and congressmen, played into Communist hands by loudly denouncing every hard-line move by the Nixon government, sponsoring marches on Washington to demand immediate surrender, and even by making well-publicized visits to Hanoi where they recorded broadcasts denouncing their own country.

Nixon meanwhile played a close hand (and he was remembered by friends from his days in the Navy as a good poker player). Using his director of the National Security Council, Henry Kissinger, he began bringing pressure on the North Vietnamese to agree to a political settlement to the war. Kissinger, a German-born refugee from Hitler's persecution of Jews, was a Harvard professor of government and a student of Metternich's grand alliance that had provided a balance-of-power era in Europe following the Napoleonic Wars. Together Nixon and Kissinger began working on Russia and China, the two major suppliers of munitions—and encouragement—to North Vietnam, to reduce their war contribution and to pressure their ally to come to a settlement.

At the same time Nixon as commander-in-chief showed the North Vietnamese that the United States was not a "paper tiger," as Chairman Mao of China had labeled it. He was reducing the number of American troops in South Vietnam and promised to continue to do so if the amount of fighting decreased, if there was progress in the Paris peace talks, and if the South Vietnamese were able to assume the burden of fighting. Yet the pressure in the United States was such that Nixon could not end the troop reductions—and the peace groups were bringing all the pressure they could muster. On October 15, 1969, they sponsored a nationwide "Vietnam Moratorium" which largely failed but which generated wide media coverage. A month later the same groups staged a "March Against Death" from Arlington National Cemetery to the White House, in which they and sympathetic newsmen estimated 250,000 participated, a greatly exaggerated figure, according to impartial observers.

Despite this pressure, in the spring of 1970 Nixon sent American troops into Cambodia to destroy Communist sanctuaries; inside that nation's borders the North Vietnamese had stockpiled weapons and supplies, using the region as a staging area for raids into Vietnam. The venture was highly successful, severely hurting the Communists and providing about one year's additional time in which to train South Vietnamese forces. But in the United States the peace groups went wild with anger at the president's "widening of the war." Demonstration followed demonstration until at last four students were killed at Kent State University in Ohio; agitators there, under the guise of patriotism, were bent on burning the ROTC building, and National Guardsmen sent in to contain them fired into a rock-throwing, obscenity-chanting, and agitator-inspired crowd.

Frantic in their efforts to thwart the Nixon bid for peace, the radical fringe elements sought martyrs and heroes. They found one in Daniel Ellsberg, a former employee at RAND Corporation (an Air Force "think tank"). Ellsberg had worked

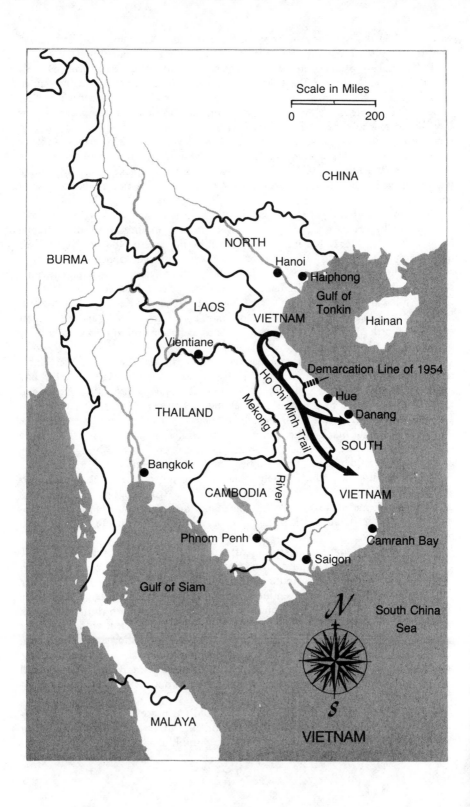

as one of thirty-six editors on a study of the war commissioned in 1967 by Robert S. McNamara; when completed, these totaled forty-seven volumes that traced the history of American involvement in Southeast Asia. These volumes were labeled Top Secret, but Ellsberg copied them and turned them over to the *New York Times,* which began publishing bits and pieces of them in June, 1970. These "Pentagon Papers" showed little even when quoted out of context. The government attempted to halt their publication, but the Supreme Court upheld the newspaper's right to publish material as long as it did not pose a threat to national security. Ellsberg, by justifying himself on the basis of "higher moral law," became an instant hero to the antiwar crowd, especially when he was indicted for his actions. (In 1973 he would be freed, not on the basis of innocence or guilt at taking government documents but on a technicality of tainted government evidence against him.)

Nixon's policy of Vietnamization was justifed in the spring of 1972 when the North Vietnamese sent division after division of their troops across the border armed with sophisticated Russian military equipment. For a time it appeared that this army might win, whereupon the president renewed the bombing of North Vietnamese targets. And he did what President Johnson had been told would widen the war to include all Asia and possibly even Russia. He mined the harbors of North Vietnam to halt their incoming supply ships; simultaneously, he publicly announced that he would end American fighting in return for an internationally supervised ceasefire and a release of Americans held as prisoners of war.

At the same time that he was winding down the war militarily—and increasing the cost of the war for the North Vietnamese—the president was moving to bring further pressure on China and Russia to halt the supplying of war materials to North Vietnam. In this he was aided by a growing rift between the two giants of the Communist world, who were almost at the point of war over disputed territory along their border. Using Kissinger as a secret envoy, Nixon engineered a visit to mainland China for the spring of 1972. The Chinese wanted this to strengthen their hand against the Russians, just as the Russians shortly announced that Nixon would be visiting that nation.

Nixon's visit to China in February, 1972, confounded the liberals, who had been urging such a move for several years, just as it angered conservatives who believed the Communist government of Chairman Mao had no legitimacy. Legitimacy or illegitimacy of the Peking regime to the contrary notwithstanding, Americans by satellite saw pictures of their president and the premier of China toasting one another. During the frank discussions between leaders of the two nations, many differences were apparently ironed out—so many that within a few months diplomatic relations were established between the two powers. Nixon's visit to China presaged a major shift in world politics, one in which the Communist Chinese government gained a patina of respectability despite its millions of murders and the revolutions it was fomenting around the globe.

Late in May, 1972, Nixon departed for Moscow. This visit came less than two weeks after the mining of the harbors of North Vietnam, yet the Russians did not cancel-out—as many liberals almost hopefully were predicting. Clearly the Russians needed the summit meeting for their own ends, which they achieved with the signing of several treaties while Nixon was in Moscow. Among these the most important was an arms limitation agreement, popularly known as SALT (from Strategic Arms Limitations Talks). This was followed in short order by increased trade between the two nations, especially the large sale of American grain; this the Soviets desperately needed because of the failure of their agricultural plans. The sale soon caused the price of wheat in the United States to soar from $1.68 a bushel to more than $6 a bushel. Nixon postured the foreign policy of his first term as reducing cold war tensions—"détente" this was called.

Linked indirectly to American foreign policy, for it did involve American prestige, were the concerted efforts of NASA to land men on the moon before the Russians could accomplish the feat. In 1957 Russia had launched Sputnik I; the first American artificial satellite was not launched until January 31, 1958. This loss of supremacy led President Eisenhower and Congress to push additional funds into the hands of NASA and an increased effort in this area. Through 1959 and 1960 both the United States and Russia sent numerous unmanned probes toward the Moon, the Sun, Mars, and Venus. With the inauguration of President Kennedy, NASA was renovated and placed under the guidance of Vice President Johnson. Kennedy even vowed dramatically that America would be first in the race to the moon. However, the Russians launched a manned orbiting satellite on April 12, 1961; the United States did not achieve this until John Glenn was lofted into orbit on February 20, 1962.

Under the Kennedy and Johnson administrations, NASA received high priority in appropriations, and space exploration continued on an intense schedule. The Mercury and Gemini manned orbital programs proved successful, giving America supremacy in such esoteric areas as manned flight, space walks, docking of vehicles in space, and lunar orbital flight. In 1968 three astronauts, Frank Borman, James Lovell, and William Anders, circled the moon ten times before splashing down in the Pacific. Finally on July 20, 1969, Neil Armstrong and Edwin Aldrin set their lunar module, dubbed *Eagle,* down on the surface of the moon; this dramatic event was witnessed via television by millions on earth. Nixon as president reaped the benefit of this event, for Americans rightfully were proud when their flag was planted on the moon. Several subsequent landings led to public boredom—while liberals chorused disapproval at the amount of money funneled into the program— but abroad American prestige rose because of the landings.

The Economy

On the home front Nixon's major fight during his first term was against inflation. The vast deficits of the Kennedy-Johnson administrations had brought uninterrupted prosperity for eight years, but at the price of 6 percent annual inflation. In a drive to cut this, the Nixon administration hiked interest rates; yet this classic measure for halting inflation failed, probably because of unbalanced budgets. In fact, two of Nixon's first four years in office saw the highest deficits in American history —coupled with five million unemployed. Vietnam was Nixon's budgetary Waterloo. Finally, in a wrong-headed attempt to halt inflation, Nixon on August 15, 1971, made a dramatic nationwide television appearance to announce a freeze on wages, prices, and rents. Three months later this was replaced by Phase II, which was a lessening of controls and an attempt to return to a free economy. Phase III, an attempt at voluntary restraint on the part of labor, industry, and businessmen, followed in 1972; however, little restraint was possible, for continued federal deficits made inflation inevitable and prices rose at an alarming rate. This inflation produced foreign fears about the value of the dollar to the extent that devaluation was made necessary twice within a year, and the United States abandoned the gold standard totally. Engineered by Secretary of the Treasury John B. Connally, a former Democratic governor of Texas who was moving toward the Republican Party, these devaluations saw the dollar quickly drop from $35 per ounce of gold to $38 to $42—while on European money markets the price of gold soared to $175 and more per ounce.

Yet another pressure on the Nixon administration's bumbling efforts against inflation was an unfavorable balance of trade. Every year the United States was buying more abroad than it was selling. To combat this the president imposed a 10 percent surcharge on imports not covered by quotas, and he negotiated limitations on specified items with certain foreign countries, notably Japan. Moreover, his diplomatic agents sought to make spectacular sales of certain American items to foreign governments, which would improve the balance of payments picture; for example, in 1972 Russia agreed to purchase American wheat in huge quantities. However, this sale, and others like it, had an adverse effect at home. The price of wheat jumped from $1.68 per bushel on the domestic market to more than $6 per bushel; domestic users were competing with foreign buyers, and the result was soaring food prices.

On other domestic issues, the president had little success. In September, 1972, came a revenue-sharing plan to give federal funds to the states, counties, and cities. This provided that some of the tax monies collected by the federal government would be given to local levels of government without strings and stipulations attached; each could use the money as it saw best. In return, however, Nixon anticipated and began implementing a reduction in certain federally funded activities at the local level—which naturally caused the local levels of government to whine endlessly. They wanted additional funds, but not at the expense of any federal reduction anywhere along the line. Yet because of huge deficits, the national government was borrowing the money it was giving to the cities, which only fueled inflation.

The Nixon administration also showed a tougher stance against campus radicals, calling for use of the National Guard and police to restore order and threatening to cut off federal funds from those campuses where the administrations did not prevent lawlessness; Nixon even asked Congress to provide a thousand additional FBI agents to investigate campus bombings and violence. The campus radicals responded by increasing their terrorist activities, as at the University of Wisconsin in the spring of 1970, when a bomb did millions of dollars worth of damage, killed one student, and destroyed years of creative work. Nixon also asked Congress for new laws with which to combat lawlessness, but the Democrat-controlled Congress refused to pass these, hoping instead to gain additional seats in the upcoming elections because of continued lawlessness (or else because some liberal Democrats and Republicans sympathized with the youthful anarchists). Campus violence wound down during 1971, however, because of the tightening job market and because legislators unhappy with the activities of certain liberal professors began cutting budgets for higher education. And declining enrollments in institutions of higher learning ended the bonanza years for professors; no longer were jobs so plentiful, and those holding positions began thinking of their own tenure rather than the revolution they had been working to promote.

Perhaps no Nixon achievement was so spectacular and influential as in his appointments to the Supreme Court. There Chief Justice Earl Warren belatedly retired, and the president named Warren Burger to his seat, giving promise of ending the leftist trend in court decisions. Then when Abe Fortas, a Johnson appointee, resigned owing to alleged irregularities, Nixon sought a Southern conservative to replace him as an associate justice. The Senate refused to confirm two of the president's nominees for basically partisan reasons, whereupon Nixon appointed Harry Blackmun. Two additional vacancies occurred in 1971, and the president named conservatives Lewis Powell of Virginia and William Rehnquist of Arizona, whom the Senate approved. Quickly these four, joined by one or more of the other justices, began moving the court to the right. For example, in May, 1972, came decisions more related to guilt or innocence, rather than placing society on trial in each case; the court decided that unanimous jury verdicts were not necessary in all criminal trials, and it said that witnesses could be required to testify without being granted total immunity from prosecution. In 1973 the court would anger many conservatives by throwing out most state regulations relating to abortion and stipulating that pregnant women did have this right; however, on balance, the court had moved decidedly to the right and away from the judicial process of legislating by court fiat (which had been the hallmark of the Warren court).

Finally in his first term Nixon confounded his liberal enemies by showing a quick willingness to spend taxpayers' money for socialistic programs. Among these was a renovation of the nation's welfare program that supposedly would emphasize "workfare," not welfare. Nixon's concept was to provide a minimum income of $1600 for every family of four while simultaneously encouraging heads of such families to go to work. Liberals helped defeat the measure on the grounds that $1600 was insufficient. Another Nixon measure was creation of the Environmental Protection Agency to consolidate all federal programs under one roof to aid in cleaning the air and water as well as conserving natural resources; this agency proved to be tough on polluters, principally automobiles, but at a high cost to purchasers of new automobiles with antismog devices. Finally, Nixon changed the Selective Service System. First, with congressional approval, he placed the draft on a lottery basis to insure fairness at a time when not all those eligible were being inducted. Gradually he shifted the emphasis to an all-volunteer armed force (the Selective Service System expired in the summer of 1973); the all-volunteer program was attended by increased salaries for members of the armed forces, by enlistment bonuses, and by additional funds for those enlistees who volunteered for combat units.

The Election of 1972

As the nation approached the election of 1972, Nixon had the economy moving —at the cost of heavy deficits—and the war in Vietnam winding down. The massive protests that had marked the late 1960s and early 1970s had ended, and the president was high on public opinion polls for his visits to China and Russia. All polls showed the president scoring high with the voters, but there was one element of uncertainty: the Twenty-sixth Amendment, adopted in 1971, provided that eighteen-year-olds could vote in national elections, and this group of new voters was an unknown factor. Almost everyone assumed that they would gravitate to the liberal —Democratic—ticket, but no one knew for sure how they would vote.

Nixon as the incumbent had only to speak the word to be renominated, and he spoke the word. At a convention in Miami Beach he and his chosen running mate, Spiro T. Agnew, were renominated easily. The self-declared agitators who wished to disrupt the proceedings mustered only a few thousand, and, despite encouragement from television and media representatives, accomplished almost nothing.

The Democratic nomination might well have settled on Ted Kennedy, the youngest brother of the former president, but his reputation had been damaged severely by an incident at Chappaquiddick, Massachusetts, in 1969. Senator Kennedy was driving a secretary, Mary Jo Kopechne, from a party when inexplicably he drove off a bridge. The secretary drowned, while Kennedy did not report the tragedy to the police until the next day. Later, in an emotion-charged television address carried nationally, Kennedy claimed that he had panicked and could offer no real vindication of his actions. The inquest was held behind closed doors with the testimony kept secret—which left the American public in doubt as to Kennedy's stability under pressure—not to mention his honesty. The Chappaquiddick incident cast doubt on the Kennedy heir's qualifications for president, and he did not actively seek the nomination in 1972.

At the Democratic convention, held also in Miami Beach, there was little excitement, for George McGovern already had won the nomination before the delegates gathered. Interestingly, McGovern, a senator from South Dakota, had headed the committee that had redrawn the rules for selecting delegates to the convention; this was based not on a democratic method of election, but rather on a quota system designed to guarantee representation to ethnic minorities, women, and the young; when there were contested delegations, as from Chicago, the regularly elected delegates were ejected, and people were seated at the convention who had not received a single vote in the primaries.

In those primaries, the early favorite of the Democratic Party, Senator Edmund Muskie of Maine, had gone down to quick defeat—largely at the hands of Governor George Wallace of Alabama. In the primaries, Wallace, running in 1972 as a "regular Democrat," outpolled most of the other candidates, but a would-be assassin's bullet cut him down in May at a rally in Maryland and left him paralyzed. Finally, the "Happy Warrior," Hubert Humphrey, failed to spark the voters, and George McGovern entered the convention with sufficient votes to win—this despite his inept campaigning style, his fuzzy economic pronouncements, and his stance on the war. The South Dakotan had publicly announced that he would crawl on his knees to Hanoi if this would end the war. His first-ballot victory was followed by a subservient convention accepting his choice for a running mate, Senator Thomas Eagleton of Missouri.

The campaign that followed was one of the most curious in American history. Within a few weeks reporters disclosed that Senator Eagleton had undergone psychiatric treatment years before. McGovern first announced that he still supported Eagleton "1000 percent," then a week later dumped him unceremoniously. The Democratic National Committee then chose the only national figure willing to take the number-two position, Sargent Shriver, a brother-in-law of John F. Kennedy. McGovern had alienated the party regulars, labor, the South, blue-collar workers, Roman Catholics—in short, all the old sources of Democratic support. Never could he get the president to debate him openly. Nixon actually made very few speeches, using second- and third-echelon Republicans to spar with McGovern. Instead the president clearly was about presidential business, trying to end the war in Vietnam by negotiation while McGovern was telling the people that he was willing to "beg" (his word) Hanoi to end it. The result of the election was a Nixon victory of landslide proportions. The president carried every state except Massachusetts and the District of Columbia, receiving 521 electoral votes to McGovern's 17. The popular vote was equally overwhelming: 45,800,000 for Nixon, 28,400,000 for McGovern. Yet the Democrats retained control of both houses of Congress.

The Watergate Affair

Only one scandal marred the Nixon victory. On June 17, 1972, five men were apprehended by police while in the Democratic national headquarters in the Watergate complex in Washington. Sophisticated electronic bugging devices were found in the party headquarters. Moreover, it soon became clear that the funds for this eavesdropping and spying had been provided by the Committee to Reelect the President, headed by former Attorney General John Mitchell. During the campaign the Democrats tried to make Watergate an issue, but the voters clearly believed that both parties indulged in this kind of spying, and it availed the Democrats nothing.

In the immediate afterglow of his stunning victory over McGovern, Nixon and his chief adviser on foreign policy, Henry A. Kissinger, sought to end the agony of Vietnam. In December, 1972, the North Vietnamese made one last attempt to win victory on the battlefield. The president responded by ordering a resumption of bombing in North Vietnam, whereupon in January, 1973, a ceasefire agreement was signed. This provided for the withdrawal of all American ground forces from South Vietnam within sixty days, internationally supervised inspections of the area, an eventual democratic vote on the future government of the region, an exchange of all prisoners of war, and the introduction of no new arms and men into Vietnam. Nixon then announced he had achieved "peace with honor," and the nation responded with a great public rejoicing as the American prisoners of war came home. Few seemed to notice that immediately the Communist North Vietnamese began violating their pledge by refusing to answer questions about Americans missing in action, just as they sent troops marching south while opposing all actions of the international ceasefire team.

Liberals at the national level needed this agreement to fail in order to justify their actions of the past several years, actions based on the premise that no military or political solution was possible and that the only American option was unilateral withdrawal from Southeast Asia. Therefore they railed at the president for his continued bombing of Communist troops in Laos and Cambodia. Their sympathizers in Congress introduced legislation to force the president to halt this bombing, and he agreed to do so by August 15, 1973. Then, by voting to cut off all aid to South Vietnam, aid promised that nation by terms of the armistice and by private promises by the president, Congress assured the eventual triumph of communism in Southeast Asia. This came with astonishing suddenness early in 1975, as the government of South Vietnam collapsed, the leaders fleeing with almost 100,000 of their fellow countrymen to the United States. In short order Cambodia also fell to the Communists, followed by a blood purge of thousands of its citizens. Liberals not only failed to denounce this killing, but also forgot their arguments that the "domino theory" had no validity. This Communist victory caused several Asian countries, such as Thailand, to reassess their foreign policy in light of the failure of American will to stand by treaty commitments.

Simultaneously, America's standing in the world community received another sharp blow, this time in the Middle East. In October, 1973, there was another

384

short Arab-Israeli war, during which the Organization of Petroleum Exporting Countries, called OPEC and consisting mainly of Arabic countries, voted to embargo shipments of petroleum to nations sympathetic to the Israelis. After the war ended and oil shipments began again, OPEC voted to raise the price of petroleum to more than $10 per barrel, almost quadrupling the cost. Highly industrialized nations, such as England, Germany, and Japan, were severely pressed to pay this price; in fact, the British pound fell to historic lows and inflation soared.

In the United States, which had come increasingly to depend on imported oil because of opposition of environmentalists to offshore drilling and the Alaskan pipeline, the price of gasoline virtually doubled in a few months, as did the prices of fertilizer, plastics, and other petrochemical products. The result was galloping inflation coupled with a reduction in the sale of automobiles that guzzled gasoline because of the antipollution devices tacked onto them at the demand of environmentalists. By 1975, however, the American balance-of-payments ledger was in the black thanks to the productiveness of farmers; the sale of farm commodities had more than offset the increased price of petroleum, although consumers were angry at the increased cost of food items at the grocery store.

Nixon's Resignation

As these events were unfolding, and while Kissinger, at last secretary of state in fact as well as in deed, was conducting his highly publicized "shuttle diplomacy," the Nixon administration was coming increasingly under fire for the burglary of the Democratic national headquarters at Watergate. Shortly after Nixon's second inauguration, the *Washington Post* and other newspapers, along with television journalists who hated Nixon, pushed the investigation until several of the five burglars talked. A Senate committee began investigating under the leadership of Democratic Senator Sam Ervin of North Carolina. Held under the glare of television lights—and growing talk of impeachment of the president—this hearing brought forth additional disclosures that forced the president to request the resignation of several of his staff members.

In the midst of this investigation came yet another blow to the Nixon administration. Vice President Spiro Agnew was implicated in a Maryland case involving alleged kickbacks and payoffs. Late in October, 1973, Agnew pleaded *nolo contendre* in court in return for a fine of $10,000 and immunity from further prosecution, and he resigned as vice president. Under terms of the Twenty-fifth Amendment, Nixon named Republican Congressman Gerald R. Ford his vice president, which the Senate confirmed after numerous delays; Ford took the oath of office on December 6, 1973—after which the tempo of the Watergate investigation assumed a new intensity, for Ford was more acceptable to liberals to succeed Nixon than Agnew had been.

During the hearings before the Ervin committee, Alexander P. Butterfield, who once had worked in the White House, revealed that Nixon had a taping system in the Oval Office to record the events of his presidency. Immediately the committee began seeking ways to secure these tapes, which would answer a question of critical importance: was the president involved in suppressing evidence of criminal activities? Nixon fought giving over these tapes, claiming executive privilege and naming a special prosecution task force to handle the Watergate situation. Time and again Nixon gave ground only to turn and fight, but the tide of battle clearly was

Bureau of Printing and Engraving

Richard M. Nixon

against him. Gradually the evidence came to light, including the tapes themselves (after the Supreme Court ruled that Nixon had to give them over). What emerged was sordid. Nixon and his close advisers in his Committee to Reelect the President had known of the crimes, had covered them up, and had paid hush money to the participants. By July, 1974, the House Judiciary Committee was holding hearings on a bill of impeachment; late that month the vote came: twenty-eight to ten in favor of impeachment. Seeing that both House and Senate were ready to vote for impeachment and conviction, on August 8 Nixon went on national television to announce his resignation. The next day, as Nixon flew west to his home in San Clemente, California, Chief Justice Warren Burger administered the oath of office to Gerald Ford.

Ford's Administration

Sixty-one years old when he assumed office, Ford was widely regarded as a moderate conservative known for his playing football at the University of Michigan and for being a "nice guy." A law graduate of Yale University and a Navy officer in World War II, he had entered the House of Representatives in 1948 from the district around Grand Rapids, Michigan, and had been reelected a dozen times. For almost ten years prior to his becoming the first nonelected president in American history, he had served as House minority leader.

Once in office, Ford almost immediately alienated many of his conservative supporters by naming Nelson A. Rockefeller, the multimillionaire former governor of New York, his vice president. Next he angered liberals and the media by issuing a blanket pardon to Richard Nixon for any crimes he may have committed as president. Then, while arguing for fiscal sanity, Ford presided over the biggest budgetary deficits in American history; estimates of the deficit in fiscal year 1976 totaled almost $60 billion. In the fall of 1975 came a timely reminder of what unlimited spending can bring; New York City, which for years had sold bonds and operated in the red in order to give lucrative benefits to its citizens, tuition-free universities to its residents, and high salaries to a horde of bureaucrats, found itself facing bankruptcy. To the mayor of the city and the governor of the state, the answer seemed simple: a raid on the national treasury. Ford met these requests with an emphatic no that all too soon turned to "maybe," provided new taxes were raised, and ended as "yes" to a federal loan. The media, headquartered in "Fun City," supported New York in its quest for easy federal money, as did liberals and their followers.

America in Transition

By late autumn of 1975 American society was at a crossroads, taking stock of where it had come from and where it was going. As the nation approached the Bicentennial of its Declaration of Independence, even the casual observer could note dramatic changes in the pattern of American life. For example, the rapid urban growth, which had marked the country from its beginnings as a republic until the census of 1950, suddenly began to slow—and even to reverse itself. America's major cities were decaying as affluent middle-class citizens moved to the suburbs and even to the country, often to escape court-ordered busing to achieve racial balance in the schools. In fact, between 1950 and 1960 four out of five of the cities with more than a million population actually declined in population. As these metropolitan areas saw their tax base eroded, spiraling welfare costs combined with a loss of income resulted. Moreover, workers in essential services in these cities—police, firemen, garbage collectors—went on strike for more and more money. Gradually there was a deterioration in services in many cities, which, combined with efforts to desegregate the schools, saw yet more middle-class whites fleeing to the suburbs; this compounded the problem because it further lowered the tax base of the cities.

This flight to the suburbs and the resulting necessity of commuting to work in the cities led to increased demands for better highways and enlarged parking facilities—and brought growing air pollution problems (caused mainly by automobile exhaust fumes). Thereby the quality of life in the cities again was diminished. In 1970 Congress tried to reverse this trend by passing the Urban Mass Transportation Assistance Act; this provided federal monies for mass transportation systems, but Americans showed a remarkable love for their automobiles and a preference for driving to work.

The noxious fumes of smog in the cities soon led many citizens to become concerned about the ecological balance in the country. Investigations showed that many American rivers were little more than sewers, that lakes were filled with industrial and sewage wastes, that the ocean had become a dumping ground for garbage, and that plant and animal life were suffering irreparable damage. Such knowledge, popularized in a host of books, led to the formation of societies and organizations to combat pollution and to protect the environment. This in turn led to excesses that slowed industrial growth. For example, a few oil spills from offshore drilling rigs brought screams from environmentalists that halted some explorations—and spurred the energy crisis. Environmentalists managed to delay construction of a pipeline across Alaska to bring petroleum from discoveries on the north shore, and the United States has had to purchase increasing amounts of petroleum from nations in the Middle East (hurting the balance of payments). Moreover, environmentalists have delayed construction of nuclear power plants, and in the summer of 1973 there were shortages of electricity in the Northeast.

The environmentalists have made excessive demands that have hurt America. Their cries for better exhaust systems have led to expensive equipment adding $400-$500 to the cost of each new automobile. Their demands for environmental protection devices on factories have caused a reduction in the number of factories— and jobs. There must be some balance between the needs of environmental protection and the realities of the American need for energy and jobs.

Other movements sweeping America in the last two decades have included diverse elements: minority groups that want a place in the economic sun; Indians and Mexican-Americans have seen that violence has brought increased federal monies to blacks, and they have reacted accordingly. Women have seen themselves discriminated against in limited job opportunities, low pay, and less prestige. In 1963 Betty Friedan published the *Feminine Mystique,* which focused attention on the problem and spurred the formation of a loosely coordinated "Women's Liberation" movement. Fringe elements of this group showed their discontent by staging marches and demonstrations, even the well-publicized burning of bras (as well as the fad of not wearing such articles). Eventually they, like the blacks, forced federal regulations that required no discrimination in the hiring, firing, and paying of women. Still not contented, these militants have pushed through Congress a proposed constitutional amendment guaranteeing females total equality in America (to date this has not been ratified by the necessary thirty-eight states).

While the blacks, Indians, Mexican-Americans, and women were challenging the "establishment," so also were campus radicals. American institutions of higher learning grew in ever-increasing numbers during the 1950s and 1960s, to the extent that students began to claim they had become numbers, not humans, in the rush to "bigness." This trend toward growth did not openly disturb students to any great extent in the 1950s; the word most often used to characterize them during this period was "apathetic." However, apathy turned to direct action during the 1960s. Riots began on the University of California at Berkeley campus in 1964, riots spawned by student demands for "free speech" (including public use of profanity), for the right to be represented on the board of regents, for the right to be consulted in the hiring and firing of faculty—and a general protest against the draft and the growing war in Vietnam. Gradually these riots became fashionable, spreading to Columbia in 1968, Harvard in 1969, and then elsewhere. Violence increasingly was employed by fringe elements, with bombs used to destroy computer centers, think tanks doing government research, and even business establishments in the vicinity of campuses.

Generally associated with these student demands were demands for the right to use drugs—marijuana, LSD, heroin, and barbiturates. Some of the other demands were equally ludicrous and others totally incompatible. For example, many demonstrators demanded that college and university officials actively recruit underqualified minority-group students and that all students be passed, yet simultaneously they wanted everyone completing a college degree to be employed at a high salary.

When society did not bow to these demands, more and more campus radicals took to "dropping out," meaning a movement away from the traditional values of America. They immigrated to communes started in rural areas, there to grow their own food (and marijuana), practice group marriage—and share their hepatitis. Others who did not drop out of society still flaunted its conventions. They dressed in clothes of any style—overalls, blue jeans, work shirts, Indian headbands, cast-off pieces of military uniforms, work boots—and no shoes. Hair for young males lengthened—and for some soap was a forgotten element. Some dressed in the most extreme fashion to show their contempt for the "straight world," while the more serious claimed the new dress code was a cry for equality with no deference for rank or wealth. Actually, however, there was rigid conformity among the nonconformists, and even older adults began imitating the young. Soon middle-aged men who sought to be stylish were adopting their fashions and their hair styles from the young.

Moving hand-in-glove with this trend toward permissiveness in fashions were Supreme Court rulings about other areas of society. For example, the Warren court decided that pornography no longer could be defined except in broad and national terms; the result was a rush to publish salacious novels and magazines. The movie industry, hard pressed by decreasing ticket sales as people stayed home to watch television, rushed to take advantage of the new permissiveness; soon main-street theaters were showing films exploiting blatant sexuality, perversions, and violence.

The young and youth-worshipers began imitating their screen idols by claiming that marriage was an outdated and outmoded custom, that "open marriage" should be the fashion. Contraceptives became widely available—even to nonmarrieds at campus dispensaries—and these ended the age-old fear of pregnancy. The result was a hedonistic society claiming to worship nonmaterialism but demanding affluence in order to enjoy the "good life." Credit cards enabled one and all to enjoy now, pay later.

Yet permissiveness left the young curiously unsatisfied and unfulfilled. Some turned to fundamental Christianity as an answer—the "Jesus Freaks." Others sought comfort in the pseudoscience of astrology, trying to read their futures in the stars. Still others began hitchhiking about the country, "trying to find myself," as they said. There was a thirst for some return to solidity, to reality, to eternal truth. But the majority of young people in this time already had found this in traditional American virtues; they did not demonstrate or riot or campaign for Eugene McCarthy or cry for a victory by North Vietnam or move to a commune. Instead they went to college or to a school for vocational-technical education, got a job, married, worked, and raised families. Many worked for the election and reelection of Richard Nixon, while their numbers in church increased. The 1920s had their expatriates, the 1950s their "beatniks," the 1960s their "hippies"—every generation has its 4 or 5 percent of dropouts. Those of the 1960s proved to be more extreme than their predecessors. The greatness of America is that it tolerated them without abridging their freedom.

An immutable law of physics holds that for every action there is an equal and opposite reaction. Fortunately for the United States, an analog of this law of physics has applied to the national political and social mood. There were gross excesses during the war in Vietnam among the radical-chic, just as there were among the youth culture. Meanwhile, as always, the majority of Americans were moderately conservative. As the United States approached the year of the Bicentennial, there was a growing mood of conservatism, a shift from the extremism of the Kennedy-Johnson years. College campuses were quiet, the Supreme Court had redefined pornography and had made it possible for local law-enforcement officials to prosecute offenders, and public opinion had rejected the youth counterculture. Only as the future unfolds will history be able to record how long this trend will continue.

Also immutable, hopefully, is the basic good sense of the American people and their willingness to work to achieve the goals of a free society. Pioneers came to this country from Europe or were born in the East and moved to the West. On the frontier they overcame hardships, deprivation, and want; they did this with sinew and spirit and great dreams. They worked and they fought. They looked upon their children and wanted something better for them. Some sought adventure and found it; some tried to start over, only to fail again; some hoped to get wealthy but few did. Yet these earlier Americans fulfilled their destiny. They kept faith with their dreams, with their ancestors, with their ideals, and with their God. They transformed a wilderness into a great nation that gives the only world leadership promising freedom, while simultaneously offering an example to other nations of what hard work and spirit can do. As the nation celebrates its two hundredth anniversary as a republic—and looks forward to the five hundredth anniversary of its discovery by Columbus—present and future Americans can afford to do no less than their ancestors.

Index

Fairbanks, Charles W., 285, 295
Fair Deal, 352–53
Fall, Albert B., 318, 321
Fallen Timbers, Battle of, 102
Farewell Address, 104
Farley, James A., 332–33
Farmers, demand reform, 269–70
Farm Loan Act, 297
Farragut, David, 200
Federal Communications Commission, 335
Federal Highway Act, 297
Federalist Papers, 93
Federalist Party, 93, 99, 105, 106, 108–18, 120, 127, 129
Federal Reserve Act, 289
Federal Reserve Bank, 330
Federal Reserve Board, 294–95
Federal revenue sharing, 381
Federal Trade Commission Act, 295
Field, James G., 253
Fifteenth Amendment, 214
Fillmore, Millard, as vice president, 178; as president, 181–83, 187
First Reconstruction Act, 213–14
Fish, Hamilton, 219
Fisk, Jim, 219
Fitzgerald, F. Scott, 324
Five Civilized Tribes, 223
Five Power Treaty, 320
Florida, 15, 17, 38, 48, 75, 79, 82, 87, 102, 120, 130, 134, 138, 195, 211, 214, 218, 221–23, 304
Food Administration, 312
Foraker, Joseph B., 255, 318
Forbes, Charles R., 321
Ford, Gerald R., as vice president, 385; as president, 387–90
Fordney-McCumber Tariff, 318
Fortas, Abe, 381–82
Fort Duquesne, 56
Fort Necessity, 55
Fort Saint Louis, 42–43
Fort Sumter, 197
Fourteenth Amendment, 212, 214, 260
Fox, George, 37
France, colonizes Canada, 18–19; and Indians, 24; in Louisiana, 39–42, 47; and American Revolution, 74–83; revolution in, 99–102; undeclared war with United States, 106–107, 119–21; war with Mexico, 166; in World War I, 309–15; in World War II, 339–45; in Cold War, 369
Franklin, 89
Franklin, Benjamin, 50, 54, 56; life of, 52–53; in American Revolution, 73–83; and Constitution, 90–92

Iroquois Indians, 19, 26; war on English, 45–46, 55–56; in American Revolution, 81
Israel, 363, 385
Italy, in World War II, 339–45

Jackson, Andrew, in War of 1812, 127; takes Florida, 134; campaigns for presidency, 139–42; as president, 142–51, 166
Jackson, Helen Hunt, 229
Jackson, Stonewall, 201, 202
James I, 22, 24; and Puritans, 27–28, 31
James II, 35–36, 44–46
James, William, 279
Jamestown, colony at, 22, 23, 26
Japan, 178, 193, 304–305, 365; in World War II, 339–48
Jay, John, 69, 73, 82, 93, 95, 102–103
Jefferson, Thomas, 50, 68; and Declaration of Independence, 73–75; 90; as secretary of state, 94–104; as vice president, 105–107; as president, 107–21
Jersey, East and West, 36–37
Johnson, Andrew, as vice president, 203, 209; as president, 209–17
Johnson-Clarendon Convention, 215
Johnson, Herschel V., 194
Johnson, Hiram, 283, 293, 297
Johnson, Hugh S., 332
Johnson, Lyndon B., 363, 366; as president, 370–76, 379, 380, 381
Johnson, Richard M., 151
Johnston, Tom, 282
Johnston, Joseph E., 199, 200
Joint stock companies, colonize, 20–24, 26–35
Joliet, Louis, 41
Jones, John Paul, 79
Joseph, Chief, 225
Joutel, Henri, 42
Judicial review, 89, 112
Judiciary Act, 95, 108, 112

Kansas, 17, 185–87, 188–90, 193, 194, 217, 237, 257, 291, 315, 323, 335, 360
Kansas-Nebraska Act, 184–85
Kearney, Stephen W., 173–76
Keating-Owen Child Labor Act, 297
Kefauver, Estes, 358, 364
Kelley, Oliver H., 269
Kellogg-Briand Pact, 323
Kennedy, Edward, 376, 383
Kennedy, John F., as president, 366–70, 371, 383
Kennedy, Robert, 363, 367, 373, 375–76

Lincoln, Abraham, debates Douglas, 190–92; as president, 194–209, 211–12, 216
Lindbergh, Charles A., 326, 340
Lisa, Manuel, 155
Livingston, Robert, 75, 86
Locke, John, 36, 69, 75
Lodge, Henry Cabot, 291, 314–17, 366
Lôme, Dupuy de, 299
London Company, 26, 28, 31
Longhorn cattle, 237–42
Long Island, Battle of, 78
Long, Stephen H., 137–38
Louisiana, 195, 211, 218, 221–23; explored, 41–43; settled, 57, 60, 62, 102; purchased by United States, 113–14; explored, 114–18
Lowell, Francis L., 146
Lusitania, 309

MacArthur, Douglas, 330, 345–48, 353–55
Macon's Bill No. 2, 121
Madison, James, 104, 109; and Constitution, 90–93; as president, 121–30
Maine, 22, 29, 35, 128, 133, 194, 221, 249, 336, 376, 383
Maine, U.S.S., 299
Mangum, Willie P., 151
Manhattan Island, 26
Manhattan Project, 348
Manifest Destiny, 163
Mann-Elkins Act, 288, 290
Marbury v. *Madison,* 112
Marquette, Jacques, 42
Marshall, George C., 343, 344
Marshall, John, 106, 109, 112, 118–19, 131–33, 143
Marshall Plan, 351–52
Marshall, Thomas R., 293
Martin, Luther, 90
Maryland, 31, 35, 56, 85, 86, 89, 90, 93, 130, 194, 197, 212, 358, 385
Mason, George, 93
Mason, James M., 206
Mason, John, 31
Mason, John Y., 178
Massachusetts, 28–31, 34–35, 45–48, 51, 56, 65, 66, 68, 69, 73, 74, 85, 89, 90, 93, 118, 130, 131, 181, 187, 194, 212, 218, 219, 229, 256, 269, 275, 315, 320, 323, 363, 366, 383
Massachusetts Bay Company, 28–31
Massachusetts Government Act, 68
Mather, Cotton, 50
Mayflower Compact, 27
Maysville Road Bill, 143
McAdoo, William G., 294, 321
McCarran Act, 358

Sanborn Contracts, 220
Sandys, Edwin, 27
San Jacinto, Battle of, 157
San Pascual, Battle of, 173
Santa Anna, Antonio López de, 156–57, 171, 177
Santa Fe Railroad, 257
Santa Fe Trade, 155–56
Saratoga, Battle of, 78
Sauk and Fox Indians, 138–39
Schurz, Carl, 218, 245
Scopes Trial, 326
Scott, Winfield, 127, 138, 145, 176, 181, 197, 199; in Mexican War, 171–75
Securities Exchange Act, 335
Sedition Act, 107–8, 313
Selective Service Act, 311, 355, 382. *See also* Conscription
Seminole Indians, 151
Serra, Junípero, 61
Seven Days' Battle, 200
Seventeenth Amendment, 294
Seven Years' War, 56–57, 60
Sevier, John, 89
Seward, William H., 194, 197, 205–6, 215
Seymour, Horatio, 217
Shafter, William R., 302
Shawnee Indians, 124
Shays' Rebellion, 89–90
Sheridan, Philip, 205
Sherman Antitrust Act, 253, 269, 288
Sherman, James S., 289, 293
Sherman, Robert, 91
Sherman, Roger, 75, 90
Sherman Silver Purchase Act, 253
Sherman, William T., 203–5
Shiloh, Battle of, 201
Short, Walter C., 343
Shriver, Sargent, 383
Sibley, Henry Hopkins, 199
Silver, 236, 253–55
Sims, William S., 311
Sinclair, Harry F., 321
Sinclair, Upton, 289
Sioux Indians, 114, 224–25
Sirhan, Sirhan B., 375–76
Sitting Bull, 225
Sixteenth Amendment, 290, 294
Slaves, 24, 26, 85, 133, 145–46. *See also* Blacks
Slidell, John, 166–67, 206
Sloughter, Henry, 45
Smith Act, 355
Smith, Alfred E., 321, 324
Smith-Hughes Act, 297
Smith, John, 22, 23, 28

Sutter, John A., 234
Sweden, 26

Taft-Hartley Act, 351, 352
Taft, Robert A., 356–58
Taft, William H., as president, 289–93, 305, 318
Tallmadge Amendment, 133
Tammany Hall, 221
Taney, Roger B., 188
Tariff, 95, 129, 139, 142, 143–45, 153, 190, 213, 251, 253, 290, 294, 318, 330, 338
Taylor, Glen H., 352
Taylor, Zachary, in Mexican War, 167–76; as president, 178–81
Tea Act, 67–68
Teamsters' Union, 367
Teapot Dome, 321
Tecumseh, 124
Tennessee, 89, 94, 138, 148, 151, 194, 197, 203, 209, 211, 212, 245, 333, 358, 364
Tennessee Valley Authority, 335, 341
Ten Percent Plan, 209
Tenure of Office Act, 216
Texas, 17, 116, 117, 120, 130, 195, 199, 211, 332, 360, 363, 366; French in, 42; Spaniards in, 42–43, 47, 60–61; Americans enter, 156–57; revolution in, 157; republic, 157–60; and Mexican War, 160–61, 167–73; and compromise of 1850, 179–81; ranching in, 236–39; railroads in, 257–59
Texas and Pacific Railroad, 257–59
Texas v. *White,* 215
Thirteenth Amendment, 211
Thoreau, Henry D., 193
Thomas, Lorenzo, 216
Thurman, Allen G., 251
Thurmond, J. Strom, 352
Tilden, Samuel J., 221–23
Timber Culture Act, 240
Timber and Stone Act, 240
Tobacco, 24
Topeka Constitution, 188
Tordesillas, Treaty of, 14
Townshend, Charles, 66
Trade Agreements Act, 338
Trail drives, 237–42
Transylvania Company, 89
Travis, William B., 156–57
Treason, defined, 118–19
Treaty of Aix-la-Chapelle, 54
Treaty of 1819, 134
Treaty of Ghent, 128
Treaty of Paris, 82–83, 302–3
Treaty of Ryswick, 45–46